DISCOVER QGIS

THE WORKBOOK FOR THE AWARD WINNING GEOACADEMY CURRICULUM

KURT MENKE, GISP

loca e
PRESS

Credits & Copyright

Discover QGIS

by Kurt Menke, GISP

Published by Locate Press LLC

Direct permission requests to info@locatepress.com or mail:
Locate Press LLC, PO Box 671897, Chugiak, AK, USA, 99567-1897

Editor   Gary Sherman
Cover Design   Julie Springer
Interior Design   Based on Memoir-LATEXdocument class
Publisher Website   http://locatepress.com
Book Website   http://locatepress.com/dqw

Contents

Foreword

It is with great pleasure I introduce you to Discover QGIS by Kurt Menke. This volume is the result of our collaboration for a decade to promote the adoption of open source software by geospatial educators and industry professionals. It reflects Kurt's deep technical knowledge and his extensive teaching experience. Kurt has long been a beacon of hope for open source advocates who share in the community of practice of QGIS and open source software. His extensive GIS consulting experience around his home base of Albuquerque, New Mexico and involvement in national healthcare and conservation societies, is reflected in Discover QGIS. He applies the geospatial technology skills defined in the US Department of Labor's Geospatial Technology Model (GTCM) to practical exercises in each of the chapters.

Kurt's decades of university, college and private teaching experience, only reinforce the quality of his pedagogical approach to the volume. In the field of geospatial technology education, his book adds greatly to the sparsely available collection of print volumes, and we will all benefit greatly from Discover QGIS for years to come. I look forward to its adoption by our GeoAcademy learners in 2016.

Phillip Davis, Ed.D
Director, GeoAcademy
Professor of Computer Science
Computer Science, Engineering and Advanced Technology Department
Del Mar College, Corpus Christi Texas, USA

About this Book

The GeoAcademy was founded in 2013, when Dr. Phil Davis brought together subject matter experts to author the first ever GIS curriculum based on a national standard—the U.S. Department of Labor's Geospatial Competency Model (GTCM). The GTCM is a hierarchical model of the knowledge, skills, and abilities (KSA's) needed to be a working GIS professional in today's marketplace. These KSA's were vetted by forty U.S. college GIS educators. Since 95% of U.S based colleges and universities use a single vendor's GIS software, it was decided the GeoAcademy should be built using free and open source software (FOSS4G). Over the summer of 2014 the exercises were beta tested on Canvas by over 3,000 students. The first edition of the GeoAcademy was released in September 2014. The GeoAcademy is therefore more of an attempt to teach GIS using QGIS, versus being a QGIS manual. (The GeoAcademy labs are licensed under the Creative Commons Attribution 3.0 Unported License. To view a copy of this license, visit http://creativecommons.org/licenses/by/3.0/)

Since its development, the GeoAcademy curriculum has been presented at several FOSS4G conferences and is being used by many professors in their GIS programs. An online GeoAcademy MOOC has over 5,000 enrollees. In 2015 the GeoAcademy team was honored to win the Global Educator of the Year Team Award by GeoForAll (http://www.geoforall.org/).

Now for the first time, this curriculum has been converted to fit into a convenient workbook format. Originally written for QGIS 2.4, the GeoAcademy material in this workbook has been updated for use with QGIS 2.14, Inkscape 0.91, and GRASS GIS 7.0.3. The material is also backwards compatible to QGIS v2.8 despite minor GUI changes. It therefore represents the most up-to-date version of the GeoAcademy curriculum.

This workbook covers GIS fundamentals, spatial analysis, data management, cartography and remote sensing. There are solution files for each exercise and most exercises have a challenge exercise. Discussion questions are also included at the end of each exercise. Some of the many highlights include learning how to: work with coordinate reference systems, create data via georeferencing and geocoding, using GRASS to conduct a supervised classification of satellite imagery, and how to work with both QGIS and Inkscape to create a publication quality map.

Thought was given to improving the content and organization for both hardcopy and electronic readers. The GeoAcademy data was reorganized to match the chapter structure of this book. Changes were made to several exercises, reflecting the newly updated integration of GRASS GIS with QGIS that came with QGIS v2.10. Portions that include working with GRASS vector maps include both GRASS 6 and GRASS 7 versions of the exercise databases. The portions using the free software Multi-Spec were rewritten using QGIS. Efforts were also made to incorporate some of the exciting new QGIS features such as Live Layer Effects into the Challenge Assignments.

It is my pleasure to work with Locate Press to bring this workbook into print and e-book formats so that more people can learn GIS with FOSS4G tools. I hope you enjoy the book!

The Data

The data for this book are available for download at http://locatepress.com/workbook/. They are organized by part and exercise. Each exercise includes solution files and answers to exercise questions.

About the Author

A former archaeologist, Kurt Menke is a Certified GIS Professional (GISP) based out of Albuquerque, New Mexico. He received a Master's degree in Geography from the University of New Mexico in 2000. That same year he founded Bird's Eye View (http://www.BirdsEyeViewGIS.com) to apply his expertise with GIS technology towards ecological conservation. Along with conservation, his other focus areas are public health and education. He is an avid open source GIS proponent, recently authoring Mastering QGIS for Packt Publishing. In 2015 he became an OsGeo Charter Member. He is an experienced FOSS4G educator and is a co-author of the GeoAcademy. In 2015 he was awarded the Global Educator of the Year Team Award by GeoForAll as part of the GeoAcademy team.

Acknowledgments

Each of the authors who contributed to these exercises is a very experienced GIS professional and I am grateful for all of their contributions. Dr. Richard (Rick) Smith (Texas A & M University – Corpus Christi) has been part of the GeoAcademy since day one, and is the original author for many of these exercises. Nate Jennings (City of Sacramento, UC Davis, Del Mar College and Sacramento City College) was the original author for the remote sensing labs. Dr. John van Hoesen performed quality checking on the GeoAcademy labs. Finally, none of this material would have been developed if it had not been for the leadership of Dr. Phil Davis (Del Mar College) who was the principal investigator for the GeoAcademy.

Part I

Introduction to Geospatial Technology

Exercise 1

Spatial Data Models

Objective – Explore and Understand Spatial Data Models

1.1 Introduction

In this exercise, you'll explore and manage geospatial data using two modules of the FOSS4G software QGIS: QGIS Browser and QGIS Desktop. QGIS Browser is an application designed to preview and manage geospatial data. It is analogous to Windows Explorer, but works specifically with geospatial datasets. QGIS Desktop is the companion application used to perform spatial analysis and make maps.

This exercise will also introduce you to the QGIS interface, which is used throughout the workbook. It is important to learn the concepts in this exercise as future exercises will require the skills covered in this exercise.

This exercise includes the following tasks:

- Task 1 – Learn to work with QGIS Browser.

- Task 2 – Become familiar with geospatial data models.

- Task 3 – Viewing geospatial data in QGIS Desktop.

1.2 Objective: Explore and Understand Geospatial Data Models

Geographic Information Systems model the real world with representations of objects such as lakes, roads and towns. Geospatial data models are the means used to represent these features. They are composed of two parts: spatial features and attributes that when combined, create a model of reality.

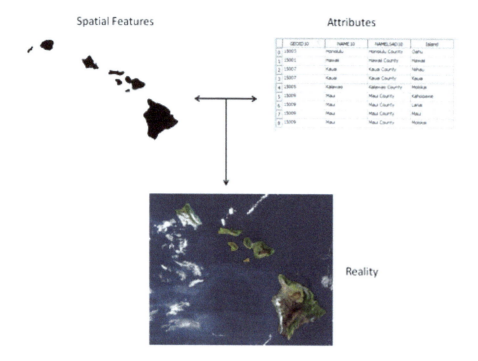

There are two main geospatial data models: vector and raster.

Vector Data Model – Best for modeling discrete objects. Vector data comes in three forms: point, line, and polygon.

Raster Data Model – This model is best for modeling continuous objects. A raster is composed of a matrix of contiguous cells, with each cell (pixel) holding a single numeric value.

1.3   Task 1 - Learn to Work with QGIS Browser

In this task, you will become familiar with QGIS Browser. The first step in working on a project with geospatial datasets is to organize your workspace. It is important that we organize datasets logically on the computer and make them easy to find. In this task, you will obtain a copy of the exercise data and explore how the data is organized using QGIS Browser.

Open QGIS Browser. The way you open QGIS Browser and QGIS Desktop will vary depending on your operating system. For this series of exercises, we will explain how to open and use QGIS using the Microsoft Windows 7 operating system.

   1. Click Start | All Programs | QGIS | QGIS Browser.

The interface to QGIS Browser is simple and clean (shown in the figure below). The File Tree is displayed on the left, which shows your computer's files and folders. (NOTE: your machine may have a different set and number of drives listed here—this is fine.) Below the drives are Database Connections. There are no connections to any databases at this point. The Display Window takes up the remainder of the window. There are Display Tabs above the Display Window that allow you to control the information you see.

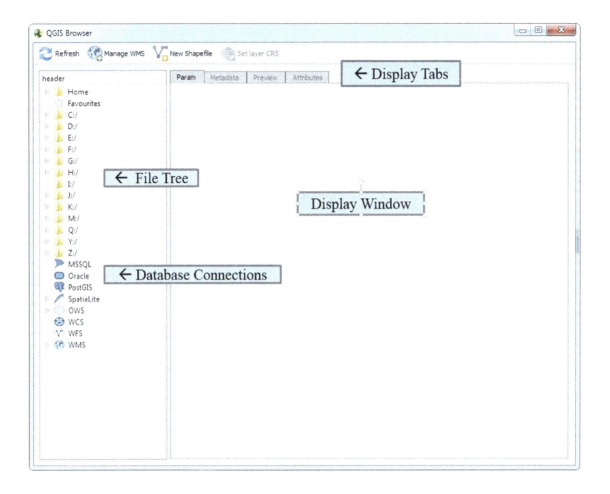

2. Look at the File Tree. Click the arrow to the left of the C: drive. You will now see all of the subfolders directly under the C:/ folder.

3. Expand the `Exercise 1 Data` folder where you stored your data in the File Tree by clicking the arrows to the left of each folder. You will now see the contents of the Data folder for the exercise (shown in figure below).

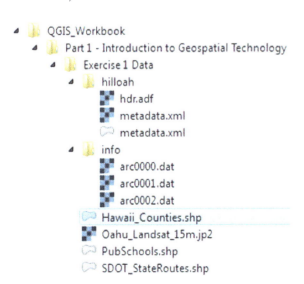

4. Take a moment to read the names of the files. There are two folders and several files listed with different

icons. The ⌣ icon indicates that the dataset is a vector layer. This icon ▓ is used to represent raster data but is also used for other files such as the XML files you see here.

1.4   Task 2 - Become Familiar with Geospatial Data Models

Now that you are familiar with the basic layout of QGIS Browser, we will explore some geospatial data.

1. Let's take a closer look at these data currently listed in QGIS Browser.

2. Select the `Hawaii_Counties.shp` layer in the File Tree. The Display Window automatically switches to the Metadata tab. This gives you some basic information about the dataset. You'll notice that the Storage type is ESRI shapefile. The Display Window also tells you that it has a Geometry type of polygon and it has 9 features (shown in figure below).

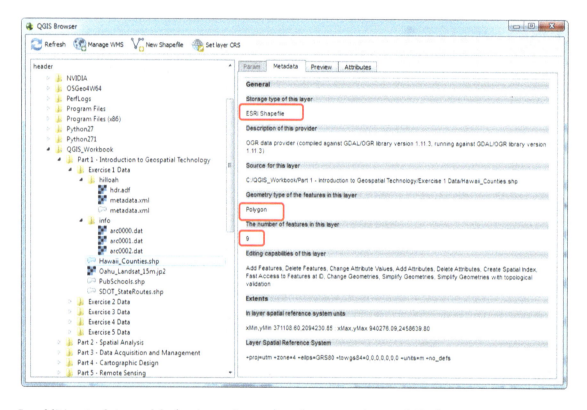

In addition to data models (vector and raster) we have to understand file formats. Some file formats are designed to store vector, and others raster data. Shapefiles are vector file format. In fact, they are probably the most common vector file format. An individual shapefile can only contain one geometry type (polygon, line, or point). A shapefile is actually a collection of files on the computer with a common name, but different extensions.

3. Now select `PubSchools.shp`. You'll see that this is also an ESRI Shapefile but that it is a point dataset with 287 features.

4. Select `SDOT_StateRoutes.shp`. This is an ESRI Shapefile with line geometry and 122 features.

5. Select `Hawaii_Counties.shp` again and click on the Preview tab. This shows you the spatial features of this GIS dataset (shown in figure below).

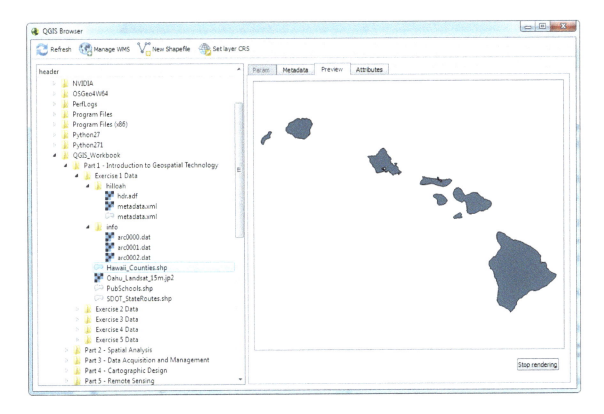

6. Click on the Attributes tab. This shows you the other component of the data model, the attributes. Each row corresponds to one polygon. The columns are things we know about the polygons such as island name (see figure below).

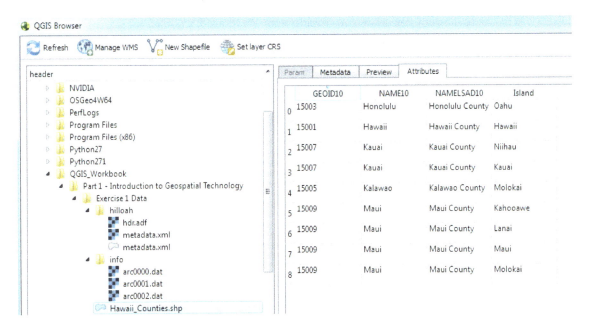

7. Select the `Oahu_Landsat_15m.jp2` dataset. Click on the Preview tab. This is an example of a raster dataset. Like a photograph, it is composed of cells. This raster is a satellite image of the island of Oahu, Hawaii (shown in figure below).

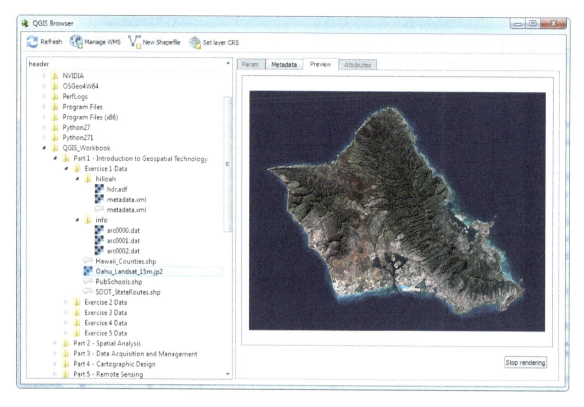

Let's look at the file formats in more detail.

8. Select the `Exercise 1 Data` folder in the File Tree. The `Param` tab is all that is available when a folder is selected (see figure below).

9. Now the Display Window is showing you what you would see in Windows Explorer.

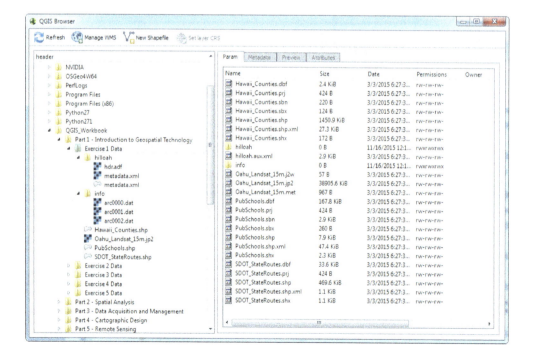

Focus on the Hawaii Counties files. Notice that the File Tree shows that Shapefile just as `Hawaii_Counties.shp` whereas the Display Window is showing seven files named Hawaii_Counties. These are all the component files of this particular shapefile. The File Tree simplifies the view of your data showing you only the *.shp* file.

For more information on ESRI shapefiles refer to this link

http://en.wikipedia.org/wiki/Shapefile

1.5   Task 3 - Viewing Geospatial Data in QGIS Desktop

Now that you know how geospatial datasets are stored on your computer, let's see what the data they contain look like. This next section will introduce you to QGIS Desktop.

1. Click Start | All Programs | QGIS | QGIS Desktop.

2. QGIS Desktop is the application you will use for making maps, editing data, and doing GIS analysis, among many other operations. QGIS Desktop has two main sections: the Layers panel and the Map Window.

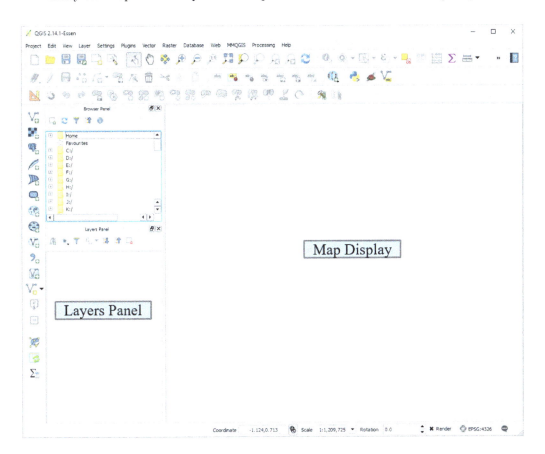

Note: Your QGIS Desktop window may look slightly different than the one pictured above. To reset your display back to the default settings, click the Settings | Options | System tab | QSettings section | Reset button, then click OK and restart QGIS Desktop.

The QGIS Desktop interface is a little cluttered by default, so let's close a few panels so we just see the Layers panel and Map Window.

3. Locate the Browser panel, and click the small 'X' button in the upper-right corner to close the panel (see

figure below).

4. Close the Shortest path panel using the same method.

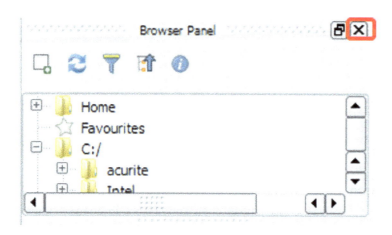

Panels can be docked and undocked from the QGIS Desktop window. To undock a panel, click and drag the panel's top title bar (outlined in figure below) and drag it away from the sides. When you release your mouse button, the panel will be floating freely.

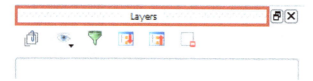

To dock a floating panel, click and drag the title bar, and drag the panel to the left or right side of QGIS Desktop until a rectangle appears underneath the panel. Release the mouse button to dock the panel (docking action shown in figure below).

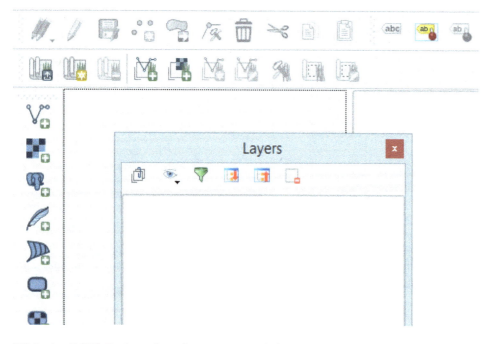

With the QGIS Desktop interface customized, let's add some data.

QGIS has Add Data buttons for each major geospatial data model (vector and raster).

5. Click the Add Vector Layer button 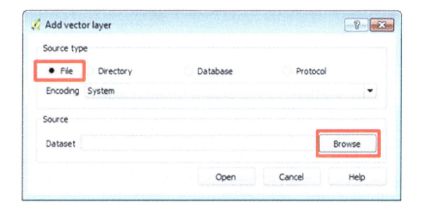. It's located on the toolbar along the left hand side of the Layers panel.

   - Alternatively, you can click Layer | Add Layer | Add Vector Layer.

6. This opens the Add vector layer window. Let's add one of the ESRI shapefiles which is a file-based dataset.

7. Keep the Source type "File" which is the default. Then click the Browse button.

8. The Open an OGR Supported Vector Layer window opens. (NOTE: OGR is a FOSS4G project with the sole purpose to read and write geospatial vector data files.) The window defaults to all files. From exploring the exercise data in QGIS Browser, you know there are several shapefiles in the exercise data folder. Take a moment to see the other available options. Click the All files dropdown box and change to ESRI Shapefiles (shown in figure below).

All files (*)
GDAL/OGR VSIFileHandler (*.zip *.gz *.tar *.tar.gz *.tgz *
Arc/Info ASCII Coverage (*.e00 *.E00)
Atlas BNA (*.bna *.BNA)
AutoCAD DXF (*.dxf *.DXF)
Comma Separated Value (*.csv *.CSV)
ESRI Personal GeoDatabase (*.mdb *.MDB)
ESRI Shapefiles (*.shp *.SHP)
GPS eXchange Format [GPX] (*.gpx *.GPX)
Generic Mapping Tools [GMT] (*.gmt *.GMT)
GeoJSON (*.geojson *.GEOJSON)
GeoPackage (*.gpkg *.GPKG)
GeoRSS (*.xml *.XML)
Geoconcept (*.gxt *.txt * GXT *.TXT)

9. Once you are finished exploring, make sure it is still set to ESRI Shapefiles. This filters what you can see in the exercise folder so that you only see the shapefiles.

10. Select `Hawaii_Counties.shp` and click Open (see figure below).

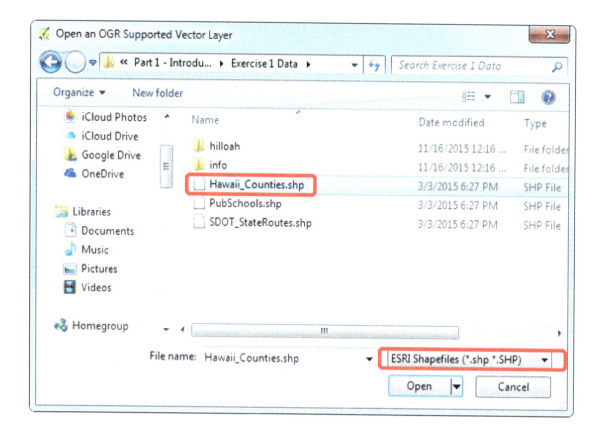

11. Now back at the Add vector layer window, click Open to add the data to QGIS Desktop (see figure below).

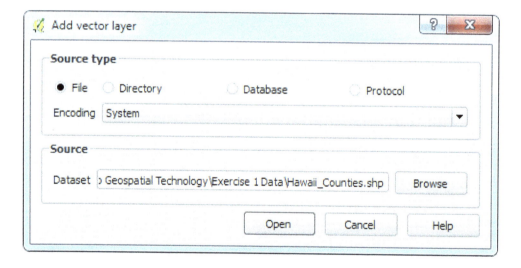

12. You will now see Hawaii_Counties in the Layers panel and the map features displayed in the map window. Vector GIS layers will come in with random colors. You will learn how to change layer styling in a future exercise.

13. Let's examine the attributes. Right-click on the Hawaii Counties layer in the Layers panel. This opens a context menu. Select Open Attribute Table (shown in figure below).

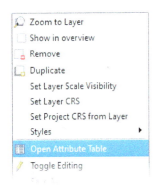

14. The attribute table opens. If you recall from exploring this dataset with QGIS Browser, it has 9 features (9 polygons). The attribute table has 9 corresponding records. There are columns with the County name (NAMELSAD10) and with the Island name (Island). Close the Attribute Table by clicking the X button in the upper right hand corner.

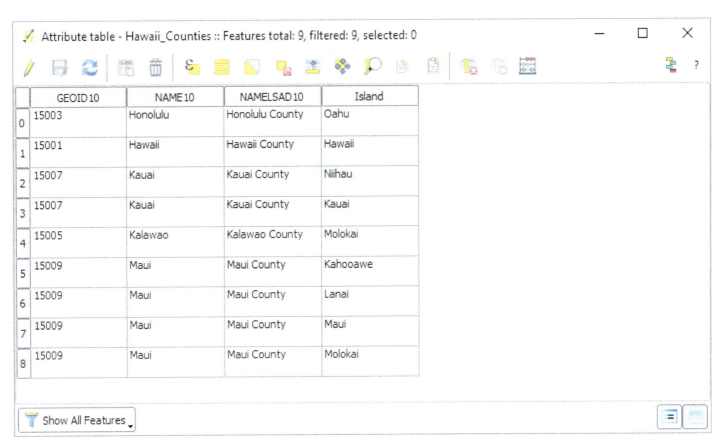

	GEOID10	NAME10	NAMELSAD10	Island
0	15003	Honolulu	Honolulu County	Oahu
1	15001	Hawaii	Hawaii County	Hawaii
2	15007	Kauai	Kauai County	Niihau
3	15007	Kauai	Kauai County	Kauai
4	15005	Kalawao	Kalawao County	Molokai
5	15009	Maui	Maui County	Kahooawe
6	15009	Maui	Maui County	Lanai
7	15009	Maui	Maui County	Maui
8	15009	Maui	Maui County	Molokai

15. Another way to interact with both the spatial features and the attributes is the Identify button.

16. Click the Identify button

17. Click on one of the features on the map. The Identify Results panel (shown in figure below) shows you the attributes for the feature you clicked on. *Note:* The Identify Results panel may initially be docked or floating.

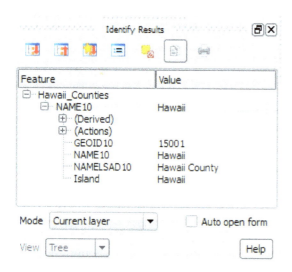

Now you will learn how to add Raster data to QGIS Desktop.

18. Click the Add Raster Layer button .

   - Alternatively, click Layer | Add Layer | Add Raster Layer.

19. The Open a GDAL Supported Raster Data Source window opens (displayed in figure below). This is a very similar workflow to adding vector data.

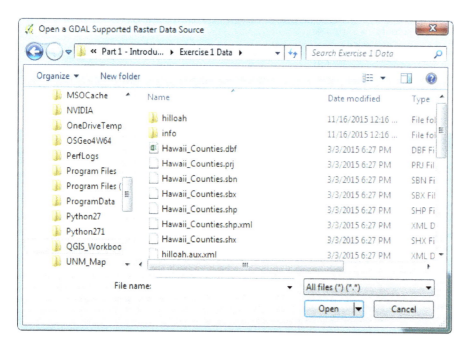

20. Whereas QGIS used OGR to open vector data files, here it uses another FOSS4G software library called GDAL. GDAL is used for reading and writing raster datasets.

21. The window's raster data filter is set to All Files by default, so you see the entire contents of the folder (Figure below).

22. Set the filter to ERDAS JPEG2000. (Also, note how many formats it will read!) In GIS there are many more raster file types than vector. Once you've set the filter you'll see the one dataset: `Oahu_Landsat_15m.jp2` (shown in figure below).

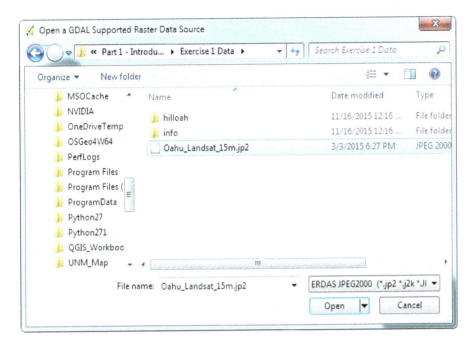

23. Select the `Oahu_Landsat_15m.jp2` raster dataset and click Open.

24. This dataset only covers a portion of Hawaii—just the island of Oahu. Right-click on the Oahu_Landsat_15m dataset in the layers panel and choose Zoom to Layer to zoom to the spatial extent of this raster (shown in figure below).

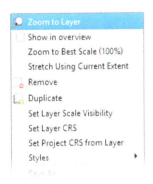

You may notice two folders in the exercise data folder that we have not discussed yet. One is named `hilloah` and the other `info`. Together, these combine to make another geospatial raster dataset format named GRID. The info folder holds the attributes and always has the name "info". The other folder is the layer name and contains the spatial data. Let's add a GRID raster to our map.

25. Click the Add Raster Layer button again.

26. Set the filter to Arc/Info Binary Grid. Double click the `hilloah` folder to enter it. Select the `hdr.adf` file and click Open to add the raster to QGIS (shown in figure below).

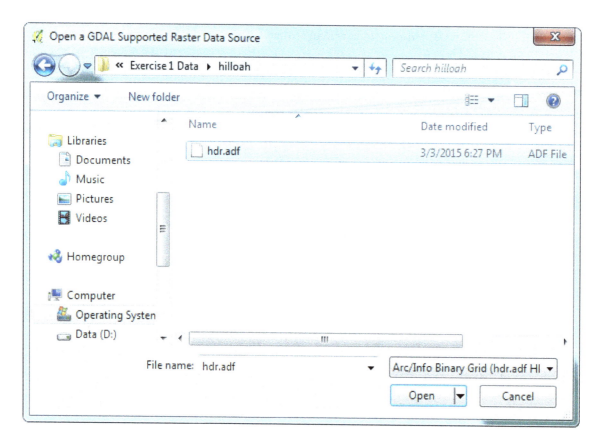

27. This raster is a hillshade image of Oahu and it represents the terrain.

QGIS Desktop also has a Browser panel that allows us to view geospatial files on our computer without having to open QGIS Browser.

28. Right-click on the blank space to the right of the Help menu. This opens a context menu showing all the toolbars and windows that you can add to the QGIS interface. Check the box next to Browser (shown in figure below). A Browser panel is added to QGIS Desktop (likely located under the Layers panel).

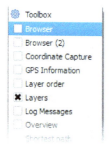

29. Look at the Browser panel. Note that there is a Favourites item. Identify folders or locations as being favorites in order for them to appear here.

Data is often stored deep inside a series of folders. It is often tedious and time consuming to navigate deep inside the folders to gain access to the data. Favorites provide a way to create a shortcut directly to any folder so that you have one-click access. Let's create a favorite to our exercise folder for practice.

30. Navigate to the `Exercise 1 Data` folder in the Browser panel. Right-click on it and choose `Add as a Favourite` (see figure below). *Note:* Currently this functionality is reserved only for the Browser tab in QGIS Desktop. However, once it is set it will show up as a favorite in QGIS Browser as well.

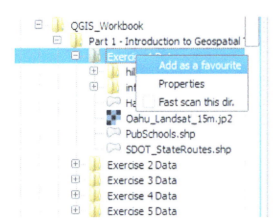

31. Now expand `Favourites` and you will see your exercise folder listed there. You can remove a favorite anytime by right-clicking on it and choosing `Remove favourite`.

32. Expand the exercise folder under `Favourites` to expose the contents. Select `SDOT_StateRoutes.shp` and drag it onto the map. This is a quick way to add data to your map.

Note: You can drag data from the QGIS Browser application to QGIS Desktop as well to add the data to the map.

1.6   Conclusion

In this exercise you explored datasets that use the two common geospatial data models: vector and raster. You have also used the QGIS Browser to preview datasets. In future exercises, you will learn how to use QGIS Desktop to make maps and perform analysis.

1.7   Discussion Questions

1. How can Browser favourites make your workflow more efficient?
2. What are the two main parts of a GIS data model?
3. Name three ways of seeing feature attributes for a vector GIS layer.

Exercise 2

Displaying Geospatial Data

Objective – Explore and Understand How to Display Geospatial Data

2.1 Introduction

In this exercise, you'll learn how to complete a well-designed map showing the relationship between species habitat and federal land ownership, as well as how to style GIS data layers in QGIS Desktop. In addition, we'll show how to use the QGIS Print Composer to design a well crafted map deliverable. The final map will include standard map elements such as the title and map legend.

This exercise will also continue to introduce you to the QGIS interface, as QGIS Desktop will be used throughout the course. It is important to learn the concepts in this exercise as future exercises will require the skills covered in this exercise.

This exercise includes the following tasks:

- Task 1 – Add data, organize map layers and set map projections.

- Task 2 – Style data layers.

- Task 3 – Compose map deliverable.

2.2 Objective: Create a Map that Meets the Customer's Requirements

Often times, you will be provided with a map requirements document from a coworker or customer. For this exercise, the you'll respond to a map requirements document from a customer who is writing a paper about the state of Greater sage-grouse habitat in the western United States. The map requirements from the customer are below.

Map Requirements from Customer:

Hi, my name is Steve Darwin. I am a wildlife biologist writing a paper on the state of Greater sage-grouse (see figure below) populations in the western United States. I need a letter sized, color, map figure that shows the relationship between current occupied Greater sage-grouse habitat and federal land ownership. I am interested in seeing how much habitat is under federal versus non-federal ownership.

I have been provided data from the US Fish and Wildlife Service depicting current occupied range for Greater sage-grouse. I also have federal land ownership, state boundaries and country boundaries from the US National Atlas. The land ownership data has an attribute column describing which federal agency manages the land (AGBUR).

I want to have the habitat data shown so that the federal land ownership data is visible beneath. I would like each different type of federal land styled with standard Bureau of Land Management colors. The map should also include a title ("Greater sage-grouse Current Distribution"), a legend, data sources and the date. The map should be a high-resolution (300 dpi) jpg image.

I trust that you will get the figure right the first time, so please just submit the completed figures to the managing editor directly.

Image attribution: By Pacific Southwest Region from Sacramento, US (Greater Sage-Grouse) [CC BY 2.0 (http://creativecommons.org/licenses/by/2.0)], via Wikimedia Commons.

2.3   Task 1 - Add Data, Organize Map Layers and Set Coordinate Reference System

In this first task you will learn a new way to add data to QGIS Desktop. You will then set the projection for the map project, organize the data layers in the Table of Contents and change the layer names.

1. Open QGIS Desktop.

In Exercise 1 you learned how to add data to QGIS Desktop by using the Add Vector Data and Add Raster Data buttons. Now you will learn another method of adding data to QGIS Desktop. You will use the QGIS Desktop Browser panel.

2. Click View | Panels and make sure Browser is checked. The Browser panel will now be displayed.

Note: The Browser panel may be docked or floating, so it may not be in the same location as in the figures in this exercise.

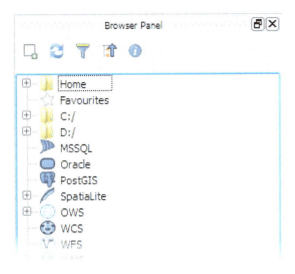

3. Using the file tree in the Browser window navigate to the `Exercise 2 Data` folder.

4. Right click on the `Exercise 2 Data` folder and choose Add as a favourite from the context menu.

5. Sometimes when recent changes have been made, such as setting a folder as a favourite, the Refresh button needs to be pressed in order to see the changes. Click the Refresh button (highlighted in figure below).

6. Now expand Favourites near the top of the file tree in the Browser window by clicking the plus sign to the left. You will see the `Exercise 2 Data` folder listed. Setting the folder as a favorite allows you to quickly navigate to your working folder.

7. You will see 5 shapefiles in the exercise data folder:

   - `Canada.shp`
   - `Land_ownership.shp`
   - `Mexico.shp`
   - `Sage_grouse_current_distribution.shp`
   - `Western_states.shp`

8. You can select them all by holding down the Ctrl key on your keyboard while left clicking on each shapefile. Select the five shapefiles (shown in figure below).

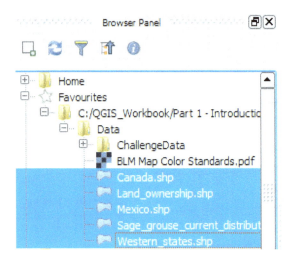

9. Drag the five selected shapefiles onto the map canvas from the Browser panel. This is another way of adding geospatial data to QGIS Desktop. QGIS Desktop should now look like figure below. The random colors that QGIS assigns to the layers may be different than the figure below but that is fine.

  - *Note:* If you do not see anything displayed in the map canvas, you may need to zoom to full extents of the map by pressing the Zoom Full button [icon]. Alternatively, you can click View | Zoom Full.

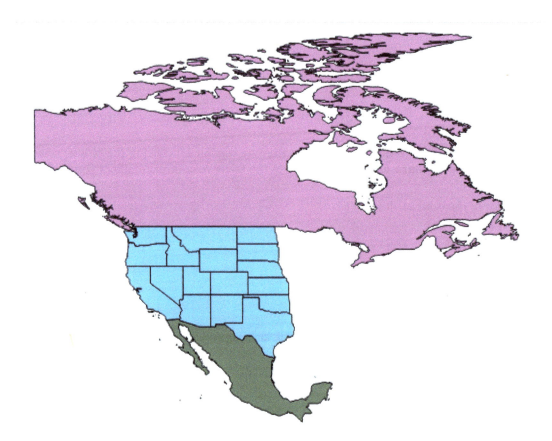

10. Let's save the QGIS project. Click on Project | Save from the menu bar. Navigate to your **Exercise 2 Data** folder and save your project as **Exercise 2**.

11. You have five layers in the map canvas, but currently all you can see are data for Canada, Mexico and the Western states. When you cannot see a dataset, one approach is to make sure the spatial extent of your map

window covers that dataset. Right click on the Sage_grouse_current_distribution layer in the Layers panel, and choose Zoom to Layer from the context menu. This will zoom you into the extent of that dataset.

12. The map is now zoomed to the western United States, but we still cannot see anything that looks like habitat data (shown in figure below).

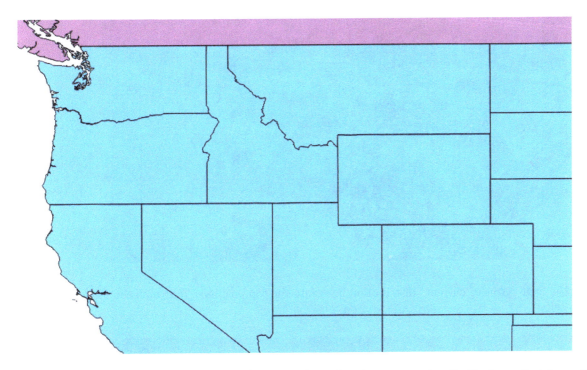

The data layers in the Layers panel are drawn in the order they appear in. So the layer that is on the top of the list in the Layers panel will be drawn on top of the other layers in the map view. Notice that the Western_states layer is in that top position. This mean that Western_states is covering up the Sage_grouse_current_distribution and Land_ownership data, since they are placed lower in the Layers panel.

Let's change this drawing order.

13. Select the Land_ownership data layer in the Layers panel and drag it to the top position. You will see a blue line as you drag this layer up the list.

14. Your map should now resemble the figure below.

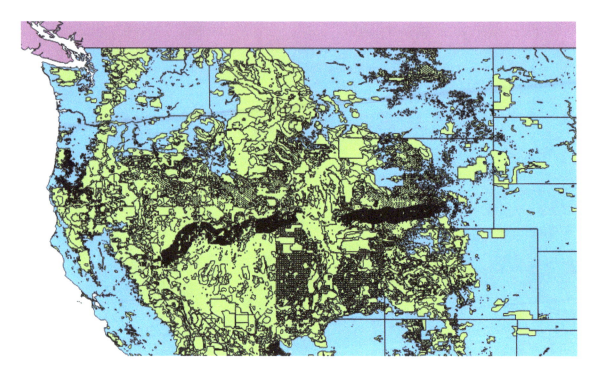

15. Now drag the Sage_grouse_current_distribution layer into the top position. Your map should now resemble the figure below.

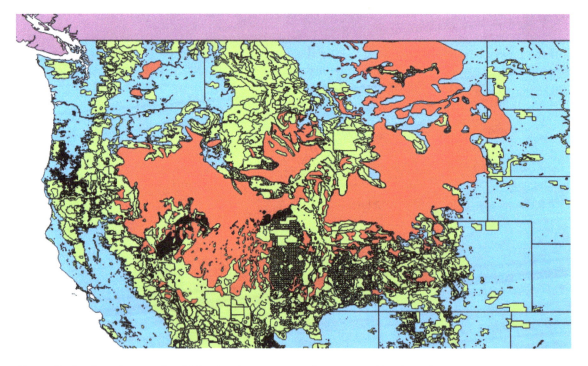

Now all the data layers should be in the correct order. Typically, data layers will be organized with point data layers on top of line layers on top of polygon layers. Raster data layers are usually placed near the bottom.

With the layers in the best drawing order, let's turn our attention to the coordinate reference system for the map.

16. Note that the lower right hand corner of QGIS displays EPSG: 4269 OTF. This is the EPSG code for the coordinate reference system (CRS) the map is currently in and an indication that on-the-fly projection is

enabled (shown in figure below).

17. Click on Project | Project Properties from the menu bar to open the Project Properties window.

18. Select the CRS tab.

The current QGIS map CRS is listed at the bottom. This is a detailed explanation of the maps CRS which is a geographic coordinate system using the NAD83 datum. This CRS makes the lower 48 look stretched out and distorted, so you'll want to change the maps CRS into something that makes the lower 48 "look correct".

19. Make sure that the Enable 'on the fly' CRS transformation option is checked. Click OK to close the Project Properties window.

Since the Sage_grouse_current_distribution layer is in an Albers projection, and the QGIS map is in a geographic CRS, that means that the Sage_grouse_current_distribution layer is being projected on the fly into the geographic projection of the map.

20. Right click on the Sage_grouse_current_distribution layer and choose Set Project CRS from Layer option on the context menu (Figure below). This will put the map into the Albers CRS of the Sage grouse layer. Note that the EPSG code in the lower right corner now reads 5070 for the Albers CRS. This CRS gives the western US an appearance we are more used to. Any other map layers not in Albers, will now be projected on the fly into Albers.

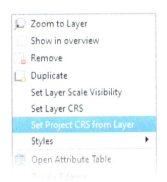

Now you will change the layer names in the Layers panel. The layer names match the names of the shapefiles by default. However, these names will appear on the legend. So you will always want to change these to proper names that your map reading audience will understand.

21. Right click on the Sage_grouse_current_distribution layer, and choose the Properties from the context menu, to open the Layer Properties window. Choose the General tab on the left. Click in the box next to Layer name and change the name to Sage-grouse Habitat (shown in figure below). Click OK to close the Layer Properties window.

   - Alternatively, you can right click on a layer in the Layers panel and choose Rename from the context menu to make the layer name editable directly in the Layers panel.

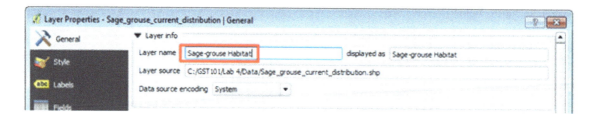

22. Change the other layers names as follows:

    - Change Land ownership to Federal Land Ownership
    - Change Western_states to State Boundaries

23. Click the File | Save to save the changes you have made to your project.

2.4   Task 2 - Style Data Layers

Now that you have set up your map, you will style your layers and begin to craft a well-designed map.

Visually you will want the land ownership and sage-grouse habitat to have the most weight. Canada and Mexico are there for reference but should fall to the background. You will make them both light gray.

1. Double-click on the Canada layer to open the Layer Properties window (this is another way to open Layer Properties).

2. Click on the Style tab.

3. In the Symbol layers box click on Simple fill (reference figure below).

4. Find the Symbol layer type box on the right side of the window. This allows you to change both the fill and outline symbols for this polygon layer. Click on the colored box to the right of Fill (shown in figure below) to open the Color picker window.

You can pick existing Basic colors or define a color via A) hue, saturation and value (HSV) or B) red blue and green (RGB) values. Set the color to Hue: 0 Sat: 0% and Val: 90%. Make sure your Color picker window matches the figure below.

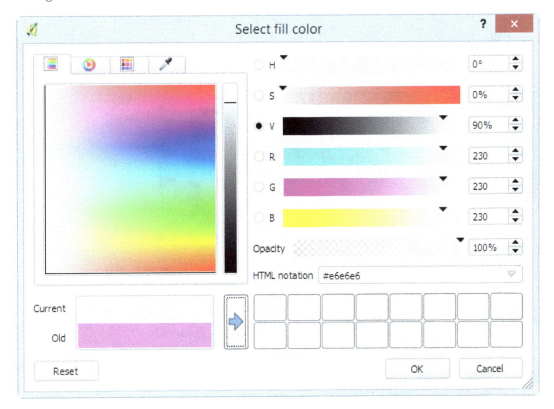

5. Click the button with the blue arrow to add the color to the custom color buttons. Click OK to close the Color picker window.

6. Back in the Layer Properties window, for the **Border style**, select Solid Line from the dropdown menu (shown in figure below).

7. Click OK on the Layer Properties window to close and style the Canada layer.

8. Open Layer Properties for Mexico. Make Mexico look the same as Canada. You can just choose the Custom color you just saved to save time.

Your map should now look like figure below.

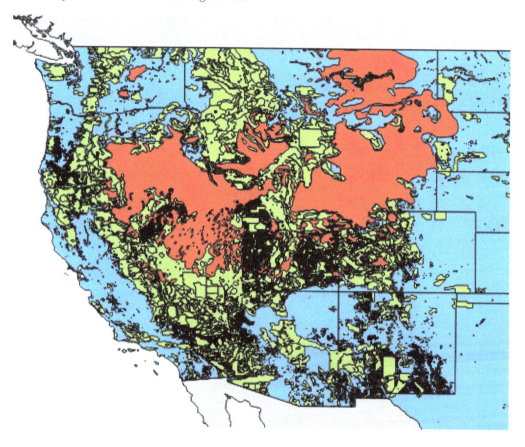

9. Using the same workflow, give the State Boundaries a white fill. You will be able to find white in the Basic colors palette.

Now you will style the Land Ownership layer. Instead of making the entire layer one color as you have done thus far, you will assign a unique color to each land managing agency. How do you know who is managing each parcel? This will be information contained in the attribute table.

10. Right click on Federal Land Ownership layer in the Layers panel, and choose Open the Attribute Table from the context menu.

There are thirteen columns of information. Can you find the one that contains the land manager?

11. Open the Layer Properties for the Federal Land Ownership layer and switch to the Style tab. So far you've used the default Single Symbol type. Now you will switch to Categorized.

12. Click the drop down menu and change from Single Symbol to Categorized (Figure below).

Now you have the option of choosing an attribute column to symbolize the layer by. The column AGBUR is the one that contains the managing agency values.

13. Click the drop down arrow and choose AGBUR for the Column.

14. Click the Classify button (shown in figure below). This tells QGIS to sort through all the records in the table and identify all the unique values. Now you can assign a specific color to each class by double clicking on the color square.

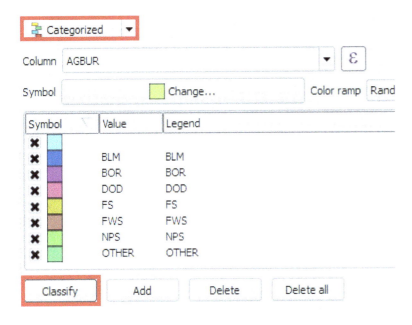

Notice that there is a symbol with no values. These are parcels with no values (NULL) in the AGBUR field. They represent private and state inholdings within federal lands. Since you are just interested in depicting federal land ownership you'll delete that symbol class.

15. Select that top symbol by clicking on it, and then click the Delete button below to remove that symbol. Now those parcels will not be included on the map.

For the remaining federal land ownership symbols you will use the BLM Standards Manual for land ownership maps http://www.blm.gov/noc/st/en/business/mapstandards/colormod.html.

- *Note:* A PDF of the BLM Map Color Standards is also available in your exercise folder and is named BLM Map Color Standards.pdf.

The BLM has designated colors for each type of land ownership. When composing a map it is important to pay attention to industry specific standards. Following them will make the map more intuitive to the target audience.

For example, people are used to seeing Forest Service land depicted in a certain shade of green.

16. To color BLM lands, double click on the color patch left of BLM in the Style window. The Symbol selector will open.

17. Click on Simple fill.

18. You will not want any border lines on these polygons. With such a complicated thematic polygon layer they are too visually distracting. Choose a Border style of No Pen.

19. Click on the Fill style color patch to open the Color Picker window.

20. In the Color Picker window, change the Red, Green, and Blue values to 254, 230, and 121 respectively (shown in figure below). This will change the color to a specific shade of tan representing BLM lands. Click OK in the Color Picker window. Then click OK in the Symbol Selector to save the BLM style.

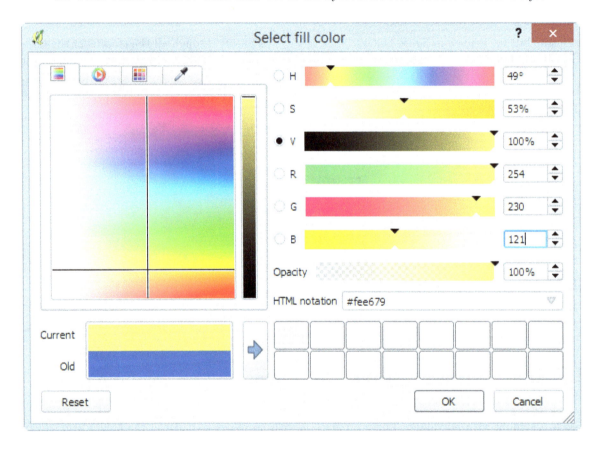

21. Use the values below to change the RGB colors for the remaining six land ownership classes. Also choose No pen for the border style.

   - BOR – 255, 255, 179
   - DOD – 251, 180, 206
   - FS – 179, 222, 105
   - FWS – 127, 204, 167
   - NPS – 177, 137, 193
   - OTHER – 150, 150, 150

22. When finished, click OK on the Layer Properties for Federal Land Ownership.

23. Turn off Sage-grouse Habitat by clicking the X next to the name in the Layers panel.

Your map should now resemble figure below.

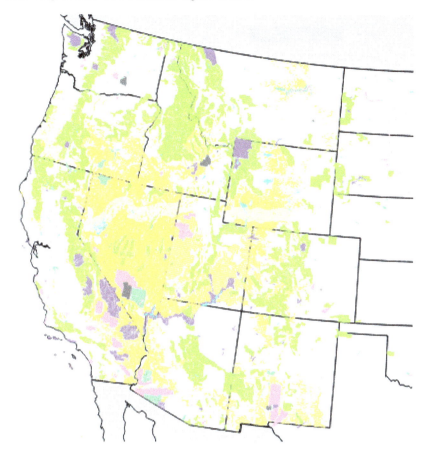

Now you will set a background color for the map. Since states are filled with white, setting a background color of light blue will serve to represent the Pacific Ocean.

24. From the menu bar choose Project | Project Properties.

25. On the General tab, click the white color patch next to Background color to open the Color Picker window.

26. Set the RGB value to: 225, 255, 255.

27. Click OK on the Color Picker window and OK on Project Properties to save the setting.

Depending on your current map extent, the area east of the states layer may be blue now too. That is fine. For the final map we will be zoomed in so you won't see that.

The states are white with a black border and serve to show non-federal land as white which is great. However, the state boundaries are obscured since State Boundaries are below Federal Land Ownership.

28. Go to the Browser panel and add `Western_states.shp` to the map again. You can have multiple copies of layers for cartographic purposes.

29. Drag the Western_states layer to the top of the Layers panel.

30. Open the Layer Properties window for the Western_states layer and select the Style tab.

31. Click on Simple fill.

32. Give the layer a Fill style of No Brush (see figure below). It will now just be the state outlines above Federal Land Ownership.

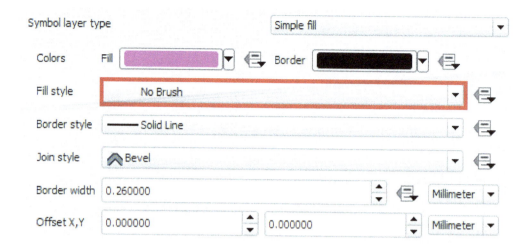

33. Click OK to save the style and close the Layer Properties window.

34. Your map should now resemble figure below.

The last layer to work with is the Sage-grouse Habitat. You will make the Sage-grouse Habitat polygons have a crosshatch pattern. This will allow the map reader to see the land ownership data beneath.

35. Turn on the visibility for the Sage-grouse Habitat layer.

36. Open the Layer Properties for Sage-grouse Habitat.

37. Click on Simple fill.

38. Change the Fill color to RGB 170, 0, 255.

39. Change the Border color to RGB 142, 0, 213.

40. Make the Fill style FDiagonal.

41. Finally change the Border width to 0.46 (reference settings in figure below).

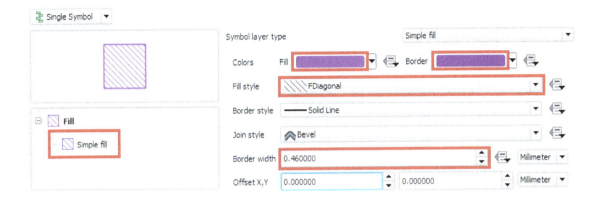

42. Click OK.

43. Save your project!

Your map should now resemble the figure below.

2.5   Task 3 - Compose Map Deliverable

Now that all the data is well styled you can compose the map deliverable.

1. Zoom in tighter to the Sage-grouse Habitat data.

   - Use the Zoom in tool and drag a box encapsulating the sage-grouse habitat. Leave a little of the Pacific Ocean visible to the west to give some context (reference figure below).

As it turns out, the data for Mexico is not needed. Sometimes you are given data that does not end up being used, but is nice to have in case you do need it.

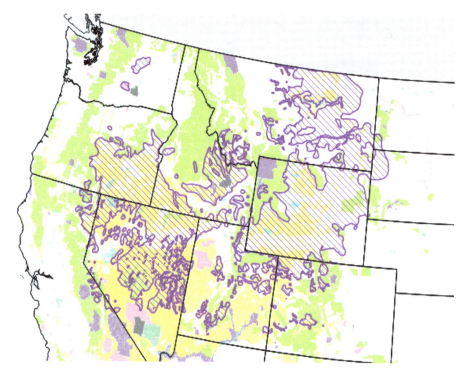

2. From the menu bar choose Project | New Print Composer.
3. Name the Composer "Exercise 2 - Sage-grouse Habitat" (shown in figure below).

4. Click OK. The Print Composer will open. This is where you craft your map.

The Print Composer is an application window with many tools that allow you to craft a map. For detailed information about the Print Composer, refer to the QGIS manual:
http://www.qgis.org/en/docs/user_manual/print_composer/print_composer.html
The main window of the Print Composer displays the piece of paper upon which the map will be designed. There

are buttons along the left side of the window that allow you to add various map elements: map, scale bar, photo, text, shapes, attribute tables, etc. Each item added to the map canvas becomes a graphic object that can be further manipulated (if selected) by the Items tab on the right side of the composer. Across the top are buttons for exporting the composition, navigating within the composition and some other graphic tools (grouping/ungrouping etc.)

5. On the Composition tab you can specify details about the overall composition. Set the Presets to ANSI A (Letter; 8.5x11 in).

6. Set the Orientation to Landscape.

7. Set the Export resolution to 300 DPI.

(These are listed as map requirements at the beginning of the exercise.)

8. Using the Add new map button 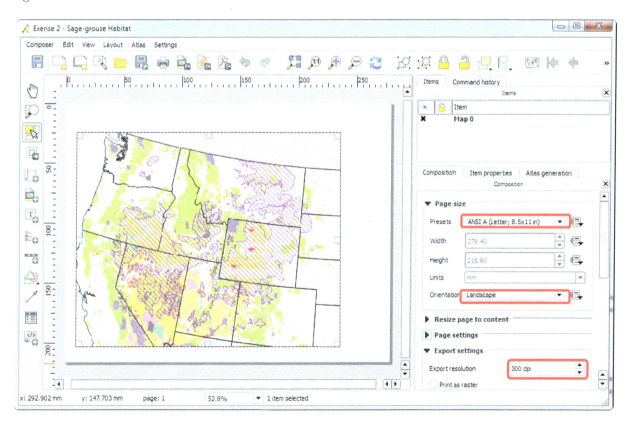 drag a box on the map canvas where you'd like the map to go. Remember that you'll need room for a title at the top of the page and a legend to the right of the map (reference figure below).

The map object can be resized after it's added by selecting it and using the handles around the perimeter to resize.

Map extent helpful hints: Generally, the map will look as it does within QGIS Desktop. However, you may need to change the map extent in QGIS Desktop, go back to the Print Composer and click the Refresh view button . It is normal to have some back and forth with QGIS Desktop and the Print Composer before getting the map just right.

Now you will add the title to your map.

9. Use the Add new label tool 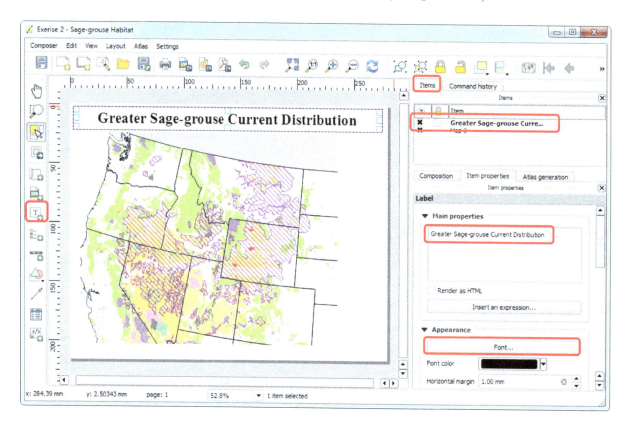 to drag a box all the way across the top of the composition. The text box can be resized after the fact by using the graphic handles.

10. Use the Item Properties to type in the title. Enter the title as 'Greater sage-grouse Current Distribution'.

11. In the Items tab, select the title. This will change the properties available in the Item Properties tab.

12. In the Item Properties tab, click the Font button and change the font to: Times New Roman, Bold, Size 36.

13. Finally align the title horizontally to the center of the map (see figure below).

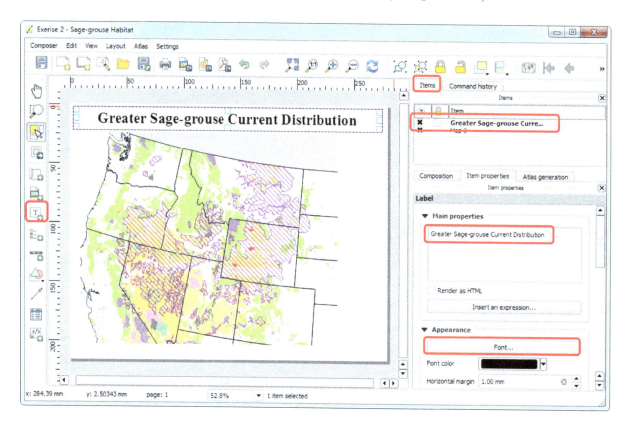

14. Now you will add a legend. Use the Add new legend tool to drag a box on the right side of the map (shown in figure below).

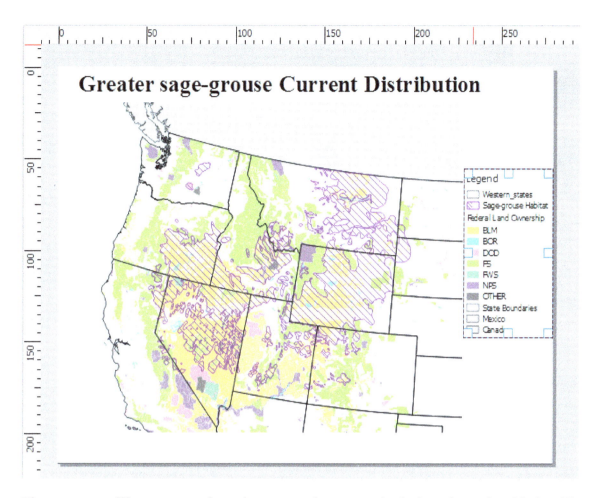

The upper most Western_states layer does not need to appear in the legend, nor does Mexico. Western_states is there purely for cartographic reasons and Mexico does not appear on the map. The Item properties tab will be used to configure the legend (see figure below).

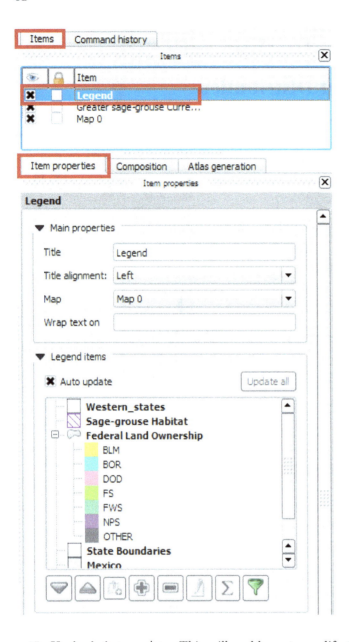

15. Uncheck Auto update. This will enable us to modify the legend, however, updates to the map will no longer be reflected in the legend unless we reenable Auto update.

16. Select the Western_states layer and click the Delete item button to remove it. Do the same for Mexico.

17. Expand the Federal Land Ownership layer.

18. Click on the BLM class and click the Edit button.

19. Change the name to "Bureau of Land Management". Go through each remaining land ownership class and edit them to match the figure below.

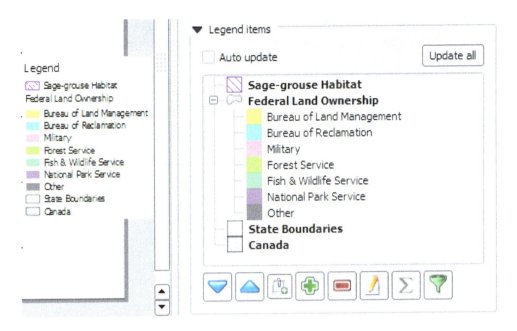

Now we will add a neatline around our map.

20. Click the tool (shown in figure below).

21. Drag a box around the map object and legend.

22. On the Item Properties tab, click the Style Change button.

23. Click Simple fill and give it a Fill style of No Brush.

24. Give it a Border width of 1.

25. Adjust the box so that it aligns with the map boundary.

You may find it necessary to lock the rectangle so you can move other map elements. To lock a map element and keep it from being selected, in the Items tab, check the box in the lock column as shown in the figure below.

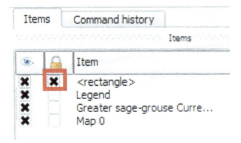

The last items to add to the map are the data sources and date.

26. Click the Add new label tool.

27. Drag a box in the lower right hand corner of the composition. Using the Item Properties type:

Data Sources: The National Atlas & USFWS

Date: Month, Day, Year

28. Make the font Times New Roman and the font size 8.

Your map should resemble the figure below.

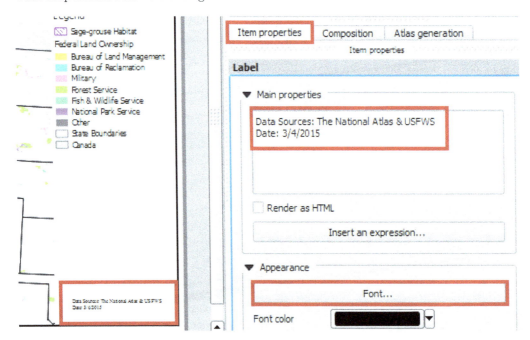

29. Congratulations your map is finished! The final step is to export it to a high-resolution jpg image.

30. Click the Export as image button.

31. Choose JPEG as the Save as type and save the image to your Exercise 2 Data folder. Name the file exercise2_Map.jpg and click Save.

32. The final map should look like the figure below.

Greater sage-grouse Current Distribution

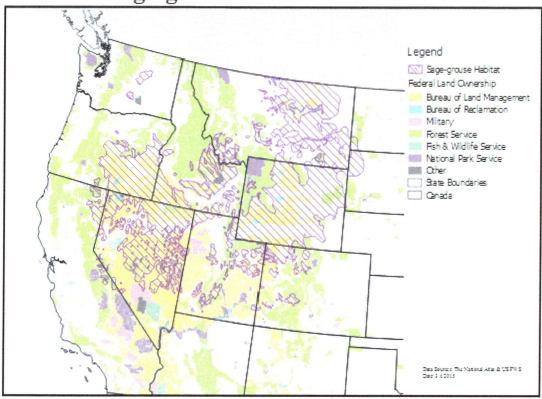

2.6 Conclusion

In this exercise you created a well-designed map using some of the cartography tools available in QGIS Desktop. You created a nice map highlighting federal land ownership within sage-grouse habitat for a client. This involved styling layers, styling layers by categorical attributes and crafting a map composition.

2.7 Discussion Questions

1. Export the final map as a high-resolution jpg for your instructor to grade.

2. What are two ways to add vector data to QGIS Desktop?

3. How would a portrait orientation change the composition of the map? Describe how you would arrange the map elements.

4. No map is perfect. Critique this map. What do you like about it? What do you dislike about it? How would you change this map to improve it? Would you add other data layers or add labels?

2.8 Challenge Assignment (optional)

Another biologist working with black bears on the east coast heard about your great work on the sage-grouse map. She would like you to create a similar map for her. The data she is providing is in the Exercise 2 Data/Challenge folder.

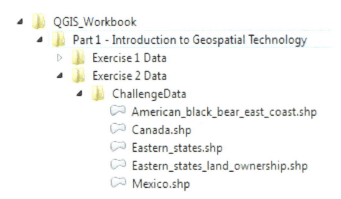

She also needs a letter sized, color, map figure that shows the relationship between black bear habitat and federal land ownership along the eastern seaboard. She is interested in seeing how much habitat is under federal versus non-federal ownership.

She is providing data from the US Fish and Wildlife Service depicting current occupied range for black bear on the east coast. She is also providing federal land ownership, state boundaries and country boundaries from the US National Atlas. The land ownership data has an attribute column describing which federal agency manages the land (AGBUR). This land ownership dataset has another category in the AGBUR field for Wilderness Areas called "Wild". These should be styled with a dark green.

She wants to have the habitat data shown so that the federal land ownership data is visible beneath. She would like each different type of federal land styled with standard Bureau of Land Management colors. The map should also include a title ("Black Bear Current Distribution"), a legend, data sources and the date. The map should be a high-resolution (300 dpi) jpg image. Perhaps you can incorporate some improvements to this map!

Exercise 3

Creating Geospatial Data

Objective – Digitize Information from a Scanned Hardcopy Source

3.1 Introduction

In this exercise, you'll learn how to georeference a scanned map. Georeferencing is the process of transforming the coordinate system of the scanned map, from the coordinate system produced by the scanning process, into a real world projected coordinate reference system. You'll then learn how to digitize information contained in the scanned map into a shapefile. The first task will be to create the empty shapefile to digitize features into. In addition, you'll learn how to edit existing vector datasets.

This exercise will continue to introduce you to the QGIS interface. It is important to learn the concepts in this exercise, as later exercises in this workbook will require the skills covered here.

This exercise includes the following tasks:

- Task 1 – Create a new shapefile.

- Task 2 – Transforming coordinate system of source data.

- Task 3 – Heads-up digitizing from transformed source data.

- Task 4 – Editing existing geospatial data.

3.2 Objective: Digitize Information from a Scanned Hard Copy Source

While there is a large amount of digital information readily available to users of GIS, there's still a large amount of information that has not been converted to digital format. For hundreds of years of hard copy paper maps contained all geospatial data. Many historic, and even newer, hard copy maps have never been digitized. It is possible to extract the information from hardcopy sources through a process called digitizing. In this exercise, you will use heads-up digitizing to digitize parcels in a portion of Albuquerque, New Mexico from a scanned map. This will be accomplished through a five-step digitizing process:

1. Create a shapefile to store the data that will be digitized.
2. Load the scanned map source data into QGIS
3. Georeference the source map
4. Digitize parcels
5. Save

3.3   Task 1 - Create a New Shapefile

In Task 3, you will be digitizing parcels from a georeferenced data source. In this first task you will learn how to create the new shapefile you will eventually digitize into.

1. Open QGIS Browser.
2. Navigate to the exercise folder in the file tree and select the Data folder by clicking once on it so that it is highlighted.
3. Click on the New Shapefile button at the top of the Browser window. This will open the New Shapefile Layer window.

 New Shapefile

4. Choose a type of 'Polygon'
5. Click the Select CRS button to open the Coordinate Reference System Selector.

The City of Albuquerque, like most American municipalities, uses the State Plane Coordinate System (SPCS) for their data. You will use the same CRS for your new shapefile.

6. In the Coordinate Reference System Selector interface type New Mexico into the Filter. This will limit the list below to just those with New Mexico in their name. These are different SPCS CRSs for New Mexico. New Mexico has 3 zones and Albuquerque is in the Central zone.
7. Select the NAD83(HARN) / New Mexico Central (ftUS) with an EPSG code of 2903 (see figure below). Click OK once you have selected this CRS to be returned to the New Shapefile Layer window.

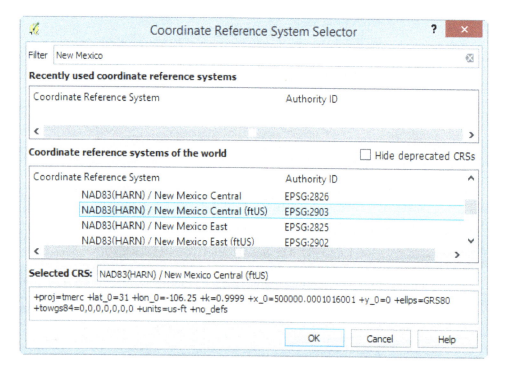

While creating your new shapefile you have the option of adding attribute columns. It is possible to add them later, but if you know of some attribute columns you will need in the layer, it makes the most sense to define them here. The ID attribute is automatically added to every shapefile you create.

For this exercise, you will need an attribute column to hold the zoning code.

8. In the New field section of the New Shapefile Layer window, define a new field named `zonecode` as Text data with a width of 5.

This means the new `zonecode` attribute column will store data as text and will only be able to accommodate five characters of data. Since our longest zoning code is 4 digits this is more than enough.

9. Click Add to fields list and you will see the new `zonecode` attribute added.

10. Click OK to approve the new shapefile options and open the Save layer as... window. Since you had the `Data` folder selected when you clicked the New Shapefile button it will default to that folder. If it doesn't just navigate to that folder now.

11. Name the shapefile `parcels.shp` and click Save to create the shapefile

Initially, the new shapefile may not display in the Browser. We need to first refresh the view to see the newly created file.

12. Click the Refresh button in the upper left hand corner of the QGIS Browser window. Expand the `Data` folder and you will see the `parcels.shp` file.

13. Select the `parcels.shp` dataset and click the Metadata tab. You'll see that it has 0 features and has the Spatial Reference System you specified. The New Mexico Central State Plane zone uses the Mercator projection since it is a north–south oriented zone.

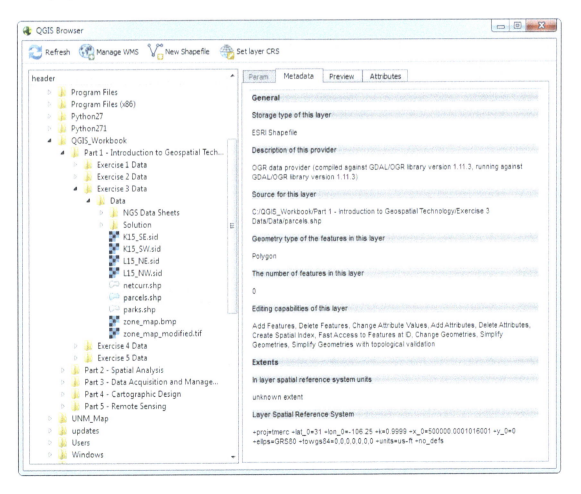

3.4 Task 2 - Transforming Coordinate System of Source Data

Now that you have created an empty shapefile to store the digitized information, you will perform a coordinate transformation (also known as georeferencing) on the source data set so that it is in an Earth-based coordinate system. In this case, the coordinate system will match your parcel shapefile (NAD83(HARN) / New Mexico Central (ftUS)).

To perform this task you will be using a plugin. Plugins are small add-ons to QGIS. Some are created by the core QGIS development team and others are created by third party developers.

1. Open QGIS Desktop.

2. Open QGIS Browser.

3. Arrange Browser and Desktop so that you can see both windows simultaneously on your desktop.

4. In Browser find the new parcels shapefile. Select it and drag it onto the map window of QGIS Desktop. This is another way to add data to Desktop.

5. From the Menu bar in QGIS Desktop, choose Project | Project Properties.

6. Click the CRS tab and Enable 'on the fly' CRS transformation. Click OK to save the setting and close the properties window.

7. The project should now have a CRS of EPSG 2903 (which is NAD83(HARN) / New Mexico Central (ftUS)) and on the fly CRS transformation is enabled. You can check this by looking at the lower right hand corner of QGIS Desktop and ensuring that EPSG: 2903 (OTF) is listed. If not right click on the parcels layer and from the context menu choose Set Project CRS from Layer.

8. Save the project to the Exercise 3 Data folder and name it exercise3.qgs.

9. From the menu bar choose Plugins | Manage and Install Plugins.

10. The Plugins manager will open. Options along the left side allow you to switch between Installed, Not Installed, New, and Settings. The plugin you will use is a Core QGIS Plugin called Georeferencer GDAL.

11. Since it is a Core plugin it will already be installed—you just need to enable it. Click on Installed plugins and check the box next to Georeferencer GDAL (shown in figure below).

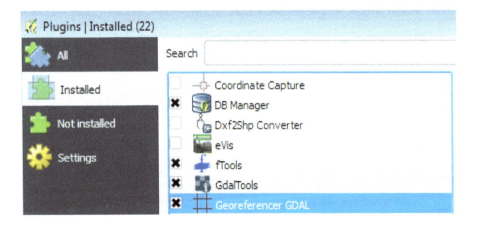

12. Click Close to close the Plugins window.

13. To open the Georeferencer plugin go to the menu bar choose Raster | Georeferencer | Georeferencer.

14. The Georeferencer window opens. Click the Open Raster button at the upper left hand side (see figure below).

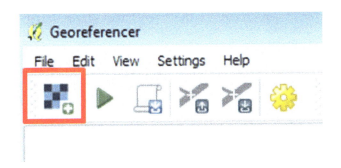

15. Navigate to the `Exercise 3 Data` folder and select the `zone_map.bmp` and click Open. *Note:* If the Coordinate Reference System Selector window opens click Cancel to close. This dataset does not yet have an Earth-based coordinate system. The source data will now be loaded in the Georeferencer (shown in figure below).

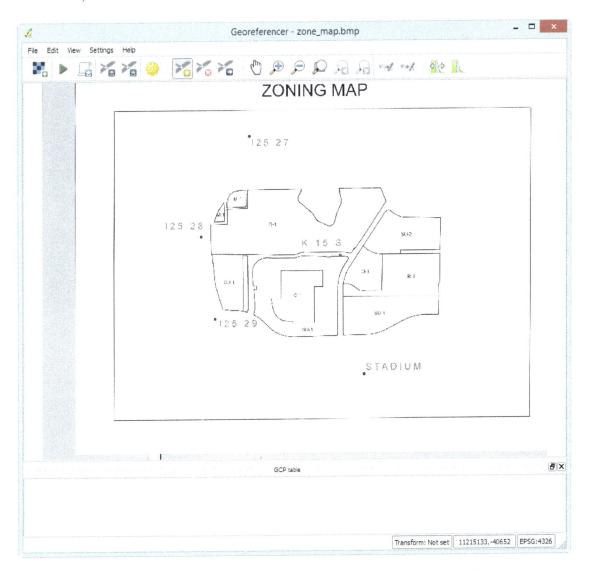

The source data is a map. On the map, there are five points with their associated names (for example, one point's name is: I25 27). These are benchmarks maintained by the National Geodetic Survey. To georeference this scanned map, you will create control points at these five locations. The plugin will then develop a georeferencing equation based off the set of source and target coordinates at these five locations. QGIS will obtain the source coordinates from your mouse click on those points. You will look up the target coordinates for these benchmarks from the NGS website.

16. The NGS website is at http://www.ngs.noaa.gov/cgi-bin/datasheet.prl. Open the site. *Note*: If you are unable to access the internet, the NGS Data Sheets have been downloaded and saved in the Exercise 3 Data/NGS Data Sheets folder. Please read the next few steps to learn how the NGS Data Sheets were acquired.

You will search for each of the benchmarks that appear on the map by searching for each benchmark's datasheet. You will use the Station Name option to do the search.

17. On the website click on the DATASHEETS button. Then click on the link for Station Name.

18. To find the first station, enter the station name of I25 27 (include the space), and then choose NEW MEXICO for the state. The search is shown in the figure below. *Note*: the station name is I25 27 with a capitalized letter i.

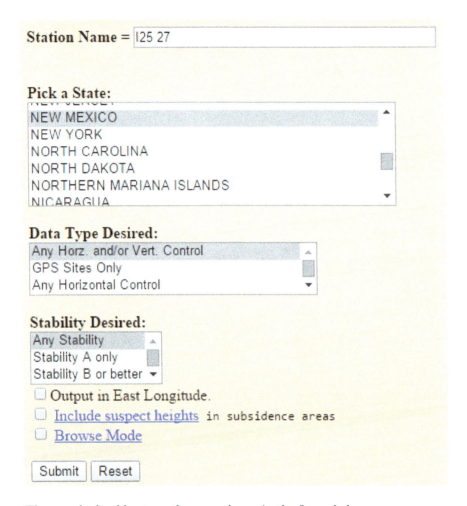

The search should return the page shown in the figure below.

Station List Results for: NM-I25 27

```
| Help |
|Dist|PID...|H V|Vert_Source|Latitude.....|Longitude.....|Stab|C|Designation ▲
|----|------|- -|-----------|-------------|--------------|----|-|-----------
|....|FO1302|2 3|29/LEVELING|N350445.73582|W1063813.49687|C...|G|I25 27
```

19. Highlight the station name and click the Get Datasheets button and you will get something that looks like the figure below.

The NGS Data Sheet

See file dsdata.txt for more information about the datasheet.

```
PROGRAM = datasheet95, VERSION = 8.6.1
1        National Geodetic Survey,   Retrieval Date = MARCH   9, 2015
 FO1302  *************************************************************************
 FO1302  DESIGNATION -   I25 27
 FO1302  PID         -   FO1302
 FO1302  STATE/COUNTY-   NM/BERNALILLO
 FO1302  COUNTRY     -   US
 FO1302  USGS QUAD   -   ALBUQUERQUE WEST (1990)
 FO1302
 FO1302                     *CURRENT SURVEY CONTROL
 FO1302  _____
 FO1302* NAD 83(1992) POSITION- 35 04 45.73582(N) 106 38 13.49687(W)   ADJUSTED
 FO1302* NAVD 88 ORTHO HEIGHT -  1545.38  (+/-2cm)    5070.1   (feet) VERTCON
 FO1302  _____
 FO1302  GEOID HEIGHT    -       -21.35  (meters)                   GEOID12A
 FO1302  LAPLACE CORR    -         7.34  (seconds)                  DEFLEC12A
 FO1302  HORZ ORDER      -   SECOND
 FO1302  VERT ORDER      -   THIRD ? (See Below)
 FO1302
 FO1302.The horizontal coordinates were established by classical geodetic methods
 FO1302.and adjusted by the National Geodetic Survey in December 1993.
 FO1302.
 FO1302.The NAVD 88 height was computed by applying the VERTCON shift value to
 FO1302.the NGVD 29 height (displayed under SUPERSEDED SURVEY CONTROL.)
 FO1302
 FO1302.The vertical order pertains to the NGVD 29 superseded value.
 FO1302
 FO1302.The Laplace correction was computed from DEFLEC12A derived deflections.
 FO1302
 FO1302. The following values were computed from the NAD 83(1992) position.
 FO1302
 FO1302;               North        East     Units Scale Factor Converg.
 FO1302;SPC NM C   -   452,447.391  464,701.544  MT  0.99991535  -0 13 20.9
 FO1302;SPC NM C   - 1,484,404.48  1,524,608.32  sFT 0.99991535  -0 13 20.9
 FO1302;UTM  13    - 3,883,070.670  350,750.959  MT  0.99987453  -0 56 27.7
```

This is an NGS Data Sheet. It gives measurement parameters for NGS benchmarks located throughout the United States. One piece of information it includes are coordinates for benchmarks in State Plane feet (highlighted in the figure above). There are two sets of State Plane coordinates on the NGS Data Sheet; one is in meters (MT) and one is in feet (sFT). Be sure to use the set in feet. *Important Note*: There is a dash before the North coordinate. It is *not* a negative number.

20. Find the data sheet for each benchmark shown in the map and fill in the coordinates below. The coordinates for the first station have been entered already. *Note*: If you are unable to access the internet, the NGS Data Sheets have been downloaded and saved in the `Exercise 3 Data/NGS Data Sheets` folder.

```
Benchmark | Northing    | Easting
I25 27      1,484,404.48   1,524,608.32

I25 28

I25 29

K 15 S

STADIUM
```

21. The next step is to enter the control points in the Georeferencer. Click on the Add point button .

It is important to be precise and click directly on the point. To help make your selection more precise, you can zoom and pan by using tools in the View toolbar (shown in figure below). If you want to redo a control point click

the Delete point button then click on the point to delete.)

22. With the Add point button selected, click on point I25 27.

23. The Enter map coordinates window opens. Enter the easting and northing State Plane Coordinates that you retrieved from the NGS Data Sheet into the two boxes. Make sure you enter them correctly. The correct coordinates are entered for I25 27 in the figure below.

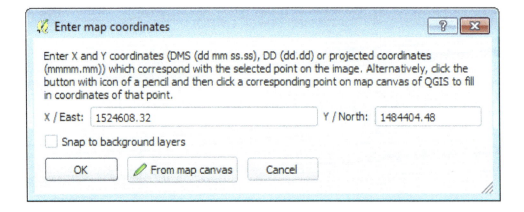

24. Click OK and a red control point will appear on the map where you clicked. The source (srcX, srcY) and

destination (dstX, dstY) X,Y coordinates will display in a table at the bottom of the window.

25. Repeat this procedure for points 'I25 28', I25 29', K 15 S' and 'STADIUM'. After the five control points have been entered your Georeferencer window should look like the figure below.

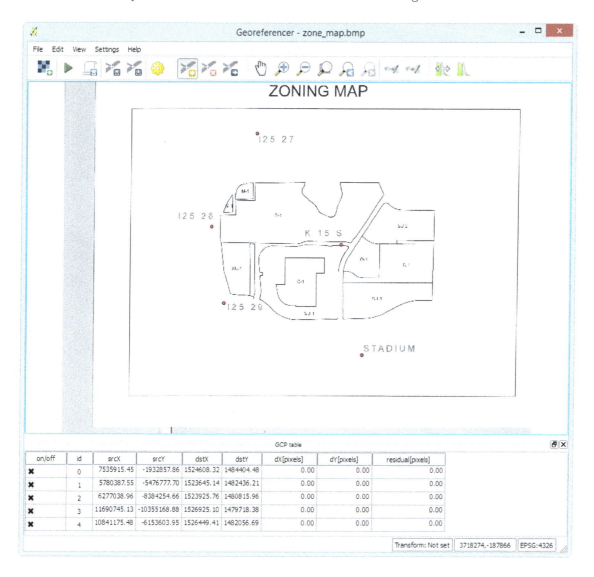

on/off	id	srcX	srcY	dstX	dstY	dX[pixels]	dY[pixels]	residual[pixels]
✗	0	7535915.45	-1932857.86	1524608.32	1484404.48	0.00	0.00	0.00
✗	1	5780387.55	-5476777.70	1523645.14	1482436.21	0.00	0.00	0.00
✗	2	6277038.96	-8384254.66	1523925.76	1480815.96	0.00	0.00	0.00
✗	3	11690745.13	-10355168.88	1526925.10	1479718.38	0.00	0.00	0.00
✗	4	10841175.48	-6153603.95	1526449.41	1482056.69	0.00	0.00	0.00

26. To perform the transformation click the Start georeferencing button ▶.

27. The Transformation settings window will open (see figure below). If beforehand you get a message saying 'Please set transformation' type click OK.

   a. In the Transformation window choose the Polynomial 1 as the Transformation type.

   b. Choose Nearest neighbor as the Resampling method. This is the standard raster resampling method for discrete data such as a scanned map.

   c. Click the browse button to the right of Target SRS. Type 2903 into the Filter.

   d. Click the NAD83(HARN)/New Mexico Central (ftUS):2903 CRS then click OK.

   e. Click the browse button to the right of Output raster. Navigate to your Exercise 3 Data folder.

   f. Create a new folder named New Data then enter the folder.

   g. Name the file zone_map_modified_spcs.tif and click Save.

   h. Check Load in QGIS when done.

i. Click OK to close the Transformation settings window and perform the transformation.

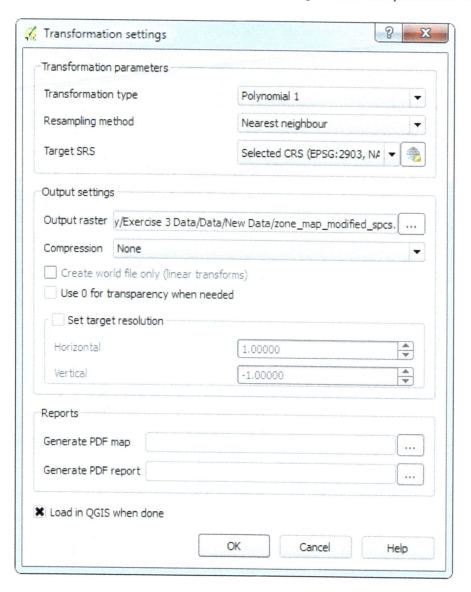

28. Close the Georeferencer and Save GCP points when prompted.

29. Right click on the zone_map_modified.tif and choose Zoom to layer extent to see the georeferenced image.

30. Using the Add Vector Layer button, add the netcurr.shp shapefile in the Exercise 3 Data folder to QGIS. This is a shapefile representing city streets produced by the City of Albuquerque. If the transformation was done correctly, the streets will line up with the georeferenced parcel map image (shown in figure below). Save your map file.

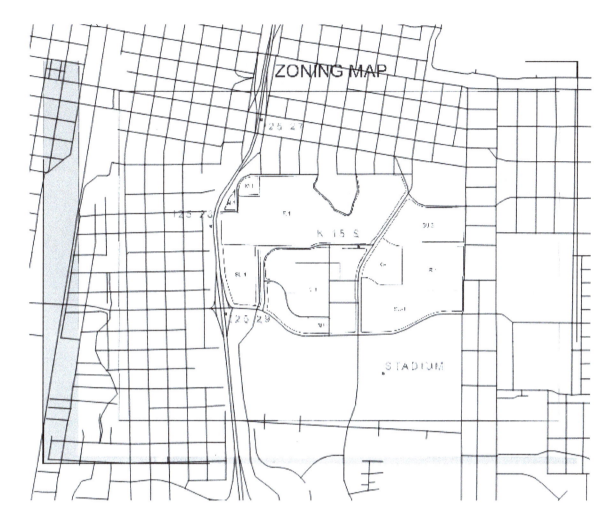

3.5   Task 3 - Heads-up Digitizing From Transformed Source Data

Now you will digitize the parcels off the georeferenced image into the parcels shapefile.

1. Drag the parcels layer above the zone_map_modified_spcs layer in the Layers panel. Right click on parcels and choose Toggle editing. This puts the parcels layer into edit mode. Notice that a pencil appears next to the layer in the Layers panel indicating that layer is in edit mode. Only one layer can be edited at a time.

2. Turn off the netcurr layer's visibility.

3. Using the Zoom in tool, drag a box around the M-1 parcels in the northwest corner of the image. You will digitize these first.

There is an Editing toolbar for editing vector datasets (see figure below). If it's not visible, go to the menu bar to View | Toolbars and turn it on. The tools available change slightly depending on the geometry of the data you are editing (polygon, line, point). When editing a polygon layer you will have a tool for adding polygon features.

4. Click on the Add Feature tool . Your cursor will change to an editing cursor that looks like a set of cross hairs.

Polygons are constructed of a series of nodes which define their shape. Here you will trace the outline of the first parcel clicking to create each node on the polygons boundary.

5. Put your cursor over a corner of one of the polygons. Left click to add the first point, left click again to add the second, and continue to click around the perimeter of the parcel. After you have added the final node finish the polygon with a right click.

6. An Attributes window will open asking you to populate the two attributes for this layer: id and zonecode. Give the parcel an id of 0 and the zonecode is M-1 (shown in figure below). Each parcel feature will receive a unique id starting here with zero. The next parcel you digitize will be id 1, the one after that id 2 etc.

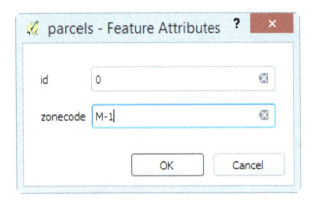

7. Click OK to close the Attributes window and complete the polygon.

If you want to delete the polygon you have just added, click the Current Edits tool dropdown menu and choose Roll Back Edits to undo your polygon.

8. Adding single isolated polygons is pretty straightforward. Zoom back to the extent of the image. You can do this by clicking theZoom last button [icon].

9. Find the big parcel in the south central area. There is a parcel with zoning code SU-1 that wraps around O-1. Zoom to that area.

10. Open the Layer properties | Style tab for the parcels layer and set the Transparency to 50%. This will allow you to see the source data underneath your parcels as you digitize.

11. Digitize the outer boundary of the SU-1 parcel ignoring the O-1 parcel for the moment. Fill in the attributes when prompted (id=0, zonecode=SU-1). The SU-1 polygon will be a ring when completed but for now it covers the O-1 parcel.

12. To finish SU-1 you will use a tool on the Advanced Digitizing toolbar. To turn that on, go to the menu bar, choose View | Toolbars, and check Advanced Digitizing. Dock the Advanced Digitizing toolbar where you would like, as shown in figure below (all toolbars in the QGIS interface can be moved by grabbing the stippled left side and dragging them to different parts of the interface.)

13. Now you'll use the Add Ring tool [icon]. Select it and click around the perimeter of the O-1 parcel. Right click to finish. This creates a ring polygon (shown in figure below).

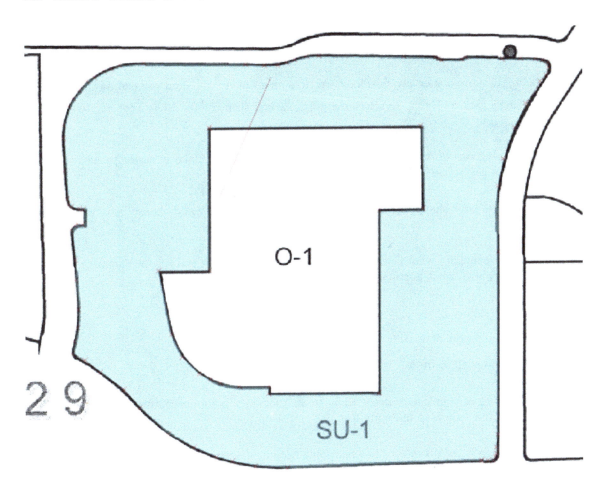

14. To Digitize O-1 you will use a tool that is part of the Digitizing Tools Plugin. First open the Plugin Manager and search for 'Digitizing Tools' in the All category. Select the Plugin and click the Install Plugin button. You should get the message *Plugin Installed Successfully*. Once it has been installed switch to the Installed plugins and make sure the Digitizing Tools toolbar is visible. Dock the toolbar.

15. On the Attributes toolbar, click the Select Features by area or single click tool and select the SU-1 polygon.

16. On the Digitizing toolbar, select the dropdown next to the Fill ring with a new feature (interactive mode) tool and select Fill all rings in selected polygons with new features tool (selection shown in figure below).

17. You will immediately be prompted to enter the attributes for the new O-1 polygon (id=2, zonecode=O-1).

18. Click OK when done and the new polygon will appear. It automatically fills the space leaving no gaps.

19. Use the Identify tool ![identify tool icon] to click on O-1 and SU-1 and verify that they are digitized correctly.

Note: If you end up needing to move one or two misplaced vertices on a finished polygon you can do that. Use the Select Features by area or single click tool ![select tool icon] to select the polygon, and then use the Node Tool ![node tool icon] to select the individual node and move it.

To digitize the remaining polygons, we will first turn on snapping options to make it easier to have adjacent polygons share vertices and/or segments.

20. To do so, first you will set your snapping environment. Go to the menu bar and choose Settings | Snapping options.

This is a window that lets you configure what layers you can snap to while editing and set the snapping tolerance. The Snapping mode lets you control what portions of a feature are being snapped to.

- To vertex will snap to vertices

- To segment will snap to any part of another layers edge

- To vertex and segment will snap to both.

The Tolerance determines how close your cursor needs to be to another layer before it snaps to it. It can be set in screen pixels or map units. In our case map units are feet.

21. For Snapping mode, change it to Advanced. The Snapping options dialog will now show a list of map layers and options.

22. Check parcels since we want to snap our parcels to that layer. Set the tolerance for parcels to 50 map units and choose a Mode of 'to vertex'.

23. Check the box under Avoid intersections to the right of Units (shown in the figure below). This enables topological editing. When digitizing a shared boundary with this option checked you can begin with one of the vertices at one end of the shared boundary. Then continue digitizing the boundary of the new polygon and end at a vertex at the other end of the shared boundary. The shared boundary will be created automatically eliminating digitizing errors.

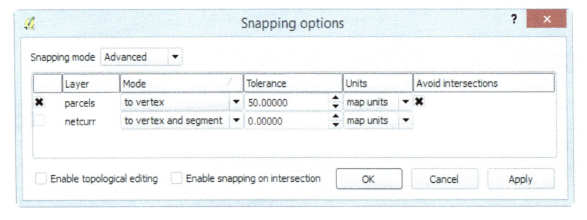

The map units are feet so when you get within 50 feet of a node (vertex) you will snap to it. This allows you to be much more precise than you could be otherwise.

24. Click OK to set the Snapping options.

If snapping is interfering with digitizing a parcel polygon you can go to Settings | Snapping options at any time (even during digitizing) and turn snapping off until you need it again.

25. Finish digitizing the polygons. Anytime you have a parcel that shares a boundary with another, use snapping to make sure you create two parcels without a gap in between.

Remember, you can adjust the snapping tolerance and what features are being snapped to vertex, segment, and vertex and segment.

26. When finished, click the Toggle Editing button to exit out of editing mode. You will be prompted to save your changes. Click Save to save the edits.

27. Turn off the zone_map_modified_spcs raster—you're done with that now. It was an intermediate step necessary to get the parcel boundaries digitized.

28. Save your QGIS project.

3.6   Task 4 - Editing Existing Geospatial Data

Now that you have digitized data into the empty shapefile you created, you will learn how to modify existing shapefiles.

1. Click the Add Raster Layer button and navigate to the Exercise 3 Data folder.

2. Set the filter to Multi-resolution Seamless Image Database (.sid, .SID).

3. Add all four SID images.

4. Drag the parcels layer above the image in the Layers panel.

5. Turn off the parcels layer.

6. Now you will make an edit to a line layer. Turn on the netcurr layer.

7. Zoom into the location highlighted in Figure below.

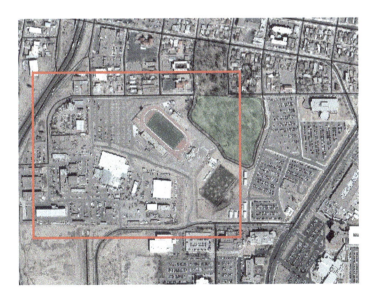

You will digitize the missing main road, shown in yellow in the figure below.

8. Toggle on editing for netcurr.

9. Set your Snapping options so that only netcurr is being snapped to, with a Mode of To vertex and a Tolerance of 20 feet.

10. Using the Add Feature tool on the Editing toolbar , digitize the new road making sure to snap to the roads at the northern and southern ends. Use the centerline of the road while digitizing.

11. There are many attributes for this layer. You will just enter a few. Enter the STREETNAME as Park, the STREETDESI as Place, the STREETQUAD as SE and the COMMENTS as Exercise 5. Click OK.

12. Toggle off editing and Save.

3.7   Conclusion

In this exercise, you have successfully digitized information using the five-step digitizing process. Additionally, you have recreated the original source data (scanned as a raster) in the vector format. Digitizing can be a time-consuming and tedious process, but can yield useful geographic information.

3.8   Discussion Questions

1. What can contribute to errors in the georeferencing process?

2. What other vector geometries (point/line/polygon) could be appropriate for digitizing a road? In which instances would you use one vector geometry type over another?

3. When you created the parcels shapefile you added a text field to hold the zoning codes. What are the possible field types? Explain what each field type contains, and provide an example of a valid entry in the field.

4. Aerial photography has a lot of information in it. What other features could you digitize from the imagery in this exercise? Explain what vector geometry you would use for each.

3.9   Challenge Assignment (optional)

You have successfully created the parcel data from a scanned map. You have also fixed the roads data in this part of town. There are some sports facilities visible: two football fields and a baseball field. Create a new layer and digitize those three facilities (include the grassy field areas at a minimum).

Create a simple page sized color map composition using the QGIS Desktop Print Composer showing your results. Show the parcels, sports facilities, parks, roads and aerial photography. Use Categorized styling to give a unique color to each zone code in the parcel data. Include:

- Title

- Legend (be sure to rename your layers so that the legend will be meaningful.)

- Date and Data Sources

You can credit the data sources as the City of Albuquerque and yourself. If you need to refresh your memory on creating a map layout, review Exercise 2.

Exercise 4

Understanding Remote Sensing and Analysis

Objective – Explore and Understand How to Display and Analyze Remotely Sensed Imagery

4.1 Introduction

In this exercise, you'll learn how to display and inspect multiband imagery in QGIS Desktop, then use QGIS data processing tools to conduct an unsupervised classification of multispectral imagery.

This exercise includes the following tasks:

- Task 1 – Display and Inspection of Image Data

- Task 2 – Unsupervised Classification

4.2 Objective: Learn the Basics of using QGIS Desktop for Image Analysis

Image analysis is one of the largest uses of remote sensing imagery, especially with imagery that has recorded wavelengths beyond the visible spectrum. There are proprietary software packages designed specifically for remote sensing work such as ENVI and ERDAS Imagine. QGIS Desktop can now be used in combination with two additional FOSS4G applications, SAGA and GRASS, to also conduct image analysis. SAGA and GRASS are both standalone software packages that can be installed separately. However, the main analysis tools from both are now bundled with QGIS Desktop. This means that no additional installations are required in order to use GRASS and SAGA analysis tools via QGIS Desktop. Some of this functionality is for more advanced users.

4.3 Task 1 - Display and Inspection of Image Data

There are many way to view multiband image data. Here you will explore some display options for a multiband image in QGIS Desktop.

1. Open QGIS Desktop and open the `Exercise_4_MultiSpectral_Imagery.qgs` project file.

2. The project contains is an aerial photograph of a portion of the Davis Purdue Agriculture Center in Randolph County, Indiana.

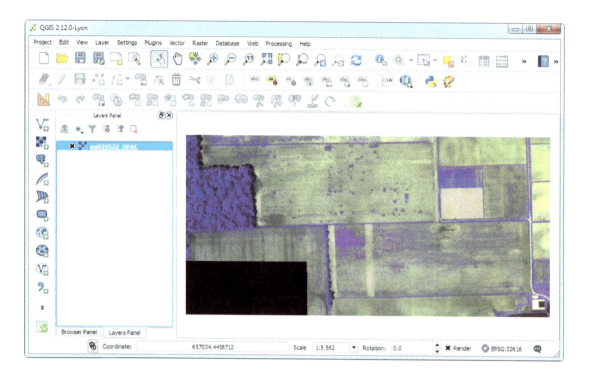

3. Double click on the layer name in the Layers panel to open the Layer Properties. Click on the General tab.

Layer info shows you the layer name, where the data are stored on your computer, and the number of columns (1,501) and rows (709). Since the CRS for the image is set when you added it to QGIS, the CRS is listed under Coordinate Reference System. Scale dependent visibility allows you to control at what scales the layer is visible. You will not set this parameter here. If you wanted the image to be visible only at a certain scale range, you could check the box and enter a scale maximum and minimum.

4. Click on the Style tab.

This image has three bands. Each band represents a segment of the electromagnetic spectrum. In this case, band 1 represents the red portion, band 2 the green portion, and band 3 the near-infrared portion. Therefore, in this image, we are able to see characteristics of the landscape that we cannot see with our eyes, since they can only detect visible light.

When an image has multiple color bands, QGIS defaults to a Multiband color rendering of that image. Colors on your computer monitor are created by combining three color channels: red, green and blue (RGB). By selecting three bands from a multiband image, and illuminating them with either red, green or blue light we create a color image. The multiband color renderer defaults to displaying Band 1 through the red channel, Band 2 through the green channel and Band 3 through the blue channel. However, we can change which bands are displayed through which channels.

5. Click the drop-down arrow for the Red band and change it to Band 3. Change the Blue band to Band 1 (see figure below).

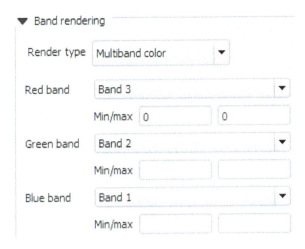

6. Click Apply and move the Layer Properties window so you can see the raster.

Note: Here is the difference between using Apply and OK: clicking OK saves the changes and closes the dialog window while apply saves the changes and leaves the window open. If you want to change a setting, see the result and change another setting, use Apply.

7. The image should now look like the figure below. This band combination creates what is known as a false color composite. Vegetation reflects a lot of near-infrared energy. You are now looking at the near-infrared through the red channel so vegetation shows up as red tones. The brighter the red, the more vigorous and healthy the vegetation.

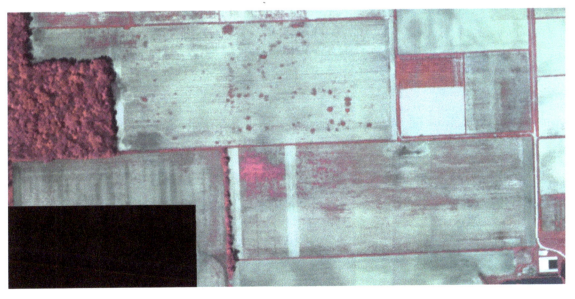

The Style tab also allows you to adjust Contrast enhancement. This setting gives you options to modify the appearance of the image when used in combination with the Load min/max values settings. Each band has values from 0-255. By default, the renderer is set to use Cumulative count cut values from 2% to 98%. This setting eliminates the bottom and top 2% of the values. Many images have some outlying very low and high data values. These outlying data values can be eliminated by using the Cumulative count cut option. The Contrast enhancement is set by default to No enhancement.

8. Click the Load button. The values currently being used for each band will appear in the Min/max boxes in

the Band rendering area.

9. Change the Contrast enhancement to Stretch to MinMax and click Apply. This setting scales the colors between the minimum and maximum values. The image gets a little brighter (see figure below) because the colors are now being stretched across the range of values. You are both applying a stretch and eliminating the bottom and top 2% of the values with the default Cumulative count cut setting.

The Accuracy setting lets you either estimate the range of values from a sample or get the actual values. Obtaining actual values can take longer since QGIS has to look at all the values in the image, instead of a sample.

10. Change the Accuracy setting to Actual, and click the Load button to see the values change slightly.

11. Now choose a Load min/max values setting of Mean +/- standard deviation and click Load. Click Apply to see the image change.

The raster gets a more saturated appearance (shown in figure below). These are the values within one standard deviation of the mean value. This is useful when you have one or two cells with abnormally high values in a raster grid that are having a negative impact on the rendering of the raster.

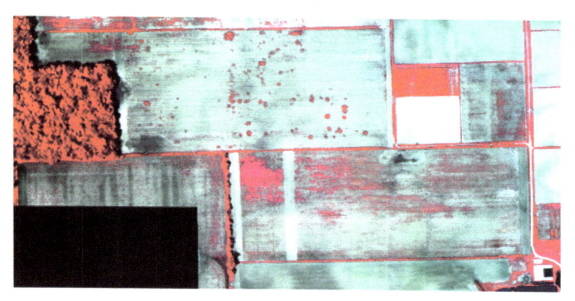

12. You can also look at one individual band. Change the Render type to Singleband gray. Choose Band 3 as the Gray band. Set the Contrast enhancement to Stretch MinMax. Click Apply.

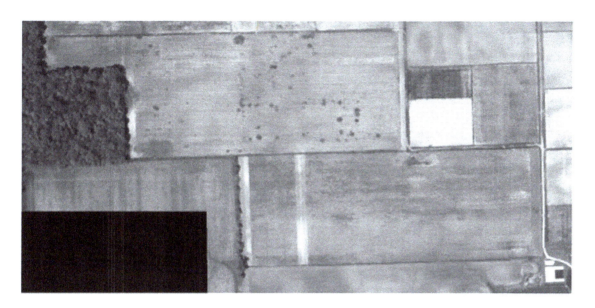

13. Change the Gray band setting to each of the other two bands and see how different they look.

14. Change back to a false color composite view:

    a. Render type: Multiband color

    b. Red band = 3

    c. Green band = 2

    d. Blue band = 1

    e. Contrast enhancement = Stretch to MinMax

    f. Click Load

    g. Click Apply

    h. In the Layer Properties, click on the Transparency tab.

    i. With the Global transparency setting you can control the transparency of the entire image.

    j. You can also define image values that you want to be transparent. Notice that in the southwest corner there is a black rectangle with no image data. On the Transparency tab click the Add values from display button [icon] then click on the black rectangle on the map. QGIS will measure the values for all three bands where you clicked and enter them into the Transparent pixel list.

    k. Click Apply. The black rectangle of no data pixels disappears.

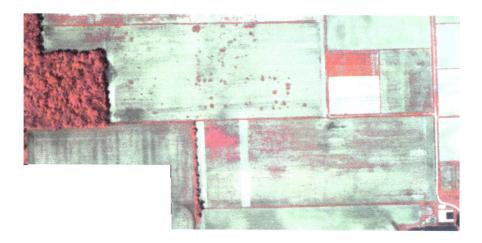

15. Click on the Pyramids tab.

Raster data sets can get very large. Pyramids help render large images more quickly. Without them, QGIS will try to render each pixel in an image even though your monitor may not have enough resolution to display each pixel. Pyramids are lower resolution versions of the image that will increase performance. This particular image is small so you will not build any now.

16. Click on the Histogram tab.

Here you can view the distribution of data values in your raster. If it is a multiband image, you can view data for each band. The histogram is generated automatically when you open this tab (see figure below). You can save the histogram as an image with the Save plot button.

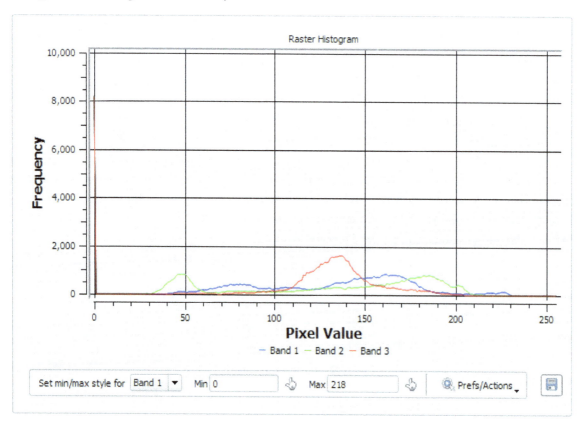

17. Save your QGIS Desktop project.

4.4 Task 2 - Unsupervised Classification

In an unsupervised classification, the software automatically classifies the image into homogenous areas. Pixels are grouped based on the reflectance values.

1. Open QGIS Desktop and then open the `Exercise 4 Data/ Exercise_4_Landsat.qgs` document.

2. This project contains a subset of a Landsat 8 scene covering Rome. There are separate rasters for bands 2, 3, 4, 5, 6, and 7. The image was acquired on June 12, 2014.

3. You will be using a Processing tool to conduct the unsupervised classification. From the menu bar, choose Processing | Toolbox to open the Processing Toolbox panel.

NOTE: Prior to QGIS version 2.14, the toolbox could be toggled between Simplifed and Advanced interfaces. At QGIS 2.14 the Simplified interface was removed. If using QGIS 2.12 or earlier, choose the Advanced interface.

1. Use the Search box at the top of the panel to help locate the tool. Type *cluster* into the Search box.

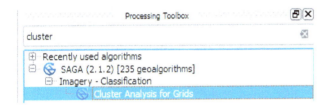

5. Double click on the SAGA tool Cluster Analysis for Grids.

6. Fill out the tool as follows (reference figure below):

   a. Click the ellipsis button to the right of Grids to open the Multiple Selection box. Click Select all and OK.

   b. Choose a Method of 2 Combined Minimum Distance/Hillclimbing

   c. Change the number of Clusters to 7.

   d. Click Run to run the cluster analysis. The result will be a temporary file.

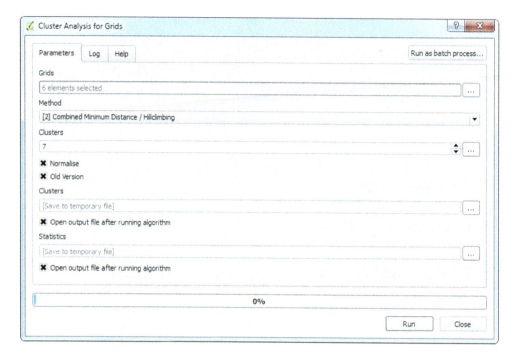

7. The temporary grid and a Statistics table are added to the Layers Panel. The Clusters grid will appear in the Map Window styled on a black to white color ramp.

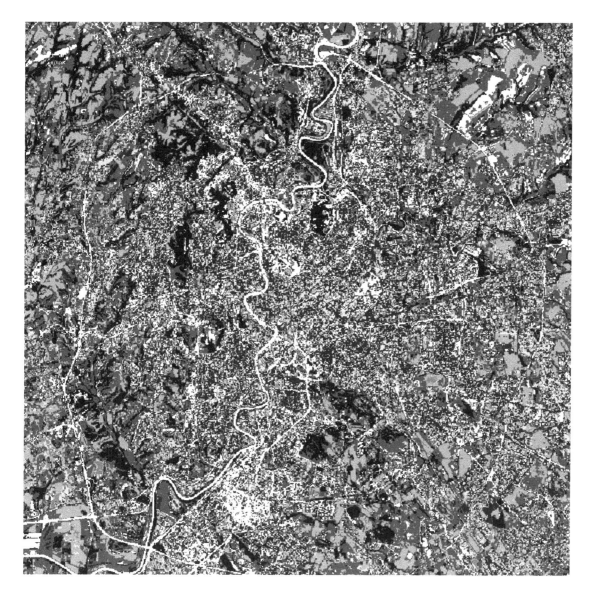

Now you will style the data.

8. Open Layer Properties for the new layer.

9. Change from a Singleband gray renderer to a Singleband pseudocolor render.

10. Change the Mode to Equal Interval.

11. Set the number of Classes to 6.

12. Change the Accuracy setting to Actual (slower) and click Load.

13. Click the Classify button.

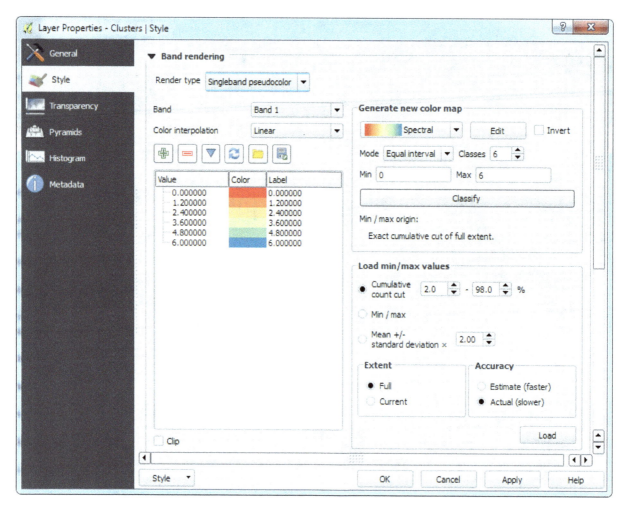

The data now shows the six classes of data. You will be able to identify those representing vegetated areas, barren soil, built up areas and water.

4.5   Conclusion

In this exercise, you have learned the basics of working with multispectral imagery in QGIS Desktop. You learned how to access data processing tools in QGIS Desktop and how to do an Unsupervised Classification. You will learn how to perform a supervised classification in Part 5 - Remote Sensing, on page 401.

4.6   Challenge Assignment (optional)

You have used QGIS to perform an Unsupervised Classification of the multispectral imagery. Create a simple page sized color map composition using the QGIS Desktop Print Composer showing your results. Include:

- Title

- Legend (be sure to rename your layers so that the legend will be meaningful.)

- Date and Data Sources

You can credit the data sources as the U.S. Geologic Survey and yourself. If you need to refresh your memory, review Exercise 2.

Exercise 5

Basic Geospatial Analysis Techniques

Objective – Use Basic Spatial Analysis Techniques to Solve a Problem

5.1 Introduction

In this exercise, the you'll explore a small set of analysis tools available in QGIS Desktop to conduct a spatial analysis and create a map of the results for a team of surveyors visiting National Geodetic Survey Monuments in Albuquerque, New Mexico. The surveyors wish to have a map showing monuments within the Albuquerque city limits. They will use this map to plan their fieldwork for the week.

This exercise includes the following tasks:

- Task 1 – Data Preparation

- Task 2 – Querying and Extracting Subsets of Data

- Task 3 – Buffering and Clipping Data

- Task 4 – Preparing a Map

5.2 Objective: Use Basic Spatial Analysis Techniques to Solve a Problem

Conducting effective spatial analysis in a GIS does not require the use of extremely complex algorithms and methods. By combining multiple simple spatial analysis operations, you can answer many questions and provide useful results. Determining the order in which these simple spatial analysis operations are executed is often the hardest part of conducting spatial analysis. Additionally, data is rarely available in exactly the format and subset that you require. A large part of almost all GIS projects is simply obtaining and preparing data for use.

In this exercise, the you'll utilize four basic geospatial analysis techniques: selection, buffer, clip, and dissolve.

- Selection uses set algebra and Boolean algebra to select records of interest.

- Buffer is the definition of a region that is less than or equal to a distance from one or more features.

- Clip defines the areas for which features will be output based on a 'clipping' polygon.

- Dissolve combines similar features within a data layer based on an attribute.

5.3   Task 1 - Data Preparation

In this task, you will obtain GIS data for this exercise by visiting several online GIS data portals, A) the National Geodetic Survey (NGS) website, B) City of Albuquerque GIS Department, C) the New Mexico Resource Geographic Information System (RGIS) and D) the Bernalillo County GIS Department. All of these websites provide free geospatial information.

Note: Copies of this data have already been obtained and are available in the Exercise 5/Data/Raw Data folder. If you are unable to obtain the data yourself, you may skip to Task 2 and use the Raw Data.

5.4   Task 1.1 - Obtain Shapefiles of NGS Monuments

We first want to go to the same National Geodetic Survey (NGS) website you visited in exercise 5. This time you will download a shapefile of the monuments in the Bernalillo County, New Mexico. This is the county in which Albuquerque is situated.

1. In a web browser, navigate to http://www.ngs.noaa.gov
2. Click on the Survey Mark Datasheets link of the left side of the page.
3. Click the Shapefiles button.
4. Use the COUNTY retrieval method:
   a. Pick a State = New Mexico then click Get County List
   b. Pick a County = Bernalillo
   c. Data Type Desired = Any Vertical Control
   d. Stability Desired = Any Stability
   e. Compression Options = Send me all the Shapefiles compressed into one ZIP file...
   f. File Prefix = Bern
   g. (Leave all other options as the default values)
   h. Click the Submit button
   i. Click the Select All button
   j. Click Get Shapefile
   k. When the dialog box appears to save the ZIP file, save it into the `Exercise 5 Data/MyData` directory.
   l. Extract the ZIP file into the `MyData` directory.

5.5   Task 1.2 - Obtain the Municipal Boundaries

Since you will identify monuments within the Albuquerque City limits, you'll need an Albuquerque City limit dataset. You will download the data from the City of Albuquerque GIS Department.

1. In a web browser, navigate to http://www.cabq.gov/gis/geographic-information-systems-data
2. Scroll down until you find the Municipal Limits data.
3. Download the Boundaries shapefile to your folder.
   a. Save the ZIP file into your `Exercise 5 Data/MyData` directory.
   b. Extract this ZIP file into the exercise directory.

5.6   Task 1.3 - Obtain the Census Tract Boundaries

You will visit the RGIS clearinghouse. This is the main source for geospatial data for New Mexico. You will download census tract boundaries for Bernalillo County.

1. In a web browser, navigate to http://rgis.unm.edu/
2. Click the Get Data button
3. In the folder tree underneath Filter data by Theme, expand Census Data
4. Expand 2010 Census
5. Click on 2010 Census Tracts
6. Download the Bernalillo County 2010 Census Tracts shapefile to your folder.
    a. Save the ZIP file into your `Exercise 5 Data/MyData` directory.
    b. Extract this ZIP file into the exercise directory.

5.7   Task 1.4 - Obtain Road Data

Finally, you will visit the Bernalillo County GIS Program to download a roads data set. This is the main source for geospatial data for New Mexico. You will download census tract boundaries for Bernalillo County.

1. In a web browser, navigate to http://www.bernco.gov/Download-GIS-Data/
2. Find the Download GIS data section
3. Find Road Inventory
4. Download the Road Inventory Zip file to your folder.
    a. Save the ZIP file into your `Exercise 5/MyData` directory.
    b. Extract this ZIP file into the exercise directory.

5.8   Task 2 - Querying and Extracting Subsets of Data

Now that you have collected the necessary data, you will add it to a blank QGIS map document. Take a moment to familiarize yourself with the data and what information it contains. As with any project, you will have to do some data preparation to make it useful for the analysis.

5.9   Task 2.1 - Working with coordinate reference systems

1. Open QGIS Desktop.
2. Using the Add Vector Layer button, add all four shapefiles to QGIS Desktop (see figure below).

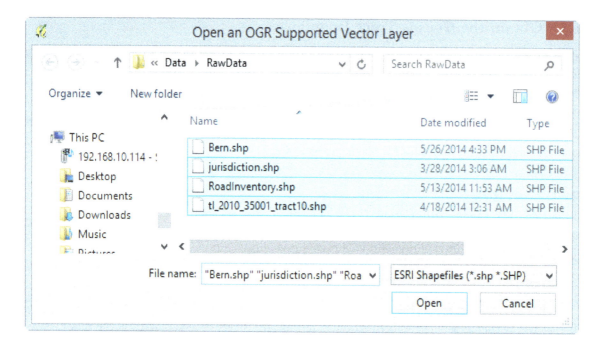

3. Organize the layers in the Layers panel so that the Bern monuments layer is on top, followed by the Road-Inventory, tl_2010_35001_tract10 (tracts), and jurisdiction.

4. Save your project to the Exercise 5 Data folder as exercise5.qgs

Does it look like all the layers are lining up together? Open the Layer properties for each layer and investigate their CRSs. Note that the Census Tracts (tl_2010_35001_tract10) and Monuments (Bern) are in geographic coordinates and the Road Inventory and jurisdiction are in the State Plane Coordinate System (SPCS).

5. From the menu bar choose Project | Project Properties.

6. Open the CRS tab and note that 'on the fly' CRS Transformation is checked. This is the default behavior if QGIS notices that Layers in the Layers panel have different CRSs. To change this default behavior, from the main menu bar, click Settings | Options | CRS tab and choose the default CRS settings.

7. While the CRS tab is still open choose NAD83(HARN)/New Mexico Central (ftUS) as the CRS for the map (EPSG: 2903).

8. Click OK to set the project CRS.

Projecting on the fly is fine for cartographic purposes. However, when conducting a geospatial analysis, the data layers involved should be in the same CRS. Typically, data layers will also be clipped to the extent of the study area to reduce rendering and data processing time. These procedures are often referred to as normalizing your data. For the typical analysis, a majority of your time is spent obtaining data and normalizing it. Once all the data is organized and normalized, the analysis can proceed.

You will want to put all four layers into the same CRS for this analysis. You will put them all into the SPCS.

9. Right-click on the Bern layer in the Layers panel and choose Save As... from the contextual menu. This will open the Save vector layer as... window (shown in the figure below).

10. Click the Browse button to the right of Save as and save it into your exercise folder as Bern_spcs.shp. (It is useful to have a naming convention for new data layers. Here you are including the CRS in the name of the copy.)

11. Click the Browse button for the CRS. The Coordinate Reference System Selector window will open.

12. From the Recently used coordinate reference systems choose NAD83(HARN) / New Mexico Central (ftUS) EPSG:2903 then click OK.

13. Check the box for Add saved file to map.

14. Click OK to save the new file in a different CRS.

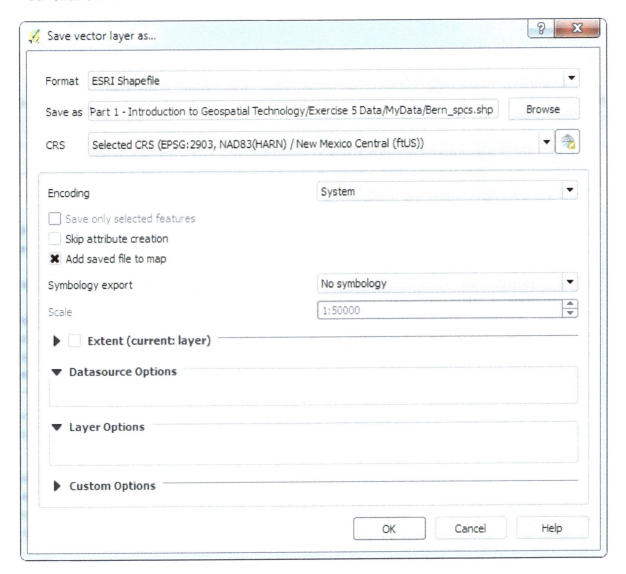

15. You no longer need the original Bern layer in your map. Right-click on the original Bern layer and choose Remove. Click OK on the Remove Objects window.

16. Repeat the above steps to save the Census Tracts (tl_2010_35001_tract10) layer in EPSG:2903.

17. Save your project.

5.10 Task 2.2 - Dissolving Tract Boundaries into a County boundary

For the map, you will need a polygon that represents the county boundary. The tl_2010_35001_tract10_spcs Census tracts collectively define the county, so you will use the dissolve spatial analysis technique to create a county boundary from the Census tracts.

1. From the menu bar choose Vector | Geoprocessing Tools | Dissolve (reference figure below).

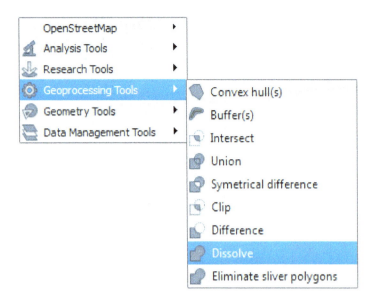

2. Set Input vector data to tl_2010_35001_tract10_spcs.

You can dissolve based on attributes. For example, if you had counties of the United States you could dissolve them based on the State name attribute and create a state boundaries layer. Here you will dissolve all the tract polygons into one to create the county boundary.

3. For Dissolve field choose — Dissolve all — (at the bottom of the list).

4. Name the output shapefile `Bernalillo_county.shp` and save it to your exercise folder (see figure below).

5. Make sure Add result to canvas is checked.

6. Click OK to run the Dissolve tool. Once the tool has executed, click Close.

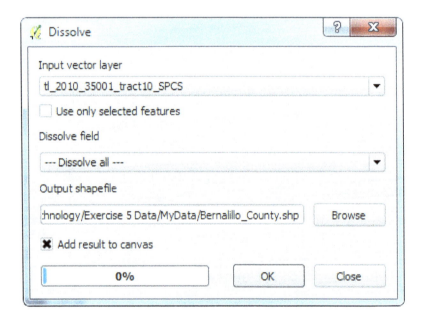

7. Remove the tl_2010_35001_tract10_spcs layer from the Layers panel. It was an intermediate dataset. All you need is the Bernalillo County Boundary.

8. Save your project.

5.11 Task 2.3 - Select Monuments

You will want to filter the monuments so that you only have the ones with the orders and classes you're interested in. Here you only want monuments that meet the following requirements:

- Elevation Order = 1

- Last recovered on or after 1995

- Satellite Observations were used for monument coordinate determination.

- a, b, and c are stored in these attribute columns:

  - ELEV_ORDER

  - LAST_RECV

  - SAT_USE

(For information on what an elevation order and class is, visit http://www.ngs.noaa.gov/heightmod/Leveling/)

1. Double-click the Bern_spcs layer to open the Layer Properties.
2. Select the General tab.
3. Find the Provider feature filter subset area. This is where you can define the contents of a layer based on the attributes. It is a way to filter a layer.
4. Click the Query Builder button to open the Query Builder. Here you can write a SQL query to filter your data.

All the attribute fields are listed on the left. Below the fields are operators you can use to build your SQL expression. The expression is built in the blank window at the bottom. When building the expression, it is best to double-click fields and field values instead of manually typing them in so that you avoid syntax errors.

5. Double-click on the field ELEV_ORDER and it will appear in the expression window surrounded by double quotes.
6. Click the = sign under operators to add it to the expression.
7. Click the All button below Values to get a list of the values contained in that field.
8. Double-click the 1 value so that your expression reads "ELEV_ORDER" = '1'.

Since you want monuments that have both an elevation order of 1 and were last recovered on or after 1994 you will now use the AND operator. The AND operator selects records that meet conditions on both sides.

9. Double-click the AND button under Operators to add it to the expression.
10. After the AND operator create the portion of the expression dealing with LAST_RECV.
11. Add another AND operator and create the third portion of the expression dealing with the SAT_USE.
12. The final expression should look like the figure below.

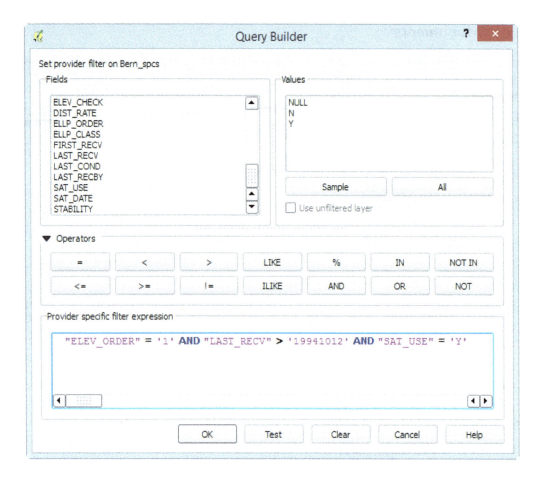

13. Click the Test button. You should get a query result of 47 rows. If you have a syntax error you will be notified and you'll have to figure out where the error lies. Any extra tics (') or quotes (") will throw an error. Click OK to dismiss the query result dialog.

14. Click OK to set the Query and close the Query Builder window.

15. Click OK again to close the Layer Properties.

It is always a good idea to open the attribute table to ensure that the layer has been filtered the way you needed.

16. Open the attribute table for the Bern_spcs layer and verify that the table only includes 47 filtered features. This will be reported on the attribute table's title bar at the top.

17. With the data properly filtered, the map should now resemble the figure below.

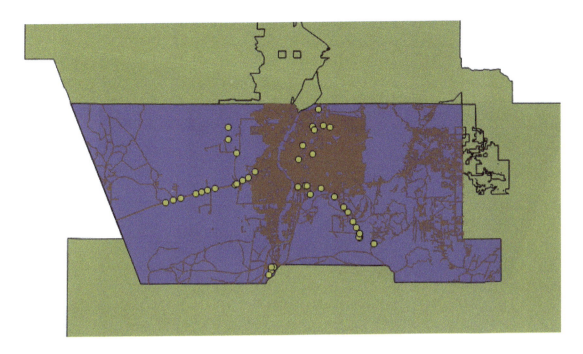

18. Save your project.

5.12 Task 3 - Buffering and Clipping Data

Now that you have prepared the county boundary and the monuments layers, you will identify just the monuments within the Albuquerque City limits. First, you will create a filter on the jurisdiction layer and the RoadInventory layer as you did for monuments.

The jurisdiction layer covers much more than Bernalillo County. Albuquerque covers just a portion of the county and jurisdiction extends north and south of the county boundary.

1. Open the attribute table for jurisdiction. The first field JURISDICTI has the city names. Notice that the majority consists of unincorporated areas. You can click the field header and you will see a small arrow appear. This lets you toggle back and forth between an ascending and descending sort of the records making it easier to find certain values. Close the Table.

2. Open the Layer properties for jurisdiction and go to the General tab.

3. Under Provider feature filter subset, click the Query Builder button and create a query that selects only the JURISDICTI of Albuquerque.

4. Click OK on the Query Builder and close the Layer Properties.

5. In the Layers panel, drag jurisdiction above the Bernalillo County layer and turn off RoadInventory. Your map should resemble the figure below.

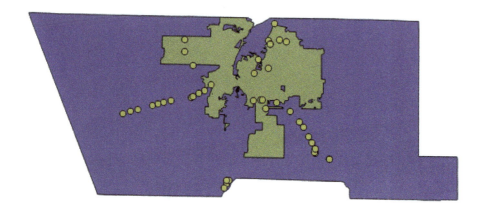

6. Open the attribute table for RoadInventory.

There is a lot of information in the RoadInventory shapefile. So far you have filtered a layer within QGIS, but left the data on disk the same. Now you will select the major roads and save them to a new shapefile. Considering the attribute table, what field would you use to select out major roads?

7. Click on the Select features using an expression button.

A similar query window opens as when you are filtering a layer. Instead of the fields being listed on the left, here you have the Expression area. In the middle, the expression functions will be listed. If you scroll down though the functions tree, you will see that one category is Fields and Values.

8. Expand Fields and Values.

9. Scroll down until you find the Class field.

10. Double-click on Class to add it to the Expression area.

11. Click the = operator.

12. Click all unique under Values.

13. Double-click the Major value to add it to the expression. Your expression should now look like the figure below.

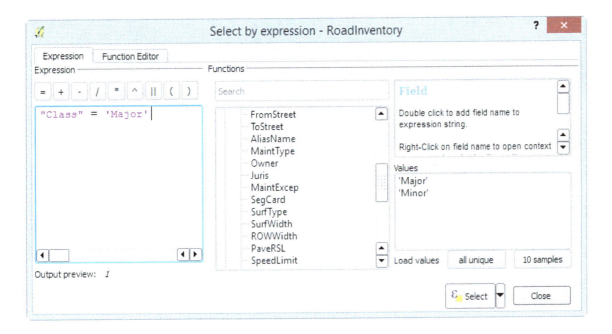

14. Click Select then Close the Select by expression window.

You now have 4,593 out of 37,963 records selected. You can use the dropdown at the lower left corner of the attribute table to show just the selected set of records (see figure below).

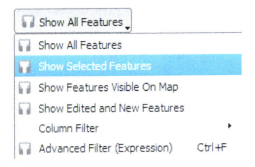

15. Close the attribute table.
16. Right-click on the RoadInventory layer and choose Save As....
17. Name the file Major_Roads.shp and save it in your exercise directory.
18. Check Save only selected features. The will only save the features currently selected to a new shapefile.
19. Verify that the dialog looks like the figure below. If so, click OK to save and add the layer to the map.

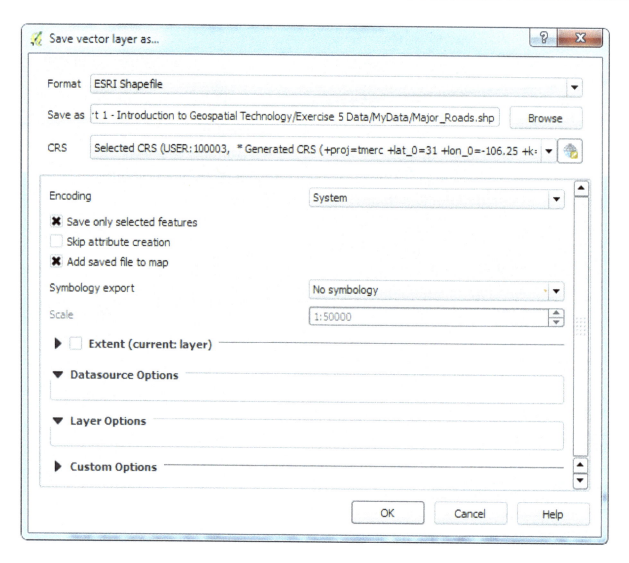

20. Remove RoadInventory from the Layers panel. All you need for your map is Major_Roads.

Now that you have the Albuquerque City limits isolated, you will buffer Albuquerque by one mile. This will allow you to identify monuments that are either inside, or close to the city limits. Buffer is an operation that creates a new polygon layer that is a buffer distance from another layer.

21. From the menu bar choose Vector | Geoprocessing Tools | Buffer(s).

22. Set the Input vector layer to jurisdiction, which now equals the Albuquerque city boundary.

23. You will enter a Buffer distance in map units. The Project CRS is a State Plane Coordinate System (SPCS), which has feet for units. Therefore, to buffer the city boundary by a mile, enter the number of feet in a mile (5280).

24. Name the output Albuquerque_buffer.shp.

25. Check Add result to canvas.

26. Your tool should resemble the figure below. If so, click OK and then Close.

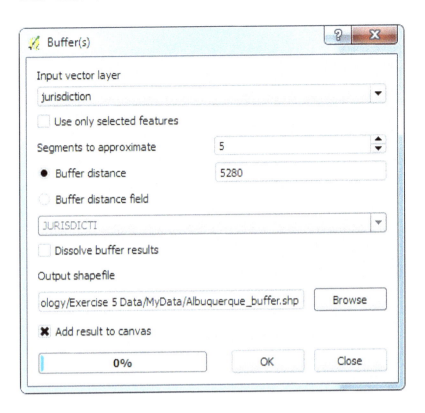

27. Drag the new buffer layer beneath jurisdiction and you will see that it is a one-mile buffer of the boundary.

Now that you have the search area for the selected monuments, you will use the Clip tool to clip the monument layer to the buffered city limits to create a new shapefile with only the monuments the surveyors should visit. The Clip tool acts like a cookie cutter. It cuts data out that falls within the clipping layer's boundary.

28. From the menu bar choose Vector | Geoprocessing Tools | Clip.

29. Set Input vector layer to Bern_spcs.

30. Set Clip layer to Albuquerque_buffer.

31. Name the output Albuquerque_monuments.shp.

32. Check Add result to canvas.

33. Your tool should resemble the figure below. If so, click OK and Close.

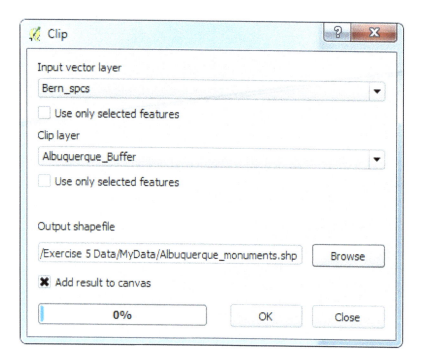

34. Remove Bern_spcs from the Layers panel.

Finally, you will label the monuments with the FeatureID attribute.

35. Open the Layer properties for the Albuquerque Monuments and select the Labels tab.

36. Check Label with and choose FeatureId as the field.

37. Select the Buffer item and check Draw text buffer with the defaults (reference figure below). This will create a white halo around the labels, which can make them easier to read against a busy background.

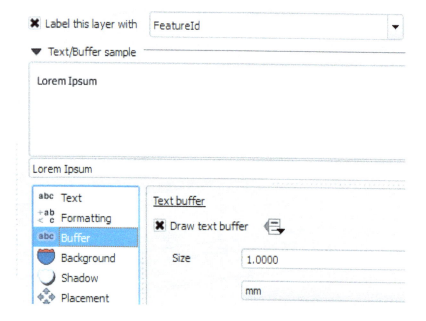

38. Click the Placement option and set an Offset X,Y of 2. This will offset the label from the point a bit giving more room for a bigger point symbol. Note that there are many options for label placement!

39. Click OK to set the labels for the monuments.

40. Label the major roads using the StreetName field. Under the Text tab, set a font size of 5.25.

41. On the Rendering tab, under the Feature options area, choose Merge connected lines to avoid duplicate labels. This will clean up duplicate labels.

42. Change the style of the layer to make the map more attractive. Choose whatever colors you prefer. As an example, reference the map in the figure below.

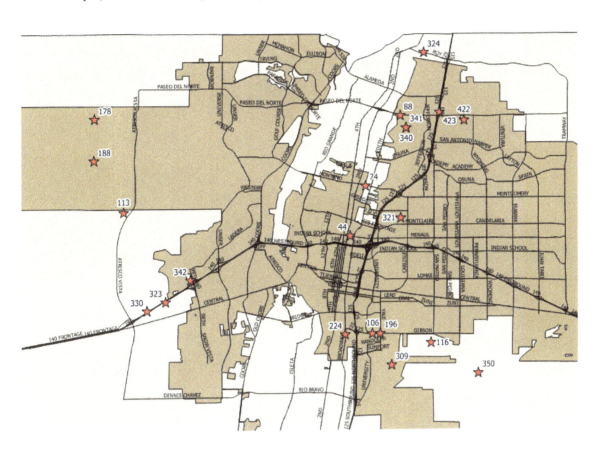

43. Save your project.

5.13 Task 4 - Preparing a Map

Now that you have identified the locations of the monuments that the surveyors should visit, you will make a map of the result of your analysis. You should show the major roads to give them a general idea of how to access the monuments.

1. Rename the layers in the Layers panel to:

   a. Albuquerque Monuments

   b. Major Roads

   c. City of Albuquerque

   d. Bernalillo County

You do not necessarily have to show the buffer layer. It was just a means of identifying the monuments to map. However, you have cartographers license on that choice!

2. Zoom In to the monuments layer so that you can show as much detail as possible.

3. Use the Print Composer to create a map layout.

4. Include the following map elements:

   - Title: Albuquerque Vertical Control Monuments
   - Legend
   - Your Name
   - Sources of Data
   - Scale Bar: Use the Add Scale Bar button 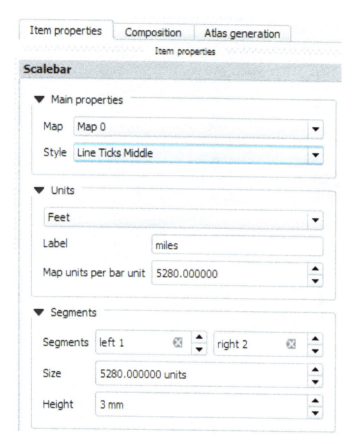 . QGIS uses map units for scale bars. Here our map units are feet. Therefore, to make a scalebar read in miles you need to enter a Map units per bar unit value of 5280 (the number of feet in a mile) (Figure below).

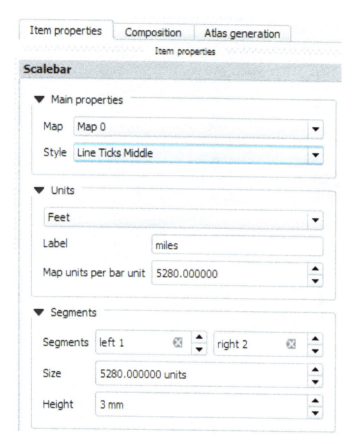

On the next page is an example of a completed map.

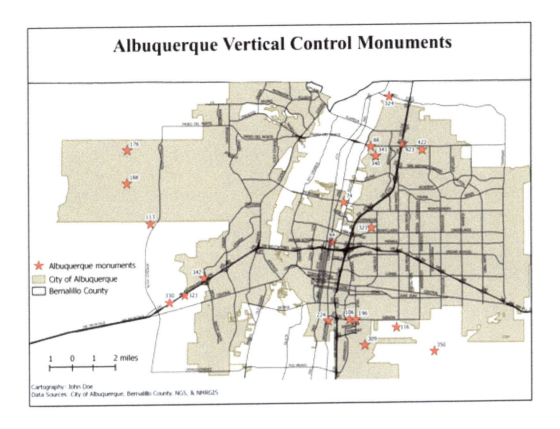

5.14 Conclusion

In this exercise, you used several basic spatial analysis techniques to prepare data for analysis and conduct the analysis. You reprojected data, queried and extracted data, conducted a dissolve operation and used buffer and clip to identify the final set of monuments. While none of these individual operations are necessarily complex, the sequence in which they were combined allowed you to answer spatial questions quickly and easily.

5.15 Discussion Questions

1. Export the final map for your instructor to grade.
2. Think of another use of a clip operation with the exercise data.
3. Could you use the dissolve tool to create a municipal boundary data set whereby all the unincorporated areas were merged together? If so describe how you would set up the tool.

5.16 Challenge Assignment (optional)

The surveyors' work was streamlined and efficient due to your GIS analysis. They now have extra time to visit The Village of Tijeras while they are in town. Generate the same analysis and accompanying map for monuments meeting the same criteria for Tijeras. You can use all the same data so you will not have to download anything else. For this map try to incorporate some of the Live Layer Effects. These can be found on the Layer Properties | Style tab under Layer rendering. Effects include: inner and outer glows and drop shadows. Visit Nyall Dawson's blog entry for more details: http://nyalldawson.net/2015/04/introducing-qgis-live-layer-effects/

Part II

Spatial Analysis

Exercise 1

Reviewing the Basics of Geospatial Data

Objective – Explore data structures, file types, coordinate systems and attributes

1.1 Introduction

This exercise features questions and activities designed to review some basic GIS and geospatial concepts. Throughout the exercise, questions will be asked for you to answer. Create a new document to write your answers and refer back using the question number.

This exercise includes the following tasks:

- Task 1 – GIS Data - Vector

- Task 2 – GIS Data – Raster

- Task 3 - Geodatabases

- Task 4 – Coordinate Systems

- Task 5 – GIS Data Attributes and Attribute Tables

1.2 Objective: Use Basic Spatial Analysis Techniques to Solve a Problem

Spatial Analysis is a crucial aspect of GIS—the tools allow the user to analyze the patterns and relationships of various data. Understanding the concepts of data structures, the variety of file formats, coordinates systems, and attributes are necessary in the design and the function of spatial analysis.

Discrete and Continuous objects:

- Discrete – Data that represents phenomena with distinct boundaries. Property lines and streets are examples of discrete data. Discrete data can be stored via vector or raster data models.

- Continuous – Data such as elevation or temperature that varies without discrete steps. Continuous data is usually represented by raster data.

There are two main data models within the GIS realm: Vector and Raster

- Vector – a representation of the world using points, lines and polygons. Vector data is useful for storing data that has discrete boundaries.

  - Points – use a single coordinate pair to define a location.

–   Lines – uses an ordered set of coordinates to define a linear feature.

–   Polygons – an area feature formed by a connected set of lines.

• Raster – a representation of the world as a surface divided into a regular grid of cells. Raster models are useful for storing data that varies continuously such as an aerial photograph.

Common Data Storage Formats:

• Shapefile (.shp) – a GIS file format for vector data.

• GeoTIFF (.tif/.tiff) – a GIS file format for raster data.

• ERDAS Imagine (.img) – a GIS file format for raster data

• Geodatabase (.gdb/.mdb/.sqlite) – a relational database capable of storing GIS data layers.

1.3   Task 1 - GIS Data – Vector

Examine the vector exercise exercise data using QGIS Browser.

1. Open QGIS Browser.

2. Navigate to and expand the `Exercise 1 Data` folder so that the data are visible in the File Tree.

3. You should see eight shapefiles, an ERDAS Imagine file, a GeoTIFF file, and several XML metadata files.

4. To study the properties of each file, select each one and choose the Metadata tab (see figure below).

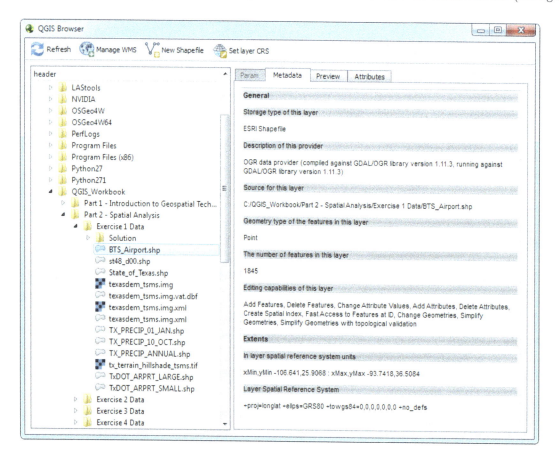

Question # 1: Studying the properties of each of the shapefiles listed below, write down the geometry type (point, line, polygon) and the number of features in the space provided below.

- BTS_Airport.shp

    – Geometry:
    – Number of Features:

- St48_d00.shp

    – Geometry:
    – Number of Features:

- TX_PRECIP_01_JAN.shp

    – Geometry:
    – Number of Features:

- TX_PRECIP_ANNUAL.shp

    – Geometry:
    – Number of Features:

- TxDOT_ARPRT_SMALL.shp

    – Geometry:
    – Number of Features:

1.4   Task 2 - GIS Data - Raster

Examine the raster datasets provided with this exercise.

1. Open QGIS Browser.
2. Expand the Exercise 1 Data folder so that the data are visible in the File Tree.
3. Along with the shapefiles you will see an ERDAS Imagine raster file and a GeoTIFF raster file along with several XML metadata files.
4. To study the properties of each raster, select each one and choose the Metadata tab.

Question # 2: Record the file format. This will be listed under the Driver section. (You can record the last line of that description which is the file format.) You will also record the pixel Dimensions in the space provided below.

- Texasdem_tsms.img

    – File format:
    – Dimensions:

- tx_terrain_hillshade_tsms.tif

    – File format:
    – Dimensions:

Question # 3: Do these look to be discrete or continuous raster datasets?

1.5   Task 3 - Geodatabase

This task will introduce you to another file format, the geodatabase. You will use QGIS Desktop to connect to and explore the data contained in a SpatiaLite database. SpatiaLite is a SQLite database engine with spatial functions added. This means that spatial data layers can be stored in the relational database.

1. Open QGIS Desktop.

2. Click the Add SpatiaLite Layer button to open the Add SpatiaLite Table(s) window.

3. Click the New button to establish a connection to a SpatiaLite database.

4. Select the `Exercise 1 Data\Geodatabase\NDG.sqlite` file and click Open.

5. Click Connect in the Add SpatiaLite Table(s) window to connect to the geodatabase and see the contents (see figure below).

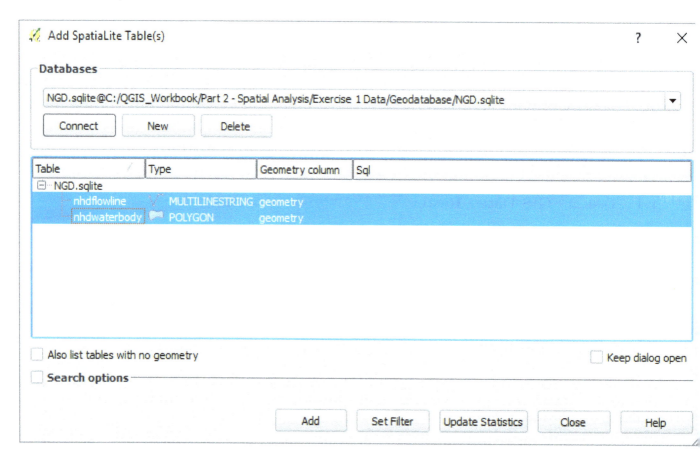

6. You will see two layers: `nhdflowline` and `nhdwaterbody`. Select both by clicking on them with the Ctrl key held down.

7. Click Add to add them to the map canvas in QGIS Desktop (see figure below).

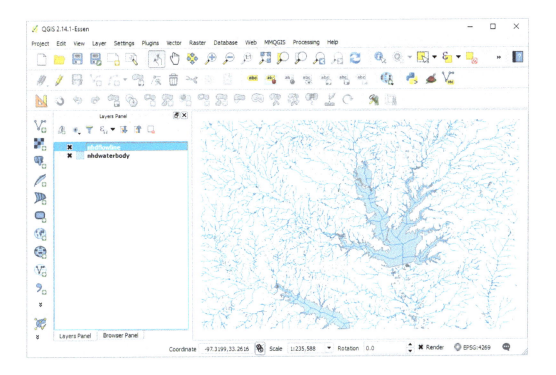

8. Now you will import a shapefile into the NDB SpatiaLite geodatabase. From the menu bar choose Database | DB Manager | DB Manager to open the DB Manager window.

9. Expand the SpatiaLite section and the NGD.sqlite geodatabase. You will see the two layers (see figure below).

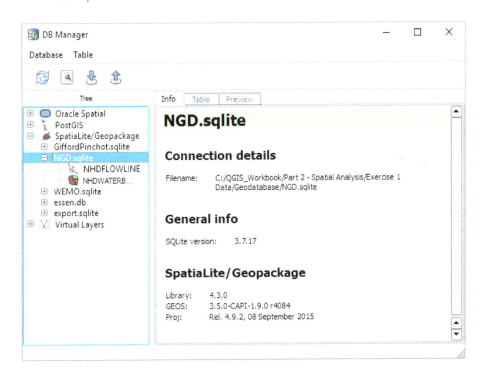

10. Click the Import Layer/File button ![button] to open the Import vector layer window.

11. Click the ellipsis ![button] button to the right of the Input section to open the Choose the file to import

window.

12. Navigate to `Exercise 1 Data\geodatabase` folder and select `NHDPOINT.shp`. Click Open.

13. Name the Output table `nhdpoint`.

14. Under Options check Source SRID and type in 4269. This is the EPSG code for the geographic coordinate system NAD83.

15. Check your options again in the figure below. If they match, click OK to import the shapefile into the database.

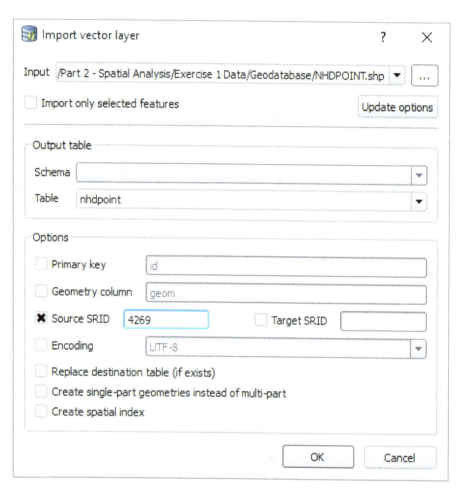

16. You should get a message that the Import was successful. Click OK.

17. Click the Refresh button on the DB Manager. You should now see `nhdpoint` listed as a new table in the database with a point icon (shown in figure below).

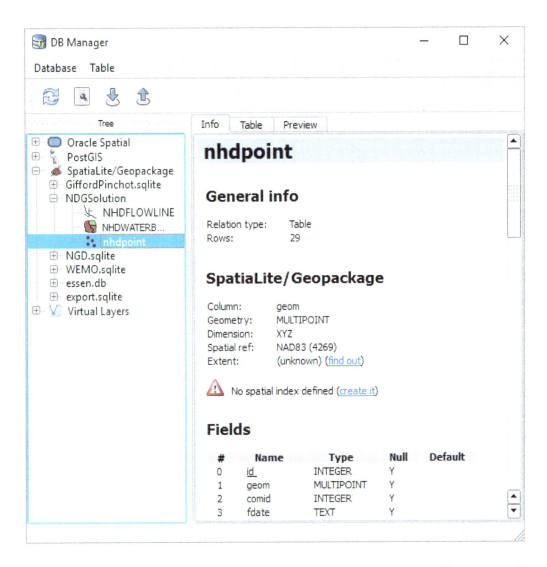

18. Right-click on the nhdpoint layer in the DB Manager and choose Add to canvas. Close the DB Manager.

19. You should now see the new point data added to QGIS (shown in figure below). You have successfully connected to a geodatabase and imported a shapefile into the database.

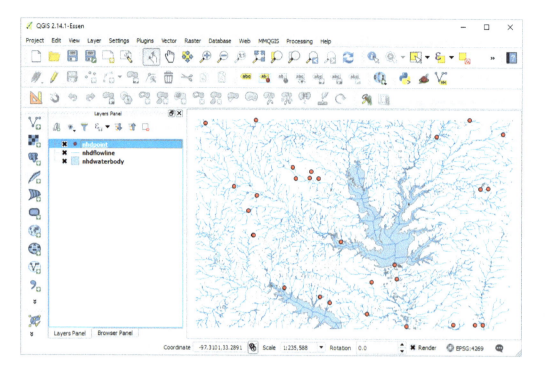

20. Open QGIS Browser. Expand the SpatiaLite database connection. Notice that you are now connected to the `NGD.sqlite` database (see figure below) and you can see the imported shapefile in the database.

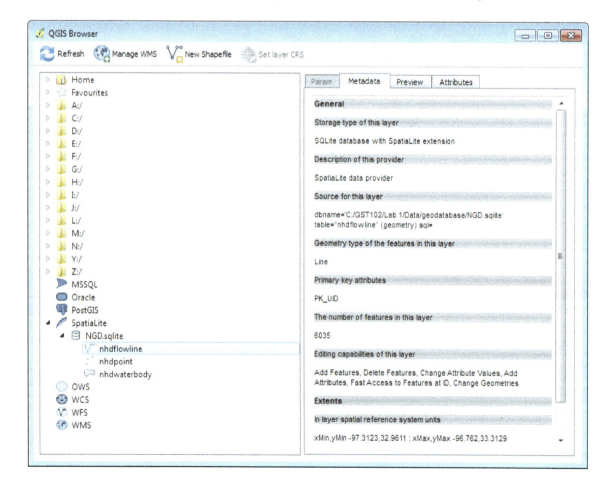

Question # 4:

What is a reason to import source data into a geodatabase?

1.6 Task 4 - Coordinate Systems

Explore the coordinate reference systems of the exercise data.

1. Open QGIS Browser.
2. Using the Metadata tab, identify the coordinate reference system for the following datasets in the Exercise 1 Data folder. Record your answers below:

Question #5:

- St48_d00.shp:

- texasdem_tsms.img:

- TxDOT_ARPRT_SMALL.shp:

1. Now, close QGIS Browser. Start QGIS Desktop, creating a new blank map.
2. Add the BTS_AIRPORT.shp shapefile to QGIS Desktop by clicking the Add vector data button and browsing for the shapefile
3. To identify the coordinate system of the BTS_Airport shapefile right-click on the layer in the Layers Panel and choose Properties from the context menu.
4. Click on the General tab in the Layer Properties window. Under the Coordinate reference system section, you will see the coordinate reference system of the layer.

Question #6: What is the current coordinate system of this data?

Let us say for purposes of our analysis that we would like to change the coordinate system of the BTS_Airport.shp layer.

1. Right-click on the layer in the Layers panel and choose Save as.... This will open the Save vector layer as... window.
2. Referencing the figure below, reproject this layer to UTM Zone 14, NAD83 and have it added to the map canvas.

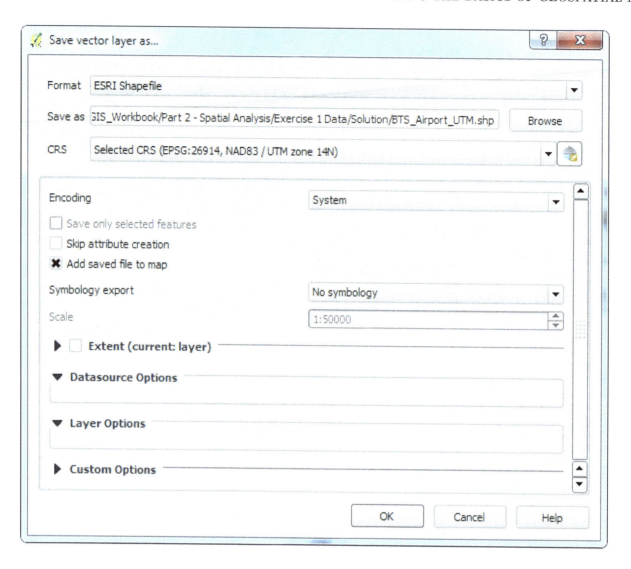

1.7   Task 5 - GIS Data Attributes and Attribute Tables

1. Open QGIS Desktop and start a new, empty project.
2. Add `State_of_Texas.shp` and `TxDOT_ARPRT_SMALL.shp` to the map canvas.
3. Open the attribute table for the `TxDOT_ARPRT_SMALL.shp` shapefile by right-clicking on it in the Layers panel then choosing Open Attribute Table from the context menu.

Question #7: How many records are in this table?

Question #8: How many attributes does this shapefile have?

1. Open the attribute table for the `State_of_Texas.shp` shapefile.

Question #9: How many records are in this table?

Question #10: How many attributes does this shapefile have?

Question #11: If you wanted to identify all Regional airports from the TxDOT_ARPRT_SMALL shapefile on the map how would you do that?

1.8 Conclusion

In this exercise, you were able to identify the data models, geometry, and number of features for several exercise data sets. You connected to a SpatiaLite geodatabase and imported a shapefile into it. You identified the coordinate reference systems of data and reprojected a dataset. Finally, you reviewed working with attribute tables. Knowing how to determine the characteristics of datasets is a necessary step in spatial analysis.

1.9 Discussion Questions

1. What is the importance of coordinate reference systems? Why are there so many different coordinate systems and map projections?

2. Describe the pros and cons of rasters and vectors.

Exercise 2

Introduction to Geospatial Analysis

Objective – Understand Attribute Table Joins and Data Classification

2.1 Introduction

GIS data comes in many formats. As you collect data from various sources on the internet, you will realize that the data you acquire will not always be spatially enabled. There may be a spatial component to the data, but it is not yet a GIS dataset. For example, you may have an Excel spreadsheet with county population statistics. The data has a spatial component, county designation, however, it is not data that is ready to be mapped. In this exercise you will learn how to perform a table join to attach data to the attribute table of an existing GIS dataset. You will then learn how to classify the data.

This exercise includes the following tasks:

- Task 1 – Data Exploration and Joins

- Task 2 – Data Classification

2.2 Objective: Explore and Understand Geospatial Data Models

In this exercise we will look at some tabular data and determine how to join it to an existing dataset. This is a common data preparation step before beginning an analysis.

Join – Appending the fields of one table, to those of another table, based on a common attribute. Typically, joins are performed to attach more attributes to the attribute table of a geographic layer.

Classification – the process of breaking up data values into meaningful groups.

2.3 Task 1 - Data Exploration and Joins

The data for this exercise includes one shapefile: U.S. County boundaries (`countyp010`). The layer only covers the contiguous lower 48 states. There is also one tabular dataset: U.S. Census data (`ce2000t.dbf`) for counties.

In order to map the data in the table, we will need to join it to the county shapefile. In order to perform such a join there needs to be a common attribute between the table and the shapefile.

1. Open QGIS Desktop and add the County shapefile.
2. Open the attribute table and examine the contents (shown in figure below).

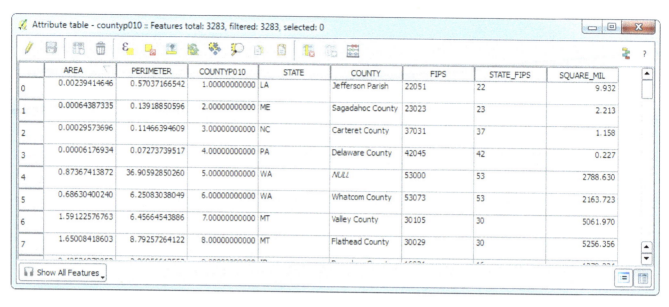

You can see that there are 3,283 records in the table. What kind of attributes does this data set have? The `Area` and `Perimeter` fields are created as part of the file format (shapefile). These represent the area and perimeter of each feature in map units. Since this dataset is in the Geographic Coordinate System these units are in decimal degrees. This is a difficult unit to work with so these values do not provide much information. The `Square_Mil` field at the far right is much more useful. This holds the area of each polygon in square miles. `CountyP010` is a unique ID. There are also fields for State abbreviation, county name and FIPS codes.

FIPS stands for Federal Information Processing Standards. They are unique codes for census designations. Each state has a FIPS code and each county has a FIPS code. This data set has a column for the `State_FIPS` but not the county FIPS alone. The first two digits in the FIPS column are the State FIPS code. The last three digits in the FIPS column are the County FIPS code. Combining both State and County FIPS codes provides a unique ID for each county in the U.S.

With this data, you can identify the state and county names and the size of each county. Now you will examine one of the standalone tables.

3. Close the county attribute table.

4. To add a table click the **Add Vector Data** button and browse to the exercise data folder. Set the file type filter to All Files (*)(*.*). Select the `ce2000t.dbf` file and add it to QGIS Desktop.

5. Right-click on the table and choose **Open Attribute Table** from the context menu. Examine the attributes.

6. This table contains many fields of socioeconomic data such as total population, population by age, population by gender etc.

What field can be used to join this to the Counties attribute table? At first you might think the `County` column would work. Click the `County` column header so that an upward facing arrow appears. (Remember that this allows you to toggle back and forth between an ascending and descending sort of the data.)

Notice that there are numerous Adams County entries from several states (shown in figure below). Therefore, County name is not a unique ID. However, the FIPS column is a unique ID that will be used to join to the FIPS column in the shapefile.

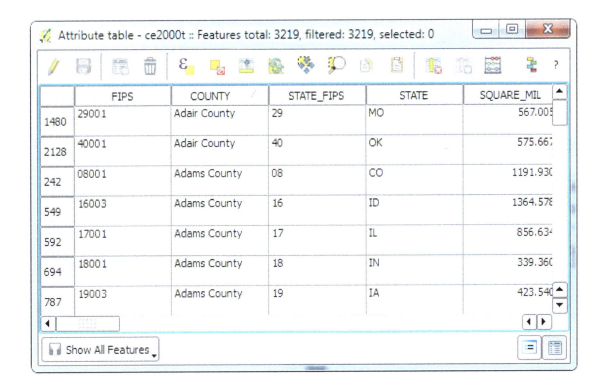

7. Close the attribute table.

8. Right-click on the countyp010 layer and choose Properties from the context menu to open the Layer Properties window.

9. Click on the Joins tab. This is where you configure joins for the layer.

10. Click the Add Join button . The Add vector join window opens.

The Join layer is the table you will join to the shapefiles attribute table. Since you only have one table in your Table of Contents there is only one choice: ce2000t. Since you've previewed both the county layer attribute table and ce2000t you know that the Join field is FIPS and the Target field is also FIPS.

11. Set the Join field to FIPS.

12. Set the Target field to FIPS.

Note: In this example both join fields have the same name. However, this is not a requirement. Both fields do need to have the same data type. For example, they need to both be text fields or both integer fields.

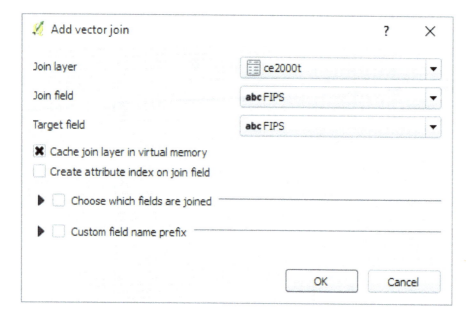

13. Click OK.

14. You will see the join show up in the Join window (shown in figure below). The join has now been created.

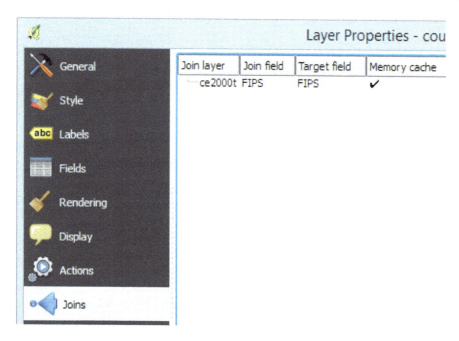

15. Click OK on the Layer Properties window to close it.

16. Reopen the countyp010 attribute table. You will see all the additional fields appended to the right side.

This join exists only within this QGIS Desktop document. In other words, the data have not been physically added to the shapefile. However, within this map document the new fields will act as all the others. Let's make the join permanent.

17. Right-click on the county layer in the Layers panel and choose Save as... from the context menu. This will allow you to save a new copy of the countyp010 shapefile with the new attributes included.

18. Name the new shapefile `countyp010_census.shp` in your exercise directory and add it to the map canvas (options shown in figure below).

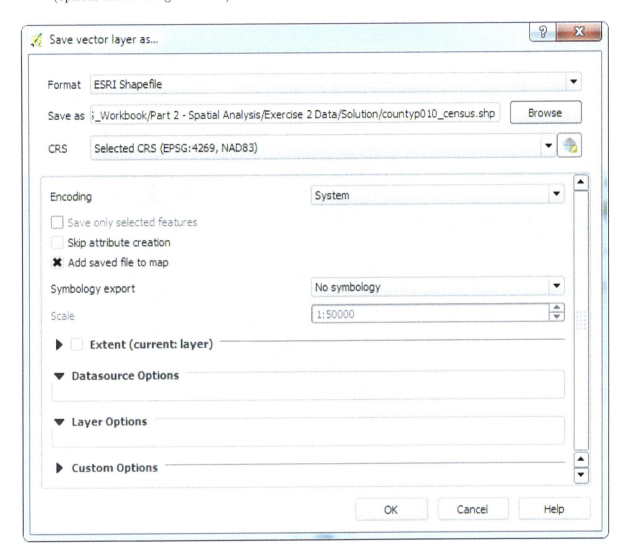

19. You can now remove the original county layer from the map by right-clicking on it in the Layers panel and choosing Remove from the context menu.

20. Save the project as `exercise2.qgs` in your exercise directory.

2.4 Task 2 - Classification

Now that you have joined data to the counties layer, you will explore different ways to symbolize the data based on the new attributes.

1. Open QGIS Desktop and open `exercise2.qgs` if it is not already open.

2. From the menu bar choose Project | Project Properties, click on the CRS tab and ensure that Enable 'on the fly' CRS transformation is checked.

3. In the Filter box type 5070. This is the EPSG code for the Albers Equal Area projection for the continental U.S.

4. Select the NAD83/Conus Albers coordinate systems for the map and click OK.

5. The data should now resemble the figure below.

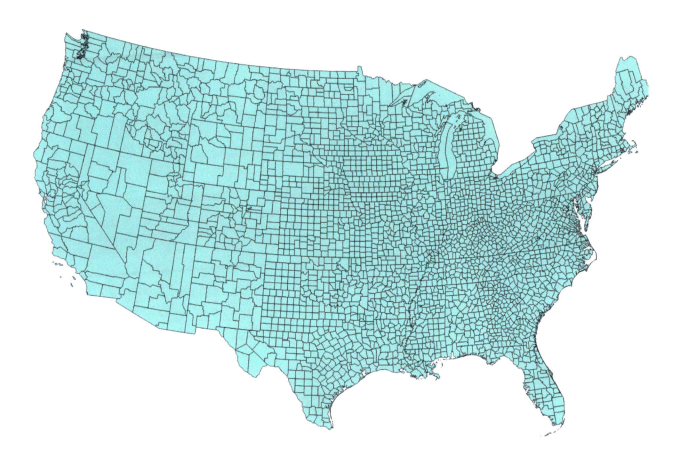

6. Open the Layer Properties for the county_010_census layer and click on the Style tab.

7. Instead of the default Single Symbol renderer, choose theGraduated renderer. This allows you to choose a numeric field and classify the data into categories.

8. Choose ce2000t_P0 as the Column. This field has the total population in 2000.

9. Click the Classify button to create five classes and assign a color to each class.

10. Keep all of the other options as their default value (shown in the figure below) and click OK.

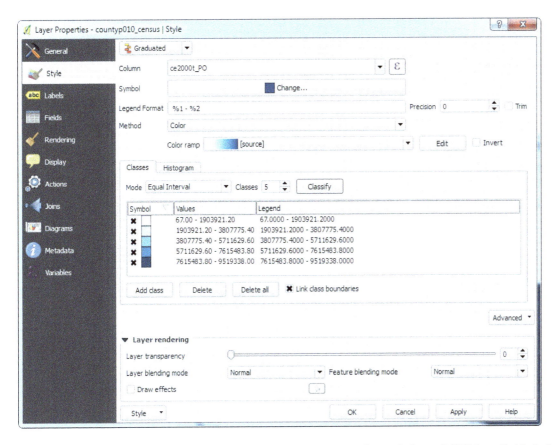

The color ramp may differ but your map should resemble the figure below. QGIS has divided the data values into five groupings and applied a color ramp across the categories. This first classification does not tell much of a story.

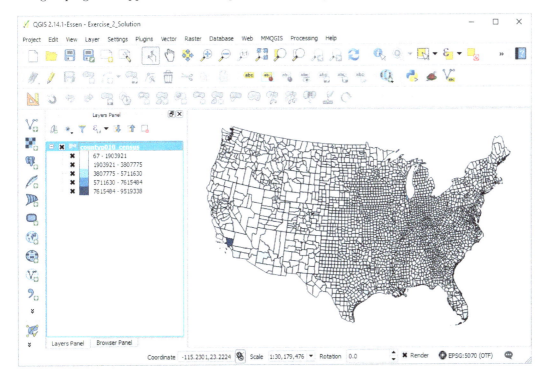

11. Open up the Layer Properties | Style tab again. The default classification Mode used was Equal Interval. This default mode attempts to create classes with the equal data value intervals.

12. Change the Mode to Natural Breaks (Jenks). Notice the data values change. This is an algorithm that calculates natural groupings of a series of data values.

13. Click OK to set the new classification.

This is a more informative portrayal of the data. There large population centers are more visible now (shown in the figure below).

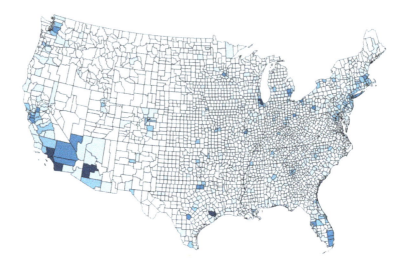

14. Open up the Layer Properties | Style tab again.

15. Change the Mode to Quantile (Equal Count). Notice the data values change. This is an algorithm that attempts to put the same number of features into each class.

16. Click OK to set the new classification.

This is a much more informative depiction of total population (shown in the figure below).

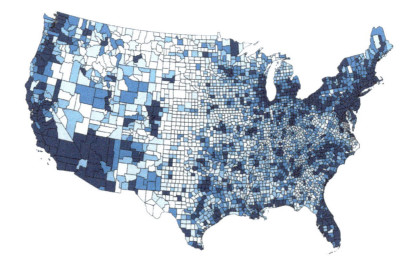

17. Open up the Layer Properties | Style tab again.

18. In addition to changing the mode, you can change the number of classes. Change the number of classes to 4 and click Apply to see the difference on the map.

19. You can also change the Color ramp. Click the drop down arrow to the right of Color ramp and choose RdBu ▬ .

20. Click Apply. This highlights rural counties with a red color (shown in the figure below).

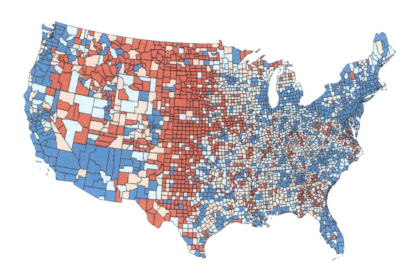

Tip: You can also click the Invert option to reverse the color ramp.

Note: Sometimes you need to change to another color ramp, and back to the one you want to use, to have the Inversion take effect.

Final Note: You can change the Legend for each class. Instead of the bottom class having values of 67-11566.75, you can double click on the label text for a class and change it. For example, you could change the least populated class label to 'Rural'. This is shown in the figure below.

Symbol		Values	Legend
✖		67.00 - 11566.75	Rural
✖		11566.75 - 25366.00	11567 - 25366
✖		25366.00 - 61098.75	25366 - 61099
✖		61098.75 - 9519338.00	61099 - 9519338

2.5 Conclusion

In this exercise, you learned to join tabular data with a spatial component to a shapefile. Once that was complete, you were able to classify the data and produce different renderings of that data. Between the various classification modes, choosing the number of classes and the color ramp you have endless possibilities for displaying numeric data. The key is to remember what data pattern you are trying to share with the map reader. Then you must find a classification theme that will tell the story. These are common techniques for dealing with numeric data on maps.

2.6 Discussion Questions

1. Describe the use of a join in GIS?

2. Why might you want to preserve a join outside of a QGIS map document by exporting the joined layer, versus just working with the join in the map document?

3. Why would you classify data?

2.7   Challenge Assignment (optional)

There are several more datasets in the `Exercise 2 Data/ChallengeData` directory. There is a `World_Countries` shapefile and two tabular datasets: `CO2_Readings_World.xls` and `RenewableEnergy_Percentages.dbf`. Both of these tabular formats can be brought into QGIS Desktop as tables. Identify the fields by which these two tables can be joined to the `World_Countries` shapefile.

Note: You can add additional joins to a shapefile by just repeating the process in Task 1.

Note: Excel files (.xls/.xlsx) do not display in QGIS Browser, so use the Add Vector Layer button in QGIS Desktop to add Excel files to the QGIS project.

Once you have joined the data make two maps: 1) Showing CO2 readings by country and 2) RenewableEnergy_Percentages by country.

Exercise 3

Advanced Attributes and Spatial Queries for Data Exploration

Objective – Understanding Attribute Queries and Spatial Queries

3.1 Introduction

In this exercise you'll explore data and decipher the data fields using a data dictionary table, then perform queries on Census data using QGIS Desktop. You'll also create a buffer and learn the importance of buffering in combination with spatial queries.

This exercise includes the following tasks:

- Task 1 – Using Data Dictionaries and Attribute Selections

- Task 2 – Buffering and Spatial Queries

3.2 Objective: Understanding Attribute Queries and Spatial Queries

The objective of this exercise is to learn how to query attribute data and how to derive information from attribute data. You will learn how to perform both attribute queries and spatial queries.

3.3 Task 1 - Using Data Dictionaries and Attribute Selections

Data dictionaries (aka lookup tables) are usually in an electronic format. They are often included with datasets so that we can understand the type of data stored in a given field. They become necessary because with some geospatial data formats (shapefile, for example) attribute column names can be restricted to a small number of characters. For example, column names in a shapefile are limited to 10 characters. Therefore, data creators often resort to using codes as field names. Often the only way to know what type of data is stored in a given field is to review the data dictionary (example shown figure below).

In this task, we will look at the data dictionary given to us with some census data for the lower 48 U.S. states. The census data captures many attributes about the U.S population from the 2010 Census. These attributes contain a lot of useful information. The ability to query the data allows us to expose trends in the data.

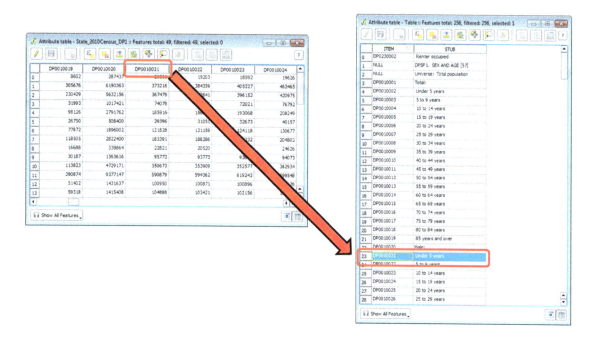

Task 1.1 - Using a Data Dictionary

1. Open QGIS Desktop.

2. Click on the Browser Panel tab. If the Browser Panel tab is not enabled from the menu bar choose View | Panels | Browser Panel.

3. Browse to the Exercise 3 Data folder, right click on the folder and choose Add as a Favourite.

4. Expand the Favourites section at the top of the tree in the Browser Panel and browse to Exercise 3/Data/Census folder (shown in the figure below).

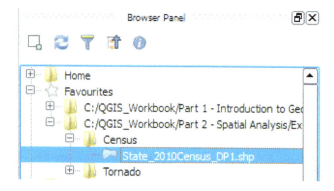

5. Select the State_2010Census_DP1 layer and drag it onto the map canvas to add it to QGIS Desktop.

6. Now you will set the coordinate reference system for the map. From the menu bar go to Project | Project Properties.

7. Enable 'on the fly' CRS transformation and put the map into NAD83/Conus Albers (EPSG:5070).

8. Save the project as exercise3_ Census.qgs in your exercise folder.

9. Open the attribute table for the State_2010_DP1 layer.

There are a lot of attribute columns. It is clear that a naming convention has been used, but there is no way to understand what data in contained in each field by the field names alone.

10. Close the attribute table.

11. The data dictionary is located in `DP_TableDescriptions.xls`. Click the Add vector data button and browse to the `Exercise 3/Data/Census` folder. If you don't see the spreadsheet, change the file filter in the lower right corner to All files (*)(*.*). Select the spreadsheet and click Open (shown in figure below).

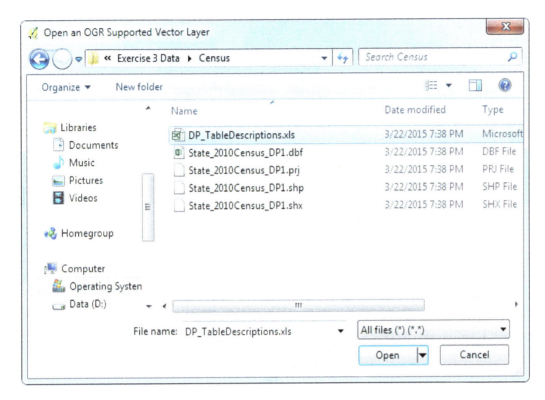

We will map the male population under age 5 for the lower 48. To determine which field in the state census shapefile contains that data, we need to consult the data dictionary table.

12. Right-click on Table in the Layers panel and choose Open attribute table from the context menu.

The data dictionary table has two columns: `Item` and `Stub`. `Item` contains the field names stored in the shapefile. `Stub` is a short description of the values stored in the field. Scroll down to see that the male under 5 years data is contained in the `DP0010021` field. Now that we know which field has the data we are interested in mapping, we can get to work.

13. Close the attribute table.

14. We will now style the layer using the under 5 years values. Open the Layer Properties of the State_2010Census_DP1 layer and go to the Style tab.

15. Use the criteria below. When finished your map should resemble figure below.

- Choose a Graduated renderer.
- Column = DP0010021
- Mode = Quantile (Equal count)
- Classes = 5
- Color ramp = Blues

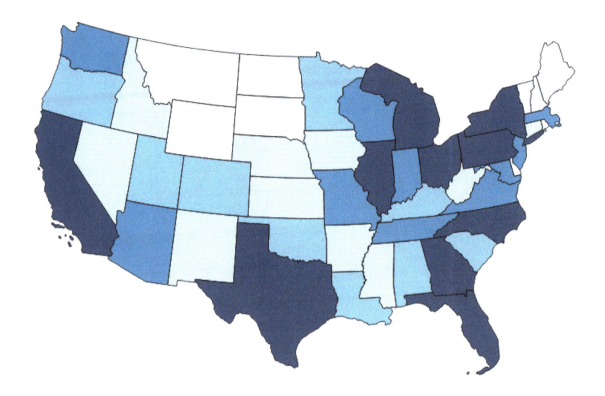

16. Save your map. You will be using this QGIS Desktop project in task 1.2

Task 1.2 - Attribute Selections

Using the map you have just created in Task 1.1, you will now perform some queries against the census data.

1. If you do not have it open, open the `exercise3_Census.qgs` project created in Task 1.1.

2. Open the attribute table for the Census layer.

3. Click the Select features using an expression button [ε]. The Select by Expression window opens.

4. You have mapped the states by the under 5 male population. Now you want to know which states have a total population less than 1,000,000. The figure below shows the layout of the Select by Expression window.

   - Fields and Values are included in the list of functions. You can expand the list to see the fields in the dataset.

   - There are a suite of operators to use in building your expression.

   - Double-clicking on Fields, Values and Operators will insert those objects into the expression window. It is best to build your expression this way instead of trying to type it. This will allow you to avoid syntax errors.

   - Select options: By default, you will create a new selection. However, you can choose to add to an already existing selection, have records removed from an existing selection, or select from an existing selected set.

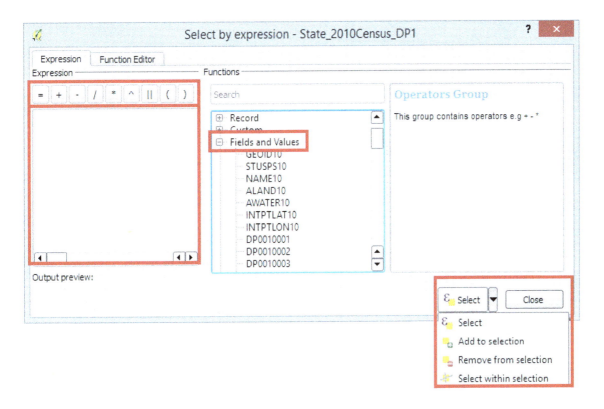

5. First, you will have to refer to the data dictionary to see which field contains the total population values. To select those states with a total population less than 1,000,000 you will:

   a. Double click on fieldDP0010001

   b. Expand the Operators in the Function list and choose '<'

   c. Type in the value of 1000000. *Note*: Since you want a specific numeric value, you will type it in here. You could choose the DP0010001 field and then click on Load values: all unique and see if there is a value of exactly 1000000. However, it is unlikely that you will find a precise even value like that. In these cases, type the value in without thousand separator commas. Also note that numeric values do not receive quotes (") or tics (').

6. If your expression looks like the figure below, click Select to perform the selection, then close the Select by expression window.

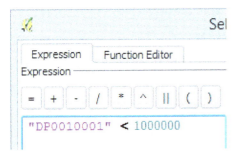

7. The selected records are highlighted in blue in the attribute table.

8. Click the Show All Features dropdown (bottom-left corner of attribute table window) and choose Show Selected Records. Now you are viewing only the seven selected records.

9. Click on the DP0010001 header to sort the selected records by total population. Now you can easily see which state has the highest and which has the lowest population among the seven selected (shown in figure below).

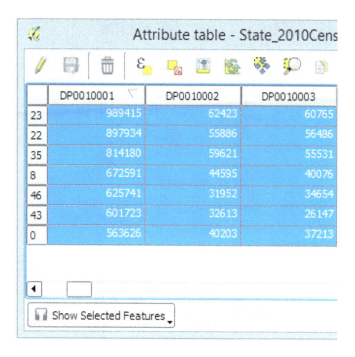

10. Close the attribute table.

11. The corresponding features are selected in the map as well. Your map should now resemble the figure below.

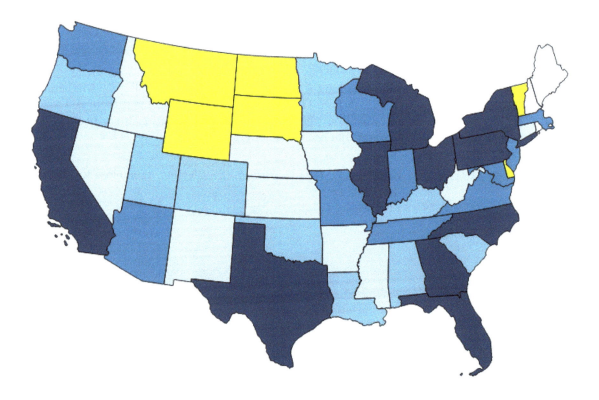

12. Reopen the attribute table and create an expression selecting the states with a total population greater than 10,000,000. Your map should now match the figure below with seven selected states.

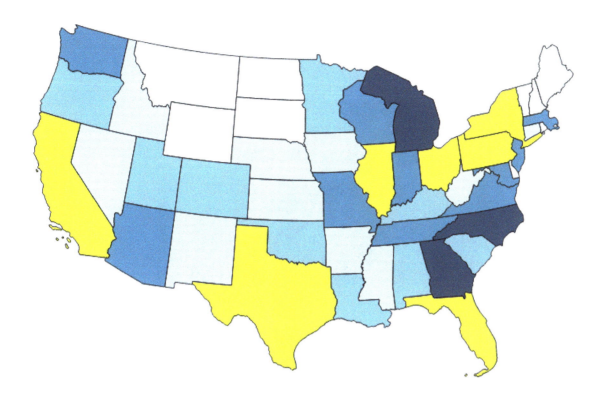

3.4 Task 2 - Buffering and Spatial Queries

Buffering is a key vector analysis tool in GIS. It gives us the ability to create a new GIS layer representing a buffer distance from some map feature(s).

Task 2.1 - Running the Buffer Tool

1. Open QGIS Desktop and open `Exercise 3 Data/Tornado/Tornado.qgs`.

2. The red line represents a tornado's path through a residential area. The approximate area of damage was 900 meters around the path. The green polygons represent schools in the area, the parcels are in yellow and the roads black lines.

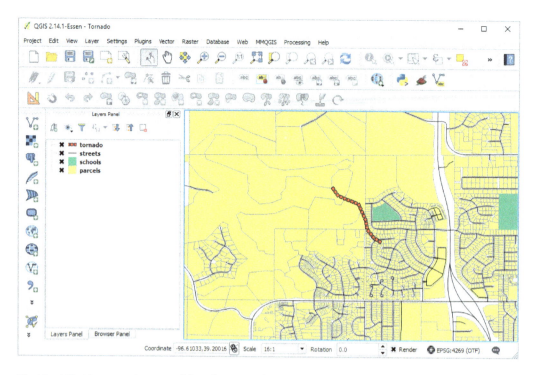

To identify the area impacted by the tornado, you will create a 900 meter buffer around the path.

3. From the menu bar choose Vector | Geoprocessing Tools | Buffer(s). Fill out the Buffer tool with the parameters seen in the figure below.

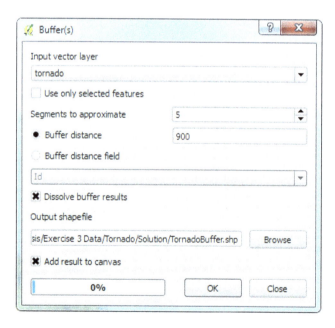

4. Click OK to run the tool, and click Close when it has finished.

A new polygon layer is created that covers all the land 900 meters from the tornado's path. You will need to make the new layer semi-transparent so that you can see what parcels, schools, and roads were affected.

5. Open the Layer Properties for the buffer layer and choose the Style tab. Set the Layer transparency to 50%

(shown in figure below).

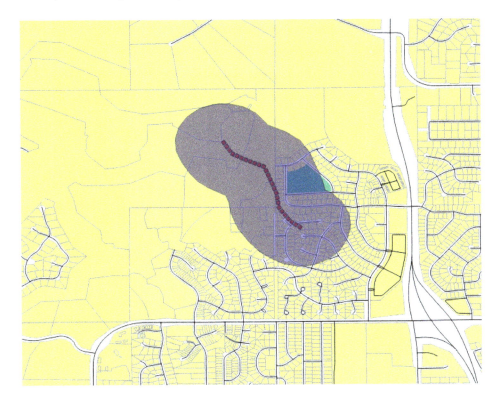

Looking at the result we can immediately see the areas affected by the tornado.

6. Save the QGIS project.

Task 2.2 Performing Spatial Queries

In this task, you will learn how to identify exactly which parcels were affected by the tornado.

1. Begin with the QGIS Desktop map as you saved it at the conclusion of the previous task.
2. From the menu bar choose Vector | Research Tools | Select by Location....

Using select by location, you can conduct spatial queries. In this case, we can determine which parcels overlap with the tornado buffer.

3. Fill out the Select by location form as in the figure below. Click OK to perform the buffer, then click Close.

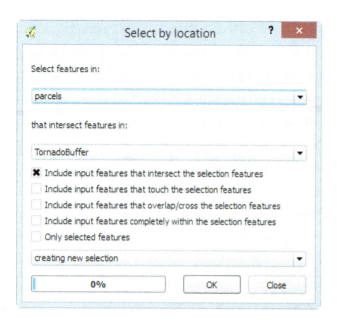

4. The parcels that intersect the tornado buffer are now selected. However, the default yellow selection color is very close to the yellow color of the parcels. To change the selection color go to the menu bar choose Project | Project Properties and click on the General tab.

5. Change the Selection color to a blue color so the selected parcels stand out better (shown in figure below).

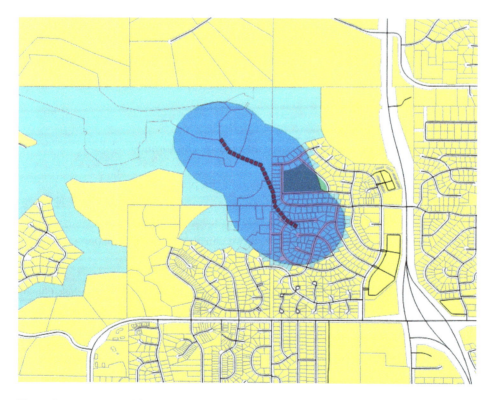

From here, you could save out the selected parcels as a new shapefile. To do this you would right-click on the parcel layer and choose Save As... then check Save only selected features. You could also open the parcel attribute table and Show Selected Features to examine the attributes of those affected parcels.

6. Finally you will examine the total value of the affected parcels. From the menu bar choose Vector | Analysis

Tools | Basic Statistics.

a. Select parcels as the Input Vector Layer.

b. Check Use only selected features.

c. Set the Target Field to TOTALVAL

d. Click OK

The results are shown in the figure below. Now you know the total value of the affected parcels! This is a great example of how you can generate information from GIS data.

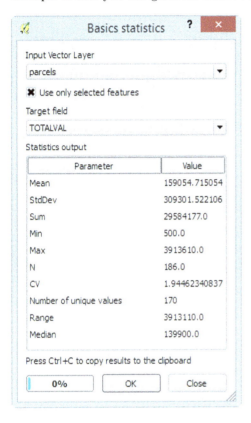

3.5 Conclusion

In this exercise, you explored the use of data dictionaries with coded field names. You experienced another example of using attribute table queries. You used a buffer operation combined with the select by location operation and basic statistics tools to determine to total value of parcels impacted by a tornado.

3.6 Discussion Questions

1. Why do we need data dictionaries?

2. How are Attribute selections useful in a GIS?

3. Why are buffering and spatial selections important to us?

3.7 Challenge Assignment (optional)

Repeat the steps in the second task to determine the roads that were impacted by the tornado. Report the affected road names to your instructor. Make a map composition of both the impacted roads and parcels. Turn in the final map to your instructor.

Exercise 4

Vector Data Analysis - Overlay Techniques

Objective - Understanding Basic Vector Analysis Using Overlays

4.1 Introduction

In this exercise, you will be learn about several powerful vector analysis tools. The tools are all considered overlay tools, since they produce outputs defined by how features overlap one another. You will be working with several datasets covering the Sierra National Forest in California.

This exercise includes the following tasks:

- Task 1 - Clip
- Task 2 - Intersection
- Task 3 - Union
- Task 4 - Join Attributes by Location

4.2 Objective Understanding Basic Vector Analysis Using Overlays

The objective of this exercise is to understand basic use of vector overlays in a geospatial analysis.

Vector Overlays – A set of tools, which work on the spatial relationships between two input datasets. The output is a new dataset derived from those spatial relationships.

Clip – Outputs the features of the input dataset that are within the features of the clip dataset. It is commonly used to cut datasets to the study area boundary.

Intersection – Takes two polygon datasets and outputs the areas common to both.

Union – A topological overlay of two polygon datasets, the output preserves the features that fall within the spatial extent of either input dataset.

Join Attributes by Location – Also known as a spatial join, this operation appends the attribute columns of one data set to another, based on the geographic intersection of the two datasets.

4.3 Task 1 - Clip

This exercise focuses on the Sierra National Forest in California. Datasets include: the National Forest boundary, Ranger Districts, and habitat data for both spotted owl and Southwest willow flycatcher. In this first task, you will be clipping data to the study area. The spotted owl is listed as Threatened and the southwest willow flycatcher is listed as endangered by the U.S. Fish and Wildlife Service.

Photo credit: Jim Rorabaugh/USFWS [Public domain]

Photo credit: John and Karen Hollingsworth; photo by USFS Region 5 (Pacific Southwest) [Public domain]

1. Open QGIS Desktop.

2. From the exercise directory, add both the `Sierra_Natl_Forest.shp` and `CA_Spotted_Owl_HmRngCore.shp` shapefiles to QGIS Desktop.

3. Move the Sierra National Forest layer below the spotted owl layer so the map canvas resembles the figure below.

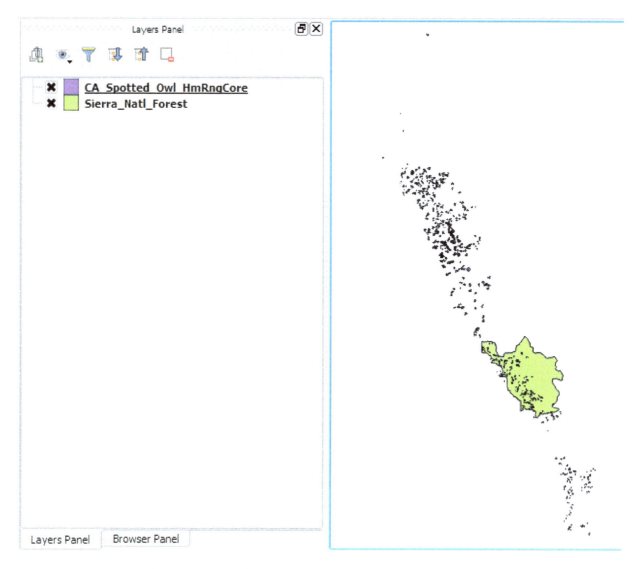

In this case, you are only interested in the data covering the Sierra National Forest. Notice that the spotted owl data covers far more territory than the forest. Therefore, you will clip the spotted owl data to the forest boundary. Clip will create a new shapefile consisting of the spotted owl polygons within the forest boundary. It is standard protocol to clip datasets to the extent of the study area. This reduces data to only that which needs to be processed, and makes processing and rendering faster.

Before conducting a spatial analysis, you need to ensure that all the involved layers are in the same coordinate reference system.

4. Open the Layer Properties for each layer, and identify the coordinate reference system.

Question # 1 – Are both layers in the same coordinate reference system? What is the coordinate reference system of each layer?

1. From the menu bar choose Vector | Geoprocessing Tools | Clip. This will open the Clip tool. Enter the following options:

   a) Input vector layer = CA_Spotted_Owl_HmRngCore

   b) Clip layer = Sierra_Natl_Forest

   c) Output shapefile = `Exercise 4 Data/MyData/Sierra_Spotted_Owl.shp`

   d) Check Add result to canvas

   e) Click OK

   f) Click Close

2. The new layer will appear in the Layers panel. Remove the original CA_Spotted_Owl_HmRngCore layer as we no longer need it.

3. Right-click on the Sierra_Natl_Forest layer and choose Zoom to Layer.

Your map should now resemble the figure below. Unlike selecting by location and exporting the selected set to a new layer, the Clip operation actually cuts spotted owl polygons at the forest boundary where they crossed the forest boundary.

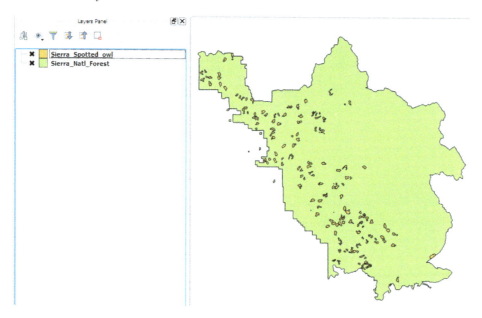

4. Save the project as `Exercise4.qgs` in the data folder.

4.4   Task 2 - Intersection

You will now include the southwest willow flycatcher habitat data in the analysis.

1. Open QGIS Desktop and open `Exercise 4 Data/exercise4.qgs` if it is not already.

2. Add `Sierra_WillowFlycatcher.shp` shapefile to QGIS Desktop. This data set falls completely within the forest boundary so there is no need to clip it.

3. Drag the Sierra_WillowFlycatcher layer to the top of the layers list in the Layers panel so it draws on top of all other layers.

4. Spend a few minutes styling your data.

   a) Give the National forest a light green color and black outline.

   b) Give the spotted owl habitat an orange fill and black outline.

   c) Give the Southwest willow flycatcher habitat a red fill and red outline.

5. Your map should now resemble the figure below.

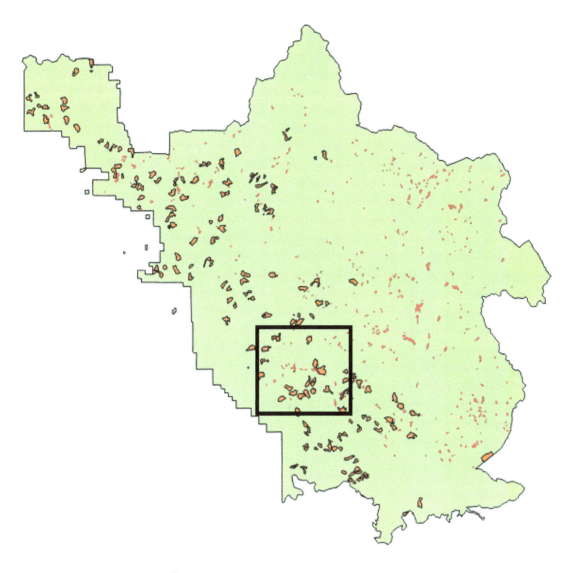

6. Use the Zoom in tool to drag a box and zoom in to the area outlined in black in the figure above.

You will notice that in this area, there is some overlap between the Southwest willow flycatcher and spotted owl habitat (shown figure below). Since these are both sensitive species, areas of habitat overlap will be important areas to protect. You could certainly conduct a spatial query to select Southwest willow flycatcher polygons that overlap spotted owl polygons. However, here you will see the value of using the Intersect tool to identify these overlapping areas.

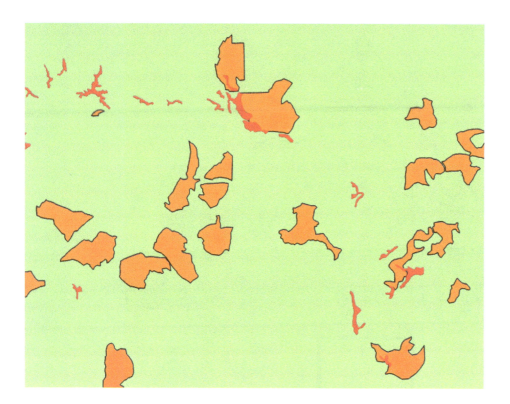

7. From the menu bar choose Vector | Geoprocessing Tools | Intersect. Fill out the form with the following (also shown in figure below):

     a. Input vector layer = Sierra_Spotted_Owl

     b. Intersect layer = Sierra_WillowFlycatcher

     c. Ouput shapefile = `Exercise 4 Data/MyData/OverlapAreas.shp`

     d. Add result to canvas: checked

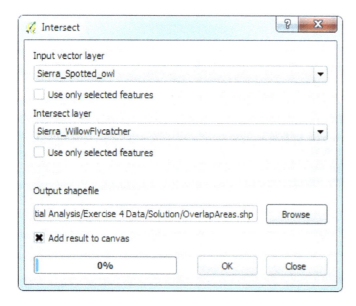

8. When finished, Click OK to perform the intersect operation, and then click Close.

9. Drag the OverlapAreas layer to the top of the layers list in the Layers panel so it draws on top of all other layers.

10. Style the OverlapAreas with a bright yellow Fill and Border. Your map should now resemble the figure below.

11. Save your map.

4.5   Task 3 - Union

You will now combine both habitat layers in different ways using both the Union and Dissolve tools. Union creates a new GIS layer that combines all the geometries of both input layers. Dissolve merges all coincident polygons together.

1. Open QGIS Desktop and open Exercise 4 Data/exercise4.qgs if it is not already.

2. From the menu bar, choose Vector | Geoprocessing Tools | Union.

3. Fill out the Union window as in the figure below:

    a) Input vector layer = Sierra_Spotted_Owl

    b) Union layer = Sierra_WillowFlycatcher

    c) Output shapefile = Exercise 4 Data/MyData/CombinedHabitat.shp

    d) Add result to canvas: checked

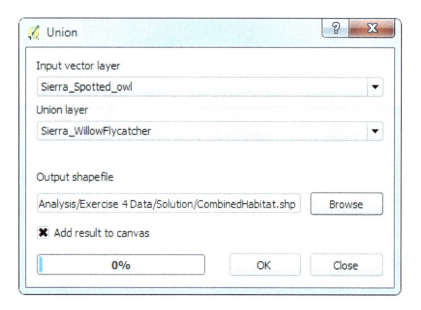

4. When finished Click OK to perform the Union operation, and then click Close.

The output contains all the polygons from both layers (shown in figure below). In addition, all the polygons retain their original attributes! Overlapping areas receive attributes from the Union layer (Sierra_WillowFlycatcher).

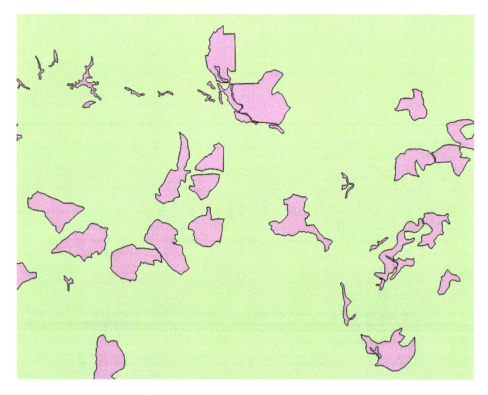

Now you will Dissolve all the polygons into one contiguous polygon layer representing areas of habitat for both species.

5. From the menu bar, choose Vector | Geoprocessing Tools | Dissolve.

6. Fill out the Dissolve window so it matches the figure below:

   a. Input vector layer = CombinedHabitat

b. Dissolve field = — Dissolve all —

c. Output shapefile = `Exercise 4 Data/MyData/CombinedHabitat_dissolved.shp`

d. Add results to canvas: checked

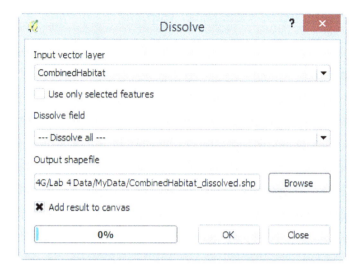

7. When finished Click OK to perform the dissolve operation, and then click Close.

8. The figure below shows the output of the Dissolve operation.

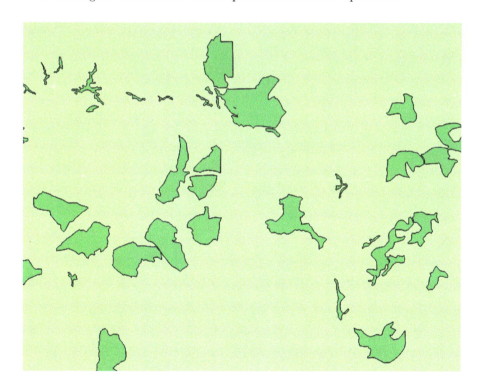

9. Save your QGIS project.

4.6   Task 4 - Join Attributes by Location

In this final task, you will incorporate the Ranger District shapefile into the analysis. There are three Ranger Districts in the Sierra National Forest. You will determine the Ranger District that each spotted owl habitat polygon is situated in. To do this you will conduct a spatial join. Unlike an attribute join done in Exercise 3, a spatial join appends attributes from one layer to another based on the location. This will allow you to attach the attributes from the Ranger District layer onto the spotted owl layer.

1. Open QGIS Desktop and open `Exercise 4 Data/exercise4.qgs`.
2. Add the `Sierra_Ranger_Dist.shp` shapefile to the project.

Remember that data layers need to be in the same coordinate reference system when conducting a geoprocessing operation between layers.

3. Open the Layer Properties for the Ranger District layer.

Question # 2 – What is the coordinate reference system of the Ranger District layer?

1. Since it is in a different coordinate reference system than the other datasets, you will first have to save it to a new coordinate reference system.
2. Right-click on Sierra_Ranger_Dist in the Layers panel and choose Save as...
3. Fill out the Save vector layer as... form as shown in the figure below. You can find the output coordinate reference system by searching on the EPSG code for CA Albers: 3310.

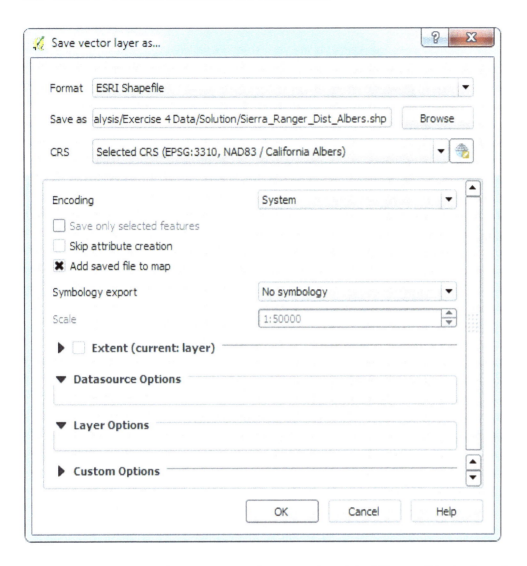

4. Once the layer has been reprojected, remove the original Ranger District layer from the Layers panel.

5. Style the new Albers Ranger District layer with a Transparent Fill and a Border of dark green (result shown in figure below).

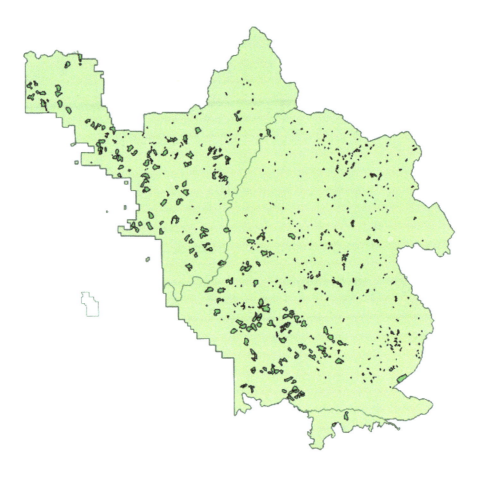

6. Now you are ready to conduct the spatial join. From the menu bar, choose Vector | Data Management Tools | Join Attributes by Location.

7. Fill out the form to match the figure below. The output will be in the form of a new spotted owl habitat shapefile with Ranger District attributes appended.

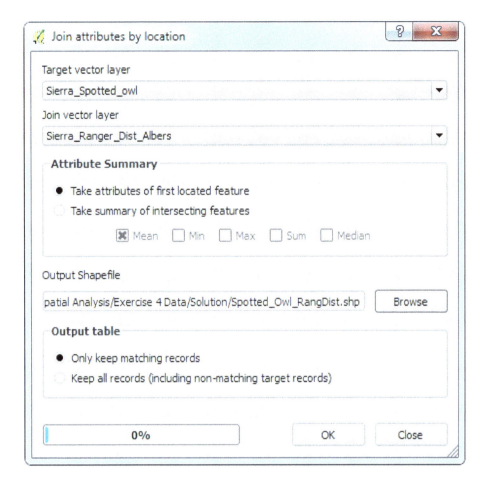

8. Click OK to perform the join.

9. When finished confirm that you want the layer added to the map.

10. Click Close to close the Join attributes by location window.

11. Select the Spotted_RangDist layer in the Layers panel by clicking on it once.

12. Now use the Identify tool to query the individual polygons of the Spotted_Owl_RangDist shapefile. You will see the additional Ranger District attribute columns added.

13. Save your project.

4.7 Conclusion

In this exercise, you explored the use of vector overlay tools with habitat data in the Sierra National Forest. There are many similar overlay tools which, when used in combination, allow you to parse the spatial relationships of multiple data layers. These tools allow you to extract data and turn it into information by narrowing down the area of interest.

4.8 Discussion Questions

1. Describe the Clip operation.

2. Describe the Intersect operation.

3. How do Intersect and Clip compare in their output?

4. Before you run an overlay tool, what aspect of your input spatial data layers should you inspect to ensure it is the same for all layers?

4.9   Challenge Assignment (optional)

The Southwest willow flycatcher data also covers multiple Ranger Districts. Conduct a spatial join between the Southwest willow flycatcher data and the Ranger districts as you did with spotted owl in the last task. Compose a map that shows the both the spotted owl and Southwest willow flycatcher data styled by the Ranger District they are situated in.

Exercise 5

Vector Data Analysis - Creating a Site Selection Model

Objective – Using the QGIS Desktop Graphical Modeler to Perform a Site Selection Analysis

5.1 Introduction

In this exercise you will learn how to streamline a workflow with a model. Using the QGIS Desktop Graphical Modeler, you will string tools together using the output of one operation as the input to the next. You can later edit model parameters and share it with others.

This exercise includes the following tasks:

- Task 1 Exploring the Data

- Task 2 Creating the Model - Part 1

- Task 3 Creating the Model - Part 2

- Task 4 Creating the Model - Part 3

5.2 Objective: Understanding Basic Vector Analysis Using Overlays

The objective of this exercise is to learn how to conduct a site selection analysis using the QGIS Desktop Graphical Modeler.

5.3 Task 1 - Exploring the Data

1. Open QGIS Desktop.
2. Add these five shapefiles from the exercise directory to a new, blank, QGIS project:
   - Airports
   - Counties
   - CityBoundaries
   - Roads
   - Water_features
3. Arrange the data layers so that points are on top of lines, which are on top of polygons. Move the City-Boundaries polygon layer above the Counties layer (reference figure below).

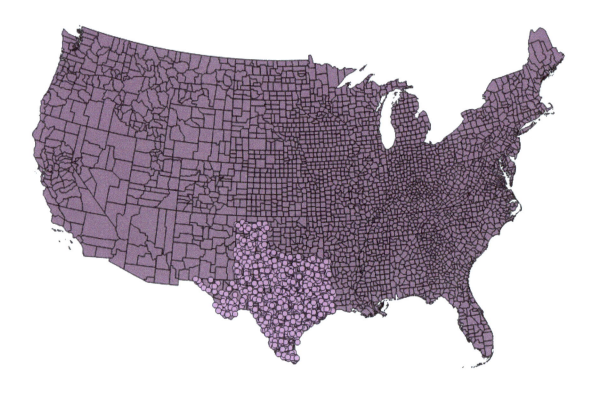

Clearly the data layers cover a variety of spatial extents. One likely step will be to Clip them so that they all cover the same spatial extent.

4. One item to check right away is the coordinate reference system of each layer. This is standard practice in any analysis. Open the Layer Properties for each layer and determine the coordinate reference system for each.

Question # 1 – What is the coordinate reference system for these layers?

Since they are all in the same coordinate reference system no re-projecting will be required.

When building a site selection model, you are usually presented with a scenario. The scenario has parameters, which you will have to address to find the solution. The scenario below describes the parameters for the site selection you will do for this exercise. The best method to solve a scenario like the one below is to extract the parameters from the description and write them down into verbal descriptions. Then from your descriptions you can transcribe them into GIS operations: buffer, intersect, =, <>, etc.

Scenario

A company is looking to lease a helipad at an airport for their company helicopter. This company is situated in Nueces County, Texas and wants the helipad to be within three miles of the Corpus Christi city limits, but not in the city limits. The pilots request that the airport or heliport be within a half mile of any source of water. It must also be within a mile from a County road. As you have some knowledge of GIS you are being asked to find the best solution.

1. Complete the descriptions below. The first two entries in Description and Extent have been entered for you. Study the data layers in QGIS Desktop and complete the table. At that point you will have a better understanding of what you have to work with.

Data Layer -- Description and Extent

Airports -- Airports, Airfields, Heliports of Texas

City Boundaries -- City Limits of Populated Areas of Texas

Water Features --

Counties --

Roads --

2. The next step is to think about the site selection analysis. Read the Scenario carefully and think about the steps required to finish it. The first two GIS Operations have been worked out for you (shown below). Complete the rest of the GIS Operations from the Scenario description. If there is a selection involved open the attribute table and determine what the field name will be and what value you will be selecting for.

Scenario Parameter -- GIS Operations

Scenario Parameter -- Select Nueces County from USA Counties and Save as a new shapefile. Attribute column = `County`. Value = `Nueces`

Airports of the USA -- Clip to Nueces County

Must be within three miles of Corpus Christi city limits but not inside city limits -- Select by Attributes Corpus Christi from CityBoundaries of Texas. The attribute column = `Name`. Value = `Corpus Christi`. Buffer three miles around the Corpus Christi City limits. Use the Difference tool to erase the Corpus Christi boundary from the buffer.

Must be within half a mile of water --

Must be within a mile of a County road --

3. Save your project as `exercise 5.qgs` in the exercise data directory.

5.4 Task 2 - Creating the Model - Part 1

Now you understand the data you have to work with. You also know that you will have to determine which airports meet the criteria laid out in the completed table above. The next task is to begin building the model.

1. Open QGIS Desktop and open `exercise5.qgs` if it is not already.
2. From the menu bar choose Processing | ToolBox.

The tools are arranged according to the provider, and a search bar is available to help you find tools. Notice that there is a section for Models. There is a default folder for models, and if saved there, they will show up as models in Toolbox | Models. You can set the location of this default folder as you will see next.

3. From the menu bar choose Processing | Options.
4. Expand the Models section.

5. Double-click the Models folder box and an ellipsis button will appear to the right.

6. Click on the ellipsis button, navigate to the `Exercise 5 Data` folder, create a new subfolder named `MyData`, and click Select the new folder (shown in figure below).

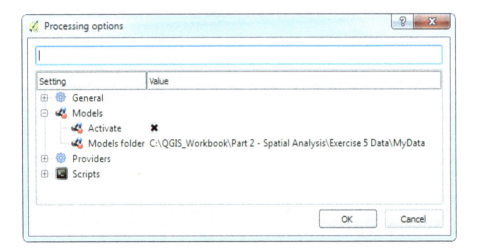

7. Click OK to close the Processing options.

8. From the menu bar now choose Processing | Graphical Modeler.

The Graphical Modeler (also known as the Processing modeler) allows you to create complex models using an intuitive graphic interface. When working with a GIS, most analysis operations are not isolated, but rather part of a chain of operations. Using the Graphical Modeler, that chain of processes can be incorporated into a single process. This allows you to run the entire analysis as a single operation. It also allows you to execute the same model on a different set of inputs! No matter how many steps and different operations it involves, a model is executed as a single operation, thus saving time and effort, especially for larger models.

The left hand panel has two tabs: Inputs and Algorithms. The model itself will be designed in the right hand window.

9. At the top of the main design window are two text fields: [Enter model name here] and [Enter group name here]. Name the model Helipad Site Selection and the Group Exercise 5 (shown in figure below).

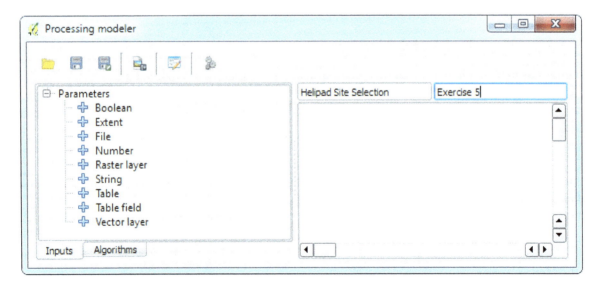

10. Next you will save your model. Click the Save button. It should now open a Save Model dialog and default to the MyData folder.

11. Name it HelipadSelection.model and click Save. It will be saved as a .model file. You should receive the Model was correctly saved message. Click OK.

The first analysis step will be to create your study area boundary. This will involve creating a Nueces County shapefile from the USA wide Counties layer.

12. The first step in creating a model is to define the inputs. All of your data is vector data. Click on the Inputs tab to the Graphical Modeler and double-click on Vector layer.

The Parameter definition window opens. Here you are simply defining the conceptual parameter. You will not actually connect it to the GIS data layer until you are ready to run the model.

13. Name the parameter Counties lyr. *Note*: The lyr will be your naming convention for parameters, which are GIS layers. Other parameters will be attributes.

14. Set the Shape type to Polygon.

15. Set the Required parameter to Yes. If your Parameter definitions look like the figure below, click OK.

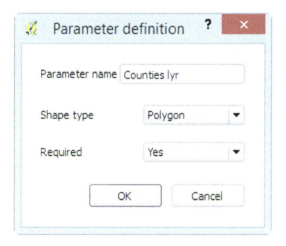

The Counties lyr parameter will now appear in the design window (shown in figure below).

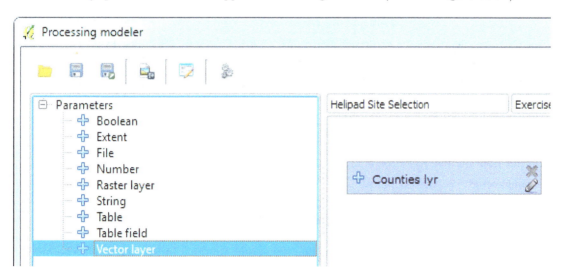

16. The next input parameter will be a Table field. Double-click on Table field.

17. Set the Parameter name to CountyName attr and the Parent layer to Counties lyr. *Note*: Ending the name with 'attr' will be the naming convention for Table field inputs.

18. If your Parameter definitions look like the figure below, click OK.

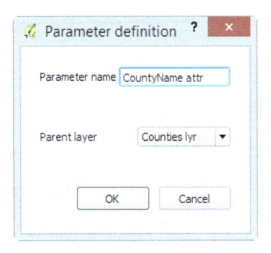

19. Drag the CountyName attr input so that it is below Counties lyr (shown in figure below). You can arrange the model elements into an attractive and intuitive flow.

20. Now you will add the Extract by attribute algorithm. Click on the Algorithms tab. It looks a lot like the Toolbox.

21. Double-click on QGIS geoalgorithms | Vector selection tools | Extract by attribute. The Extract by attribute window opens. Fill it out as follows (reference figure below):

a. Input layer =Counties lyr

b. Selection attribute =CountyName attr

c. Operator =

d. Value (Refer to your notes in the table above)
   Note: It will not need quotes, just type it in as it appears in the attribute table.

e. Output<OutputVector> = NuecesCounty

Note: There is a slight difference here between a Graphical Modeler tool and a standard Toolbox tool. Here the output can be saved as a temporary file that will be used as input to the next algorithm, or it can be saved to a permanent layer that you will specify when you run the model. Typing in anything in this space tells the Modeler that this output will be saved. The text you supply will be the description for the output when executing the model. You will choose the actual name of the shapefile and its location when you execute the model. Since you may want the Nueces County boundary for cartographic reasons you will choose to save it as a layer.

22. Click OK to set the parameters for the Extract by attribute algorithm.

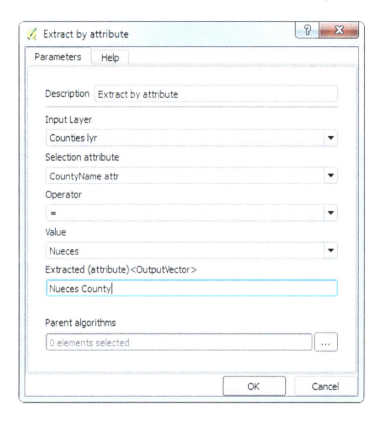

The first complete algorithm has been added! You can drag the parameter boxes to arrange them as you would like and the connecting arrows will follow (example in figure below). You can also click on the Edit button on any model parameter at any time. This will reopen the algorithm window or model parameter window, from there you can make changes if necessary.

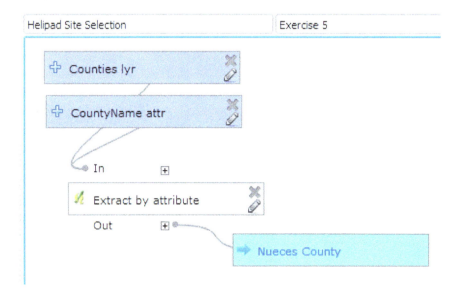

23. Save the model and close the Graphical Modeler window.

24. From the Processing Toolbox panel, expand Models | Exercise 5. There is your model (shown in figure below).

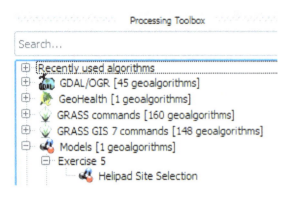

Your model is obviously not yet complete. However, it is already a geoprocessing tool that you can open, set parameters for, and run. Let's try the model out to see what happens with its current configuration.

25. Double-click on the Helipad Site Selection model in the Processing Toolbox to open the model as a tool.

26. Set Counties lyr to `Counties`, CountyName attr to `COUNTY` and keep Nueces County as a temporary file for now—do not fill it in (reference figure below).

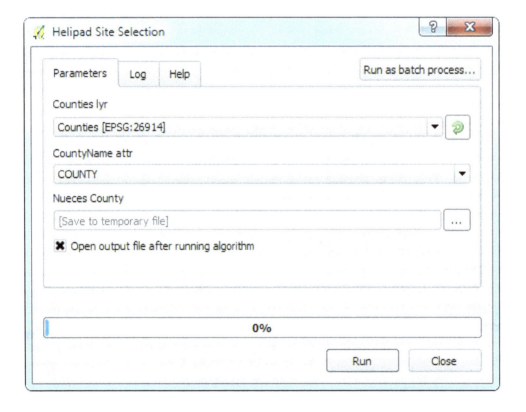

27. Click Run. The temporary NuecesCounty layer will be added to QGIS Desktop. Zoom in and verify that Nueces county was correctly selected using the tool.

28. For now, remove this layer from QGIS Desktop and then save your QGIS project.

5.5   Task 3 - Creating the Model - Part 2

Now that your basic model is set up, you will add additional functionality to it. In this task you will work on geoprocessing the data for the CityBoundaries, Roads, and Water_features layers. You will also clip the airports to Nueces County.

1. Open QGIS Desktop and open `exercise 5.qgs` if it is not already.

2. From the menu bar now choose Processing | Graphical Modeler.

3. Once the Graphical Modeler opens, click the Open Model button 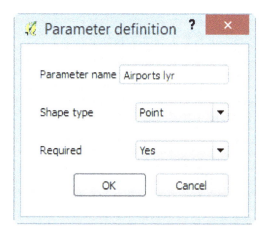 and open the Helipad Site Selection model (if it is not already open).

4. Now you will add a parameter for Airports. Click the Vector layer input parameter and fill out the Parameter definition as in the figure below.

5. You will clip Airports with the Nueces County layer. Click on the Algorithms tab and select QGIS geoalgorithms | Vector overlay tools | Clip. The Clip tool will open.

6. Set the Input layer to Airports lyr and the Clip layer to 'Extracted (attribute)' from algorithm 'Extract by attribute' (reference figure below).

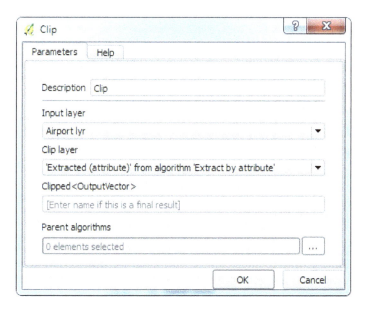

Your model should now resemble the figure below.

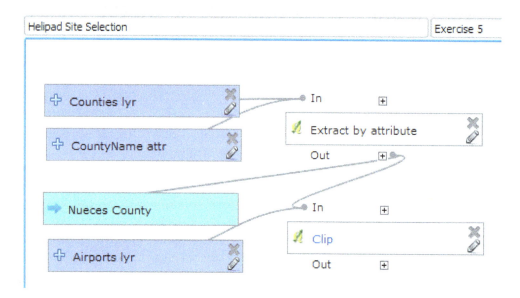

Now you will work with the CityBoundaries. This is the most involved parameter because the site must be both within three miles of Corpus Christi and beyond the Corpus Christi city limits.

7. Add a Vector layer Input for CityBoundaries

   a. Parameter name = CityBoundaries lyr

   b. Shape type = Polygon

   c. Required = Yes

   d. Click OK

   e. Situate it below the Airport lyr

8. You will need to do an Extract by attribute on CityBoundaries in order to extract the Corpus Christi boundary. Therefore, you will need another Table field attribute. Click on Inputs tab and choose Table field.

   a. Parameter name = CityBoundaries attrC

   b. Parent layer = CityBoundaries lyr

   c. Click OK

   d. Situate it below the CityBoundaries lyr

9. Add another Extract by attribute algorithm to the model with the following parameters:

   a. Description = Extract city boundaries by attribute

   b. Input layer = CityBoundaries lyr

   c. Selection attribute = CityBoundaries attr

   d. Select the = Operator

   e. Value = Corpus Christi

   f. Output = leave blank

   g. Click OK

10. The next step for processing the CityBoundary site selection parameter is to buffer the Corpus Christi layer by three miles. Click on the Algorithms tab and choose QGIS geoalgorithms | Vector geometry tools | Fixed distance buffer. Use the following parameters:

a. Input layer = 'Output' from algorithm 'Extract city boundaries by attribute'

b. Distance = 4828.03 (3 miles in meters; we are using meters since the data is in UTM meters)

c. Segments = 5

d. Dissolve result = Yes

e. Buffer - leave blank

f. Click OK

The last parameter detail related to the boundary of Corpus Christi is that the airport needs to be located outside the city limits. Therefore, you need to take the three mile buffer output, and run a Difference algorithm on it, with the Corpus Christi output as the Difference layer. This will take the buffer and erase from it the portion within the city limits, leaving a three mile ring around the city limits.

11. Click on the Algorithms tab and choose QGIS geoalgorithms | Vector overlay tools | Difference

12. Use the following parameters:

a. Input layer = 'Buffer' from algorithm 'Fixed distance buffer'

b. Difference layer = Output from algorithm 'Extract' city boundaries by attribute'

c. Difference - leave blank

d. Click OK.

Your model should now resemble the figure below.

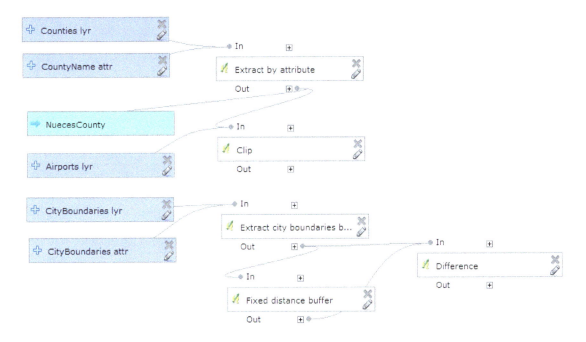

Now you will work on the Roads parameter. First, the County roads will be selected, then buffered by one mile.

13. Add a Vector layer input for Roads with the following parameters:

a. Parameter name =Roads lyr

b. Shape type = Line

c. Required = Yes

d. Situate it below the CityBoundaries attr input

   e. Click OK.

14. Add a Table field input with the following parameters:

   a. Parameter name = Roads attr

   b. Parent layer = Roads lyr

   c. Situate it below the Roads lyr

   d. Click OK

15. Add another Extract by attribute algorithm to the model with the following parameters:

   a. Description = Extract roads by attribute

   b. Input layer = Roads lyr

   c. Selection attribute = Roads attr

   d. Operator = =

   e. Value = C

   f. Output = leave blank

   g. Click OK

16. Now you will buffer the County roads by one mile. Add another Fixed distance buffer algorithm and use the following parameters:

   a. Description = Fixed distance buffer for roads

   b. Input layer = Output from algorithm 'Extract roads by attribute'

   c. Distance = 1609.34 (1 mile in meters)

   d. Segments = 5

   e. Dissolve result = Yes

   f. Buffer - leave blank

   g. Click OK

Your model should now resemble the figure below.

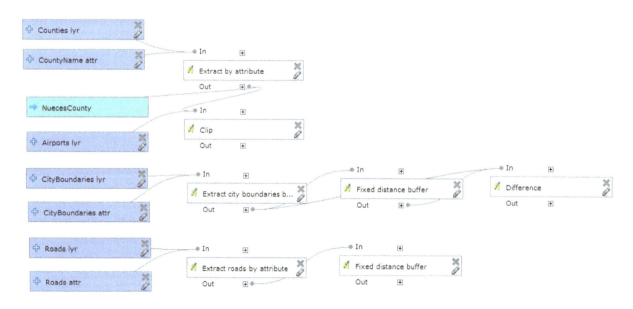

The last parameter to address the distance to Water Features which be buffered by 0.5 miles.

17. Add a Vector layer input for WaterFeatures with the following parameters:

    a. Parameter name = Water lyr

    b. Shape type = Line

    c. Required = Yes

    d. Situate it below the Roads attr input

    e. Click OK.

18. Now you will buffer the Water Features by 0.5 miles. Add another Fixed distance buffer algorithm and use the following parameters:

    a. Description = Fixed distance buffer for water

    b. Input layer = Water lyr

    c. Distance = 804.67 (0.5 miles in meters)

    d. Segments = 5

    e. Dissolve result = Yes

    f. Buffer - leave blank

    g. Click OK

Your model should now resemble the figure below.

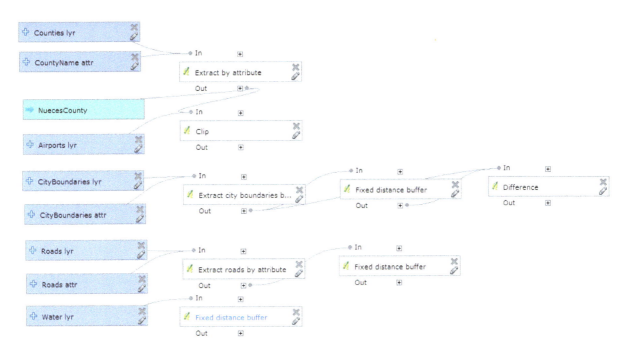

19. Save the model.

5.6   Task 4 - Creating the Model - Part 3

In this final task, you will combine all the individual parameters into one layer representing the combination of all parameters. This will represent the acceptable area for helipad locations. Then you will run a clip algorithm on airports to determine which airports meet all the criteria.

    1. Open QGIS Desktop and open `exercise5.qgs` if it is not already.

2. From the menu bar now choose Processing | Graphical Modeler. Once the Graphical Modeler opens, click the Open Model button [📁] and open the Helipad Site Selection model.

You can combine the water buffer, county roads buffer and the three mile ring around Corpus Christi using the Intersect algorithm. This will compute the area of overlap between the three layers.

3. Click on the Algorithms tab and choose QGIS geoalgorithms | Vector overlay tools | Intersection. Use the following parameters:

    a. Input layer = 'Difference' from algorithm 'Difference'

    b. Intersect layer = 'Buffer' from algorithm 'Fixed distance buffer for roads'

    c. Intersection - leave blank

    d. Since we need to Intersect more than two layers, we need to set two parent algorithms. Click the ellipsis button for the Parent algorithms parameter. When the Multiple Selection window opens check the bottom two Fixed distance buffer representing the roads and water buffers (reference figure below).

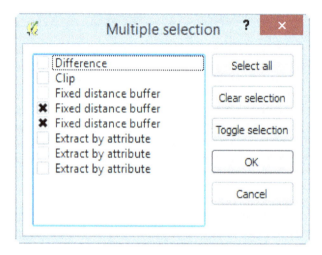

4. Click OK to set the Multiple Selection.

5. Click OK to set the Intersection parameters.

The model will now look like the figure below with the Intersect algorithm taking all three inputs.

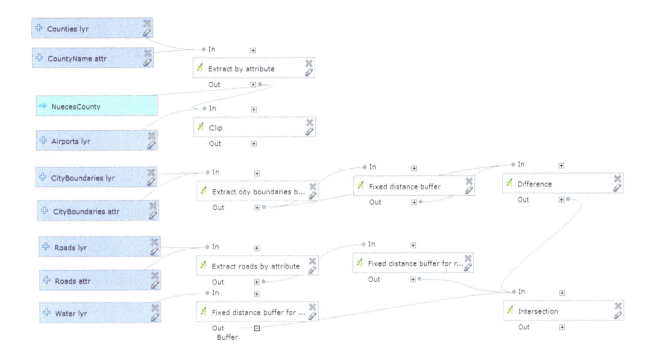

6. Finally, you will clip the airports with the output of the Intersect giving you the final solution. Click on the Algorithms tab and choose QGIS geoalgorithms | Vector overlay tools | Clip. Use the following parameters:

   a. Input layer = 'Clipped' from algorithm 'Clip'

   b. Clip layer = 'Intersection' from algorithm 'Intersection'

   c. Clipped - Final Solution

The final model should resemble the figure below.

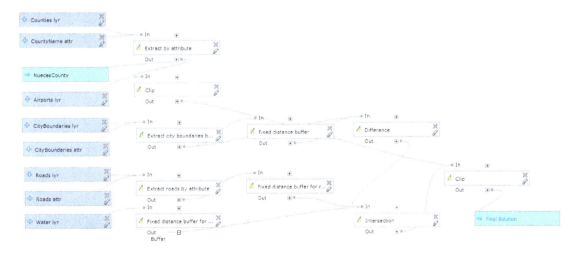

Note on the Final Clip Algorithm: At this time, there is a new bug that may prevent the final clip from working in the model. The error will be reported in the Log tab on the final step in red and it will read: *Error executing algorithm 9 [Errno 9] Bad file descriptor See log for more details.* This bug is not present on all installations and all platforms. If you do not get this you can ignore this note. However, if you receive this error, simply end the model with the Intersection, and save the output of the Intersection to your MyData folder. You can then perform the final clip manually.

7. Save the Model and Close it.

8. Congratulations! You have created your first geoprocessing model!

9. From the Toolbox panel, expand Models | Exercise 5.

10. Double-click on Helipad Site Selection. Fill out all the parameters as shown in the figure below. Click Run when ready.

If the model ran correctly, the FinalSolution layer should contain Cuddihy Field as the only selected airport (shown in figure below).

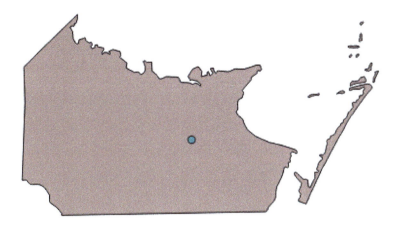

Note on Running Models: Models can also be run from the Graphical Modeler interface. You can click the Run model button [icon] You will be prompted to Save the model, then you will be presented with the same model window shown in the figure below.

Note on Debugging Models: Here we have written out the vast majority of outputs to temporary files. If you get an error or an incorrect result, it can be helpful to save out questionable intermediate datasets. For example, say you are getting an error or an unexpected result from a buffer operation. Try outputting the result of the Extract by attribute dataset that feeds into the buffer algorithm. This will let you determine if the prior step is working correctly. To do this all you have to do is enter a name for the output in question like you did for Nueces County and the Final Solution.

5.7 Conclusion

In this exercise you have been exposed to both site selection modeling and the use of Graphical Modeler in building a workflow. Building the model is certainly time consuming. However, the benefits are many, especially if this is a workflow you will have to perform many times.

By clicking on the Export as image button [icon] in the Graphical Modeler you can export the model to a graphic. This graphic can then be included in a report or a presentation. This can help you explain the technical workflow to others.

If the client changed their mind on the distance from Corpus Christi, you could simply adjust that buffer distance in the model, and rerun it to see how the solution changed. Without the model, you would be starting from scratch in this scenario.

This model can now be run against similar set of data at a different site such as Seattle or Boston. If you were to run it against another set of data, some of the parameters of the Extract by attribute would have to be edited. However, that is easily done. Models allow you to streamline big workflows.

5.8 Discussion Questions

1. How does Graphical Modeler make spatial analysis easier?
2. Export your model as a graphic and turn in with your exercise.

5.9   Challenge Assignment (optional)

The client has decided that they can expand the Corpus Christi parameter from 3 miles to 3.5 miles. Edit the buffer distance in the model for the Corpus Christi buffer and determine how that changes the number of airports meeting their needs. Make a map of each scenario to show the client. You may want to output some intermediate datasets such as the Intersection or Buffers to be able to show these criteria on your maps.

Exercise 6

Vector Data Analysis - Network Analysis

Objective – Learn the Basics of Network Analysis

6.1 Introduction

In this exercise, you will learn how to conduct analyses related to linear networks. You will learn how to determine the shortest path from origin to destination and how to allocate a linear network into service areas.

This exercise includes the following tasks:

- Task 1 Basic Network Analysis
- Task 2 Allocating Service Areas

6.2 Objective: Learn the Basics of Network Analysis

The objective of this exercise is to learn how to conduct basic network analysis. You will use the Road Graph plugin in QGIS Desktop, and be introduced to the GRASS 7 plugin. You will use some of the networking tools in GRASS to allocate service areas.

6.3 Task 1 Basic Network Analysis

In this task, you will use the Road Graph plugin to determine the shortest distance between two points via a San Francisco streets layer. You will do this both by shortest overall distance and by time traveled.

1. Open QGIS Desktop.
2. Add the `MTA_DPT_SpeedLimits` shapefile to QGIS Desktop.
3. Right-click on the layer and choose Set Project CRS from layer from the context menu.

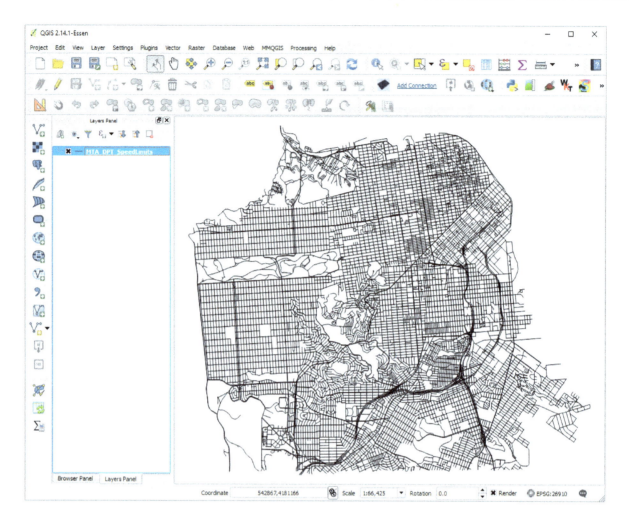

4. This is a street network for the City of San Francisco. Open the attribute table to see what kind of data you have to work with. Notice that in addition to having the street name and type, there is a column populated with speed limits for each road segment. Close the attribute table.

5. Open the Layer Properties | Style tab and symbolize the data by speed limit.

   a. Choose a Categorized renderer

   b. Column = speedlimit

   c. Color ramp = Greys

   d. Click Classify

   e. Click OK (see figure below)

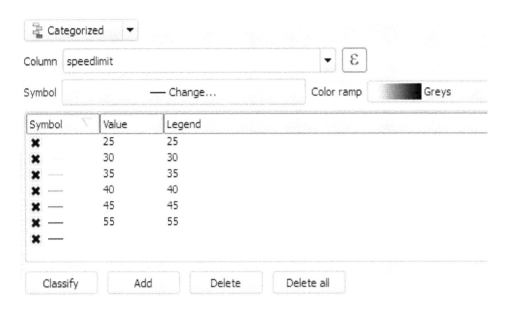

Your map should resemble the figure below. You can now distinguish the major arteries.

6. Save your map as `exercise6.qgs`.

7. You will use the QGIS Road Graph plugin to find the shortest distance between two points on the network. From the menu bar choose Plugins | Manage and Install Plugins.

8. Select the All tab, and type Road into the Search bar.

9. Check the box next the Road graph plugin to enable it. Click Close.

10. A new panel, named Shortest path, will appear below the Layers panel. If it does not, click View | Panels | Shortest path.

11. Before you begin you need to configure the Road graph plugin. From the menu bar, choose Vector | Road Graph | Settings. The Road Graph settings window opens. Choose the following settings (reference figure below):

   a. Time unit: hour

   b. Distance unit: kilometer

   c. Topology tolerance: 10

   d. Layer: MTA_DPT_SpeedLimits

   e. Direction field: Always use default

   f. Speed field: speedlimit km/h

   g. Click OK to set the settings

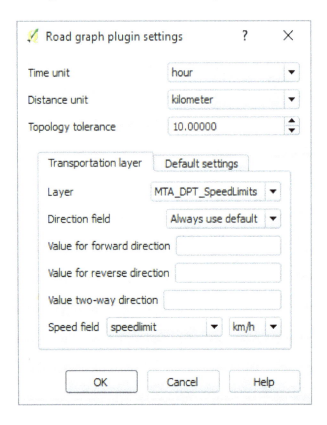

12. Now you will populate the Shortest path panel (below the Layers panel). Click the Start location button and click on a spot anywhere on the map. Do the same for the Stop location via the Stop location button. Small dots will appear where you have clicked.

13. Set the Criterion as Length.

14. Click Calculate to find the shortest path between the two points. After some processing, a red line will appear as the solution (example shown in figure below).

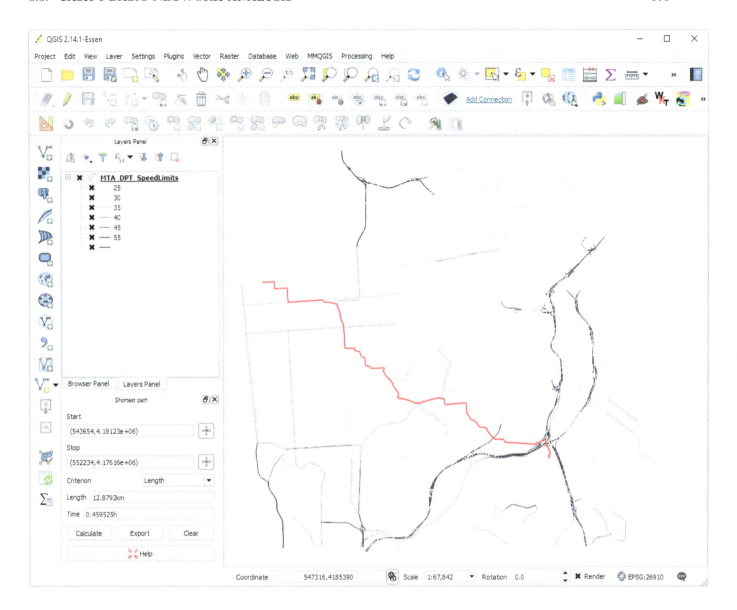

15. To save the shortest path click the Export button.

16. Choose New temporary layer as the Select destination layer. Click OK. The shortest path will now appear in your Layers panel and on the map canvas.

17. To make this layer permanent right-click on it and choose Save As... Save the data to a shapefile in the `Exercise 6 Data` folder named `ShortestPath.shp` (see figure below),

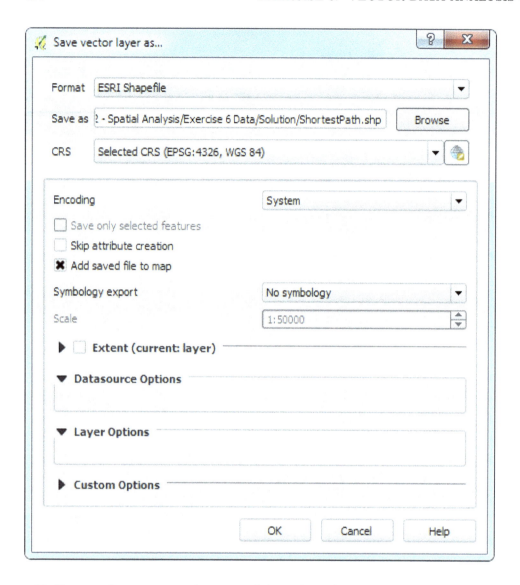

18. Remove the temporary shortest path layer from the Layers panel.

19. Now you will determine the shortest drive time between the two points. In the Shortest path panel, change the Criterion to Time.

20. Click Calculate. With this Criterion, you may get a very different solution, depending on the points you chose.

21. Click Export to save this layer to a New temporary layer, and again, save that temporary file out to a shapefile. Name this file `FastestRoute.shp`.

22. Remove the temporary layer from the map, leaving just the street network and two solutions.

23. Click Clear on the Shortest path button to remove the temporary red line showing the fastest route.

24. Style the ShortestPath layer as a red line with a thickness of 0.46 and the FastestRoute layer with a dark blue line of equal thickness. With the points I chose, I had two very different solutions (figure below).

25. Save your map file and close QGIS Desktop.

6.4 Task 2 Allocating Service Areas

Now you will use some GRASS tools to allocate portions of the road network served by each San Francisco Police Station. GRASS is a mature and powerful free and open source (FOSS) GIS software package. It has a unique data structure that can be initially intimidating. Fortunately, QGIS Desktop has a GRASS 7 plugin that provides a much more intuitive interface to the large suite of GRASS analysis tools.

NOTE: On Windows machines you will need to have the 32 bit version of at least QGIS 2.12 with GRASS installed to complete this particular task. The GRASS vector data structure changed from GRASS6 to GRASS7. Therefore, this exercise has both a GRASS6 and a GRASS7 database so you can use the version that corresponds with your version of GRASS. The instructions will focus on GRASS7.

1. Using QGIS Desktop 2.14 with GRASS, open `Exercise 6 Data/Exercise6_Task2.qgs`
2. This project has three layers loaded: SF_Police, SF_FireStations and SF_Streets.

GRASS uses its own file format. These layers are stored in a GRASS Database, which is essentially a folder containing GRASS data. The Grass Database is found in `Exercise 6 Data/GRASS7db`. These data sets have been imported into GRASS from shapefiles. In QGIS Desktop they will behave just like any other layer. However, since they are stored as GRASS Vectors, you can also use the suite of GRASS tools with them. These tools include a set for network analysis.

3. First, you will enable the GRASS 7 (or GRASS 6) plugin. From the menu bar choose Plugins | Manage and Install Plugins.
   The GRASS 7 plugin is a core QGIS plugin. This means it is already installed and all you need to do is enable it.

4. Click on the Installed tab. Find GRASS 7 and check the box to turn it on. Click Close when done.

Enabling the GRASS 7 plugin turns on a new panel (shown in figure below). If the panel does not appear, click View | Panels | GRASS Tools.

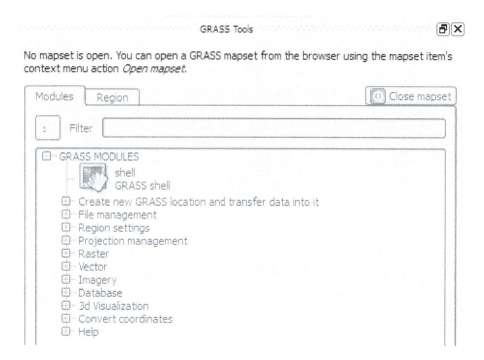

The data is already set up for you in this QGIS Desktop project. The following is simply an explanation to get you oriented to the GRASS data structure and show you how the GRASS data was loaded in to QGIS Desktop. Remember GRASS data is stored in a GRASS database, which again is simply a folder. Inside the database will be folder(s) called Locations and inside a Location will be folder(s) called Mapsets.

GRASSdb | Locations | Mapsets

Locations represent a certain spatial extent and coordinate reference system that you identify when you create one. Mapsets are a way to organize data and are the data tier that actually contains data layers. Every Location contains a default Mapset named PERMANENT. Additional Mapsets can be set up for individual users (Tom, Mary, Alice etc,) or for categories of data such as hydrology, transportation, boundaries etc.

This QGIS project has three data layers from a GRASS Database, however, you need to open a Mapset to begin working with GRASS tools. Additionally, the Mapset you have open determines where your outputs will be saved. For this exercise there is an empty Mapset called MyData that you will open to complete Task 2.

5. From the Browser Panel in QGIS Desktop, navigate to the `Exercise 6 Data` folder. Expand the folder to expose the `GRASS7db` database. It will have a GRASS icon next to it. Expand the `GRASS7db` database folder. Right-click on the `MyData` mapset and from the context menu choose Open mapset.

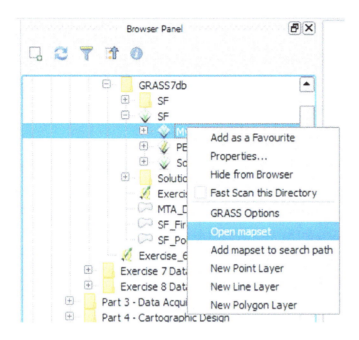

6. There will be two changes that occur. 1) You will see a red box appear around your data on the map. This represents the Region of study (shown in figure below), which in this case is equal to the Location settings. It is the spatial extent of your study area. 2) The GRASS Tools panel is now active.

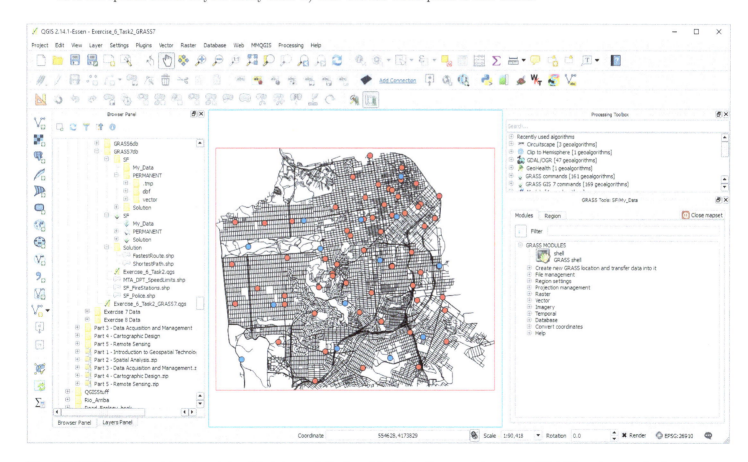

The GRASS Tools panel has two tabs: Modules and Region. Modules allows you to access GRASS tools organized by theme. Region shows you your GRASS Region settings.

7. The first step in doing a network analysis in GRASS is the build a network dataset. In the GRASS Tools panel, expand Vector | Spatial Analysis | Network analysis and click on the v.net - Network Maintenance tool. This will open the tool in a new tab to the right of the Region tab.

This tool will create a linear network of San Francisco streets and attach nodes representing the Police stations. Additionally, the tool itself has three tabs: Options, Output, and Manual. The Options tab is where you fill out your parameters before running the tool. When you run the tool, it will switch to the Output tab and you will see details about the running process. The Manual tab contains the documentation for the tool.

8. Enter the parameters described below and shown in the figure below: *Note*: The inputs are listed as LayerName@Mapset.

   a. Name of input vector map: SF_Streets (SF_Streets@PERMANENT 1 line)

   b. Name of input point vector map: SF_Police (SF_Police@PERMANENT 1 point)

   c. Operation to be performed: Connect still unconnected points to vector network by inserting new line(s)

   d. Arc layer: 1

   e. Node layer: 2

   f. Threshold: 300

   g. Name for output vector map: SF_Network

   h. Click Run

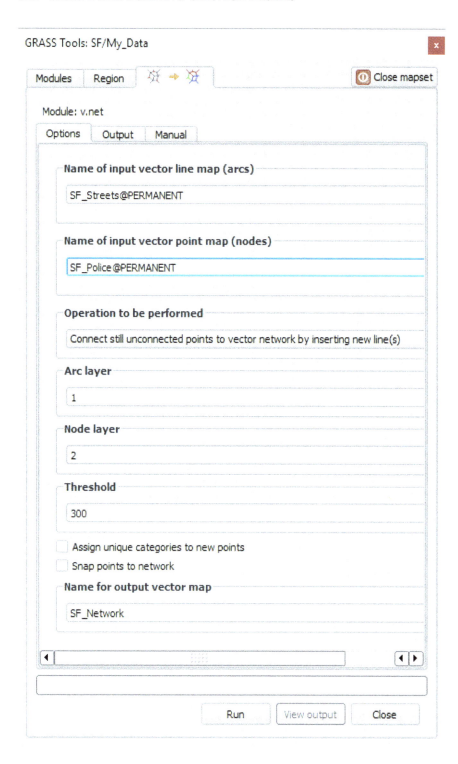

While running the Output tab will be visible (shown in figure below).

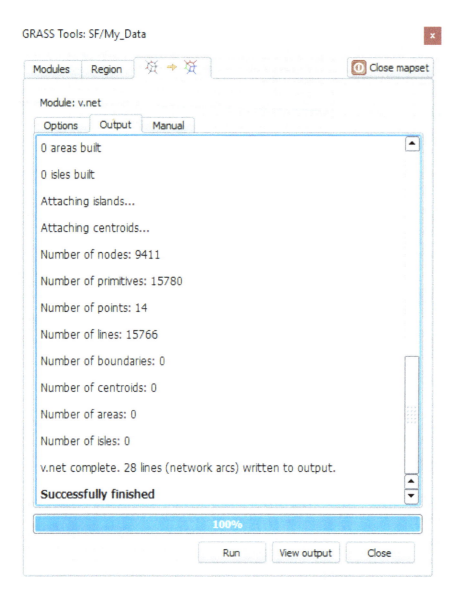

9. Click the View output button to add the network dataset to QGIS and close the v.net tool by clicking the Close button to the right of the View output button.

10. Turn off the SF_FireStations and SF_Police layers.

In addition to the linear network, this operation produced nodes for each police station point. The View output only added the linear network to QGIS, so you will now add the network nodes to QGIS.

11. In the Browser Panel click the Refresh button. Expand the MyData Mapset and expand the SF_Network network dataset. Notice that there are two layers. Right-click on the 2 Point layer and choose Add layer from the context menu. (Remember when you ran the v.net tool you specified that the ID for the Arc layer was 1 and the node layer 2.)

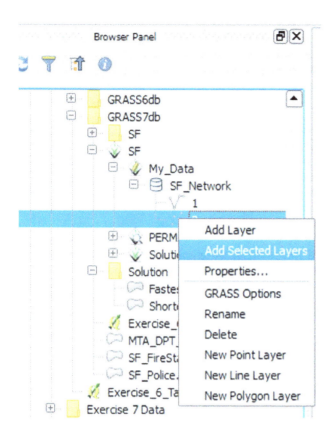

12. Open the attribute table for the SF_Network_2 node layer. It has one column named `cat` with values for each of the 14 police stations (1-14). Close the table.

Now that the network dataset is constructed, you will identify the road territory that each police station should serve.

13. In the GRASS Tools Panel switch back to the Modules tab.

14. Click on v.net.alloc – Allocate network tool. The tool will open in yet another tab.

15. Fill out the tool form as described below and as seen in the figure below.

    a. Input arcs: SF_Network

    b. Input nodes: SF_Network

    c. Cats: 1,2,3,4,5,6,7,8,9,10,11,12,13,14
      Note: these are the values for each police station from the SF_Network_2 node attribute table.

    d. Name for output vector map: PoliceSt_Allocation

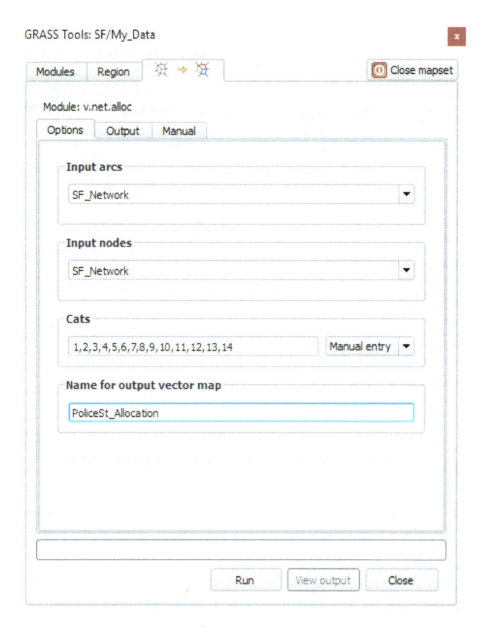

16. When the tool is set up correctly, click Run. When complete click View output.

17. Turn off the visibility of the SF_Network and SF_Streets layers.

18. Open the attribute table for the PoliceSt_Allocation layer. Notice that it simply has the `cat` ID of each of the 14 police stations.

19. Switch to the Browser Panel.

20. Click the Refresh button.

21. Expand `MyData` and `PERMANENT`. You will see the data layers listed in each Mapset (see figure below).

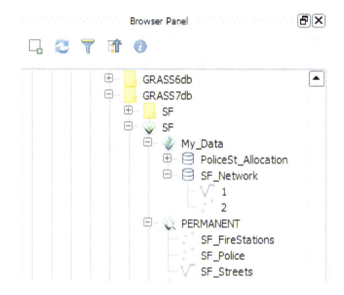

22. To see the results of your analysis you will Style the PoliceSt_Allocation layer. Open the Layer Properties | Style tab. Choose the following parameters:

    a. Renderer: Categorized

    b. Column: cat

    c. Color ramp: Random colors

    d. Click Classify

    e. Click OK

23. Now turn OFF the SF_Network 2 layer and turn ON the SF_Police layer.

24. Drag the SF_Police layer above the PoliceST_Allocation layer in the Layers panel.

25. Next you will label the Police stations with their name. Open the Layer Properties | Labels tab for the SF_Police layer.

    a. Select Show labels for this layer from the drop-down box

    b. For Label with choose FACILITY_N

    c. Click the Text tab below and make the font size 9 and Bold

    d. Click the Buffer tab and click Draw text buffer and make the size 1.0

    e. Click OK.

26. Your map should resemble the figure below.

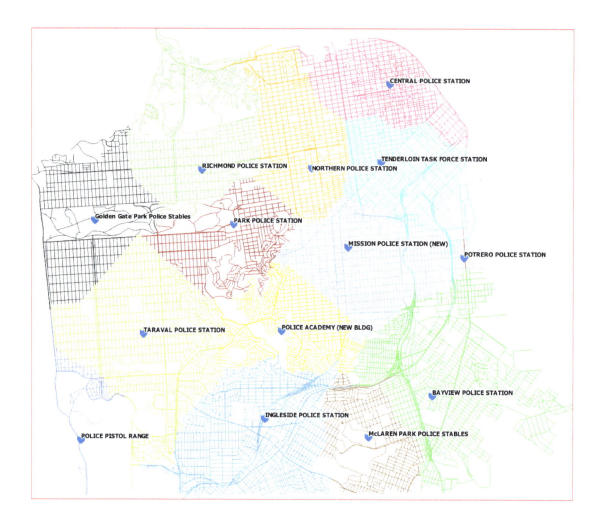

6.5   Conclusion

In this exercise, you were exposed to basic network routing and allocation analysis. You calculated the shortest distance between two points via both time and distance. You then determined which portions of the network that should be allocated to each police station. There are many applications for this type of analysis including emergency management, parcel delivery, and general navigation.

6.6   Discussion Questions

1. What is a real world application of network analysis? Explain.

2. How can a network analysis benefit the logistics industry?

3. What other linear networks could this apply to other than roads?

6.7   Challenge Assignment (optional)

The San Francisco Police Department has shown your analysis to their colleagues at the Fire Department and they were impressed. Now the Fire Department would like the same analysis done for their stations. In the PERMANENT mapset there is a SF_FireStations GRASS vector layer. Repeat the steps in the second task to create the same allocation analysis for the Fire Department. Compose a map of the results of the Fire Department analysis.

Exercise 7

Raster Data Analysis - Working with Topographic Data

Objective – Learn the Basics of Terrain Analysis

7.1   Introduction

In this exercise, you will learn about topographic data and how to use it for analysis. You will learn how to create datasets such as slope, aspect, and hillshades using QGIS Desktop. You will then learn how to combine them using raster algebra.

This exercise includes the following tasks:

- Task 1 Terrain Analysis
- Task 2 Reclassification
- Task 3 Raster Calculator

7.2   Objective: Learn the Basics of Terrain Analysis

The objective of this exercise is to learn the basics of terrain analysis using QGIS Desktop.

7.3   Task 1 Terrain Analysis

In this task, you will use a digital elevation model to create several terrain related datasets: slope, aspect, and hillshade. These elevation derived datasets can be important in site selection and other terrain based spatial analyses.

1. Open QGIS Desktop.
2. Add the `35106-B4.dem` raster from the exercise directory to QGIS Desktop using the Add Raster Layer button.

This raster layer has elevation values for each cell. This type of data is referred to as a digital elevation model, or DEM, for short. This particular dataset covers the Sandia Mountains on the east side of Albuquerque, New Mexico (shown in figure below). The light areas have the highest elevation and the dark areas the lowest elevation.

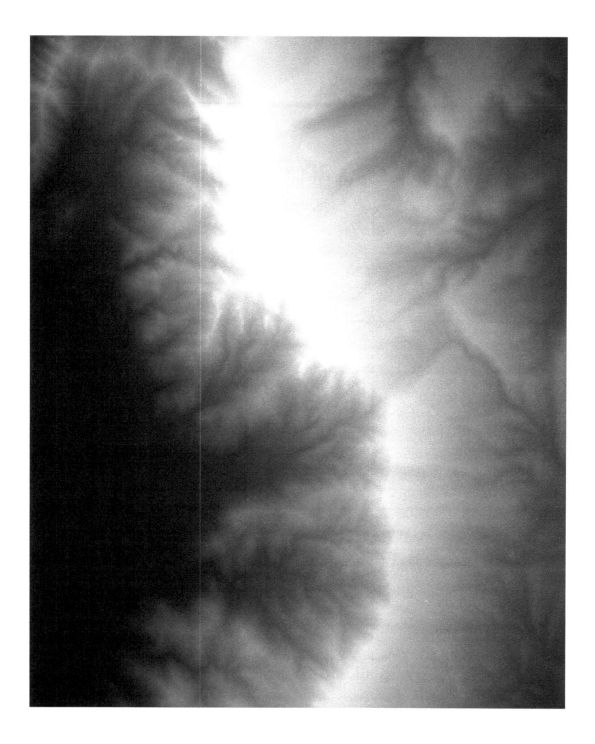

3. Let's explore the properties of the raster dataset.

   a. Open the Layer Properties for the DEM and choose the General tab. Notice that the raster is in the UTM coordinate system. UTM has X/Y coordinate values in meters.

   b. Now switch to the Metadata tab. Find the Properties section and scroll down until you see the Pixel Size properties. Notice that the Pixel size is 10 x 10. This means each cell represents a 10 by 10 meter area.

   c. Now switch to the Style tab. The elevation values (Z) of a DEM are typically either feet or meters. For me, the min value reads 1841 and the max value 3094. Your values may differ slightly. By default, the Load min/max values is set to Cumulative count cut and the Accuracy is set to Estimate (faster). Switch the Load min/max values to Min/Max and the Accuracy to Actual (slower) and click the Load button. The values should now read 1775 to 3255. The Sandia Mountain range reaches 10,678 feet above sea level. Therefore, you can deduce that these elevation units are in meters. Before working with DEMs, it is important to understand what unit the X, Y, and Z values are in. In this case, all three are in meters.

   d. Close the Layer Properties window.

4. Save your project as `Exercise7.qgs` in the exercise directory.

5. You will use the Raster Terrain Analysis plugin to create the three elevation related datasets. From the menu bar choose Plugins | Manage and Install Plugins.

6. Type 'Terrain' into the Search bar.

7. Find the Raster Terrain Analysis plugin and click the box to enable it. Close the Plugins window.

8. First you will create a hillshade image which will allow you to get a better feel for the terrain in this area. Hillshade images are very useful for creating nice maps of an area. From the menu bar choose Raster | Terrain Analysis | Hillshade.

9. Use the following parameters (shown in figure below).

   a. Elevation layer = 35106-B4

   b. Output layer =`Exercise 7 Data/MyData/Hillshade.img`

   c. Output format = Erdas Imagine Images (.img)

   d. Z factor – 1.0 (this is a conversion factor between the X/Y and Z

   e. units. Since all three are meters you can leave this at 1.0)

   f. Check Add result to project

   g. Leave defaults for Azimuth and Vertical angle (sun position).

   h. Click OK.

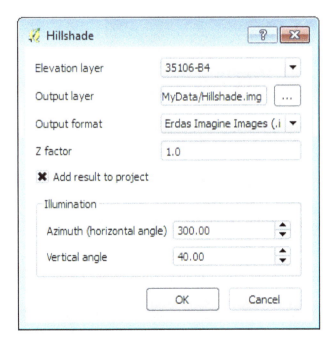

The resulting hillshade should resemble the figure below.

This is a grayscale hillshade rendering. Now you will use both the original DEM and the hillshade to create a color hillshade image.

10. Drag the Hillshade below the DEM in the Layers panel.

11. Open the Layer Properties | Style tab for the DEM (35106-B4)

12. Set the following Style properties (shown in figure below):

   a. Change the Render type to Singleband pseudocolor

   b. Change the color ramp to BrBG.

c. Change the Load min/max values to Min/max and the Accuracy to Actual (slower).

d. Click Load

e. Click Classify

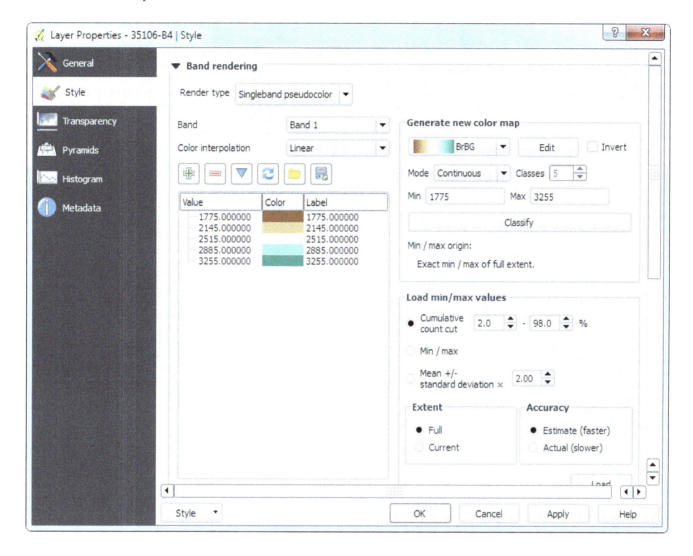

13. Switch to the Transparency tab and set the Global transparency to 50%.

14. Click OK and close the Layer Properties.

15. Your map should now resemble the figure below.

16. Now you will create a Slope dataset. From the menu bar choose Raster | Terrain Analysis | Slope.

17. Fill out the Slope tool as shown in the figure below then click OK.

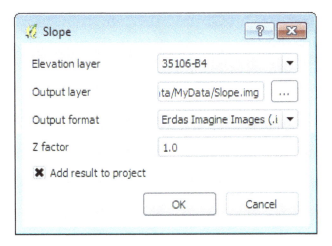

The slope raster shows the steepest areas in white and the flattest terrain in black. The tool determines the steepness of each pixel by comparing the elevation value of each pixel to that of the eight surrounding pixels. The slope values are degrees of slope (shown in figure below).

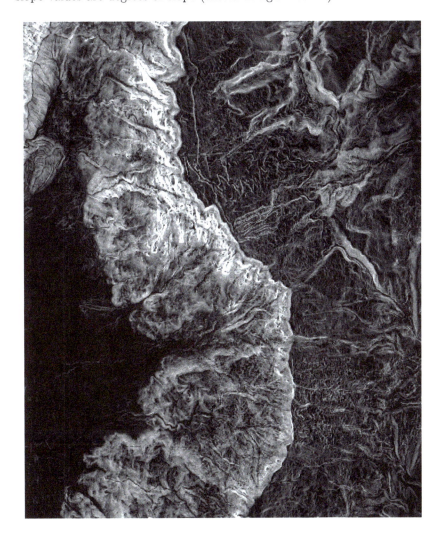

Now you will create an Aspect raster. Aspect measures which cardinal direction the terrain in each pixel is facing (north facing vs. south facing etc.)

18. From the menu bar choose Raster | Terrain Analysis | Aspect.

19. Fill out the Aspect tool as shown in the figure below then click OK.

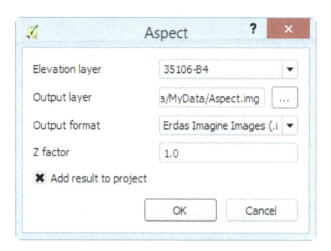

The output should resemble the figure below with values ranging from 0-360 representing degrees (0=north, 90= east, 180 = south and 270 = west).

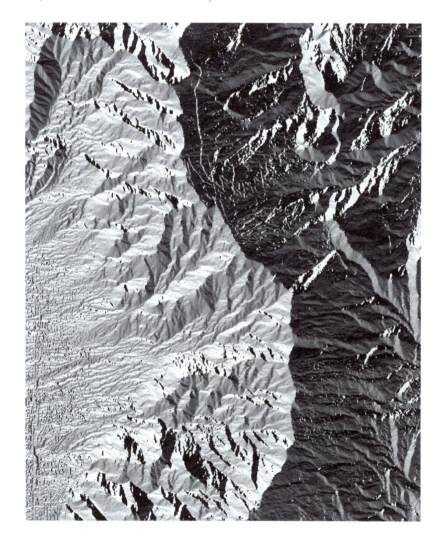

20. Save your project.

7.4   Task 2 Reclassification

Now that you have created the slope and aspect data you will reclassify them into meaningful categories. Raster reclassification is a method for aggregating data values into categories. In this case, you will be reclassifying them into categories important to identifying habitat suitability for a plant. Once the slope and aspect data have been reclassified you will combine them in Task 3 to identify suitable habitat areas.

In the previous exercise you worked with the GRASS 7 plugin, which not only allows you to execute GRASS algorithms, but allows you to save into a GRASS database. Here you will use GRASS algorithms directly out of the Processing Toolbox. This approach allows you to use GRASS tools without having your data in a GRASS database.

1. Open QGIS Desktop and open **Exercise 7 Data/Lab7.qgs** if it is not already open.

2. This plant requires steep slopes. You will classify slope raster into three categories: 0-45, 45-55, and > 55. First you will create a text file that contains the classification rules.

   a. Open NotePad or a similar text editor and create a text file in the format of the figure below.

   b. The first line tells QGIS to recode cells with slope values between 0 and 45 degrees with a new value of 1.

   c. Cells with slope values from 45-55 degrees will receive a new value of 2 and those cells with values greater than 55 will receive a new value of 3.

   d. Save the text file to the **Exercise 7 Data/MyData** folder and name it **Slope_Recode_Rules.txt**. Close the text editor.

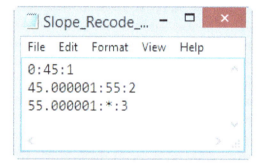

3. From the menu bar choose Processing | Toolbox.

4. Expand and open the GRASS commands | Raster (r.*) | r.recode - Recodes categorical raster maps.

5. Set the tool options to the following (shown in figure below):

   a. Set the Input layer to Slope.

   b. Navigate to the **Exercise 7 Data/MyData** folder and select the **Slope_Recode_Rules.txt** as the File containing recode rules.

   c. Name the output file **Slope_ReCode.img**.

   d. Click Run.

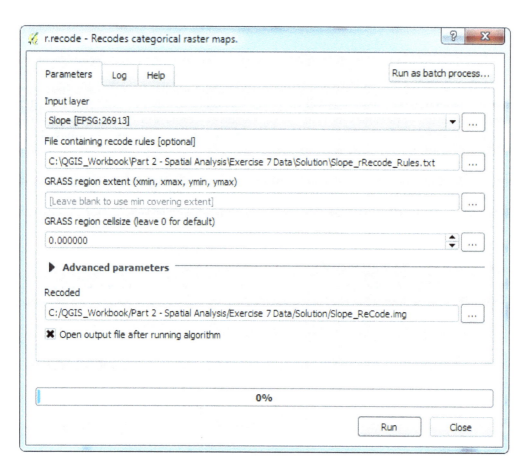

6. The new layer will be called Output raster layer in the Layers panel. It appears to have only two categories: 1) black and 2) white.

7. Open the Layer Properties | Style tab and set the following options:

   a. Change the Render type to Singleband pseudocolor.

   b. Change the color ramp to RdYlGn.

   c. Change the Mode to Equal Interval.

   d. Set the number of classes to 3.

   e. Change the Load min/max values to Min / max.

   f. Change the Accuracy to Actual (slower).

   g. Click Load.

   h. Click Classify.

   i. Before closing Layer Properties go to the General tab and change the Layer name to Slope Reclassified.

   j. Click OK to set the Layer Properties.

8. Now the best habitat in terms of slope has a value of 3 and the worst a value of 1 (shown in figure below).

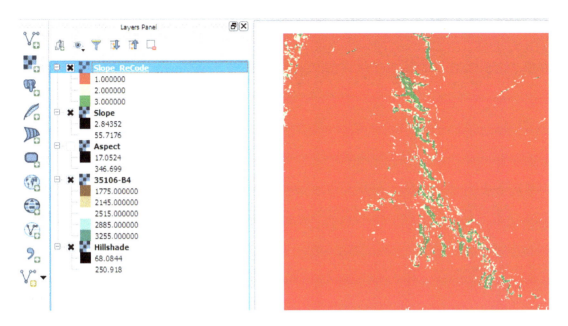

Now you will recode the Aspect data in the same fashion. This plant prefers west facing slopes. Hence the west facing slopes will be set to 3, the north and south are the next best location so set them to 2, and the eastern slopes can be set 1. Remember that the values of the aspect raster are compass bearings or azimuths (270 is due west, 0 is north, 180 is south and 90 is east). You will classify the aspect data into eight cardinal directions.

9. Open Notepad and create a text file that looks like the figure below. Save the text file to your MyData folder and name it Aspect_Recode_Rules.txt.

10. Close the text editor.

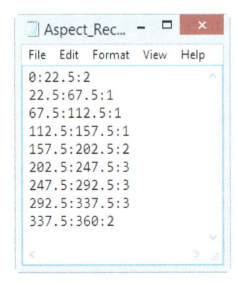

11. In the Processing Toolbox, expand the GRASS commands | Raster (r.*) | r.recode - Recodes categorical raster maps.

12. Set the following tool options (shown in figure below):

   a. Set the Input layer to Aspect.

   b. Navigate to the Exercise 7 Data/MyData folder and select the Aspect_Recode_Rules.txt as the File containing recode rules.

    c. Name the output file `Aspect_ReCode.img`.

    d. Click Run

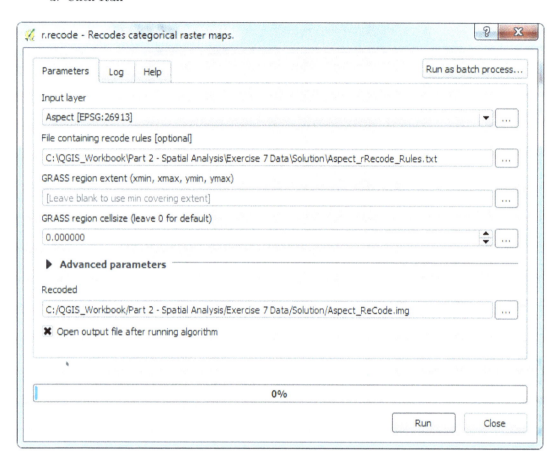

13. Rename the newly reclassified Aspect layer from Output raster layer to Aspect Reclassified.

14. Save your QGIS project.

7.5   Task 3 Raster Calculator

Now you will use the Raster Calculator to combine the reclassified slope and aspect data. The Raster Calculator allows you to combine raster datasets mathematically to produce new outputs. For example, raster datasets can be added, subtracted, multiplied, and divided against one another. This procedure is also known as raster algebra. In this task you will add the two reclassified rasters together. Since each raster has ideal conditions coded with the value '3', an area that ends up with a pixel value of 6 would be ideal.

1. Open QGIS Desktop and open `Exercise 7 Data/Lab7.qgs` if it is not already opened.

2. From the menu bar choose Raster | Raster Calculator. The loaded raster datasets are listed in the upper right window. Below it is a panel of operators and an expression window (see figure below).

3. Do the following to add the two reclassified rasters:

    a) Double click on `Slope Reclassified@1` to place it in the Raster calculator expression.

    b) Click the addition sign.

    c) Then click on the `Aspect Reclassified@1` raster.

    d) In the Result layer section name the output layer `Exercise 7 Data/MyData/PlantHabitat.img`.

    e) Choose an Output format of Erdas Imagine Images (*.img)

f) Click OK.

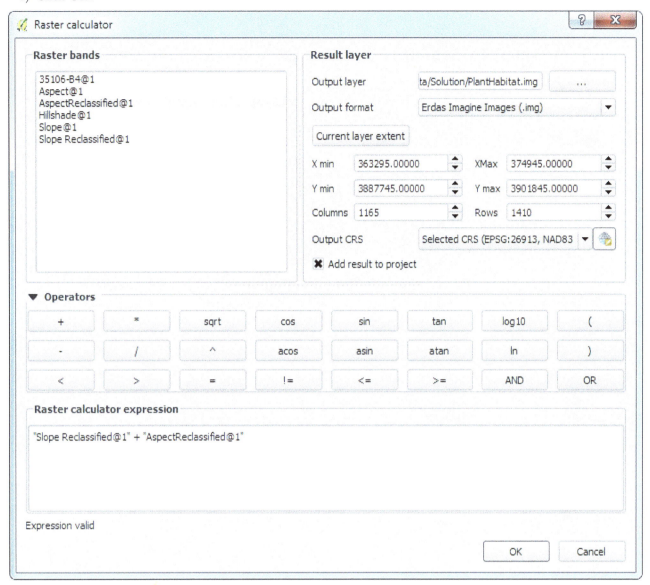

4. Open the Layer Properties of the PlantHabitat layer and symbolize the data with a pseudoband color with 6 equal interval classes.

5. The final raster will resemble the figure below.

6. Save your QGIS project.

7.6   Conclusion

In this exercise, you were exposed to terrain analysis, creating derived datasets from elevation data (DEMs). You then went on to reclassify two terrain related datasets (aspect and slope), and combine them to produce a suitable habitat layer for a plant species. This is another method of doing site selection analysis. Raster data are well suited for these types of analyses.

7.7 Discussion Questions

1. What other real world applications of terrain analysis can you think of?

2. How does this suitability analysis compare to the site selection analysis done with the vector data model in Exercise 5?

3. What other linear networks could this apply to other than roads?

7.8 Challenge Assignment (optional)

Another scientist is interested in developing a map of potential habitat for another species that prefers rugged, steep west facing slopes. Use the Raster Terrain Analysis plugin to develop a Ruggedness Index. Recode the Ruggedness Index into three categories:

```
0:20:1
```

```
20:40:2
```

```
40:*:3
```

Combine the resulting recoded ruggedness index with the recoded slope and aspect from the exercise to create the final result. Compose a map showing the results.

Exercise 8

Raster Data Analysis - Density Surfaces

Objective – Learn Density Analysis Methods

8.1 Introduction

In this exercise you'll learn about performing point density analysis. Density analysis can be used to show areas where there is a high occurrence of data. The exercise will also cover converting between vector and raster data.

This exercise includes the following tasks:

- Task 1 Point Density

- Task 2 Raster to Vector Conversion

- Task 3 Vector to Raster Conversion

8.2 Objective: Learn Density Analysis Methods

The objective of this exercise is to learn about density analysis methods and look at the conversion between the raster and vector data models.

8.3 Task 1 Point Density

Point density analysis can be used to show where there is a concentration of data points. In this task, you will use a core QGIS plugin called Heatmap, which generates point density surfaces.

Radius (aka neighborhood) – With the Heatmap tool you can define the search radius. The tool will use this distance when searching for neighboring points. A given pixel will receive higher values when more points are found within the search radius, and lower values when fewer points are found. Therefore, you can get very different results by changing the radius value.

Note: *In QGIS version 2.8, a bug was introduced that causes the Heatmap tool to not work correctly.* This problem has been solved since QGIS version 2.10. Due to this issue, both the `TownDensity.tif` and `TownPopDensity.tif` rasters have been created and placed for you to use. If you choose to use these files, read down until the `TownPopDensity.tif` is created and continue from there. The files can be found in the Exercise 8 Data/ Solution/Task 1 Raster Files folder.

1. Open QGIS Desktop.
2. Use the `Add Vector Layer` button to add the `Texas.shp` and `Place_names.shp` from the `Exercise 8 Data` folder.

3. Save your project as `Exercise 8.qgs` in the exercise directory.

4. For this task, you will use the Heatmap plugin. From the menu bar choose Plugins | Manage and Install Plugins.

5. Choose the All Plugins tab.

6. Type 'Heat' in to the Search box and locate the Heatmap plugin. This is a Core QGIS plugin and should be installed already—if not, install it. Once it is installed, check the box to enable it. Close the Plugin manager.

7. From the menu bar choose Raster | Heatmap | Heatmap.

8. Enter the following options in the tool (shown figure below).

    a) Input point layer = Place_Names

    b) Output raster = `Exercise 8 Data/MyData/TownDensity.tif`

    c) Output format = GeoTIFF

    d) Radius = 80000

    e) Check Add generated file to map

    f) Click OK to run the Heatmap Plugin

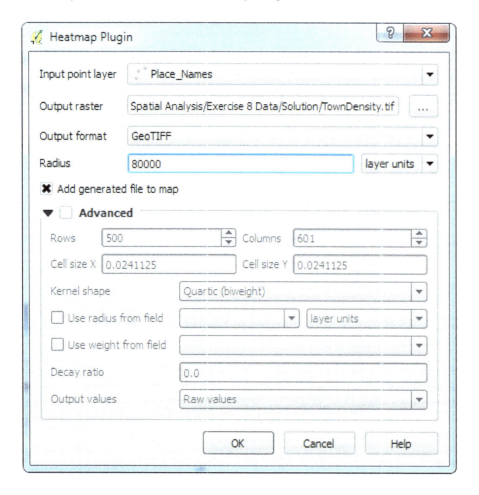

9. Restyle the Texas layer with a Fill style of transparent (No Brush) fill and a thick yellow border. Drag the Texas layer to the top of the Layer panel (figure below).

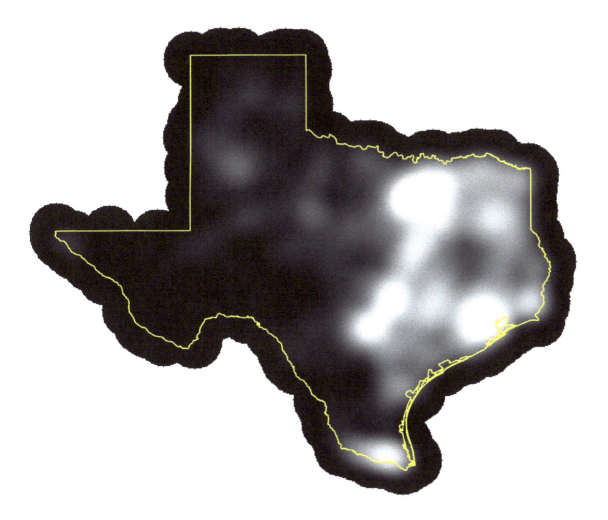

10. Now you will run the plugin again but you will weight the town points by their population. Run the Heatmap Plugin again. This time name the Output raster TownPopDensity.tif.

11. Check the Advanced box and check Use weight from field.

12. Choose POPULATION as the weight field. This will create a heat map based on the population values of each town (figure below). Click OK to execute the tool.

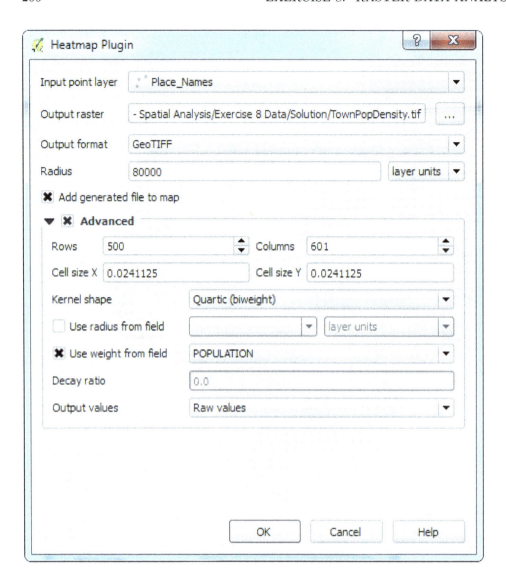

13. Move the newly created heatmap above the previous heatmap in the Layers panel.

Weighting the heatmap by a field provides a much more accurate picture of where the population centers are, rather than just town density (figure below).

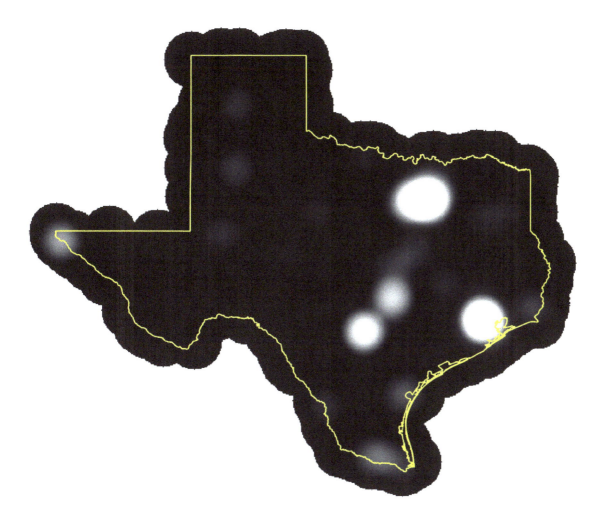

14. Save your project.

8.4 Task 2 Raster to Vector Conversion

Sometimes it is necessary to convert data between the two main data models: vector and raster. Here you will convert the population-based heat map to a vector dataset. Having the data in the vector data model allows for easier area calculations and different cartographic options (border and fill).

#. Open QGIS Desktop and open the `Exercise 8 Data/Lab8.qgs` project file you saved during Task 1.

1. Open the Layer Properties | Style tab for the TownPopDensity raster. Set the following parameters:
    a) Render type = Singleband pseudocolor
    b) Color map = YlOrRd
    c) Mode = Continuous
    d) Accuracy = Actual (slower)
    e) Click Load
    f) Click Classify
    g) Click OK to apply and close the Layer Properties.

The map will now resemble the figure below. (**Note:** Here, the state outline has been changed to black for better contrast.)

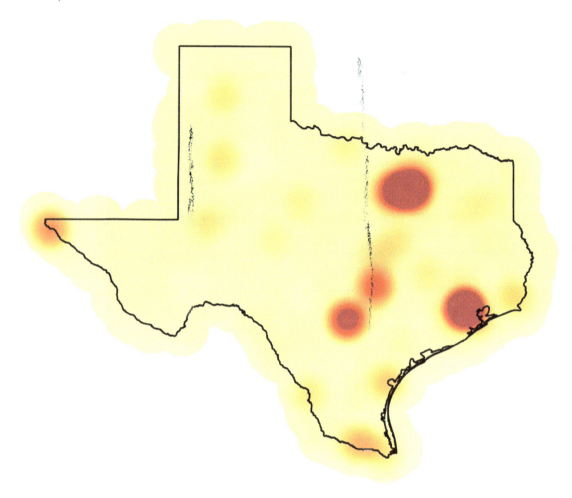

This is a more pleasing rendering and is very useful for a visual interpretation of population centers. However, if you wanted to have an actual layer of these population centers, the heat map needs to be processed further. You will now identify the highest population centers.

3. First, you need to decide on a threshold value that will constitute the population centers. There are a couple ways to do this: you can look at the values from the layer classification or look at the Layer Properties | Histogram. Here you will use values greater than 800,000 as the threshold for population centers.

4. From the menu bar choose Raster | Raster Calculator.

   a) Double-click on `TownPopDensity@1`

   b) Click on the > operator

   c) Type 800000 in as the value

   d) Output layer = `Exercise 8 Data/MyData/PopulationCenter.tif`

   e) Output format = GeoTIFF

   f) Click OK (figure below).

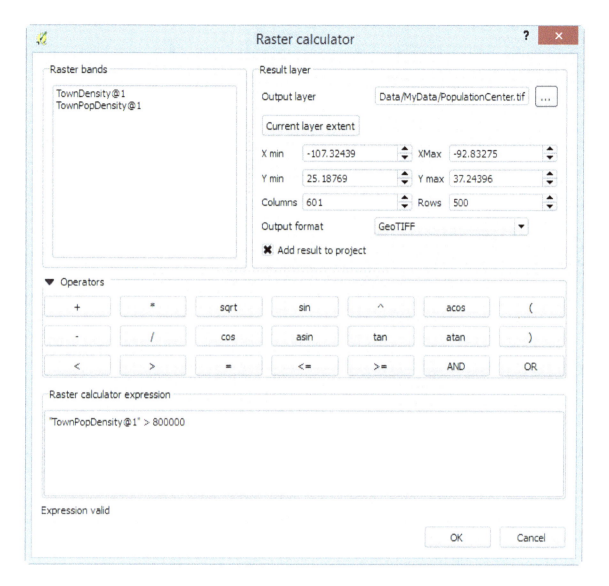

5. All the cells in the PopulationCenters raster input layer that had pixel values greater than 800,000 now have a value of 1, and the remaining pixels have a value of 0.

6. You will now convert the output to a vector layer. From the menu bar choose Raster | Conversion | Polygonize (Raster to Vector).

   a) Input file (raster) = PopulationCenter

   b) Output file for polygons (shapefile) = MyData/PopulationCenters.shp

   c) Check the box for Field name

   d) Click OK. (figure below)

   e) Click Close when complete.

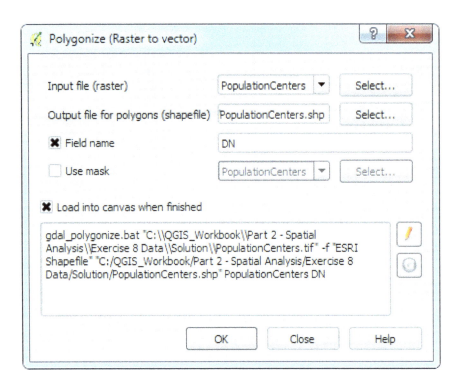

7. When the processing is complete, make sure the new polygon layer is above the raster layer in the Layers panel so that it is visible.

Since the output represents all the pixels in the raster you need to eliminate the non-population center polygons from this layer. To do this you will put the layer into Edit mode, select those polygons with a value of 0 and delete them.

8. Right-click on the PopulationCenters polygon layer in the Layers panel and choose Toggle editing from the context menu.

9. Open the attribute table for the layer. Click the Select features using an expression button $\mathcal{E}$.

10. Expand Field and Values. Double-click on DN to place it in the Expression window. Click the = operator. Now click the all unique button and double-click on the 0 value to place it in the expression. (figure below)

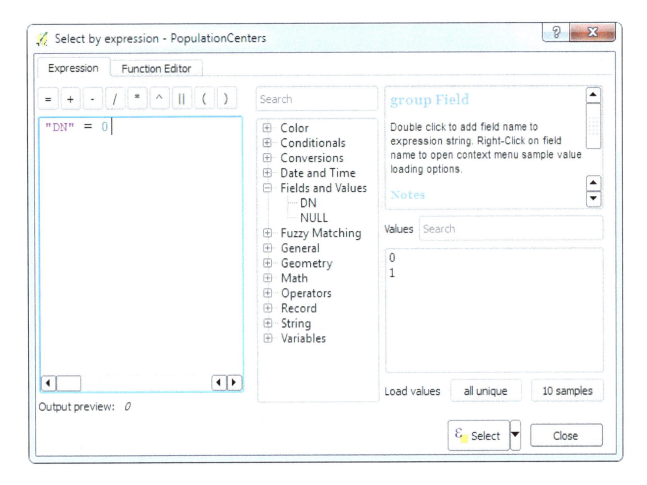

11. Click Select to execute the selection then click Close.

12. Now that the records with a value of zero are selected, and the layer is in edit mode, click the Delete selected features (DEL) 🗑 button.

13. Lastly click the Toggle editing mode button 🖊 and Save the changes.

The population centers are now a polygon layer you can use in a final map, or perhaps to feed into another analysis (figure below).

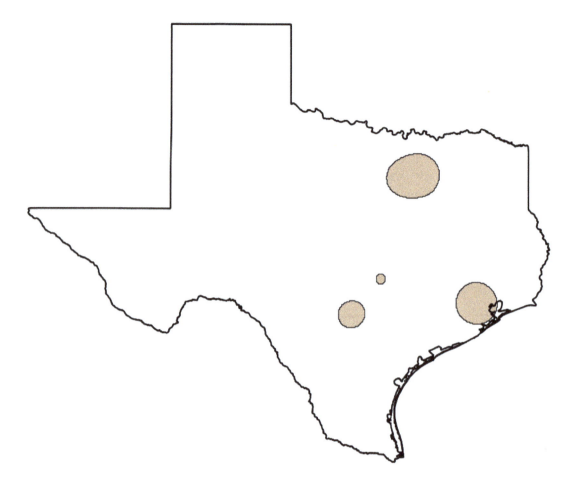

Now that the data are in polygon form, it is straightforward to calculate their acreage. QGIS calculates areas in the units of the coordinate reference system, therefore the layer needs to be in a Cartesian coordinate system with units of feet or meters. Currently it is in a Geographic coordinate system with values of decimal degrees. You will save the layer to a new coordinate reference system; then you can calculate the square meters of the polygons and convert those to acres or square miles, etc.

14. Right-click on the PopulationCenters polygon layer in the Layers panel and choose Save As...

    a) Save the layer as `PopulationCenters_albers.shp`

    b) Click the Select CRS button to open the Coordinate Reference System Selector. Type 'Texas' into the Filter window.

    c) Choose the NAD/83 Texas Centric Albers Equal Area EPSG:3083 CRS. Click OK.

    d) Check Add saved file to map

    e) Click OK

15. Open the attribute table for the PopulationCenters_albers polygon layer.

16. Click the Toggle editing mode button.

17. Click the New column button 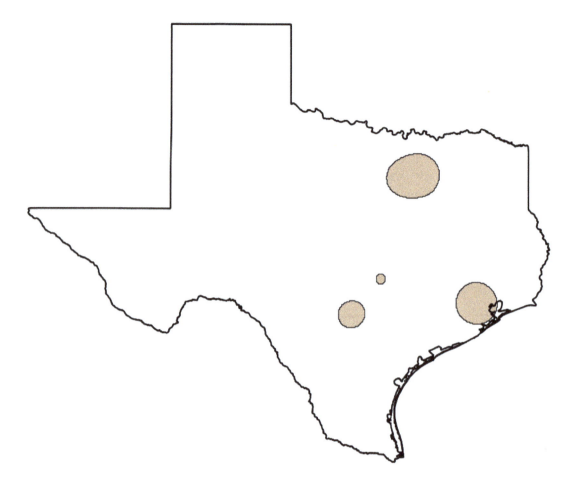.

18. Name the column `Acreage` and make it a Decimal number (real) column. Give it a Width of 7 and a Precision of 1 (figure below).

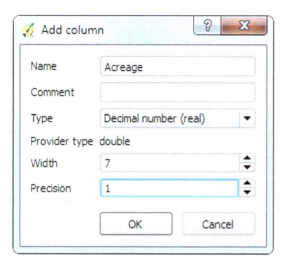

19. Click the Open field calculator button .

    a. Click the Update existing field option

    b. Choose `Acreage` as that field

    c. Expand the Geometry Function list and double-click `$area`

    d. Click the * operator

    e. Enter the conversion factor from square meters to acres 0.000247105 (figure below)

    f. Click OK.

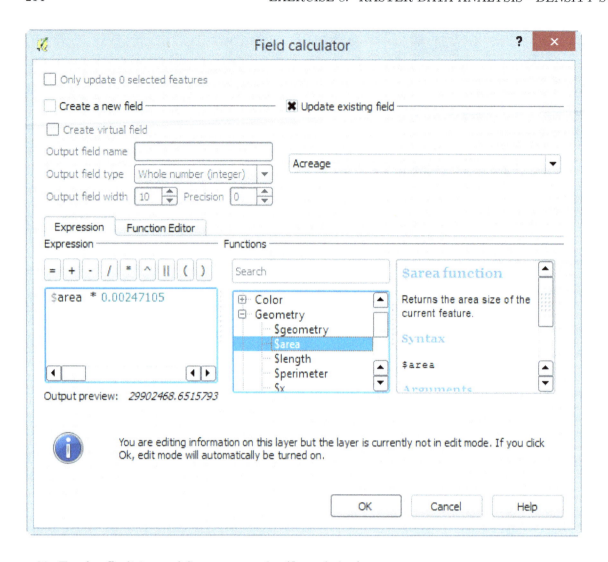

20. Toggle off editing and Save your results (figure below).

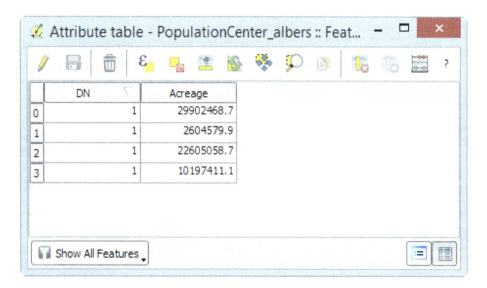

21. Now you have a layer of population centers and you have calculated their acreage!

22. Save your project.

8.5   Task 3 Vector to Raster Conversion

It can also be very useful to have data represented in the raster data model. Rasters are very useful for analysis. In the last exercise, you saw how rasters can be combined via the Raster Calculator. You can convert points, lines and polygons to a raster format. One must be cognizant of the effects of cell size. The data will be generalized when the conversion from precise vector locations to cells occurs. Here you will convert a vector layer to raster.

1. Open QGIS Desktop and open `Exercise 8 Data/Lab8.qgs`.
2. Add the `Nueces_Roads.shp` to QGIS Desktop.
3. Right-click on the Nueces Roads layer in the Layers panel and choose Zoom to layer (figure below).

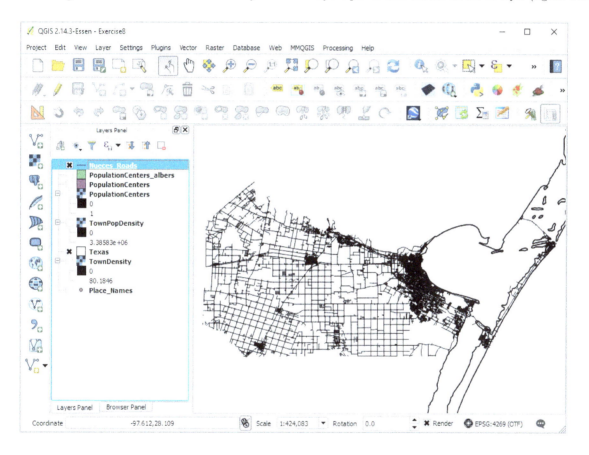

4. From the menu bar choose Raster | Conversion | Rasterize (Vector to Raster).
   a. Input file (shapefile) = Nueces_Roads
   b. Attribute field = `TLID` (*Note*: this can be any numeric attribute. Often it will be a field that assigned some sort of weight to the output raster cells. Here we will simply use the `TLID` column.)
   c. Output file for rasterized vectors (raster) = `MyData/Roads_raster.tif` (*Note*: If you get the message 'The output file doesn't exist. You must set up the output size or resolution to create it.' Click OK.)
   d. Take the remaining defaults.
   e. Click OK. (figure below). Click OK and Close.

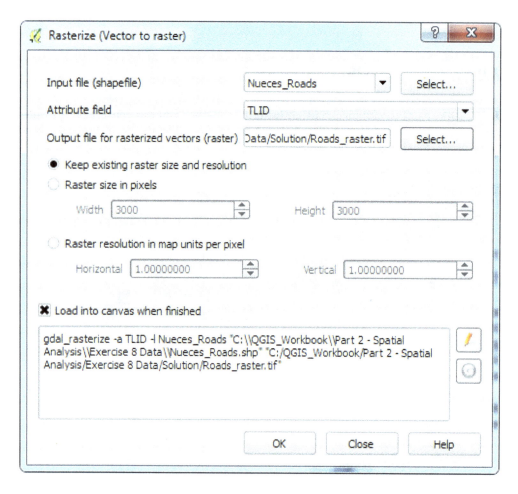

5. The resulting raster has values matching the TLID values for road pixels and values of 0 for the remaining pixels (figure below).

8.6 Conclusion

In this exercise, you learned how to use the Heatmap Plugin to generate point density rasters based off of both point densities and attribute values (population). Density analyses are often used to analyze data related to crimes, or the amount of fast food stores in an area. The output provides a nice overview of how close the points are, and you can choose our own variables to weight the output. Finally, using the conversion tools we can convert between raster and vector. Having data in raster form allows you to perform raster algebra operations via the Raster Calculator. Having the data in vector form allows for geometries to be easily calculated (acreage), and for more sophisticated cartographic options (border and fill).

8.7 Discussion Questions

1. Discuss the different uses of point density.

2. Explain how weighting a feature via an attribute changes the outcome.

3. Is there anything we can do about the degradation of data in the conversion between vector and raster?

8.8 Challenge Assignment (optional)

In the **Exercise 8 Data/Challenge** folder there is a shapefile containing crime data for Surrey in the United Kingdom. There is a column for crime type (**Crime_type**). Use this field to generate two heatmaps: one for

'Violent Crimes' and one for 'Drugs'. You will have to select records corresponding to each crime type, and save the selected features to a new shapefile for each. The heatmaps will be generated against the resulting shapefiles.

Part III

Data Acquisition and Management

Exercise 1

Reviewing the Basics of Geospatial Data

Objective – Explore and Understand Geospatial Data Models and File Formats

1.1 Introduction

There are two main data models for GIS data: vector and raster. Additionally, GIS data comes in many file formats. When gathering data for a project, it is common to acquire data from several sources. Therefore, it is also common for the data to be in several different file formats. In this exercise, you will review GIS data models and file formats.

This exercise includes the following tasks:

- Task 1 GIS Data Models
- Task 2 GIS File Formats

1.2 Objective: Explore and Understand Geospatial Data Models and File Formats

The objective of this exercise is to explore and understand geospatial data models and file formats.

1.3 Task 1 GIS Data Models

This task will be a review of the data commonly stored in the vector and raster data models. You will explore the exercise 1 data and answer some questions.

1. Open QGIS Desktop.
2. Use the Add Raster Layer button to add the 35106-B4.dem file from the exercise data directory.

Question # 1 – Is this a continuous or categorical raster?

Question # 2 – In a DEM what do the pixel values represent?

3. Now use the Add Raster Layer button again and add the 05_35106b47.tif raster. This is a multiband raster image with red and green light combined with color infrared to create a false color image.

Question # 3 – What is the pixel resolution of this raster?

4. Now use the Add Raster Layer button and add the LandFire_EVT.img raster.

Question # 4 – Is this a continuous or categorical raster?

5. Use the Add Vector Layer button  and add both `Road.shp` and `Trail.shp` shapefiles to the map canvas.

Question # 5 – What is the coordinate reference system for the Road.shp layer?

Question # 6 – How many features are in the Trail.shp layer?

Question # 7 – What are the two easiest methods in QGIS Desktop, for answering question number 6?

1.4   Task 2 GIS Data File Formats

There are many different file formats commonly used in GIS. Some formats are designed to store vector data and some raster data, while others contain a myriad of other types of information. In this task, you will explore the file formats included with the exercise data.

Question # 8 – In Task 1 you added three raster datasets. What were the three file formats that those were stored in?

LandFire_EVT:

05_35106b47:

35106-B4:

1. Open QGIS Browser and navigate to the `Exercise 1 Data` folder. The folder contains three raster datasets, three shapefiles, two XML files, and two text files.
2. There are also two folders: an `info` folder and a folder named `vegetation`.
3. Expand the `vegetation` folder and select the `metadata.xml` file with the polygon icon next to it. QGIS Browser will switch to the Metadata tab.

You can see that it is a line layer with 15,953 features and the coordinate reference system is UTM. However, you probably do not know the storage type for this layer. This is an older file format for storing vector data called a Coverage. The `info` folder holds the attributes. The `vegetation` folder is the layer name and stores the spatial features. Sometimes you will see data files ending in `.e00`. This is an exported coverage. This format is for data sharing as it is a file containing the info and layer folders, and is more easily transferred. QGIS can also natively read e00 files.

4. Open QGIS Desktop and click on the Add Vector Layer button to open the Add vector layer dialog.
5. Up to this point, you have always used the default Source type of File. Now switch the Source type to Directory and the Source Type to Arc/Info Binary Coverage (see figure below).

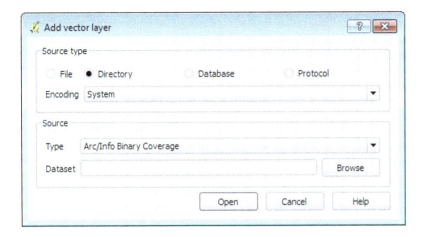

6. Click the Browse button and navigate to the **Exercise 1 Data** folder.

7. Select the **vegetation** folder (do not enter it just select it) and click Select Folder.

8. Click Open.

9. The Select vector layers to add... window opens. Here you are being asked to choose which components of the coverage to add to QGIS. This is because of a special property that coverages have: they can store multiple geometries. While a single shapefile stores either point, line, or polygon geometry, a single coverage can store all three geometries. This vegetation dataset has two polygon components (PAL & landfire_evt) a line component (Arc), and a point component (CNT).

10. Select the landfire_evt layer and choose OK (see figure below).

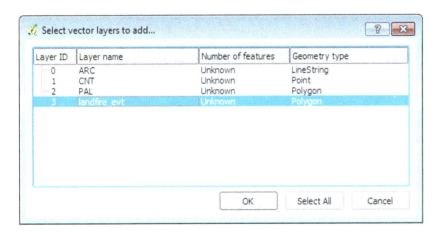

11. The layer is added to QGIS (see figure below). This is a vector version of the LandFire_EVT raster layer.

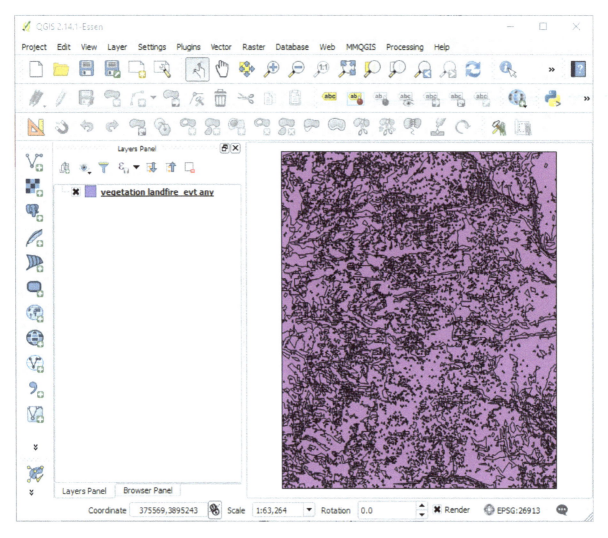

Question # 9 – What attribute column would you use to map these vegetation types using a Categorical renderer?

Question # 10 – How would you convert the vegetation coverage to a shapefile?

12. Open QGIS Browser again and navigate to the exercise data folder.

13. Select the `Exercise 1 Data` folder so that the contents are visible in the Param tab (in the figure below). Notice the `Recreation_Site_pt.kmz` file. This does not appear as a GIS layer in the layer tree. KMZ is compressed KML (Keyhole Markup Language). This is the native format for Google Earth and is a very common geospatial file format. In order for QGIS Desktop to read this data the KMZ file must be decompressed.

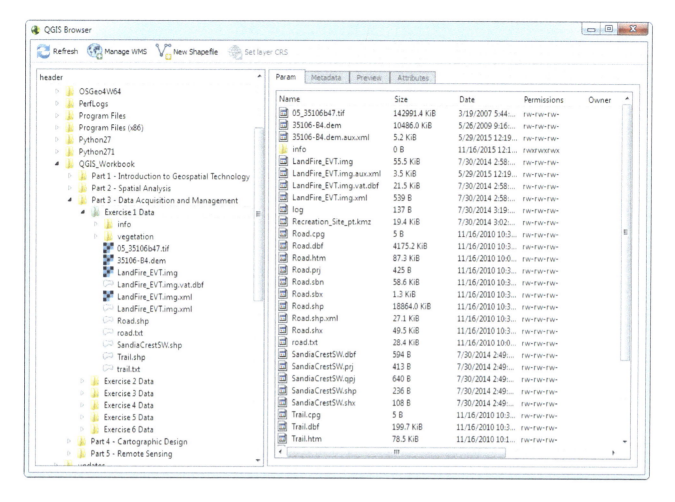

14. Uncompress/unzip `Recreation_Site_pt.kmz`.

Note: The method for doing this will depend on your operating system (Windows, OSX, or Linux). Each operating system comes with compression software that allows you to compress and uncompress files. Additionally, there are many good third party software applications available. If you are using Windows or Linux, try 7-Zip. Macs may not recognize KMZ as files that can be uncompressed. Therefore, select the File | Open With | Other | The Unarchiver to uncompress it. Once the data has been uncompressed you will be left with a KML file.

15. In QGIS Desktop, click the Add Vector Layer button. Set the Source type to File, and click Browse. Navigate to the Exercise 1 Data folder and change the file format filter in the lower right corner to Keyhole Markup Language (KML) (in the figure below).

16. Select the `Recreation_Site_pt.kml` file and click Open to add this to QGIS Desktop.

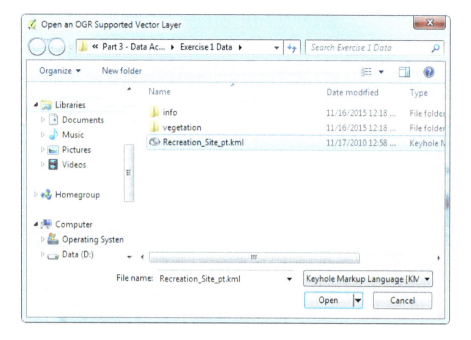

17. Click Open again. You are presented with the Select vector layers to add... window. There are many different feature layers within this KML file.

18. Select Picnic site and Trailhead (hold the Control key to select multiple entries) and click OK (selections shown in the figure below).

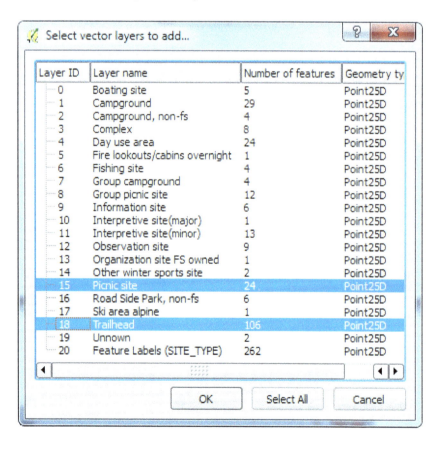

1.5 Conclusion

In this exercise, you reviewed the raster and vector data models. You have explored several file formats and have been introduced to two new vector formats: the coverage and Keyhole Markup Language (KML).

1.6 Discussion Questions

1. What are the strengths of both the vector and raster data models?
2. List the vector and raster file formats you are now familiar with.
3. How does a coverage differ from a shapefile?

1.7 Challenge Assignment

Convert the KML and coverage data to shapefiles.

Exercise 2

Setting Up a Project Database

Objective – Learn How to Normalize Data and Import It into a SpatiaLite Database

2.1 Introduction

There are two main data models for GIS data: vector and raster. Additionally, GIS data comes in many file formats. When gathering data for a project, it is common to acquire data from several sources. Therefore, it is also common for the data to be in several different file formats. In this exercise you will create a project geodatabase for the Gifford-Pinchot National Forest in Washington State. First, you will normalize the data. This means you'll put all datasets in the same coordinate reference system (CRS) and clip them to the study area boundary. Lastly, you'll put them all into the same file format: a SpatiaLite geodatabase.

This exercise includes the following tasks:

- Task 1 Investigate and Normalize Project Data

- Task 2 Create a New Database

- Task 2 Populate the New Database

2.2 Objective: Learn How to Normalize Data and Import it into a SpatiaLite Database

The objective of this exercise is to explore and understand geospatial data models and file formats.

2.3 Task 1 Investigate and Normalize Project Data

In this task, you will familiarize yourself with the exercise data and will begin to normalize the data.

1. Open QGIS Browser, navigate to and expand the `Exercise 2 Data` folder.

There are eight vector layers here. There are four shapefiles, two KML files, and two coverages (shown in the figure below). Each of these file formats will be treated differently. (*Note*: when there are multiple coverages in the same workspace they share the same info folder.)

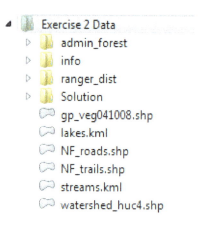

2. All the data for this project will need to be in UTM, Zone 10, NAD83. Unfortunately, not all of the data are in that coordinate system, so we will need to convert it.

3. Open QGIS Desktop.

4. Click the Add Vector Layer button and change the Source type to Directory. Then change the Type to Arc/Info Binary Coverage.

5. Browse to the exercise Data folder and select the admin_forest folder. Click Open.

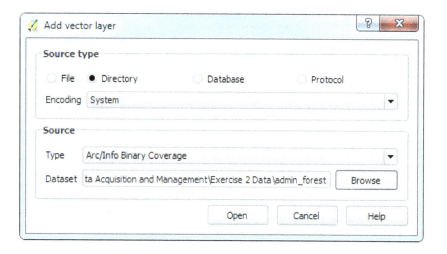

6. In the Select vector layers to add window choose 3 PAL (Polygon layer). Click OK.

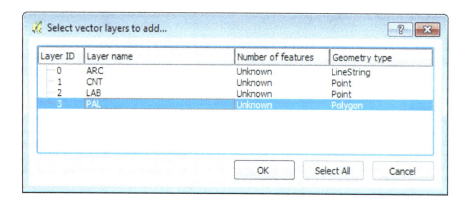

7. Save your project as Exercise2.qgs.

This layer is in a custom Albers Equal Area coordinate system. Since it is in a custom CRS, there is no EPSG code to use during import into a database. Therefore, we will first save this out to a shapefile in the desired CRS.

8. Right-click on the layer in the Layers panel and choose Save as...

9. Save the resulting dataset as a shapefile named `Forest_boundary.shp` to the exercise `Data` folder.

10. Set the CRS to UTM Zone 10 NAD83 (EPSG 26910) (completed dialog shown in figure below).

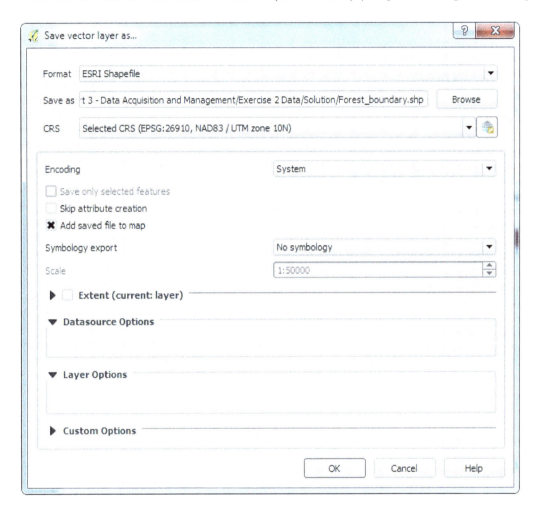

11. Click OK to save the new shapefile and add it to the map.

12. Remove the PAL layer from the map as we no longer need it.

13. Export the ranger_dist coverage PAL polygon to a shapefile with the same coordinate system as the Forest_boundary layer. Once this has been completed, the map should resemble the figure below.

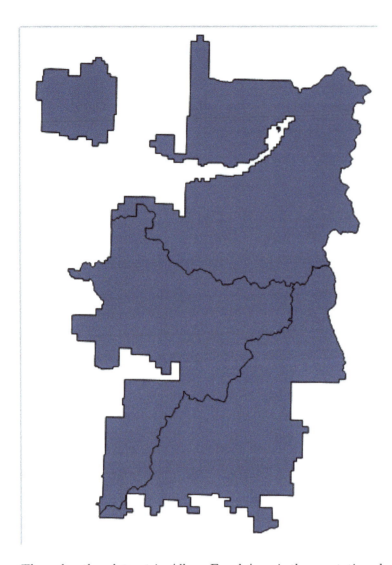

The only other dataset in Albers Equal Area is the vegetation shapefile.

14. Add the `gp_veg041008.shp` shapefile to QGIS Desktop and save this as a new shapefile in UTM Zone 10 NAD83.

15. Add the NF_roads, NF_trails, and watershed_huc4 shapefiles to QGIS Desktop.

These last three layers are all shapefiles in the correct CRS. However, they extend beyond the forest boundary. We need to clip the layers to within the forest boundary.

16. Use the Vector | Geoprocessing Tools | Clip tool to clip the roads, trails, and watershed to the forest boundary (example clip parameters shown in the figure below). You can give them the same output name, but end it with clip. For example, NF_roads will become NF_roads_clip.

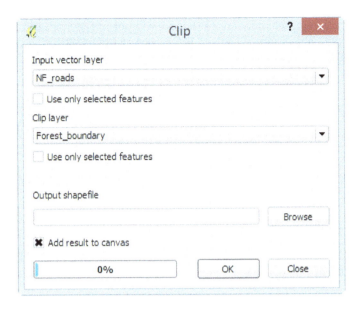

17. Remove the original unclipped roads, trails, and watershed layers once the three clip operations are complete. Your map should now resemble the figure below (note that not all layers are visible in the figure below).

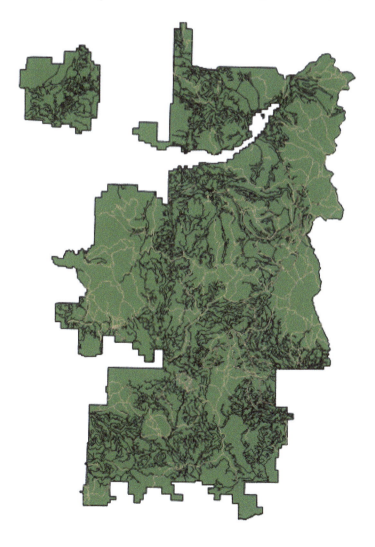

You have taken the initial steps to normalize the data. There are two more layers that we will put in the SpatiaLite database; rivers and lakes. However, KML files are always in a geographic CRS of WGS 1984 (EPSG:4326). These KML files can be reprojected when importing into the SpatiaLite database without having to be converted to another format.

18. Save your project.

2.4   Task 2 Create a New Database

Now that you have taken the initial steps to prepare your data, you will create a new empty SpatiaLite database that you will import your datasets into.

1. Open your `Exercise2.qgs` project in QGIS Desktop if it not already open.

2. Find the Browser Panel. If your Browser Panel is not visible, click View | Panels | Browser Panel to turn it on.

3. Find the SpatiaLite database connection below your hard drives. Right-click on it and choose Create database (figure below).

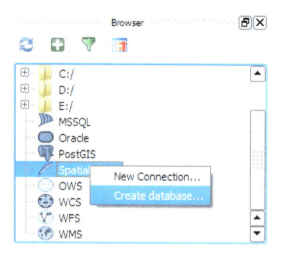

4. Navigate to the exercise `Data` folder and name the new database `GiffordPinchot.sqlite` and click `Save` (figure below).

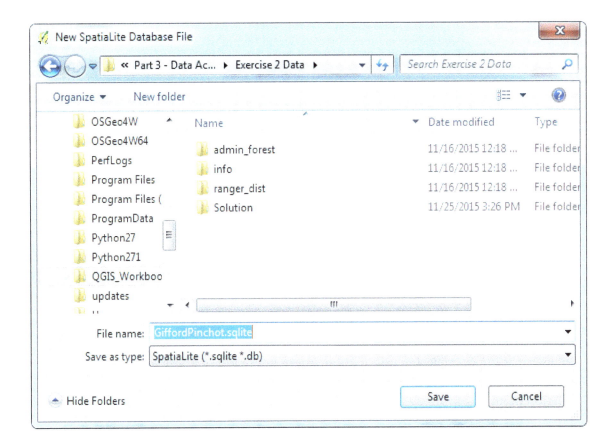

5. A dialog will appear stating that the database has been created. Click OK to dismiss.

The database will now appear under the SpatiaLite database connection.

6. Save your project.

2.5   Task 3 Populate the New Database

Now you will populate the SpatiaLite database with the eight layers.

1. Open your `Exercise2.qgs` project in QGIS Desktop if it is not already open.

2. Add the streams and lake KML layers to QGIS Desktop.

3. From the menu bar choose Database | DB Manager | DB Manager. Expand the SpatiaLite database connection. You will see the `GiffordPinchot.sqlite` database. If you expand the database, you will see many tables but no GIS layers yet (shown in figure below).

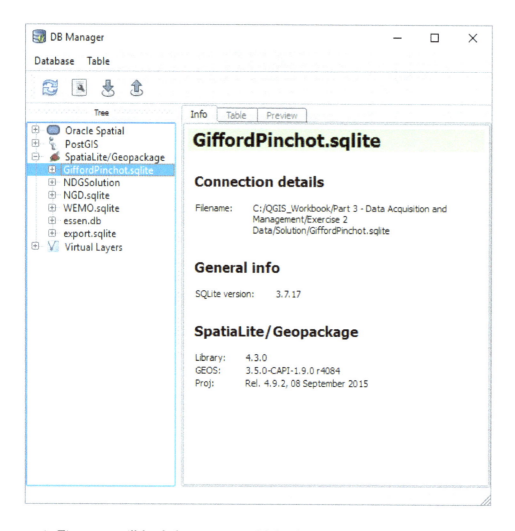

4. First, you will load the streams and lakes layers. Since these are KML, they are in a geographic CRS with an EPSG code of 4326. This is the case for all KML datasets.

5. Click the Import layer/file button

6. Set up the Input vector layer window as follows (shown in figure below):

   a. Set the Input as lakes

   b. Name the table `lakes`

   c. Check Source SRID and enter 4326

   d. Check Target SRID and enter 26910

   e. Check Create spatial index

   f. Click OK

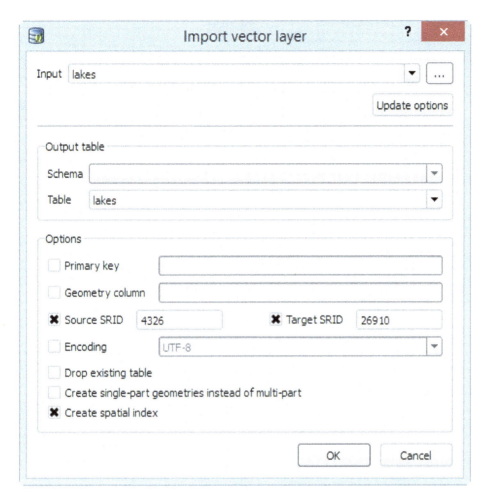

7. Once the operation has completed successfully click the Refresh button 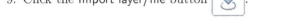 to see the lakes layer in the database.

8. Repeat the previous steps to import the streams KML.

Streams and Lakes were the final two layers that required a CRS reprojection. The remaining six UTM layers can now be imported. The only change is that both the input and target SRID's will be 26910 (UTM Zone NAD83).

9. Click the Import layer/file button 📥.

10. Set up the Input vector layer window as follows (shown in figure below):

   a. Set the Input as NF_roads_clip

   b. Name the table roads

   c. Check Source SRID and enter 26910

   d. Check Target SRID and enter 26910

   e. Check Create spatial index

   f. Click OK

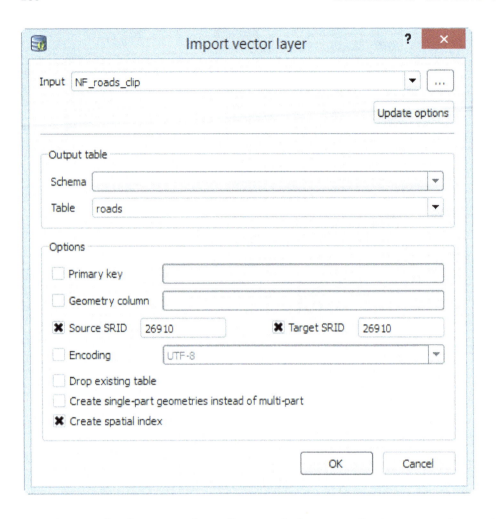

11. Repeat the above steps for trails, watersheds, ranger districts, vegetation, and forest boundary layers.

12. Now that all eight layers have been imported you can remove the original layers from the map.

13. The layers in the database can be added via the DB Manager or the Add SpatiaLite Layer button.

14. If using the DB Manager, right-click on a layer and choose Add to canvas.

15. If using the Add SpatiaLite Layer button   , select the database and click the Connect button. Once the layers appear, you can select them and click Add, which will add them to QGIS (figure below).

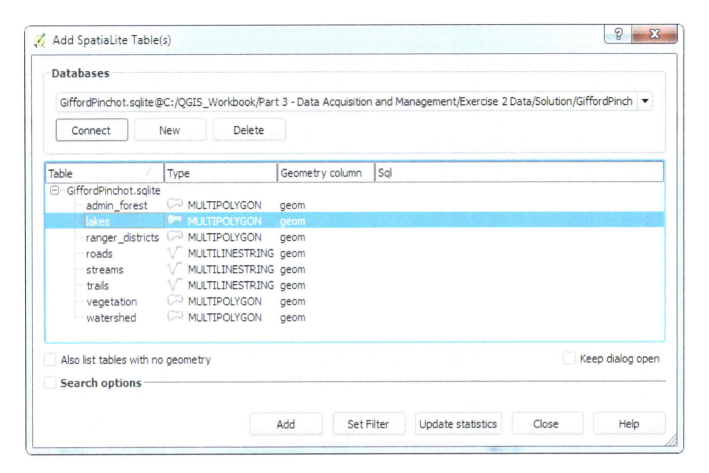

2.6 Conclusion

In this exercise, you took data in several different file formats and CRSs and normalized them. They are all now in the same CRS, clipped to the forest boundary, and in a geodatabase. This methodology has the benefit of creating a working copy of the data—the raw data still exist. If you accidentally delete or corrupt a dataset, you still have the original files. Additionally, the data now all reside in a tidy database. Since they are all in the same CRS, you can run any geoprocessing or analysis tools against them knowing they are all in UTM Zone 10 NAD83.

2.7 Discussion Questions

1. What are the steps involved in setting up a SpatiaLite database?
2. What are the advantages of normalizing project data?

Exercise 3

Vector Data Quality

Objective – Learn to Verify the Quality of Vector Data with Topology Rules

3.1 Introduction

GIS data are referred to as models because they are simplified representations of actual real world objects. As the real world is represented, this often results in data with thousands of records and complex spatial relationships. With so many records, it can be challenging to verify the quality of such large data by visual means alone. Additionally, to verify that spatial relationships have been maintained, we can test the data using topology rules and ensure that it is well constructed.

This exercise includes the following tasks:

- Task 1 Topology Rules - Part 1

- Task 2 Topology Rules - Part 2

- Task 3 Fixing Topology Errors

3.2 Objective: Learn To Verify the Quality of Vector Data with Topology Rules

In this exercise you will be explore the spatial relationship between points, lines, and polygons. You will build topology rules and validate them to identify data errors.

3.3 Task 1 Topology Rules - Part 1

In this task, you will use the Topology Checker plugin to investigate the quality of two datasets: bus routes and bus stops.

1. Open QGIS Desktop and add the `parcels.shp`, `Bus_stops.shp`, and `Bus_routes.shp` layers from the exercise `Data` folder to the map (shown in figure below).

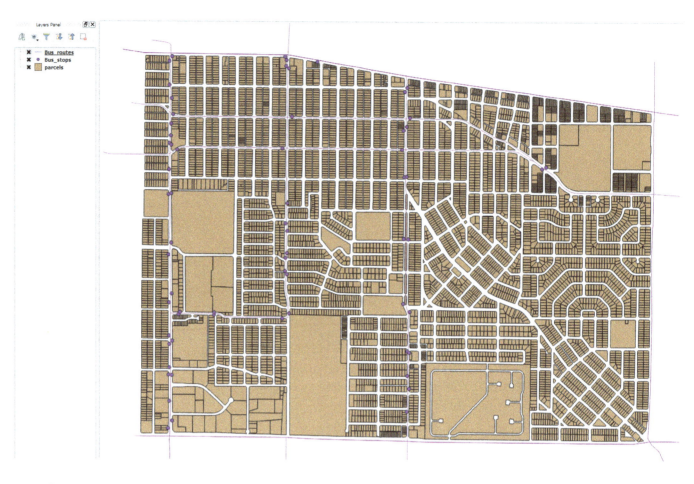

2. Save your project as `exercise3.qgs` in the exercise folder.

3. From the menu bar, choose Plugins | Manage and Install Plugins.

4. Select the Installed tab and enable the Topology Checker plugin.

5. Click Vector | Topology Checker | TopologyChecker, or, click on the Topology Checker button 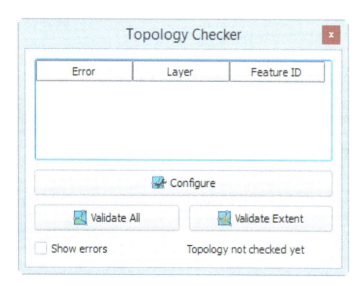 to open the Topology Checker panel (figure below).

First, you will investigate the integrity of the Bus Stops layer.

6. Click the Configure button in the toolbar of the Topology Checker panel. This opens the Topology Rules Settings window. Here you can set up a variety of topology rules.

7. Under Current rules choose Bus_stops as the layer. Click the second drop down to see what topology rules are available for point layers. Choose must not have duplicates. This rule will check to make sure there are no stacked points, in other words, a bus stop situated directly over another. This type of error is difficult to identify without a topology rule.

8. Click the Add Rule button to have the rule established (shown in figure below).

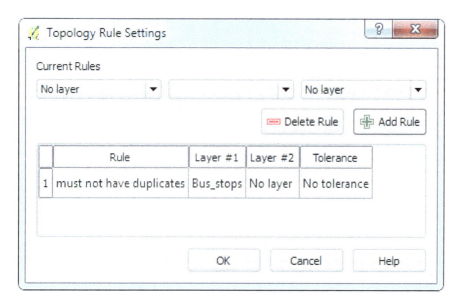

9. Click OK to close the Topology Rule Settings.

10. In the Topology Checker panel, click the Validate All button.

Note: You can also choose to zoom into a particular area and just validate the topology rule within the current extent by clicking the Validate Extent button.

11. The topology checker finds three duplicate geometries which are listed in the Topology Checker panel with their Feature IDs and the rule they are violating. (shown in figure below).

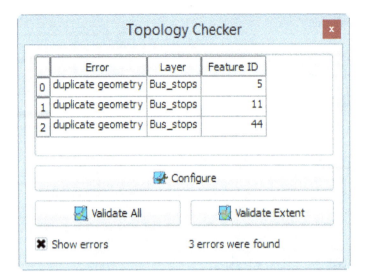

Additionally, the duplicated points are highlighted in red on the map. Again, these errors would be difficult to find any other way. However, once identified they are easy to fix. Simply toggle on editing, select the duplicates and delete them.

Now you will examine the topology of the Bus_routes layer.

12. In the Topology Checker panel, click the Configure button again.

13. Select and delete the Topology rule for the Bus Stops.

14. Create a new rule for the Bus_routes, using must not have dangles. This means the endpoint of a dangling line will be identified. You might expect that since these data are only a portion of an urban area, and there are bus routes heading off the map that those dangling endpoints will be identified. However, there should not be any in the middle of the network.

15. Click the Add Rule button and click OK (topology rule shown in figure below).

16. Validate the topology. The Topology Checker finds 25 errors of this type. Many are the expected ones, for example lines heading off the map edge. However, there are several in the middle of the network. Zoom in to some of these errors and investigate.

17. Save your project.

3.4   Task 2 Topology Rules - Part 2

Now you will implement topology rules to check the integrity of the parcels layer.

1. Open your `exercise3.qgs` project in QGIS Desktop if it is not already open.
2. Open the Topology Checker panel.
3. Click the Configure button.
4. Select any existing rules and click the Delete Rule button to remove them.
5. Configure three rules for the parcels layer: must not have gaps, must not overlap, and must not have duplicates (rules shown in figure below).

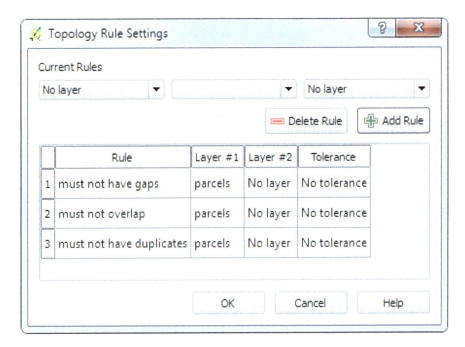

6. Click OK to set the topology rules.
7. In the Topology Checker panel, click Validate All.
8. The Topology Checker will report violations for each rule, seventeen errors in all.
9. Save your project.

3.5   Task 3 Fixing Topology Errors

Now you will edit the parcel layer to eliminate the seventeen topology errors.

1. Open your `exercise3.qgs` project in QGIS Desktop if it is not already open.
2. Re-validate the topology rules if they are not appearing.
3. First, you will work on the duplicate geometries. Right-click on the parcels layer in the Layers panel and choose Toggle Editing.
4. Double-click on the first **duplicate geometry** error in the Topology Checker panel to zoom to that location.

5. Use the Select Feature by Rectangle tool 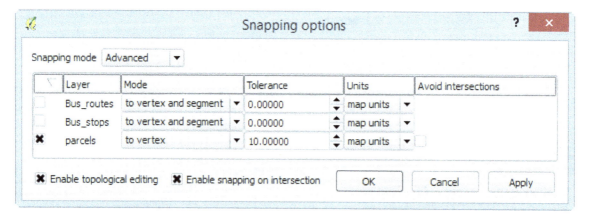 and drag a small rectangle to select the duplicate parcels on the map.

6. Open the parcels layer attribute table.

7. Change the display filter in the lower left corner to Show Selected Features.

8. Notice that for the two selected features, all of the attributes are identical.

9. Select the feature with the higher row number by clicking on the row number. This leaves just one selected record.

10. Click the Delete selected features 🗑 button to remove the duplicate parcel.

11. Repeat these steps to delete the remaining duplicate geometry topology errors. The attribute table should now show a total of 6,968 records.

Now that the duplicate geometry errors are fixed, we will turn our attention to fixing the overlaps and gaps errors. To fix these errors, we will first set our snapping tolerances to make editing significantly easier and more precise.

12. From the menu bar choose Settings | Snapping Options.

13. Set the Snapping mode to Advanced.

14. In the left-most column, uncheck Bus_routes and Bus_stops and check parcels.

15. Set the Mode for parcels to to vertex and the Tolerance to 10 map units.

16. Check Enable topological editing.

17. Check Enable snapping on intersection.

Topological editing maintains common boundaries in polygon mosaics. With this option checked, QGIS detects a shared boundary in a polygon mosaic and you only have to move the vertex once—QGIS will take care of updating the other boundary.

The selected snapping options are shown in the figure below.

18. Click OK to set and close the Snapping options.

19. From the menu bar choose Settings | Options and click on the Digitizing tab.

20. Set the Search radius for vertex edits to 10 pixels (shown in figure below). Setting this to something other than zero ensures that QGIS finds the correct vertex when editing.

21. Click OK to set the digitizing options.

22. Open the Layer properties for the parcels layer and from the Style tab set the transparency to 50.

23. Click OK to close the Layer properties.

24. On the Topology Checker panel, uncheck Show errors.

25. Double-click on the error for Feature ID 624. The map will zoom to the location of the error. With errors turned off and the transparency set, you can see the overlap issue (shown in figure below).

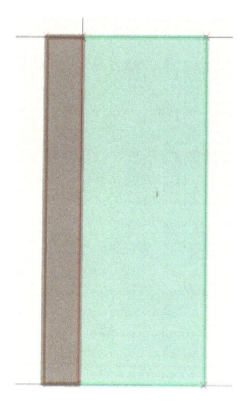

There are two parcels involved in the overlap. Here, the western (left) overlapping parcel boundary needs to be moved west (left) so that it does not overlap with the eastern parcel (parcel on the right).

26. Use the Select Feature by Rectangle tool to select the western (left) overlapping parcel. The vertices of the selected feature will appear as red Xs.

27. Enable the Digitizing toolbar by clicking View | Toolbars | Digitizing.

28. On the Digitizing toolbar, click on the Node Tool . This tool allows you to move individual feature vertices.

29. Click on a vertex of the selected feature and the vertices will show as red boxes (shown in figure below). If the vertices for a different feature appear, try clicking on a vertex, then clicking between that vertex and another vertex of the same feature along the connecting line.

30. Click on the upper right vertex and the selected vertex will turn blue (figure below).

31. Drag that selected vertex west (left) until it snaps to the boundary of the parcel it is overlapping.

32. Repeat for the lower right vertex.

33. In the Topology Checker panel, click Validate All and the overlap topology error will no longer be listed and the overlap will be resolved (shown in figure below).

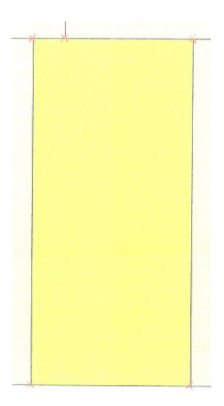

There is one other issue with this parcel. There is a tiny overlap in the northwest corner (figure below). This very small overlap cannot be seen at this scale.

34. To resolve this, simply select the affected vertices with the Node tool, and snap them back into place. The overlap is so small you won't see them move, however, the overlap will be resolved due to the Topological editing setting.

35. The remaining overlaps can be fixed in the same fashion.

36. From the Topology Checker panel click on the first Gap error in the list (for Feature ID 0). Again you will be zoomed to the location of the error (shown in figure below).

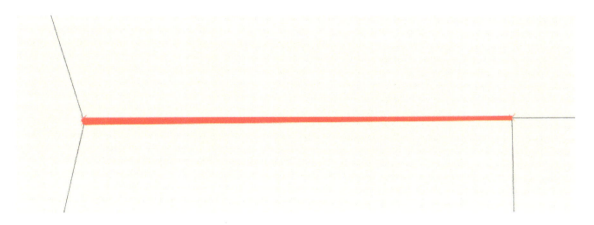

37. In the Topology Checker panel, uncheck Show errors.

38. There is a small sliver between the parcels. Select the parcel to the north and then click on the Node Tool.

39. Select the vertex in the southwestern corner of the selected parcel. Drag it until it snaps with the parcel vertex to the south, closing the gap.

40. Click Validate Extent to ensure that the issue has been resolved.

41. You can repair other gap errors the same way.

42. When you are done repairing the topology errors, save your edits.

43. Save your project.

3.6   Conclusion

In this exercise, you learned how to test the integrity of your vector data with topology rules. These rules can involve features in two different layers or can be set to test the features in a single layer. There are different rules for points, lines and polygon features. You also learned how to use Topological editing to resolve the issues found.

3.7   Discussion Questions

1. What are the steps involved creating and testing a topology rule?
2. How would topology be useful for property data?

3.8   Challenge Assignment (optional)

See if you can think of other topology rules that could be implemented against these data sets. Use topological editing to fix all the errors found.

Exercise 4

Spatial Data Quality

Objective – Learn to Assess Data Quality, Work with Metadata and Aggregate Data

4.1 Introduction

Spatial data is becoming more common and readily available via the Internet. However, the accuracy of the data is always a concern. As we are experiencing a growth in data availability, we should choose our sources wisely. When it comes to data accuracy, not only do we look at the spatial component, but the attribute component as well. Metadata is becoming a large component to data and it is a key factor in determining the completeness of data.

This exercise includes the following tasks:

- Task 1 Exploring Data Accuracy

- Task 2 Metadata

- Task 3 Data Aggregation

4.2 Objective: Learn to Assess Data Quality, Work with Metadata and Aggregate Data

This exercise focuses on data and its accuracy. You'll be looking at the metadata and the standards of the metadata that some datasets require. You'll also look at assessing the accuracy of the data and if it is usable or not.

4.3 Task 1 Exploring Data Accuracy

Data accuracy is an important concept and this goes for the spatial data as well as the attribute data. The spatial and attribute data can be edited and changed, but what if it is a noted problem in the data? Can we overlook certain points in the data that we know have been captured erroneously? We must be aware of the errors that are inherent in the data and the fixes that are provided. In this first task, you will create a point layer of shipwrecks from a text file containing the X and Y coordinates. You will then assess its accuracy.

1. Open QGIS Desktop and add the `great_lakes.shp` shapefile from the exercise directory.

2. Click the Add Delimited Text Layer  button. Fill out the form as in the figure below.

   a. File Name: Browse to the exercise data folder and select `shipwrecks.csv`

   b. Layer name: Shipwrecks

   c. File format: CSV (comma separated values)

251

 d. Check First record has field names

 e. Geometry definition: Point coordinates

 f. X field: `X_COORD,N,15,6`

 g. Y field: `Y_COORD,N,16,6`

 h. Click OK

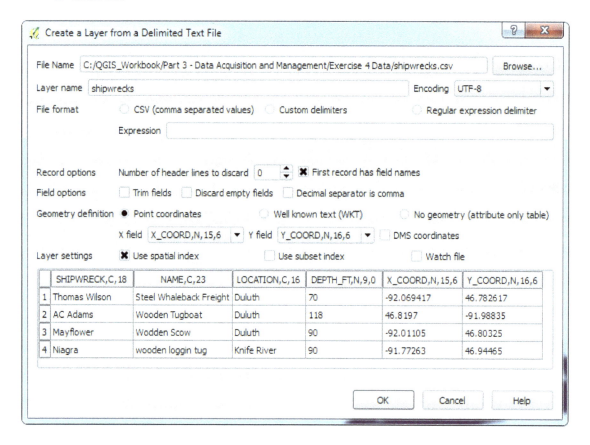

3. The Coordinate Reference System Selector will appear. Choose WGS 84 (EPSG:4326) and click OK.

4. Right-click on the Shipwrecks layer in the Layers panel and choose Zoom to layer.

5. Notice that one point is well away from the others.

6. Open the attribute table for shipwrecks. Notice the coordinate values for the AC Adams. The X and Y values are in the wrong columns. This was a data entry error. Close the attribute table and remove the shipwrecks layer.

Note: Another common issue that occurs with coordinate data are rounding errors or truncated coordinates. For example, people may round UTM coordinates to the nearest thousand when working off of USGS topographic maps. This may be due to the fact that these maps list the UTM coordinate values every thousand meters.

Note: When creating a point layer from a delimited text file, the coordinates are being mapped just within the current QGIS Desktop program instance. The data are still not in a GIS format, such as a shapefile. To create a permanent GIS layer, you would right-click on the layer and save it as a shapefile or other format.

7. Using a text editor such as Notepad or a spreadsheet program such as Open Office Calc or Microsoft Excel, open the `shipwrecks.csv` file and correct the incorrect coordinates, then save your edits.

8. Recreate the layer from the corrected delimited text file.

9. The data points should all fall near the western end of Lake Superior.

10. One must always be careful about data and not take their accuracy for granted. It is your responsibility to discover and fix errors. You cannot rely on the software to understand such mistakes.

4.4 Task 2 Metadata

In this task, you will be looking at the metadata section of spatial data. When data is purchased, or published online by an agency or organization, we expect to have a complete dataset. This includes the spatial data, the attribute data, and the metadata. Metadata is data about data, and is the one sure way we can understand the source, how it was created, what scale it was created at, what the spatial reference is, what kinds of accuracy can we expect, etc. All datasets have some error associated with them. After all, they are simplified models of the real world.

1. Open QGIS Desktop and start a new project.

2. Add the `tl_2010_35_place10.shp` shapefile to QGIS. This is the metropolitan areas of New Mexico.

3. You can open the Layer properties and click on the Metadata tab to see some basic information regarding the layer (at the bottom under Properties).

However, actual metadata is a U.S. Federal standard maintained by the Federal Geographic Data Committee (FGDC). One of the files that composes a shapefile is a metadata file. It can take several forms: text, HTML or XML. These can be opened in a text editor or a web browser. However, there is also a QGIS plugin to read and edit metadata files.

4. From the menu bar choose Plugins | Manage and Install plugins.

5. Click on the Settings tab and click the Show also experimental plugins option.

6. Click on the All tab and search for Meta.

7. Locate the Metatools plugin and install it (shown in figure below). Close the Plugins window.

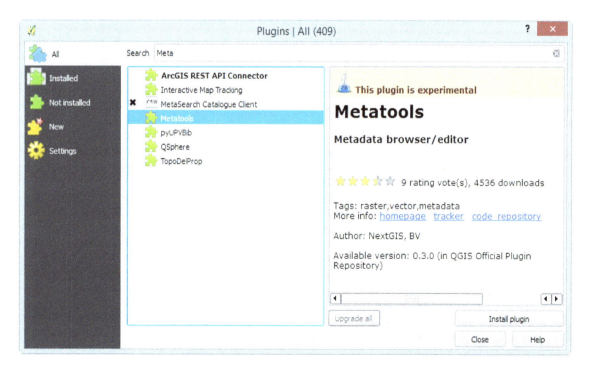

8. This is an experimental plugin at this point. However, it is well conceived and very useful. It loads a toolbar with several tools (shown in figure below).

Note: If you are working on a Windows computer you will need to open the Python Console for the tool to run. To do this click Plugins | Python Console. Other operating systems such as MAC OSX and Linux may not require this step.

9. Select `tl_2010_35_place10` in the Layers panel and click the View metadata button.

10. The Metadata Viewer will open (shown in figure below).

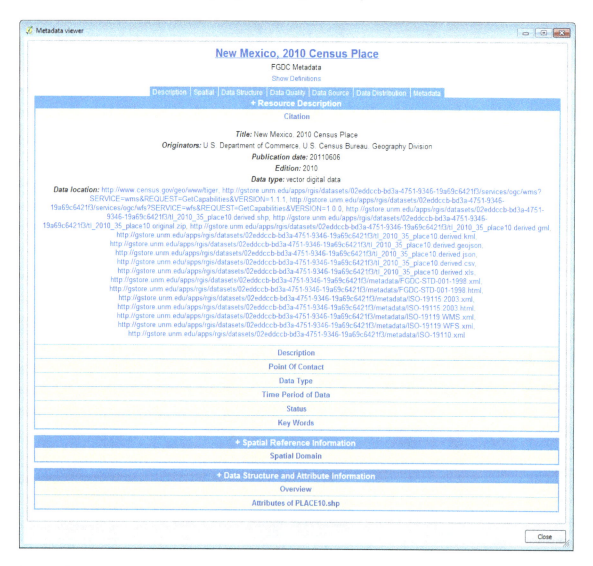

Metatools parses the metadata file and presents it in an easily readable format.

The FGDC Metadata Standard contains six major sections as seen below.

- **Identification Information** – Includes the data title and abstract

- **Data Quality Information** – Information about the accuracy and precision of the data, including the processing steps taken to produce it.

- **Spatial Organization Information** – Information about the file format.

- **Spatial Reference Information** – The coordinate reference system used including: projection/coordinate system, datum, and other parameters.

- **Entity and Attribute Information** – Explanations on the field types and data contained within each attribute column.

- **Distribution Information** – Contact information of the data provider.

11. Click on Description to expand that section. This provides an abstract and purpose for the data.

12. The viewer is not completely parsing this metadata file. If you click on the Data Quality section it is blank.

13. To see the Data Quality section, open the `Exercise 4 Data\tl_2010_35_place10.shp.xml` file in a web browser. You should be able to double click on it and have your operating system locate the associated program. This is the raw XML metadata.

14. This is certainly harder to look at than the parsed display in Metatools. Fortunately, because of the FGDC standard, all metadata files have the same sections in the same order.

15. Scroll down past the abstract and you will find a tag called dataqual. This section contains the Logical Consistency Report, which details the tests used to determine the data quality (shown in figure below).

```
- <dataqual>
    - <attracc>
          <attraccr>Accurate against Federal Information Processing Standards (FIPS), FIPS Publication 6-4, and
              FIPS-55 at the 100% level for the codes and base names. The remaining attribute information has
              been examined but has not been fully tested for accuracy.</attraccr>
      </attracc>
      <logic>The Census Bureau performed automated tests to ensure logical consistency and limits of shapefiles.
          Segments making up the outer and inner boundaries of a polygon tie end-to-end to completely enclose
          the area. All polygons are tested for closure. The Census Bureau uses its internally developed geographic
          update system to enhance and modify spatial and attribute data in the Census MAF/TIGER database.
          Standard geographic codes, such as FIPS codes for states, counties, municipalities, county subdivisions,
          places, American Indian/Alaska Native/Native Hawaiian areas, and congressional districts are used
          when encoding spatial entities. The Census Bureau performed spatial data tests for logical consistency of
          the codes during the compilation of the original Census MAF/TIGER database files. Most of the codes for
          geographic entities except states, counties, urban areas, Core Based Statistical Areas (CBSAs), American
          Indian Areas (AIAs), and congressional districts were provided to the Census Bureau by the USGS, the
          agency responsible for maintaining FIPS 55. Feature attribute information has been examined but has
          not been fully tested for consistency. For the TIGER/Line Shapefiles, the Point and Vector Object Count
          for the G-polygon SDTS Point and Vector Object Type reflects the number of records in the shapefile
          attribute table. For multi-polygon features, only one attribute record exists for each multi-polygon rather
          than one attribute record per individual G-polygon component of the multi-polygon feature. TIGER/Line
          Shapefile multi-polygons are an exception to the G-polygon object type classification. Therefore, when
          multi-polygons exist in a shapefile, the object count will be less than the actual number of
          G-polygons.</logic>
      <complete>Data completeness of the TIGER/Line Shapefiles reflects the contents of the Census MAF/TIGER
          database at the time the TIGER/Line Shapefiles were created.</complete>
    - <lineage>
        - <srcinfo>
            - <srccite>
                - <citeinfo>
                      <origin>U.S. Department of Commerce, U.S. Census Bureau, Geography Division</origin>
                      <pubdate>Unpublished material</pubdate>
                      <title>Census MAF/TIGER database</title>
                  </citeinfo>
```

16. Slightly farther down you will find the attribute section. This section details all of the attribute columns.

17. Close the web browser with the metadata XML displayed.

18. Close the Metadata Viewer in QGIS Desktop.

19. Click on the Edit Metadata [ ] button to open the Metadata editor. Expand metadata and you will see abbreviated listings of the six FGDC metadata sections (see figure below).

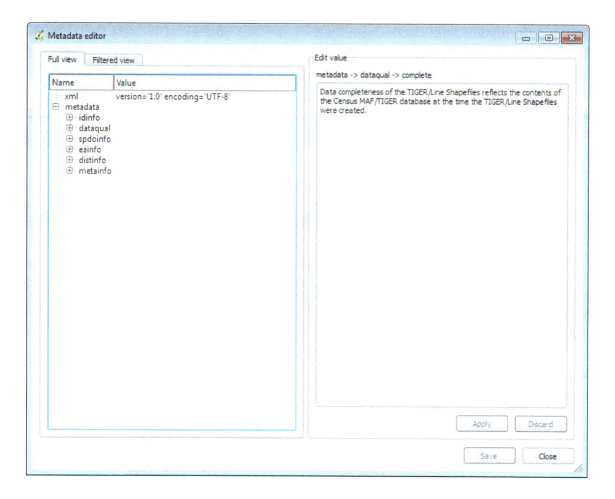

20. Expand dataqual. If you click on an entry such as logic you will see that entry. You can use this editor to edit the text and save the metadata.

21. Close the Metadata Editor.

The Import and Export buttons allow you to save out a copy of the metadata. Many organizations will set up a metadata template with items that will be the same from metadata file to metadata file, such as contact information. If you have such a template, you can use the Import tool to import it. The Metadata Editor can then be used to complete the record.

4.5   Task 3 Data Aggregation

Data aggregation is the process where data is joined, merged, or generalized to suit a need. This may be done in such a way to protect the information at a lower level.

1. Open QGIS Desktop and start a new project.

2. Add the countries.shp shapefile to QGIS.

3. From the menu bar choose Vector | Geoprocessing Tools | Dissolve.

4. Set up the dissolve tool to dissolve based on the SubRegion attribute field. Name the output Sub_Regions.shp (shown in figure below).

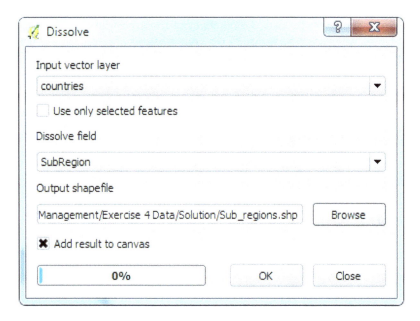

The result is an example of data aggregation. All the data in the map will be mapped using those regions (shown in the figure below). In this scenario, all data by country will be aggregated to the sub region level.

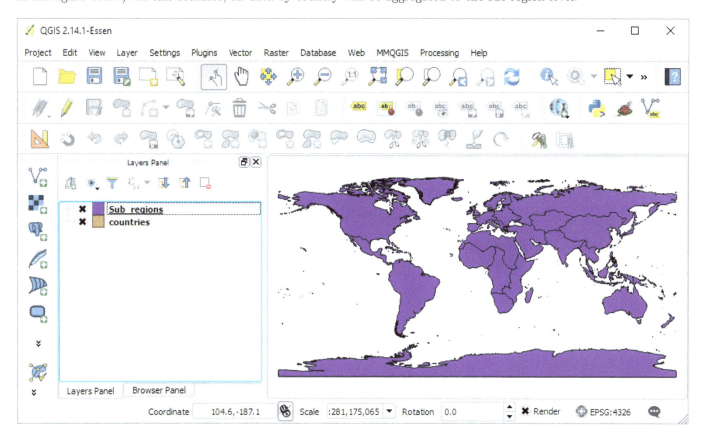

4.6   Conclusion

Spatial and attribute data accuracy is important. Having a complete data set and keeping track of all the edits and errors is also important. Metadata provides background on the data provided to us. It supplies us with vital information regarding the use and resolution of the data. If you read the metadata, you may be able to determine that the data is not a good fit for your project before trying to edit and manipulate it. Data aggregation is a way to abstract the data and to remove data levels from the data. In Task 3, you changed the lowest level in the data from countries to sub regions. This is important, but we need to be aware of the consequences of our actions when mapping data and how the accuracy is changed when we manipulate it.

4.7   Discussion Questions

1. Does metadata need to be written for all datasets? Explain.
2. Why do we need a metadata standard?
3. How can data aggregation be problematic in a real world mapping scenario?

4.8   Challenge Assignment (optional)

Add the `NM_Game_Management_Units` shapefile to QGIS. View the metadata. Take note of the Horizontal Coordinate System.

What is provided as the Positional Accuracy?

Aggregate the Game Management Units into Cougar Zones.

Add a Delimited Text layer of cougar_sample_points.

Note: once mapped, the CRS for the cougar sample points will need to be defined. QGIS will default to a geographic CRS and you will have to redefine the CRS in Layer Properties. They are in the same CRS as the Game Management Units.

Do all the cougar sample points fall correctly in New Mexico? If not can you identify the issue with any points that are not falling in the correct location?

Exercise 5

Raster Data Structure

Objective – Work with the Raster Data Model

5.1 Introduction

Raster data is a data model in which the data is presented in a grid. Each grid cell contains one data value or attribute. For example, a digital elevation model (DEM) has cell values that represent the elevation. One important characteristic of raster data is the resolution. Raster resolution is a measure of the cell dimensions, which means the area that each cell covers in the real world. For example, a satellite image may have a resolution of 30 meters, which means that each cell covers 30 square meters in the real world. You can use raster data simply as cartographic backdrops, as datasets for digitizing, or for analysis.

This exercise includes the following tasks:

- Task 1 Merging and Clipping Raster Data

- Task 2 Raster Pyramids

5.2 Objective: Work with the Raster Data Model

This exercise focuses on working with raster data within QGIS.

5.3 Task 1 Merging and Clipping Raster Data

Raster data are often provided in tiles, such as USGS Quadrangles. In such cases, it is necessary to merge the raster tiles together to form a seamless raster covering the study area.

1. Open QGIS Desktop and add the four DEM raster datasets (35106-A4.dem, 35106-A5.dem, 35106-B4.dem and 35106-B5.dem) (shown in figure below).

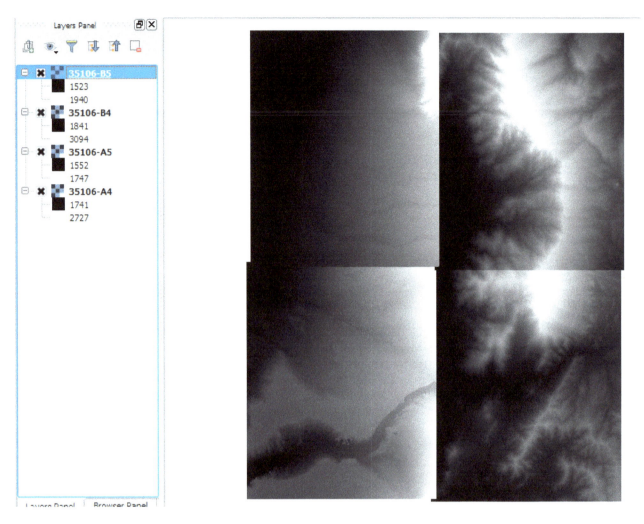

Each of these has cell values representing the elevation above sea level. Each is styled with the values stretched across a black to white color ramp. Since each dataset has different minimum and maximum cell values, the boundaries between datasets is obvious.

2. Save your project as `exercise_5.qgs`.

3. Double-click on the `35106-B5.dem` layer to open the Layer Properties.

4. Click on the Metadata tab.

In the Properties window you will find information about the file format (Driver), cell statistics (Band 1), Dimensions, Origin, Pixel size (10 meters), the No Data value and the Data Type.

Raster datasets are always rectangular. If the data content does not fill the rectangular area, the extra cells will be assigned a value that signifies that there is no data there. Here the No Data value is -32767.

5. Close the Layer Properties.

6. Turn on the Processing toolbox by clicking on Processing | Toolbox.

7. From the Toolbox choose SAGA | Raster tools | Mosaick raster layers (shown in figure below).
   NOTE: In versions of QGIS prior to v2.14 this tool will be found here: SAGA | Grid-Tools | Mosaick raster layers

8. Fill out the Mosaic raster dialog with the following parameters:

a. Input Grids = Click the ellipsis button ⌈ ... ⌉ in the upper right corner and select all four DEM rasters. Click OK.

b. Preferred data storage type = [6] 4 byte signed integer.

c. Interpolation = [1] Bilinear Interpolation

d. Overlapping cells = [1] last value in order of grid list

e. Mosaicked grid = Save to file: `Exercise 5 Data\Merge.tif.sdat`

f. When parameters match the figure below, click Run.

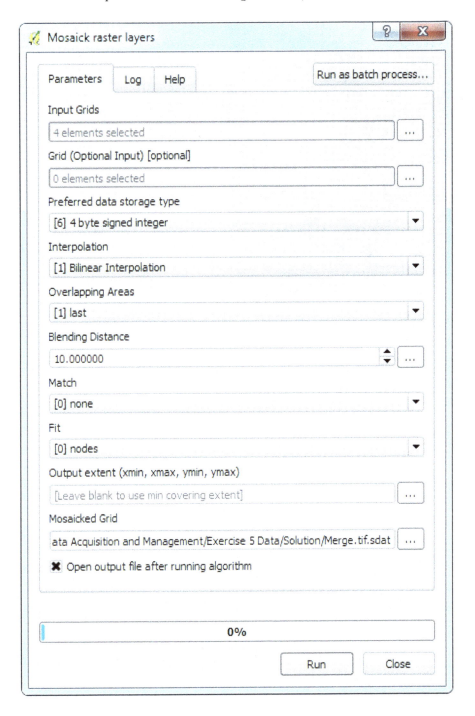

10. Turn off the input DEMs in the Layers panel. You now have a seamless raster (shown in figure below).

11. Now you will clip the mosaicked DEM to the project study area.

12. Add the `StudyArea.shp` shapefile to QGIS Desktop.

13. From the menu bar choose Raster | Extraction | Clipper.

14. Set the following parameters for the Clipper (shown in figure below):

   a. Input file (raster) = Merge

   b. Output file =`Exercise 5 Data\StudyArea.tif`

   c. Clipping Mode = Mask Layer

   d. Mask layer = StudyArea

   e. Click OK.

   f. Click Close when done.

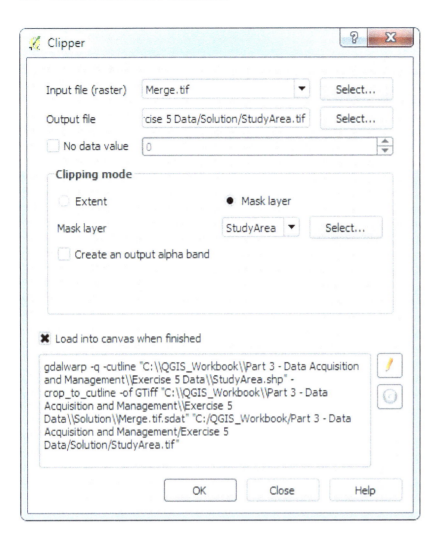

15. Turn off the visibility for the StudyArea and Mosaick layers to see the clipped raster.

16. Save your project.

This is a common workflow to get raster data set up for analysis.

5.4 Task 2 Raster Pyramids

Pyramids are lower resolution versions of a raster dataset that are more suitable for display on a monitor. Without pyramids, the computer will attempt to render each and every pixel in a raster dataset, whether the computer monitor can display all the detail or not. Having pyramids greatly decreases the time it takes to render a raster on screen.

1. Open `exercise_5.qgs` in QGIS Desktop.

2. Open the Layer Properties for the Merge raster layer.

3. Click on the Pyramids tab. Currently this raster has no pyramids. The available resolutions are listed on the right side (shown in figure below).

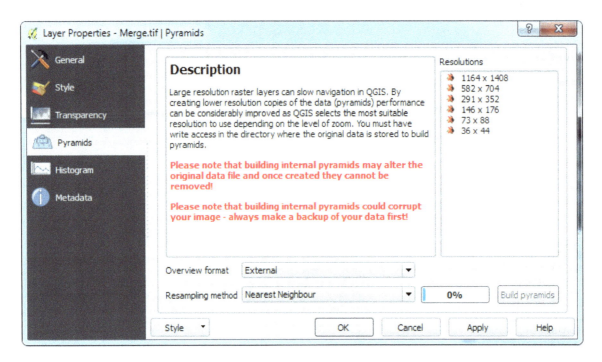

Pyramids can be embedded within the raster file, or built externally. It is safer to build them externally as this does not alter the original dataset. The external pyramid file can always be deleted if it does not have the desired results.

4. Select all 6 resolutions: 1164 x 1408 to 36 x 44.

5. For the Overview format, select External.

6. Set Resampling method to Cubic.

Generally nearest neighbor technique is most suitable for discrete rasters since it will not change the values of the cells. The average, gauss, and cubic techniques are more suitable for continuous rasters such as this DEM. They will cause some smoothing of the data and may result in some values that are beyond the original range.

7. Click Build pyramids.

8. Click OK to close the Layer Properties.

9. Zoom in and out on the raster to see how quickly the raster renders on the screen.

Note: This dataset is small enough that you may not notice an improvement in drawing speed. However, it can be quite dramatic for large rasters over 100 Mb in size.

10. Re-open the layer properties for the Mosaick raster layer.

11. Switch to the Metadata tab.

12. In the Properties section, scroll to the Dimensions section. Under Dimensions you will see multiple dimension entries indicating that the pyramid resolutions were built.

13. Open a file browser (for example: Windows explorer or Finder) and navigate to the Exercise 5 Data folder. You will see a Merge.tif.ovr file. This is the file containing the pyramids.

5.5 Conclusion

In this exercise you focused on preparing raster data so that it seamlessly covers a study area. You also learned how to build pyramid files for a raster dataset.

5.6 Discussion Questions

1. What is a raster dataset?
2. Compare and contrast raster and vector data models.
3. Why might you use raster data? Give two examples.

5.7 Challenge Assignment (optional)

Using the National Map (http://viewer.nationalmap.gov/basic/), download DEMs for an area interesting to you.

1. Select an area of interest using the Download by Draw Rectangle tool ■. With this tool, drag a box around an area roughly the size of a large county or several small counties.
2. Select the Elevation Products (3DEP) option, and Select 1/9 arc-second DEM.
3. Click the Find Products button.
4. All the available DEMs with be listed.
5. Click the Add to Shopping Cart 🛒➕ button for those items you'd like to download. Note that there may be more than one DEM covering an area. Pay attention to the coordinates embedded in the file name.
6. Once you have all the DEM's added to your cart, click the View Cart button.
7. Finally, click the Download link for each item to download it.

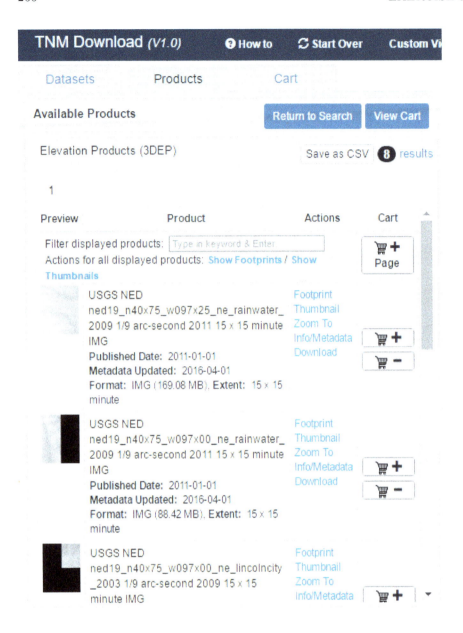

Exercise 6

Data Sources

Objective – Learn to Map Address Data via Geocoding

6.1   Introduction

Data collection is an important task in the creation of a GIS. Data can come from several sources such as GPS receivers, text files, or from the Internet as shapefiles—you may even receive a coverage. The GIS can manage all of this data. We may receive data with an address that we want to display on a map. We can geolocate items using an address via a process known as geocoding. This tool helps us take point features from a text file and tie it to an address.

This exercise includes the following tasks:

- Task 1 Geocoding
- Task 2 Build a Map

6.2   Objective: Learn to Map Address Data via Geocoding

The objective of this exercise is to learn how to geocode address-based data provided in a text file and create a map from various data sources.

6.3   Task 1 Geocoding

In a geocoding operation, address data contained in a table or text file are mapped against a street network dataset. The street network dataset needs to have attribute fields for address ranges on the left and right side of each road segment. Mapping addresses has many applications including mapping: the customer base for a store, members of an organization, public health records, and crime locations. Once mapped, the points can be used to generate density surfaces and can be tied to parcels of land. This can be important in cadastral information systems.

1. Open QGIS Desktop and add the `Streets.shp` shapefile.
2. Open the Attribute table for Streets and examine the available fields of data. Notice that in addition to the `STREETNAME` and `STREETDESI` columns that the data include fields called `LEFTLOW`, `LEFTHIGH`, `RIGHTLOW`, and `RIGHTHIGH`. These fields hold the address range for each road segment. These are necessary in a geocoding operation.
3. Close the attribute table.
4. Click the Add Vector Layer button and add the `Addresses.csv` table to QGIS Desktop.
5. Open the attribute table for the Addresses layer.

6. This file has an `ADDRESS` column that combines the street number, street, street type (ex: BLVD, AVE, ST), and city quadrant. There are additional fields with that address parsed out into `STREET`, `NUMBER` and `QUAD`. The tool you will be using requires separate fields in the address data for street and street number.

7. Now that you are familiar with the data, close the Addresses attribute table.

8. To geocode you will use a Plugin called MMQGIS. From the menu bar choose Plugins | Manage and Install Plugins.

9. Choose the All tab and type 'MMQGIS' into the Search bar.

10. Find the plugin named `mmqgis` and click Install plugin (shown in figure below).

11. When complete click Close.

MMQGIS appears as a separate menu in QGIS Desktop.

12. From the menu bar choose MMQGIS | Geocode | Geocode from Street Layer.

13. Click the Browse button, navigate to the `Exercise 6 Data` folder and choose the `Addresses.csv` table. Fill in the remaining choices as shown in the figure below.

   a. First set the fields that hold street name and number in the `Address.csv` file.

   b. Then assign the field in the Streets shapefile that contains the street name.

   c. The Bldg. Setback field allows you to specify how far from the street arc to place the points. Street GIS data are known as street centerlines. The line falls where the median is on a large boulevard. Using this setting allows you to place the points more closely to the building's actual location. We'll set this to 20. The map units of this dataset are in feet. This distance roughly corresponds to the width of two road lanes.

   d. The result will be a point shapefile. Name the Output Shapefile `Street_Geocode.shp` and save it to the `Exercise 6 Data` folder.

e. Geocoding operations rarely have 100% success. Street names in the street shapefile must match the street names in the CSV file exactly. The tool will save out a list of the unmatched records. Set the Not Found Output List field to `Steet_Geocoded_notFound.csv` in the `Exercise 6 Data` folder.

f. Click OK to run. This process may take several minutes. The status of the geocoding will display in the bottom-left corner of QGIS Desktop.

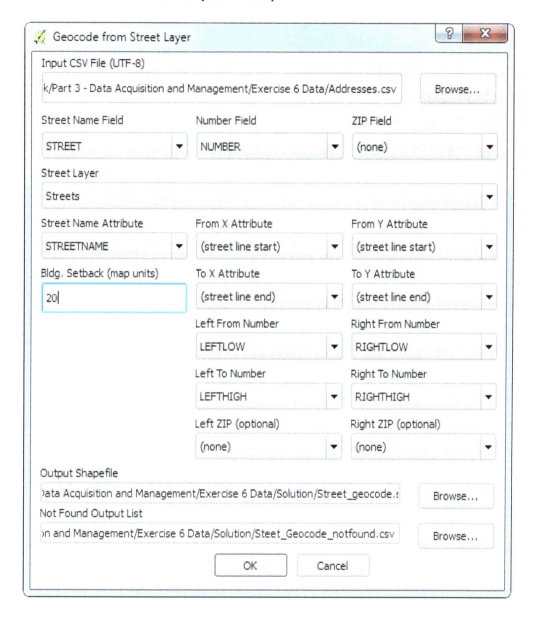

14. When complete the new layer is added to QGIS Desktop. The process should successfully geocode 199 of the 203 addresses (shown in figure below).

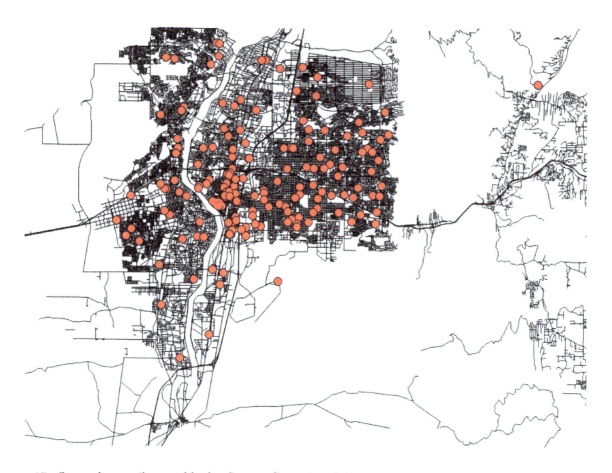

15. Open the attribute table for Street_Geocode. All of the attributes from the CSV file are brought in as attributes to the output shapefile.

16. Right click on the Street_Geocode layer and choose Zoom to Layer. All of the points look to be well mapped.

17. Zoom into a concentration of points and then zoom in farther to some within the city. Use the Identify tool

    to inspect the mapped points and the roads to ensure that the operation was successful. Never take a GIS operation for granted. Check your results with a critical eye.

18. You can also add the Street_Geocode_notFound.csv file to QGIS Desktop and study it to try and determine why the four records did not find a match.

19. These are good geocoding results. Now you will try the other method available: geocode using the Google Geocoder.

20. From the menu bar choose MMQGIS | Geocode | Geocode CSV with Google/OpenStreetMap.

21. This tool uses the same geocoding engine that is used when you type an address into Google maps. *Note:* This tool requires an Internet connection.

22. Fill out the Web Service Geocode parameters so they match the figure below:

    a. Click the Browse button, navigate to the Exercise 6 Data folder and choose Addresses.csv as the Input CSV File (UTF-8).

    b. Address Field = STREET

    c. City Field = CITY

    d. State Field = STATE

    e. Country Field = COUNTRY

f. Web Service = Google Maps

g. Output Shapefile = `Google_Addresses.shp`

h. Not Found Output List = `Google_notFound.csv`

i. Click OK to run. Again, this may take a while and progress is displayed in the lower-left corner of QGIS Desktop.

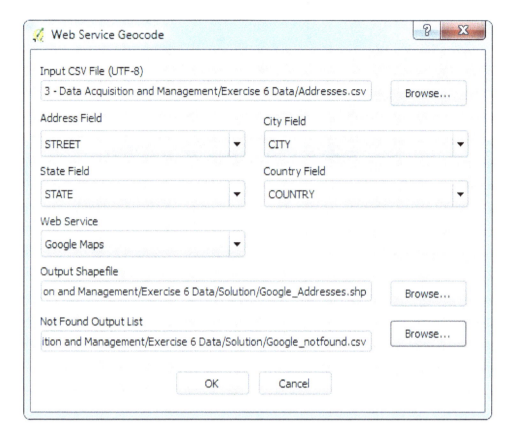

23. This may take several minutes to run and in part depends on the speed of your internet connection.

24. This technique matches all 203 records. The figure below shows the Google Addresses in yellow and the street layer geocoded addresses in red. Note that they differ!

25. Right-click on `Google_Addresses.shp` and choose `Zoom to Layer`. These, too, seem to be well mapped. Although there is a discernible difference between the address point locations identified by the two tools. The `Google_notfound.csv` is an empty text file since Google found a match for each record.

26. Again, zoom in to some sample address points and spot check the results to determine if the points are on the street they should be. Can you determine which output is more accurate?

27. Congratulations! You have created points from a table of addresses!

28. Save your map as `exercise_6.qgs`.

6.4   Task 2 Build a Map

At the end of your data collection, a product is usually required. In this case, a map is necessary to complete the exercise. Data from several sources have been downloaded and included in your exercise data folder.

1. Open `exercise_6.qgs` in QGIS Desktop if necessary.

2. Add the jurisdiction, biketrails, and council shapefiles. Jurisdiction is the municipal boundaries for Albuquerque, New Mexico. Council is the City Council Districts. Bike trails are municipal bike trails.

3. Using QGIS Desktop, style the layers and use the Print Composer to compose a letter sized color map highlighting the different Facilities (Google_Addresses) by City Council District.

4. You will have to style the Google Addresses and City Council Districts using Categories.

5. Symbolize Bike Trails, Streets, and Jurisdiction as you see fit.

6. If you need a refresher on how to compose a map you can refer to Part 1 - Introduction to Geospatial Technology, Exercise 2 - Displaying Geospatial Data, on page 33.

7. Submit a jpg of your final map.

6.5 Conclusion

In this exercise you learned how to geocode address data using the MMQGIS plugin. Geocoding is an important vector data creation process. There are many data organized by address. Mapping such data allows you to generate density maps, measure proximity of points, and perhaps even characterize the neighborhoods the points fall in with socioeconomic data from the Census. Maps are often part of a final product of a GIS project or analysis. Data can come from various sources and be manipulated to fit the project. The data should be normalized in respect to the file format, spatial extent and coordinate reference system. Remember GIS data are often free, and there is a wealth of it on the Internet. Just use it with caution and check the accuracy of the data if at all possible. One should explore the data as much as possible before using and endorsing it.

6.6 Discussion Questions

1. Which tool created better output, the Geocoding by Street Layer or the Google Geocoder?
2. What are the advantages and disadvantages of having all the data on the Internet?
3. What are some applications of geocoding? Describe.

6.7 Challenge Assignment (optional)

Use the data in the `Exercise_6 Data\Challenge` folder to compose a map to do with pollutants in Nueces County, Texas. The data include:

- Airports
- Cities
- Roads
- Water_features
- Places
- Counties

Use the MMQGIS Geocode CSV with Google/OpenStreetMap tool to geocode the address data in the `NuecesCounty.csv` file. These addresses are Toxic Release Inventory sites from the EPA. As such, they are potential source points for pollutants.

In order to compose the map you will have to utilize Feature subsets (Layer Properties | General tab) to limit some of the data to Nueces County.

You will have to check the coordinate systems to ensure that all data are in the same coordinate reference system.

Style data layers such as airports and rivers.

Submit a jpg of your final map.

Part IV

Cartographic Design

Exercise 1

Creating a Colorful Map of the United States of America

Objective – Explore and utilize style properties in QGIS to design a colorful map of the United States of America

1.1 Introduction

In this exercise, you'll explore and utilize style properties in QGIS Desktop to create a colorful map of the United States of America (USA).

This exercise will focus primarily on setting style properties to create an attractive, colorful map of the USA. Throughout the exercise, you'll create three maps: one of the lower 48 states, one of Alaska, and one of Hawaii. In the next two labs, these three maps will be refined and completed to create the final map.

This exercise includes the following tasks:

- Task 1 – Designing the Lower 48 Map

- Task 2 – Basic Labeling of States

- Task 3 – Saving and Loading QGIS Layer Style Files

- Task 4 – Designing the Alaska Map

- Task 5 – Designing the Hawaii Map

1.2 Objective: Explore and Utilize Style Properties in QGIS to Design a Colorful Map of the United States of America

To achieve a properly designed map, the features on the map must be easily distinguishable, attractive to the map reader, and stand out from the grounds (supporting background information/data). In this exercise, you'll learn how to utilize the style properties in QGIS to achieve a properly designed map. Additionally, you'll learn how to save, load, and manage styles so they can be applied to multiple projects and/or data layers. To show you where we're headed, the map below is the final design.

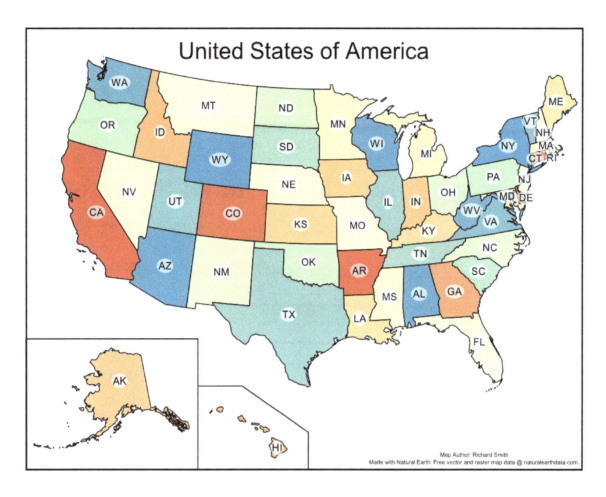

1.3   Task 1 Designing the Lower 48 Map

In this task, you will load and stylize the data that will be used to design the map. We'll focus on selecting the fill colors of the states, and the line color and thickness for the state boundaries.

1. Open QGIS Desktop.
2. In QGIS Desktop, add the vector layer USA States Area.shp to the project by clicking Layer | Add Layer | Add Vector Layer from the menu bar.

As the Lower 48 states are going to be the focus of this task, we will zoom in on them to fill the display.

3. Use the Zoom In tool ⊕ to drag a box around the Lower 48 states to zoom in as close as possible without any part of a state exceeding the display area. Your display should look similar to:

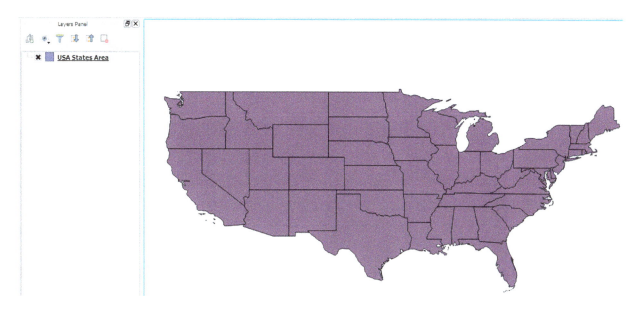

We now will set the style for each state. The general strategy will be to randomly assign each state a color from a color ramp that we like, set the line color and thickness, and finally change state colors where they are too similar to their neighbors.

4. In the Layers panel, right-click 'USA States Area' then choose Properties. This will open the Layer Properties dialog.

5. In the Layer Properties dialog, click the Style tab to view the styling options for the layer.

6. In the Classify drop-down box, select Categorized (the drop-down box initially displays Single Symbol).

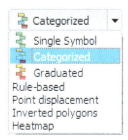

7. In the Column, choose name. We will use the name of the state as a unique value to classify the data by so we can assign a unique color to each state by name.

8. For the Color ramp, choose Spectral.

9. Click the Classify button. This will add all values from the name column and apply a unique color to each state.

10. Your Style properties should look like the figure below. If it does, click OK, otherwise, change your style properties to match.

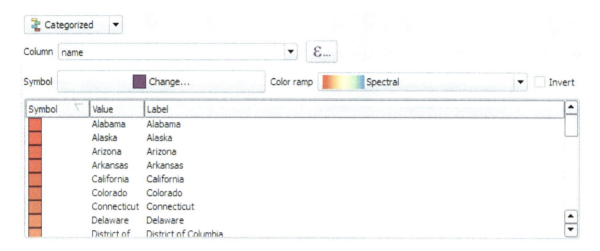

You now have a colorful map of the lower 48 states with each state having a unique color. While this color ramp generally produces a pleasing set of colors, there are multiple problems with the map we need to address going forward.

First, while the black state outlines are generally reasonable, they could be thickened a little to really set each state apart and make each state's color 'pop'.

Second, there are multiple instances of neighboring states that share too similar of a color. This is a problem because neighboring states of similar colors may be perceived as a single state, or, a pattern may be perceived to exist where there is none. We need to change the colors to avoid both of these problems.

Third, the red colors tend to dominate the map and distract the eye towards a few states too much. If the reds were used on smaller states, it may not be as distracting, however, in our case, some of the larger states have too strong of a red color. We need to tone down the reds to bring them into parity with the other colors on the map.

Fourth, and finally, the map is not projected to a reasonable map projection. We'll defer dealing with this problem until Exercise 2 where we will choose an appropriate map projection.

Let's get started with choosing a new line thickness for the state outlines.

11. In the Layers panel, right-click 'USA States Area' then choose Properties. Choose the **Style** tab to view the layer's style properties.

12. Click the Symbol **Change...** button (shown in figure below) to view the Symbol selector dialog.

13. In the Symbol layers box, choose **Simple** fill. This will allow us to change the border color, style, and width.

14. As the border color is black, and the border style is a solid line, only change the **Border width** to 0.4. This will thicken the solid black border lines for each state.

15. If your Symbol properties look like the figure below, click OK to close the Symbol selector dialog, then click OK again to close the Layer Properties, otherwise make your properties match the figure below.

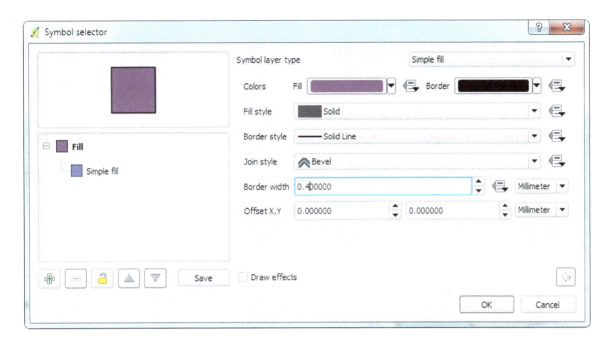

At this point, your map should look like the figure below.

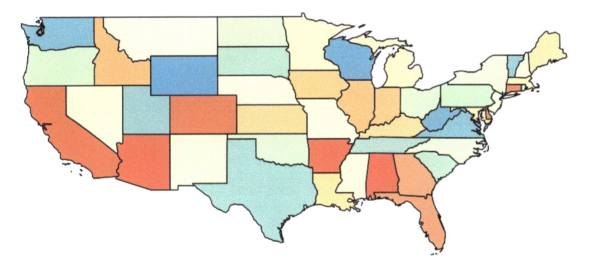

Now that the state outlines look good, let us deal with neighboring states with similar colors and with the very red states. There are five states that we will have their color changed: Illinois, Florida, New York, Alabama, and Arizona.

16. In the Layer panel, right-click 'USA States Area' then choose Properties.

17. In the Layer Properties dialog, click the Style tab.

18. Consider the states bordering Illinois—they're all a similar color. Since there is no green state close to Illinois, lets change its color to the same as Texas. Find 'Texas' in the Classification List, right-click on 'Texas' and choose Change color.

19. Note the Red, Green, Blue colors: 123, 187, 172 respectively. We will use those values to make Illinois the same color as Texas. Click OK to close the Change Symbol Color dialog.

20. Find 'Illinois' in the Classification List, right-click on 'Illinois' and choose Change color.

21. Set the Red, Green, Blue values to 123, 187, 172 respectively.

22. Click OK to set Illinois to the new color.

23. Click OK to apply the changes and dismiss the Layer Properties Dialog.

Now that Illinois is a different color than its surrounding states, the states stand out more from each other.

24. Using the steps above, change the colors of Florida, New York, Alabama, and Arizona to other, complementary colors that will reduce the brightness of the red states and remove the homogeneous colors of neighboring states. The figure below shows an example of what the final colors could look like.

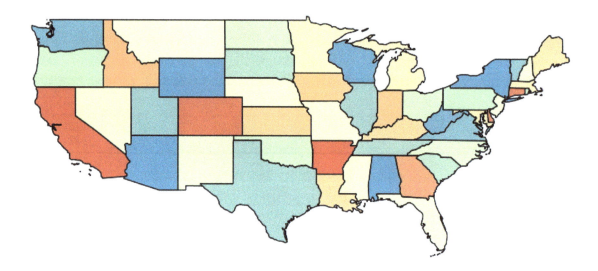

25. We are finished designing the Lower 48 states map for now. Save your QGIS Project as `Lower 48 States.qgs` in your exercise folder by clicking Project | Save.

1.4   Task 2 Basic Labeling of States

This task will walk you through the process of applying basic labels to the map. Exercise 7, on page 383 covers advanced labeling techniques—for this map, we will keep the labeling fairly simple and focus on overall map design, layout, and projection choices.

1. Open the Layer Properties for 'USA States Area', then choose the Labels tab.

2. At the top of the Layer Properties dialog, check Label this layer with and choose `postal` from the field selector dropdown box.

3. Click OK to see the labels on the map. You should see something like the figure below.

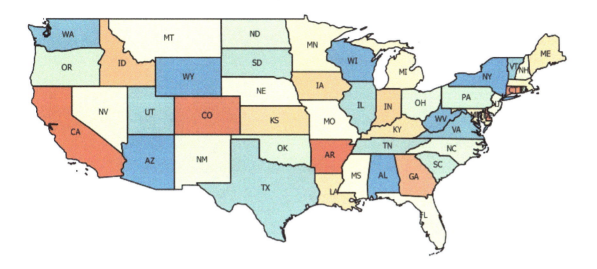

Let's consider the labels for a few moments. First, the size may be too small to reliably read. Second, the labels are offset from center in some states, which looks awkward. Third, in the smaller states along the east coast, the labels are difficult to read because they overlap with state boundary lines. Lastly, some states may not be labeled (there may/may not be states missing labels). Let us correct each of these issues.

First, we will increase the font size to make the postal codes larger and easier to read.

4. Reopen the Label Properties.

5. Choose Text from the properties list on the left-hand side of the Label properties tab (see figure below).

6. Set the following text properties:

- Font: Arial
- Style: Normal
- Size: 14.0 points

7. Click OK to see the changes on the map.

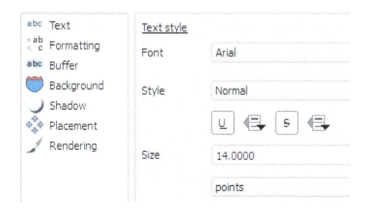

Now we are getting somewhere. The labels are now clearly visible size-wise. However, now we need to adjust the placement of the labels to put them in more desirable locations. Let's work on that next.

8. Reopen the Label Properties.

9. Choose Placement from the properties list on the left-hand side of the Label properties tab.

10. Set the following placement properties (see the figure below):

- Placement: Around centroid
- Centroid: visible polygon

11. Click OK to see the label placement change on the map.

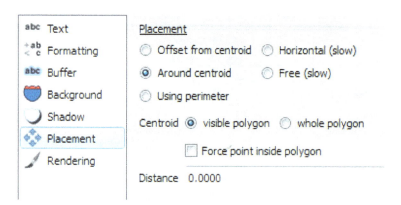

Now the labels are really coming together. There are a few labels that are still not placed optimally (e.g. LA, RI, NJ, DE, MD, and FL), however, the other states have nicely placed labels. We will deal with the non-optimal label placement in Exercise 3, on page 315 when we work on the layout.

Now we will address the smaller states and the difficulty in reading their labels due to overlap with state boundaries. Let's apply a buffer to the labels to provide a nice white canvas for them to sit on.

12. Reopen the Label Properties.

13. Choose Buffer from the properties list on the left-hand side of the Label properties tab.

14. Set the following Buffer properties (see figure below):

- Check Draw text buffer
- Transparency: 20
- Pen join style: Round

15. Click OK to see the labels. They should look similar to the map below.

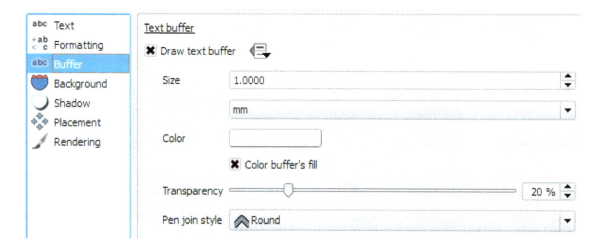

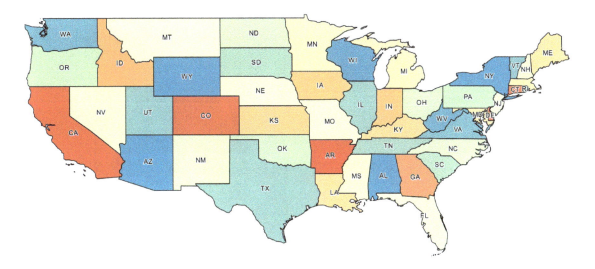

While the labels are now easier to read, we can do something a little non-traditional and put a different background behind the labels to make them easier to read. Instead of a buffer that follows the strokes of the letters, let us put semi-transparent white ellipsis behind the text.

16. Reopen the Label Properties.

17. Choose Buffer from the properties list on the left-hand side of the Label properties tab.

18. Uncheck Draw text buffer to turn off the buffers.

19. Choose Background from the properties list on the left-hand side of the Label properties tab.

20. Set the following Background properties (see figure below):

   - Check Draw background
   - Shape: Ellipse
   - Size type: Buffer
   - Size X: -0.5 mm
   - Size Y: -0.5 mm
   - *Note*: The negative sizes will make the ellipse smaller and tighter around the label.
   - Transparency: 40

21. Click OK to see the labels with ellipses as their background.

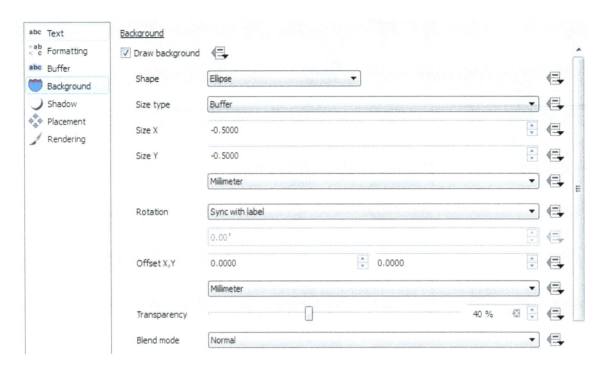

Your map should look similar to the figure below.

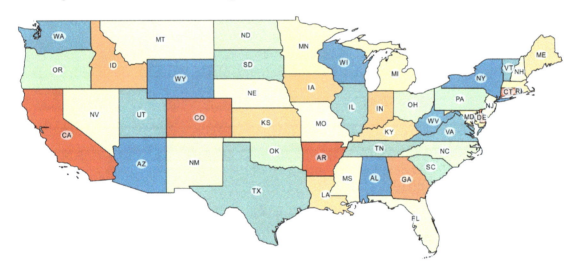

Each state now has an easily readable label. If you prefer the buffer to the ellipse, feel free to change it back, or, better yet, explore labeling options to find one that you prefer. However, for the remainder of this and Exercise 2, on page 291 and Exercise 3, on page 315, the assumption is that you have ellipses behind the labels, so if you do not, you may need to adapt the exercise instructions to fit your label choices.

The fourth issue we identified with the labels earlier is that some states may not have labels. Additionally, with the backgrounds added to the labels, Massachusetts now does not have a label. First, let us discuss why some states may not have labels by using Florida and New York as examples. Because Florida and New York are composed of multiple polygons, stored as a single feature in the shapefile, the QGIS labeling engine may be attempting to label one of the very small polygons and finding that it is too small to label, therefore, it does not apply a label. If you zoom in to New York or Florida, it will eventually place a label on the largest polygon. Other states that are composed of multiple polygons are not afflicted by this, however, so there is some inconsistencies in either a) how QGIS decides how to label multi-part polygons, or b) the order in which the polygons are stored in the shapefile. In either case, labels for those missing states will need to be added in manually; this will be handled in Exercise 3, on page 315.

Moving on to Massachusetts, its label disappeared because the backgrounds of Connecticut and Rhode Island overlap slightly with the Massachusetts label. QGIS, by default, does place features that conflict with other labels. We will need to override this behavior to get Massachusetts labeled.

22. Reopen the Label Properties.

23. Choose Rendering from the properties list on the left-hand side of the Label properties tab.

24. Set the following Rendering parameters (see figure below):

    - Check Show all labels for this layer...
    - Suppress labeling of features smaller than: 1.00 mm
        - This setting tells QGIS not to label features that render smaller than a set size. By setting this to 1.00 mm, this will prevent Washington DC from being labeled on the map.

25. Click OK to see that Massachusetts is now labeled.

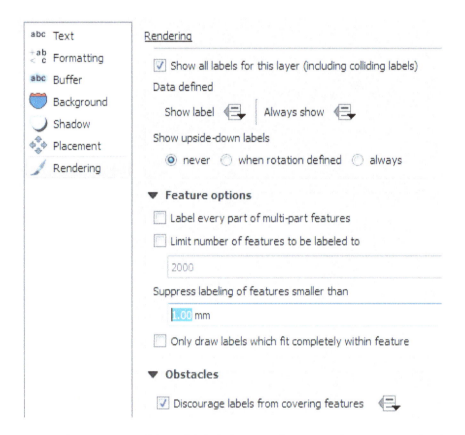

We now have a reasonably well labeled map. There are a few tweaks still to be made, however, we will stop working with labels for now and will revisit them in Exercise 3, on page 315.

1.5 Task 3 Saving and Loading QGIS Layer Style Files

With your color and label choices for the Lower 48 set, lets save those color and label choices to a style file so you can reuse the style in other QGIS projects as well as reapply the style to your current map.

Currently, the style for the USA States layer is stored inside the QGIS project file (.qgs). If you start a new QGIS project, and add the same USA States layer to the new project, the color choices you made in Task 1 and the label choices you made in Task 2 will not transfer over—styles are not stored inside of the GIS data (shapefile in this case). In order for the style to be used in other QGIS projects, or to apply the style to other layers, it must first be saved out to a separate file. When saved to the style file, you can transfer it along with the GIS dataset that it will be applied to, or apply its saved style to a different GIS dataset.

To preserve our color and label choices for use later, let's save our style as a QGIS Layer Style File (.qml).

1. Open the Style properties for the USA States Area layer.

2. In the lower-left corner, click Style | Save Style | QGIS Layer Style File from dropdown button. This will open the Save layer properties as style file dialog box.

3. Name the file USA States Colors.qml in your exercise directory.

4. Click Save to save the style file to disk.

The style has now been saved to disk. Let us tempt fate and change the style of the layer, then load our newly saved style to see how it works.

5. Change the color ramp to any other color ramp.

6. Click the Delete All button, followed by the Classify button. This will change the colors of the states.

7. Click Apply to see the change on the map. We have now changed our style.

8. We will now load our saved style to restore the previous color choices. Click Style | Load Style from the Style button in the lower-left corner, and open the USA States Colors.qml file. This changes the colors of the states back to our previously set colors.

9. Click Apply to see the change on the map. Voilà! The style has been reapplied.

10. Save your QGIS project.

1.6   Task 4 Designing the Alaska Map

In this task, you will load and stylize the data that will be used to design a map of the state of Alaska. As we have already saved a QGIS Layer Style File, we will load that style for Alaska to keep a consistent feel in colors and line thickness between the two maps.

1. In QGIS Desktop, start a new project by clicking Project | New.

2. Add USA States Area.shp to the project.

3. Zoom in close to Alaska.

4. Open 'USA States Area' layer properties and click the Style tab.

5. Click Style | Load Style and open USA States Colors.qml. This will load the style we created in Task 1 and Task 2, and saved in Task 3.

6. Click OK to apply the style to the map.

Alaska is a bright red, and should be toned down or changed to a different color.

7. Change the color of Alaska to another complementary color. The figure below shows an example color choice for Alaska.

8. Save the current style as a QGIS Layer Style File and replace the existing USA States Colors.qml file. By overwriting this style file, it stores the new color of Alaska so we don't have to set it again.

9. We are finished designing the Alaska map for now. Save your QGIS Project as `Alaska.qgs` in your exercise folder by clicking Project | Save.

1.7   Task 5 Designing the Hawaii Map

In this task, you will load and stylize the data that will be used to design a map of the state of Hawaii. As we have already saved a QGIS Layer Style File, we will load that style for Hawaii to keep a consistent feel in colors and line thickness between the two maps.

1. In QGIS Desktop, start a new project by clicking Project | New.

2. Add `USA States Area.shp` to the project.

3. Zoom in close to Hawaii.

4. Open 'USA States Area' layer properties and click Style tab.

5. Click Style | Load Style and open `USA States Colors.qml`. This will load the style we created in Task 1 and Task 2, and saved in Task 3.

6. Click OK to apply the style to the map. Hawaii should look similar to the figure below.

7. We are done designing the Hawaii map for now. Save your QGIS Project as `Hawaii.qgs` in your exercise folder by clicking Project | Save.

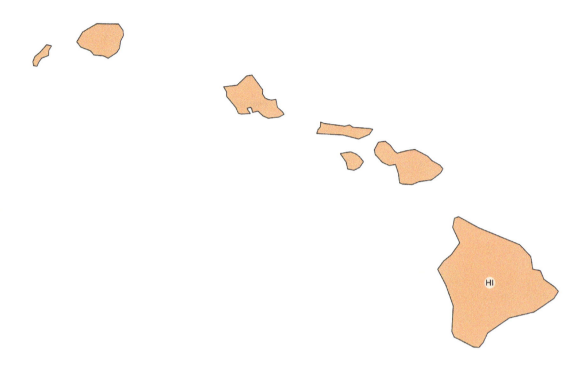

1.8   Conclusion

In this exercise, you have learned how to apply style properties to geometry and apply styles to labels. While the map still has some work to be completed, the basic design structure has begun to be built. In Exercise 2, on the facing page we will focus on map projections and coordinate systems and which one(s) would be most appropriate for mapping the United States. In Exercise 3, on page 315, you will learn how to add the supporting map elements (e.g. legend, title, metadata) and create the final map layout.

1.9   Discussion Questions

1. Thinking about the way in which colors were chosen for the map, are you surprised that the exercise asked you to change colors of selected states? Reflect on whether you tend to accept the default behavior of mapping software and whether that default behavior is really the best choice.

2. Save the three QGIS Projects (Lower 48, Alaska, Hawaii) as JPGs for submission. To export the map as a JPG, click Project | Save as Image. Submit these three images for grading.

1.10   Challenge: Design a Colorful State Map (optional)

Now that you have designed a map at a national level, your next challenge is to choose a state that contains multiple smaller administrative units (e.g. county, parish) and make a colorful map of that state. In the map, choose a pleasing color scheme, and label all counties and the state. Additionally, make the state outline thicker than the county outlines. This may require some creative thinking on your part.

To accomplish this challenge, the 2013 TIGER County boundaries have been placed in the exercise directory. The county shapefile is named US Counties 2013 - TIGER.shp.

Exercise 2

Exploring Coordinate Systems and Map Projections

Objective – Explore and Understand Coordinate Systems and Map Projections

2.1 Introduction

In this exercise, you'll explore the effects of various map projections on the characteristics of a map using QGIS.

This exercise will focus primarily on shape and area distortions and will examine projections useful for mapping on the global scale as well as on the national and state level.

This exercise includes the following tasks:

- Task 1 – Setting Map Projections and Coordinate Systems in QGIS Desktop
- Task 2 – Exploring World Map Projections
- Task 3 – Exploring National Map Projections
- Task 4 – Exploring State Map Projections
- Task 5 – Select an Appropriate Map Projection for Colorful Map of the USA
- Task 6 - Exploring the Universal Transverse Mercator (UTM) Coordinate System

2.2 Objective: Explore and Understand Map Projections and Coordinate Systems

The map projection is a fundamental part of the mapping process, and provides the backbone, or framework, for the map. It is important for the GIS Specialist to understand the qualities of the mapped region that are preserved by a given projection, and the qualities that will be distorted or skewed. Additionally, for cartographers, selection of an appropriate map projection is a crucial part of the map design process. This is because we are all used to seeing different parts of the world mapped using specific standard projections that make these areas "look right."

The transformation of the ellipsoid shape of the earth onto a two-dimensional surface cannot be accomplished without some element of distortion, through shearing, tearing, or compression. For mapping small Earth areas (large-scale mapping), projection is not a major issue, but as the scale becomes smaller, as in the mapping of continents or subcontinents, distortion becomes a significant factor. Distortion of area, shape, distance, and direction become properties to consider. It is impossible for one projection to maintain all of these properties simultaneously.

Projections are classified according to the properties they preserve. Equal-area (or equivalent) maps, for example, preserve area relationships, but tend to lose conformality (preservation of shape). Conformal projections, on the other hand, maintain shape over small areas but produce areal distortion. In thematic mapping, it is important to maintain correct area properties. Therefore, shape is at times compromised through the choice of an equivalent projection. For small-scale maps, in fact, conformality cannot be maintained over the entire area; rather, the projection may preserve shape best along a standard line, with shape distortion increasing with distance from the line. Another property to consider is distance preservation (equidistance), which preserves distance measurements along great circle arcs. Finally, direction preservation (azimuthality) maintains correct direction from one central point to all other points.

There are hundreds of possible projections from which to choose. Some distort less in certain ways than others. It is up to the map designer to select the projection that produces the least amount of unwanted distortion. Many computer mapping software packages now allow the GIS specialist to easily switch between various projections, allowing the choice of the one most appropriate. In the selection of a projection, several key elements must be considered:

- Projection properties - Are the properties of the projection suitable to the map's purpose? Considering the properties of shape, distance, direction, and area, which ones must be preserved, and which can be sacrificed? Or is compromise of all four the best choice?

- Deformational patterns - Is the amount of deformation acceptable?

- Projection center - Can the projection be centered easily on the area being mapped?

- Familiarity - Is the appearance of the map recognizable to the map reader or will it detract from the map's purpose?

2.3   Task 1 - Setting Map Projections and Coordinate Systems in QGIS

In this task, you will explore the effects of various projections on the characteristics of a map. We will focus primarily on shape and area distortions. We will examine projections useful for mapping on the global scale.

In Exercise 2 you added data to QGIS Desktop. Here you will open an existing QGIS project.

1. Open QGIS Desktop.
2. In QGIS Desktop, open the project, `World View.qgs` by clicking Project | Open. You should see the map shown in the figure below.

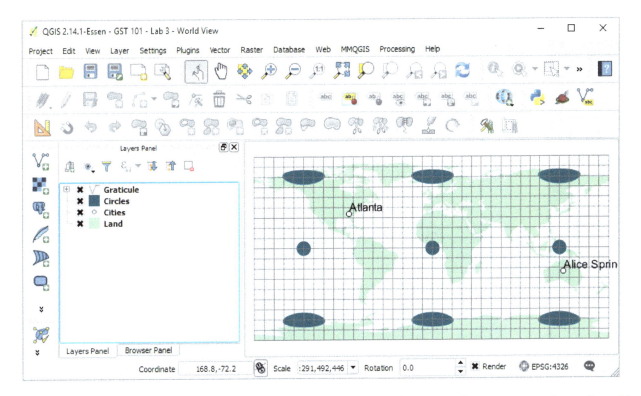

`WorldView.qgs` is a QGIS project file. A project file contains information about a map such as: list of layers, coordinate system, symbols, labels, custom tools, map elements, and much more.

An individual GIS layer in the Layers Panel is known as a theme. In the project file, there are two polygon themes, Circles and Land, a point theme, Cities, and a line theme, Graticule. If these circles were displayed on a globe they would be perfect circles. Here you can begin to visualize the distortion in the projection by the distortion in the Circles theme. On this map, a projection has not been chosen in QGIS. The software is using latitude and longitude measured in geodetic decimal degrees, which displays a simple rectangular coordinate system in which the length of one degree of longitude is consistently equal to one degree of latitude. In QGIS, when a projection has not yet been selected, distance calculations remain true, since the software computes distance using the spherical coordinates of latitude and longitude along a great circle arc, just as if you were actually measuring at the Earth's surface. Although a projection has not yet been chosen by the user, the display is essentially a Plate Carrée projection. On a projection that preserves shape, the polygons on the Circles theme appear as true circles. In a Plate Carrée projection, linear scale, area, and shape are all distorted increasingly toward the poles as demonstrated with the Circles theme.

The circles will be used in this exercise for illustrating the areal and shape distortion that occurs with various projections. While this method does not actually quantify the distortion, as does Tissot's indicatrix[1], it does visually demonstrate the skewing, tearing, and shearing that occurs with certain projections.

First we will examine the map units and distance units set for this "unprojected" map.

3. From the menu bar, select Project | Project Properties.

4. Click the CRS tab to view the Coordinate Reference System information for the project file (shown in figure below).

---

[1] https://en.wikipedia.org/wiki/Tissot%27s_indicatrix

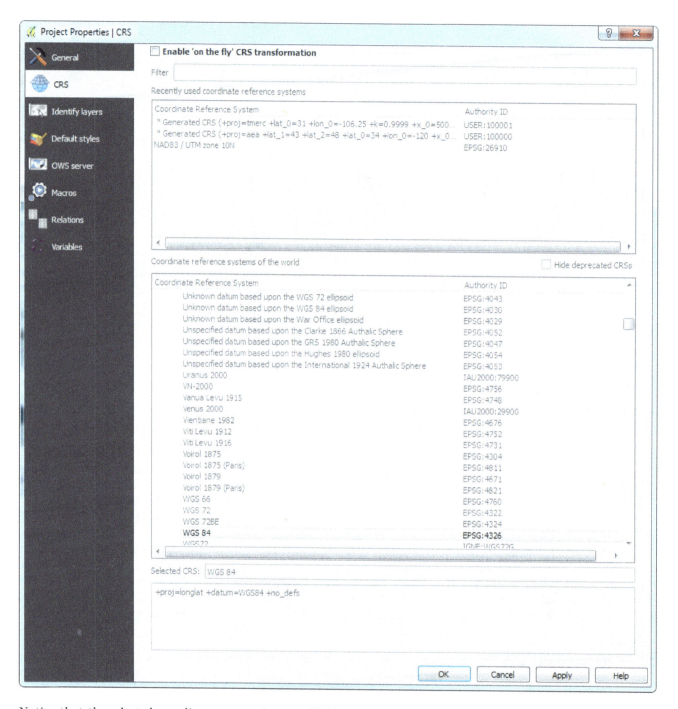

Notice that the selected coordinate system is set to WGS 84, which is an unprojected coordinate system.

5. Click Cancel to close the Project Properties dialog box.

Now we will do some distance measurements on this map for later comparison to maps in which a projection is set.

6. Click on the Measure Line tool, ▭ ▾ , on the Attributes toolbar. The Measure box will appear (figure below).

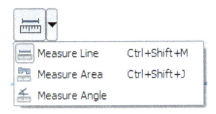

7. Click on the point for Atlanta, in the United States.

8. Move the cursor to the point for Alice Springs, Australia, then right-click to end the line. The distance between Atlanta and Alice Springs will be displayed in metric in the Measure box (Figure below).

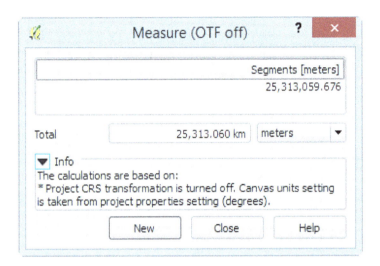

The measured distance is about 25,300 kilometers (your distance will vary slightly). This is not the actual distance between Atlanta and Alice Springs. Since on the fly CRS transformation is turned off, QGIS measures directly between Atlanta and Alice Springs (along your measure line) heading east from Atlanta. What it should do is measure to Alice Springs by heading west from Atlanta instead of east, since heading west is a shorter distance. However, QGIS does not know that the "World is round," so-to-speak, since on-the-fly transformation (OTF) is turned off. With OTF turned on, it treats the coordinate system as a selected world-based coordinate system. This view does not maintain spherical distance measurements, and distorts shape, direction and area.

We need to tell QGIS that we are, in fact, working with a world-based coordinate system and wish to measure on a round world.

9. From the menu bar, select Project | Project Properties.

10. Click on the CRS tab.

11. Check the Enable 'on the fly' CRS transformation option.

12. Select the WGS 84 coordinate system from the list of Coordinate reference systems of the world (figure below).

Coordinate reference systems of the world

Coordinate Reference System	Authority ID
WGS 72	EPSG:4322
WGS 72BE	EPSG:4324
WGS 84	EPSG:4326
WGS72	IGNF:WGS72G

13. Click OK to view the map.

14. Using the Measure tool, measure the distance between Atlanta and Alice Springs again (figure below).

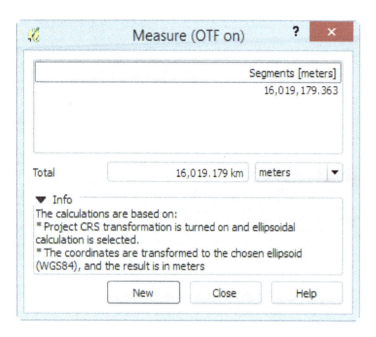

The measured distance is about 16,000 kilometers (your distance will vary slightly). This is the actual distance between Atlanta and Alice Springs. This view maintains spherical distance measurements, but distorts shape, direction, and area.

Next we will change the projection on this view to the Mercator projection.

15. Open the Project Properties and select the CRS tab.

16. In the Filter box, type in 3395, which is the EPSG code for the WGS 84 / World Mercator projected coordinate system. This filters the long list of Coordinate Reference Systems so we can easily find the one we are searching for.

EPSG Codes are unique codes for each projection/coordinate system. To learn more about EPSG codes, visit http://www.epsg.org/.

17. Select WGS 84 / World Mercator from the filtered Coordinate Reference System list (figure below).

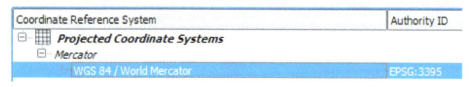

18. Click OK to view the map. You should see the map shown in the figure below.

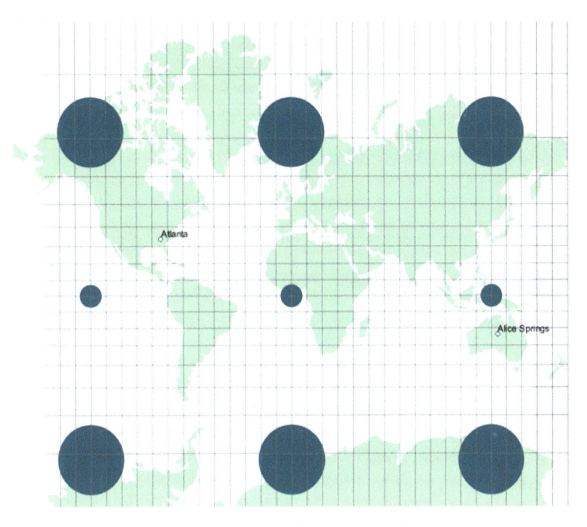

The Mercator projection, a conformal projection (except at the poles), has straight meridians and parallels that intersect at right angles. Scale is truest along the equator, and becomes more distorted at higher latitudes, as evidenced by the increasing size of the circles. The Mercator projection was designed for marine navigation and gives all straight lines on the map as lines of constant compass bearing. For global scale thematic maps, however, the Mercator has too much areal distortion for accurate use.

The Mercator is best for larger scale projections of areas at low latitude. Small-scale maps have much distortion of area and distance.

The Mercator map is much less desirable for mapping continents than other projections as it has significant distortion and can promote geographical misconceptions. In general, rectangular maps are not recommended for use in mapping the world. Equivalency (the property of equal area) and conformality are better preserved using non-rectangular maps. Task 2 will examine a map projection more suitable for mapping the world.

Keep the `World View` QGIS project open, it will be used in Task 2 as well.

2.4 Task 2 - Exploring World Map Projections

We will examine a map projection more suitable for mapping the entire world: the Eckert IV projection. This projection is an equal-area pseudocylindrical map projection with straight parallel latitude lines and equally spaced meridians.

Let's change the projection to Eckert IV:

1. Open the Project Properties and select the CRS tab.

2. In the Filter box, type in Eckert. This filters the long list of Coordinate Reference Systems so we can easily find the one we are searching for by name.

3. Select Eckert IV/World_Eckert_IV (EPSG:54012) from the filtered Coordinate Reference System list.

4. Click OK to view the map. You should see the map shown in the figure below.

   - *Note:* Due to occasional rendering issues, the projected map may look "blocky". If this happens, either zooming in, or temporarily switching the CRS to another CRS and back will sometimes fix the issue.

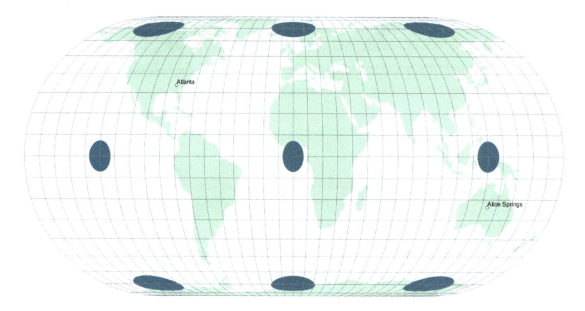

The Eckert IV is useful for world maps as it is equal-area and is pleasing to the eye. Its standard parallels are at 40° 30'N and 40° 30'S. This map is only distortion free where the standard parallels intersect the central meridian.

We will see how the distance property fares.

5. Using the Measure tool, measure the distance from Atlanta to Alice Springs.

The distance measures approximately 20,848 kilometers. The Eckert IV is therefore not an equidistant projection and should not be used for distance measurement.

2.5 Task 3 - Exploring National Map Projections

Projections suitable for mapping the world are not necessarily the best for mapping smaller areas, such as continents or countries. When mapping at such a scale in the mid-latitudes it is important to use a projection that centers on the area being mapped and has a standard line, or lines, passing through the area being mapped.

In this task, we will look at a map of the contiguous United States using a few different projections.

1. In QGIS Desktop, open the Country View.qgs project (figure below) by clicking Project | Open.

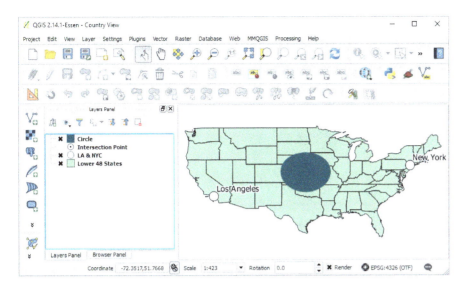

Country View.qgs is an unprojected map of the lower 48 states comprised of three themes: United States, LA & NYC, and Circle (centered on -97.50, 39.00). You can see it does not look quite right given the default projection. The circle shows some obvious skewing.

The distance property is more difficult to judge. The known distance between Los Angeles and New York is approximately 3,962 kilometers. We can see how the unprojected map controls distance distortion.

2. As before, use the Measure tool to measure the distance between Los Angeles and New York City in kilometers.

If OTF is off, the distance in the unprojected view returns an answer 44.8 meters! If you receive this short distance, enable on-the-fly CRS transformation so the correct distance will be returned.

3. From the menu bar, select Project | Project Properties.

4. Click on the CRS tab.

5. Check the Enable 'on the fly' CRS transformation option.

6. Select the WGS 84 coordinate system from the list of Coordinate reference systems of the world (figure below).

7. Click OK to view the map.

8. You may need to right click on the Lower 48 States and choose Zoom to Layer Extent.

9. Measure the distance between Los Angeles and New York again.

The measurement will now be virtually the same as the actual distance of 3,962 kilometers. Remember, for this projection in QGIS, coordinates are treated as spherical latitude and longitude. Distance is calculated as if along a great circle arc and so the actual ground distance is preserved. Shape and areal properties, however, are distorted.

Now we will project the data using the Eckert IV projection. The Eckert IV did a nice job with the whole world, but we will see how it fares with a single mid-latitude country.

10. Open the Project Properties, select the CRS tab, and choose World_Eckert_IV from the recently used coordinate reference systems box.

11. Click OK to set the CRS. You may need to zoom full ⬚ to see the lower 48 states (figure below).

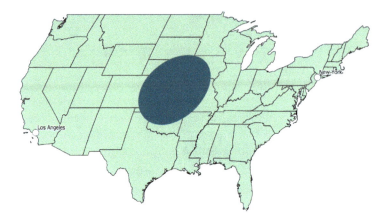

There clearly is a great deal of distortion using this projection, most obviously the shearing. Part of the problem lies in the fact that this projection is centered at 0 degrees longitude. We can center the projection on the United States by creating a custom CRS based on the World_Eckert_IV projection.

12. Click Settings | Custom CRS... from the menu bar. This will open the Custom Coordinate Reference System Definition dialog box.

13. Click the Copy existing CRS button ▤ to open the Coordinate Reference System Selector.

14. Select World_Eckert_IV from the recently used list. Make sure that the CRS parameters show at the bottom of the selector. If not, temporarily select a different CRS, then select World_Eckert_IV again (see figure below).

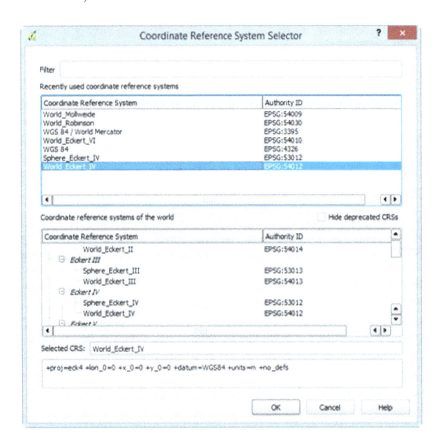

15. Click OK to return to the Custom CRS Definition dialog. The Parameters will now be filled with the copied CRS parameters (shown in figure below).

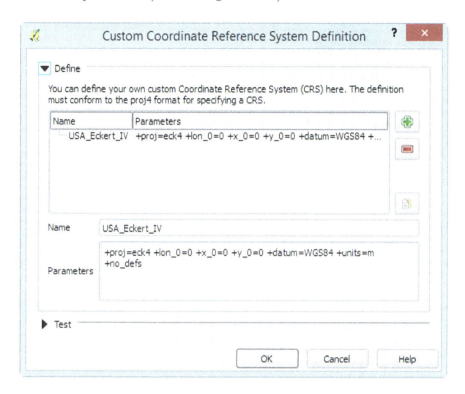

We need to change the central meridian so that the projection is centered at -96.000 degrees longitude instead of 0.000. This will center the projection down the middle of the country.

16. To accomplish this, replace `lon_0=0` with `lon_0=-96.0` (essentially replacing the central meridian of 0 with -96.0). The CRS Parameters should now look like:

```
+proj=eck4 +lon_0=-96.0 +x_0=0 +y_0=0 +datum=WGS84 +units=m +no_defs
```

17. In the Name box, enter USA_Eckert_IV. This will serve as a name of our new Custom CRS.

18. Click OK.

Our custom CRS is now added to QGIS Desktop for us to use. We can then choose our USA_Eckert_IV projection to see how it projects our map.

19. Open the Project Properties, select the CRS tab.

20. In the Coordinate reference systems of the world list, scroll all the way to the bottom until you see
    ⊞··👤 **User Defined Coordinate Systems**

21. Expand the User Defined Coordinate Systems entry.

22. Choose USA_Eckert_IV.

23. Click OK to set the CRS. You may need to zoom full 🧩 to see the lower 48 states (figure below).

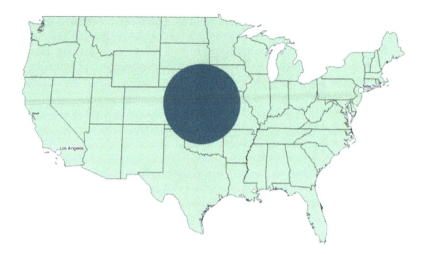

This is a distinct improvement in shape, but there is still some skewing. The Eckert IV projection is primarily used for mapping the entire world. For mapping large countries, at mid-latitudes, such as the United States, other projections are more appropriate.

The Lambert azimuthal, Albers equal-area, Bonne equal-area, and Lambert conformal conic projections are examples of suitable projections for mapping the entire U.S.

Because it has two standard parallels, the Albers equal-area projection is particularly good for larger countries with a significant east-west extent. We can also try Albers on our map.

24. Once again, open the Project Properties, select the CRS tab, and choose USA_Contiguous_Albers_Equal_Area_Co (EPSG: 102003) as the CRS.

25. Click OK to set the CRS. You may need to zoom full to see the lower 48 states (figure below).

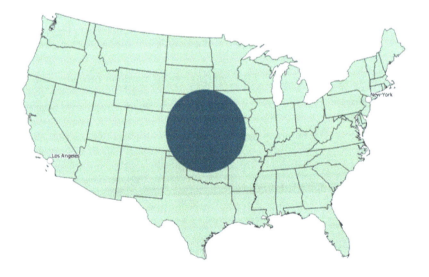

The Albers conic projection has low scale distortion for an area the size of the U.S. As the area being mapped decreases in size, distortion is less of an issue.

We will try another map projection to see what changes.

26. Open the Project Properties, select the CRS tab, and choose USA_Contiguous_Lambert_Conformal_Conic (EPSG: 102004) as the CRS.

27. Click OK to set the CRS. You may need to zoom full to see the lower 48 states.

Not too much changed between Albers and Lambert. They are both similar map projections. Lambert does have more options in its CRS parameters list, so let us examine the custom options so we can more fully understand what options can be set when creating a custom CRS.

28. Click Settings | Custom CRS... from the menu bar. This will open the Custom Corodinate Reference System Definition dialog box.

29. Click the Add new CRS button ![plus icon] .

30. Click the Copy existing CRS button ![copy icon] to open the Coordinate Reference System Selector.

31. Select USA_Contiguous_Lambert_Conformal_Conic from the recently used list. Make sure that the CRS parameters show at the bottom of the selector. If not, temporarily select a different CRS, then select USA_Contiguous_Lambert_Conformal_Conic again.

32. Click OK to copy the parameters.

33. Change the Name to Modified_USA_Contiguous_Lambert_Conformal_Conic. Your Custom CRS Parameters should look like the figure below.

Name	Modified_USA_Contiguous_Lambert_Conformal_Conic
Parameters	+proj=lcc +lat_1=33 +lat_2=45 +lat_0=39 +lon_0=-96 +x_0=0 +y_0=0 +datum=NAD83 +units=m +no_defs

34. Click on Project | Project Properties and change the maps projection to the newly created Modified_USA_Contiguous_Lambert_Conformal_Conic

There are many ways that we can customize this CRS. You can customize one of the projection selections so that it is centered on the area in question, in this case the United States, simply by redefining the particular cartographic settings, such as the central meridians, standard parallel(s), reference latitude, or false eastings and northings. The choice of parameters varies depending on which projection is being used.

We need to briefly define these terms and where they can be modified in the CRS Parameters. Each term will be followed by the parameter in the CRS Parameters inside of parenthesis.

Note: Proj.4 is another FOSS4G project used by QGIS, like OGR and GDAL. This project is for managing coordinate systems and projections. For a detailed user manual for the Proj.4 format used to specify the CRS Parameters in QGIS, visit

ftp://ftp.remotesensing.org/proj/OF90-284.pdf

- False easting (x_0) – in QGIS, the x-coordinate value for the x-origin. For example, if the central meridian for your projected map is -96.00, and the false easting is set to 0.00, then all locations along that meridian are assigned a value of 0.00. All locations to the west of the central meridian (x-origin) are assigned a negative value, and all locations to the east of the central meridian are assigned a positive value, as in a typical Cartesian plane.

- False northing (y_0) – in QGIS, the y-coordinate value for the y-origin. For example, if the reference latitude for a conic projection is 37.00, then all locations along that parallel are assigned a value of 0.00. All locations to the south of the reference latitude (y-origin) are assigned a negative value, and all locations to the north of the reference latitude are assigned a positive value, as in a typical Cartesian plane.

- Central meridian (lon_0) – the longitude on which a map is centered (x-origin).

- Standard parallel(s) (lat_1, lat_2) – the latitude on which a map is centered (sometimes the y-origin), or for conic projections, the parallels along which the cone touches the earth.

- Latitude of Origin (lat_0) – the latitude on which a map is centered (y-origin).

For now, we will leave the default settings for the central meridian, latitude of origin, standard parallels, and false easting and northing. In setting map projections, the choice of spheroid, or reference ellipsoid, is also an important consideration. In this example, the spheroid is currently set to GRS_1980.

- Spheroid (ellps) – a model of the earth's shape used in transforming a projection. The reference spheroid, or ellipsoid, is generated by choosing the lengths of the major and minor axes that best fit those of the real earth. Many such models are appropriate for different locations on the earth.

Closely related to the concept of the spheroid is the concept of the datum. The North American Datum of 1927 (NAD27) uses the Clarke 1866 reference ellipsoid, whereas the North American Datum of 1983 (NAD83) uses the Geodetic Reference System (GRS) 1980 reference ellipsoid.

- Datum (datum) – selecting and orienting a specific spheroid to use for a location.

- Coordinate Units (units) – Coordinate Units are used to define distances when setting x and y coordinates.

Now we can see the effect of the 0.00 settings for the false easting and northing. The x-origin is approximately -95.85 and the y-origin is approximately 37.16.

35. In the Layers panel, turn off the Circle layer to see southeastern Kansas, the location where the x and y origins intersect.

36. Turn on the Intersection Point layer to see where the x and y origins intersect.

In the figure below, a white circle with a centered, black dot illustrates the intersection of the x and y origins. At this intersection in the view, the x and y coordinates are 0.00, 0.00. As you move to the northeast, both the x and y coordinates are positive.

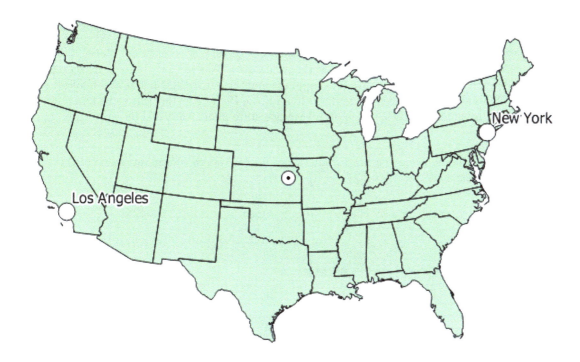

You can view the coordinates of your mouse cursor in the bottom-right corner of QGIS. The figure below shows an example.

The values of the x and y coordinates are expressed in meters from the origin. As you move to the southwest of the intersection, the x and y coordinates are both negative. Experiment with the changing coordinate values and other projections on your own.

The conic projections function quite well for mapping the larger states in the U.S. In terms of thematic mapping, it is important that maps at this scale are equal-area. Any other properties important to the particular map should also be considered when selecting a proper projection. We will now examine projections and grid systems for large-scale maps, such as for small states, counties, or local regions.

2.6 Task 4 - Exploring State Map Projections

The State Plane Coordinate System (SPCS) was developed to provide a simple rectangular coordinate system for large scale mapping use (i.e. small areas of the earth), such as surveying and engineering projects.

The SPCS is a series of separate coordinate systems, each covering either an entire state, or a portion of a state. The SPCS is only used in the United States of America and, therefore, it is not appropriate to use SPCS for other countries or regions of the World. SPCS is popular due to its high accuracy in large-scale mapping because of the relatively small size of each SPCS zone. The SPCS is composed of 120 zones which follow county boundaries (except in Alaska) and often divides a state into multiple zones. There are two main projections used with the SPCS. States with a north-south axis are mapped using the Transverse Mercator projection, and designate zones between a range of 'North' and 'South' (e.g. Minnesota North). States with an east-west axis are mapped with the Lambert Conformal projection and designate zones between a range of 'East' and 'West' (e.g. New Mexico Central).

The original state plane system, developed in the 1930s, was based on the North American Datum of 1927, with coordinates measured in feet. Today the state plane system is based on the North American Datum of 1983, and coordinates are in meters.

The coordinate grids cover small areas with minimal areal or distance distortion. For small states, one grid is sufficient, while for larger states, more are required to cover the entire area. Alaska, for example, needs ten grids. The state plane system, therefore, is only appropriate for mapping small Earth areas, such as the smallest states, city grids, or local regions. Your study area will need to fit within a State Plane Zone for this to be an appropriate choice of coordinate system. The smallest states, which only have one state plane zone, can be represented in their entirety using the SPCS.

Let's create a map display of Vermont, using the State Plane Coordinate System. Vermont is one of the smaller states and only has one state plane zone.

1. In QGIS, open the project, `Vermont.qgs` by clicking Project | Open.

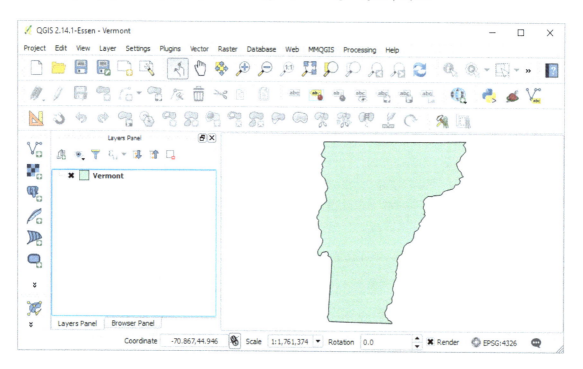

2. Open the Project Properties, then click on CRS tab.

Note that the projection selected is WGS 84. This is selected because the Vermont shapefile is the only layer, is projected in the WGS 84 coordinate system, and first added layer in the map, so QGIS sets the project's coordinate system to match. Also note that on the fly CRS transformation is not enabled, therefore, we are seeing Vermont in an unprojected state.

To make the map of Vermont in SPCS, we have two options:

- Enable 'on the fly' CRS transformation, and select NAD27 / Vermont coordinate system, EPSG: 32045.

- Project the Vermont shapefile in to NAD27 / Vermont and set the Project's coordinate system to match.

Enabling on the fly CRS transformation will allow us to work with data that are in different map projections in the same QGIS Project. However, sometimes it is best to project the data in to the coordinate system we wish to map at, since it will have the advantages of not requiring QGIS to calculate the transformation on the fly, and analysis operations will be more predictable and accurate.

So, let's project the Vermont shapefile into the NAD27 / Vermont coordinate system and set the Project coordinate system to match.

3. In the Layers panel, right-click on the Vermont layer and from the context menu choose Save As... (figure below). This will open the Save vector layer as... dialog box.

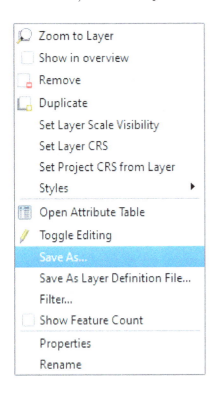

4. Set the following options to project the Vermont layer, save it to a new shapefile, and add it to the map (figure below shows correct options).

   a. Format: ESRI Shapefile

   b. Click Browse

   c. Find your Exercise 2 Data folder and save within that folder under the name Vermont_SPCS.shp

   d. CRS: NAD27 / Vermont (EPSG:32045)

   e. Check Add saved file to map.

   f. Your dialog should now look like the one in the figure below.

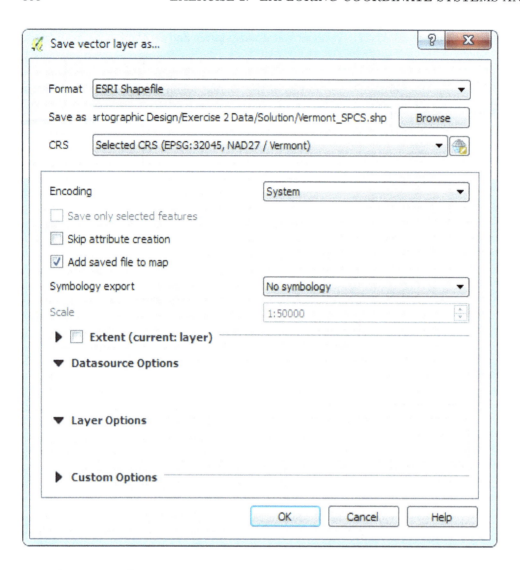

5. Click OK. QGIS will project the Vermont layer and add it to the map. It will look like the figure below, but the color of the newly-added Vermont layer may differ. Remember that styling is random on layers added to QGIS.

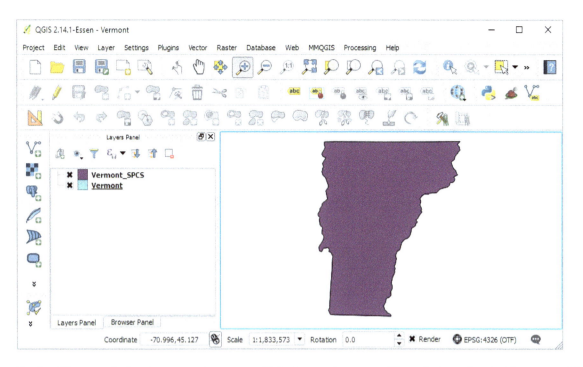

So far, Vermont looks the same, but you will find out why soon. First, let's make the Vermont_SPCS layer look the same as the Vermont layer.

6. Open the Project Properties, select the CRS tab.

Notice that on the fly CRS transformation is enabled (remember, it was not enabled before) and WGS 84 is the project's current CRS. This happened because QGIS realized that layers in the project had different CRS. With on the fly CRS transformation enabled, the two Vermont layers still display on top of each other. If on the fly CRS transformation was not enabled, the two Vermont layers would not display on top of each other or, even, on the same map at all! If you wish to modify the behavior of QGIS and its automatic management of on the fly CRS transformations, you can set the behavior options by clicking Settings | Options | CRS tab from the main QGIS menu bar.

Let us now change the project CRS to match our SPCS Vermont shapefile. First, we will set the style of the SPCS Vermont to match the WGS 84 Vermont.

7. Click OK to close the Project Properties.

8. Right-click on Vermont in the Layers panel, and select Styles | Copy Style. This copies the style definition of this layer.

9. Right-click on Vermont_SPCS in the table of contents and select Styles | Paste Style. This sets the style of this layer based on the previously copied style.

10. Right-click on Vermont_SPCS and choose Set Project CRS from Layer from the context menu.

You should now see that Vermont got 'skinnier' as it is not being displayed in the NAD27 / Vermont SPCS and not WGS 84.

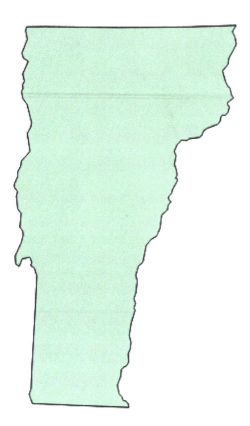

11. Open the Project Properties, select the CRS tab. Notice that on the fly CRS transformation is still enabled, but now NAD27 / Vermont is now the selected CRS.

Look at the Selected CRS Parameters at the bottom of the properties window (shown in figure below). Note that the projection used is Transverse Mercator (`proj=tmerc`) and the scale factor is (k=0.999964286). The spheroid is Clarke 1866, however this is not shown in the CRS Parameters because the default spheroid is Clarke 1866 if not specified (otherwise, it would be specified as `ellps=clrk66`). The central meridian is -72.5 (`lon_0=-72.5`), which runs through the center of the state. The reference latitude, or y-origin, is 42.5 (`lat_0=42.5`), which is just south of Vermont. The false easting is set to 152,400.30480 meters (`x_0=152400.3048006096`), which is equivalent to 500,000 feet. The false northing is set to 0.00 (`y_0=0`). So, the false origin will be to the west (500,000 feet west of -72.5) and south (42.5) of the state of Vermont.

Selected CRS: NAD27 / Vermont

```
+proj=tmerc +lat_0=42.5 +lon_0=-72.5 +k=0.999964286 +x_0=152400.3048006096 +y_0=0 +datum=NAD27
+units=us-ft +no_defs
```

12. Click OK to close the Project Properties.

GIS layers can be removed from the Layers panel (and map window) as easily as they were added. For example, we do not need the original Vermont layer. We can just work with the version of Vermont in SPCS. To remove a layer simply right click on it within the Layers panel and choose Remove from the context menu. A confirmation dialog will appear. Click the OK button to confirm the removal of the layer.

13. Remove Vermont from the Layers panel (not Vermont_SPCS!).

Scroll around the state and notice the changing coordinates. If you have a USGS topographic map of any part of Vermont, based on NAD27, the coordinates displayed here will match the UTM coordinates shown on the hardcopy map.

2.7 Task 5 Select an Appropriate Map Projection for Colorful Map of the USA

Now that you know how to select and modify map projections in QGIS, you will use what you learned to choose the best projection for the map you started in Exercise 1, on page 277 (the Colorful Map of the USA).

The Albers Equal Area Conic projection has low scale distortion for an area the size of the U.S., Alaska, and Hawaii, and holds relative sizes true. As this is a popular map projection for mapping the United States, there are three commonly-used Albers Equal Area Conic map projections: one for the contiguous United States, one for Alaska, and one for Hawaii. We will now project our three maps in to their respective map projection.

1. Open the `Lower 48 States.qgs` project file that you created in Exercise 1, Task 1.
2. Open the Layer Properties for the 'USA States Area' layer.
3. Select the General tab.

Note that the coordinate system of the shapefile is EPSG:4326, WGS 84; an unsuitable coordinate system for mapping. We have two options for changing the display of the map: 1) enable on the fly CRS transformation and set the CRS to the Albers projection, or, 2) project the shapefile to the Albers CRS and save it as a new shapefile. While both methods are reasonable, it is best to have the data projected to the coordinate system/map projection that you will be working in. Therefore, we will project this shapfile to the EPSG:102003 – USA Contiguous Albers Equal Area Conic map projection.

4. Click OK to close the Layer Properties.
5. Right-click on 'USA States Area' in the Layers panel then choose Save As.... This will open the Save vector layer as... dialog.
6. Set the following options (shown in the figure below):
   - Format: ESRI Shapefile
   - Save as:USA States Area - Albers Equal Area Conic.shp
   - CRS: EPSG: 102003 - USA_Contiguous_Albers_Equal_Area_Conic
   - Check Add saved file to map

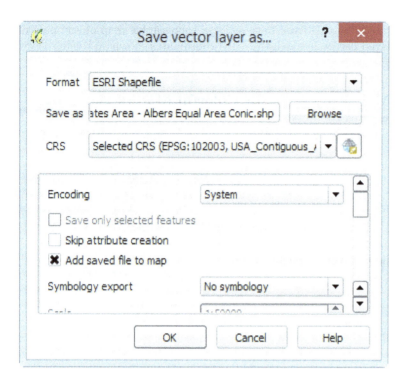

7. Click OK to save the new shapefile. The shapefile will be added as a new layer to the map.

8. Remove the USA States Area layer with the WGS 84 CRS.

9. Load the `USA States Color.qml` QGIS Layer Style File to apply the color and labels to the newly created layer.

10. Right-click on the USA States Area layer and then choose Set Project CRS from Layer. Your map should now look similar to the figure below.

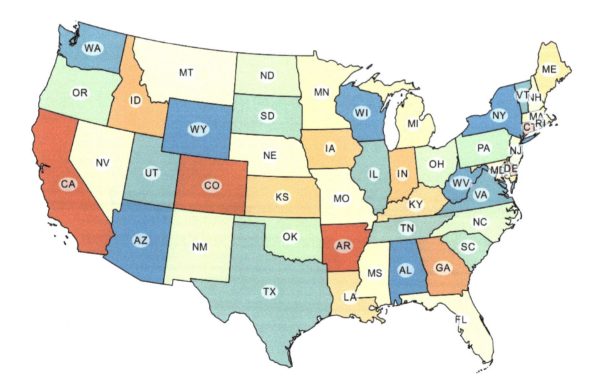

11. Save your QGIS Project. You will use this project file in Exercise 3.

12. Repeat the previous steps for **Alaska.qgs**. Set the CRS of both the layer and project to EPSG:102006 – Alaska Albers Equal Area Conic. Save the projected shapefile to a new file (do not overwrite the Lower 48 shapefile). Save the project file when done.

13. Repeat the previous steps for **Hawaii.qgs**. Set the CRS of both the layer and project to EPSG:102007 – Hawaii Albers Equal Area Conic. Save the projected shapefile to a new file (do not overwrite the Lower 48 shapefile). Save the project file when done.

2.8 Task 6 Exploring the Universal Transverse Mercator (UTM) Coordinate System

The Universal Transverse Mercator (UTM) grid (shown in the figure below) is a plane coordinate system that spans almost the entire globe. It is probably the best known plane coordinate system of international scope. For the UTM system, the globe is divided into sixty zones, each comprised of six degrees of longitude. Each zone has its own central meridian. The limits of each zone are 84 degrees north and 80 degrees south. UTM uses the Transverse Mercator projection. The zones are numbered 1 to 60, where zone 1 begins at -180° longitude and zones increase heading east back to +180° where zone 60 ends.

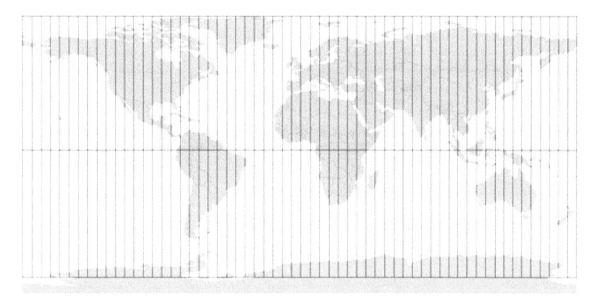

1. There are separate versions of both the Country View and World View QGIS project files with a UTM Zone polygon theme. In each QGIS project document, the UTM theme is labeled with the UTM zones so you can see what zones cover your part of the country.

2. These QGIS project documents are named **World View UTM.qgs** and **Country View UTM.qgs**

3. Using what you have learned in this exercise, experiment with the putting these UTM World and Country View maps into the UTM system.

4. Open up one of these projects. (for example: Project | Open | Country View UTM.qgs)

5. Once the map opens, from the Project menu choose Project Properties and open the CRS tab.

6. Via the Filter, search for UTM. Choose a UTM zone in your part of the country to put the map into. There are UTM definitions with different datums. Choose one from the NAD83 UTM zone projection series.

Note: Many U.S. federal agencies use this system, such as the U.S. Forest Service and the U.S. Bureau of Land Management. Like the State Plane Coordinate System, it is important that your study area fit within a UTM zone.

For more information on the UTM Coordinate system, read the USGS Fact Sheet 077-01, available at http://pubs.usgs.gov/fs/2001/0077/report.pdf

2.9 Conclusion

In this exercise, you have explored coordinate systems and map projections. Each map projection distorts the earth differently. You are able to modify the map projections provided in QGIS to suit your mapping needs. It is important that you set the correct map projection for each data layer, and for the project.

When you import spatial data into QGIS, you must know the projection, if any, the grid system, and the datum, of your data. Mostly you will find the data in decimal degrees, that is, latitude and longitude coordinates. Base maps with underlying coordinates that are geodetic decimal degrees are the most versatile when constructing a map database. It is important that if you plan on doing any spatial analysis with your data, that you first project the data into the same coordinate system to get maximum accuracy.

2.10 Discussion Questions

1. Based on the world map projections covered in this exercise, which industries would best be served by each projection (provide two examples)? Does the entire industry need to agree on a single one? What problems could arise from the use of different projections?

2. Can your GIS data be in a different Coordinate Reference System than your QGIS project? Explain.

3. What UTM zone does Nevada fall into?

4. Inspect the CRS Parameters for the three Exercise 1 maps (`Lower 48.qgs`, `Alaska.qgs`, `Hawaii.qgs`). List the two standard parallels for each map projection. Explain why you think the standard parallels were placed where they were.

Exercise 3

Map Elements and Design

Objective - Add map elements QGIS and design a layout in Inkscape to complete the colorful map of the United States of America

3.1 Introduction

In this exercise, you'll learn how to add map elements to a print composer in QGIS and use Inkscape v0.91 to complete the design of a colorful map of the United States of America (USA) that was started in Exercise 1. Inkscape is a free, open source vector graphics software useful for creating maps, among other products: https://inkscape.org/en/download/.

Note: If you have not yet completed Exercises 1 and 2, the `Exercise 3 Data` folder contains a copy of the completed data for you to use. It does not contain the data required to complete the challenge.

This exercise will focus primarily on adding map elements to the print composer and exporting those elements to be used in Inkscape for final map design. By the end of the exercise, you'll have a completed color map of the USA.

This exercise includes the following tasks:

- Task 1 – Composing and Exporting Maps

- Task 2 – Basics of Inkscape

- Task 3 – Importing and Arranging Maps in Inkscape

- Task 4 – Designing the Final Map Layout

- Task 5 - Challenge: Complete Challenge from exercise 1 (optional)

3.2 Objective: Utilize QGIS and Inkscape to Complete the Design of the Colorful Map of the United States of America

To achieve a properly designed map, the features on the map must be easily distinguishable, attractive to the map reader, and stand out from the grounds (supporting background information/data).

3.3 Task 1 Composing and Exporting Maps

In this task, you will use the QGIS Print Composer to prepare and export the Lower 48, Alaska, and Hawaii maps that you made and refined in Exercises 1 and 2. Print Composer can export the maps in a vector format which allows us to modify the individual features, if needed. After we export the maps, we will import them into Inkscape to compose our final map layout.

1. Open QGIS Desktop.
2. Open the `Lower 48 States.qgs` QGIS project file that you created in Exercises 1 and 2.
3. Click Project | New Print Composer from the main file menu.
4. Enter 'Lower 48 States' as the Composer title.
5. Click OK. This will set the title and open a new print composer window.

We need to take a moment to refresh our memory on the Print Composer. The figure below identifies the components of the Print Composer, along with brief descriptions of the components.

- **Composition View**: Displays the map composition.

- **Information Panels**: A collection of panels that allow you to set the properties of the composition, any selected map element, and atlas generation.

- **Command History**: A list of commands that you have performed on the composition.

- **Composer Items**: Commands that add, select, pan, and move map elements to the composition.

- **Composer**: Commands that save, create, print, and export the map composition.

- **Paper Navigation**: Tools to navigate around the virtual paper (on which you compose your map) in the Composition View.

- **Composer Items Actions**: Commands to group, lock, order, and align selected map elements.

- **Atlas**: Commands used to generate an atlas—will not be used in this exercise.

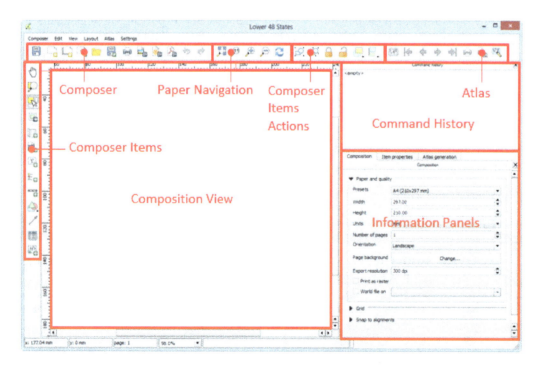

We are going to use the Print Composer to create a map of the Lower 48 States and then export it for use in Inkscape later. As we will be producing our final map on a 8.5 x 11 inch piece of paper, in landscape orientation, we will first set a few composition options, then add the map to the composition view.

6. Click the Composition tab in the Information Panels. Set the following options:

   - Presets: ANSI A (Letter; 8.5 x 11 in)
   - Orientation: Landscape

7. Click the Add new map button on the Composer Items toolbar. Drag a large box on the Composition View. This will create a map view showing the Lower 48 States.

8. To maximize the size of the map, set the position and size to use the entire 8.5x11 inches of the paper:

   - Click the Select/Move item tool  and select the map. You should have one item selected. You can check to see how many items are selected at the bottom of the composer window (shown in figure below).
   - Click the Item Properties tab in the Information Panels section of the Print Composer.
   - Expand the Position and size section.
   - Set the following properties:
     - X: 0 mm
     - Y: 0 mm
     - Width: 279.4 mm
     - Height: 215.9 mm

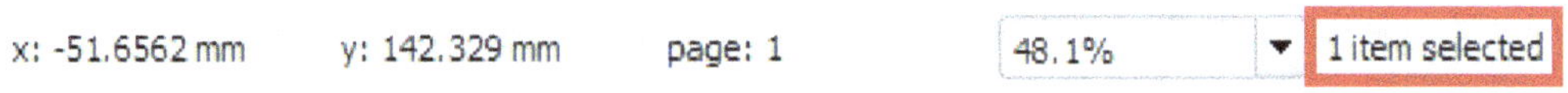

x: -51.6562 mm   y: 142.329 mm   page: 1   48.1%   ▼   1 item selected

These properties set the map's origin to 0,0, which is the top-left corner of the page. The width and height are set in millimeters. 279.4 mm and 215.9 mm are 11 inches by 8.5 inches respectively. By setting these values, we are maximizing the size of our map on the page.

9. Now we can re-synchronize the extent with what we had set in QGIS. Click the Item Properties tab in the Information Panels section of the Print Composer.

10. Click Set to map canvas extent. This will set the map extent to match the extent we have set in the QGIS project.

11. Still in the Item properties tab, set Scale to 18000000.

    - If your map is still not centered, either:
      - Change the map extent using the zoom and pan tools in QGIS
      - Use the Move item content tool on the Composer Items toolbar to move the map inside the Composition View.

With the map composed how we like it, we'll now prepare it for exporting to PDF format. PDF format is preferred for exporting vector data as the format preserves the vector data and does not rasterize it. This allows for vector editing without loss of quality of the data. To prepare for export, we'll set the export resolution and set the background as transparent.

12. Click the Composition tab in the Information Panels. Set the following options:

    - Page background: Change | Transparency: 100%
    - Export Resolution: 300 dpi

13. Select the map, then click the Item properties tab in the Information Panels. Set the following options:

    - Background: unchecked

14. Click Composer | Export as PDF...

15. Save the PDF as `Lower 48 States.pdf` in your exercise folder.

16. Using what you have learned in this Task, export Hawaii and Alaska as PDF files using similar settings as above. For each export, set the scale to show the states as large as possible without showing any part of the Lower 48.

3.4   Task 2 Basics of Inkscape

This task will teach you the basics of Inkscape, an open source vector-editing program that we'll use to complete our map design. The reason we are using Inkscape to complete the map design is because QGIS does not allow for multiple QGIS Project maps to be displayed on a single print composer (there is a work-around way to do this, but it is clunky and confusing). Exporting maps for final composition in a graphics-editing program is a common workflow for cartographers and so we are not working outside of what would be considered a normal workflow.

1. Open Inkscape.

The figure below shows the interface, and the following text describes the sections of the Inkscape interface.

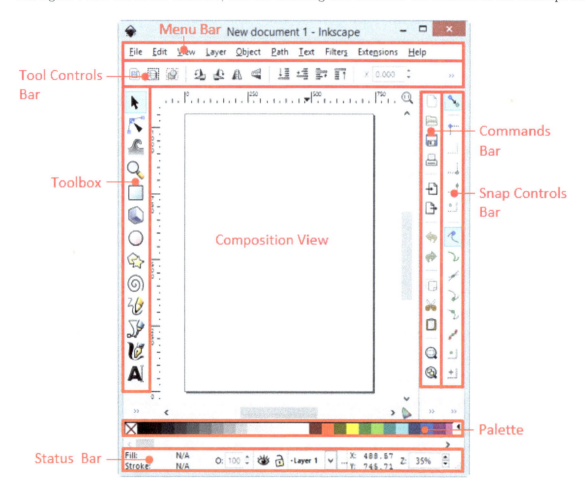

- **Composition View**: Displays the composition.

- **Menu Bar**: Provides access to Inkscape's capabilities. Many of these capabilities are also provided in the other bars on the interface for faster access.

- **Tool Controls Bar**: Contains tools to select, rotate, position, scale, and arrange objects and nodes in the composition.

- **Toolbox**: Tools that allow for selection, vertex editing, zooming, drawing, and text editing, among others.

- **Commands Bar**: Provides quick access to open, save, print, import, export, copy/paste, and quick zoom commands.

- **Snap Controls Bar**: Provides quick access to a variety of snapping controls—will not be used in this exercise.

- **Palette**: Quick access to colors. Click to set a fill color, shift-click to set a stroke (line) color.

- **Status Bar**: Displays location of mouse cursor, selected colors, active layer, and layer visibility and locked status.

Any of the above bars may be shown or hidden by clicking View | Show/Hide.

Inkscape is quite powerful and has hundreds of commands at its disposal. For this exercise, you will only use a small subset of commands to design your map layout. You are encouraged to further explore Inkscape's capabilities as many may be useful for future map designs. The following is a list of commands that you will rely on heavily when designing your map.

- Select and transform objects tool ▸ | (toolbox) – This tool allows you to select objects in the composition. Once an object is selected, its handles will appear, and you can select those to scale and transform the objects.

- Zoom in or out tool (toolbox) – Left-click or drag a box to zoom in. Right-click to zoom out.

- Create rectangles or squares (toolbox)

  - **Click and drag to create a rectangle. Hold down the Control key on** your keyboard to create a square or integer-ratio rectangle. You can set the fill and stroke color to different colors.

- Draw Bezier curves and straight lines (toolbox) – Click and drag, then drag and click to create a Bezier curve. Click, move, then click again to create a straight line segment. Double-click to complete the line or curve. Hold down the Control key on your keyboard to have the line rotate in 15° increments.

- Create circles, ellipses, and arcs ◯ (toolbox) – Click and drag to create a circle. Hold down the Control key on your keyboard to create a square or integer-ratio ellipse. You can set the fill and stroke colors to different colors.

- Create and edit text objects **A** (toolbox) – Click to start a text object then type in the desired text.

- Import a bitmap or SVG image... (commands bar) – This command will open the import dialog for you to select a file to import in to the inkscape document.

- Group selected objects (commands bar) – With objects selected in the composition view, this command will group the objects together. The objects will then be considered a single object and will move, scale, and transform together. Grouped items can be ungrouped with the Ungroup selected objects command.

- Ungroup selected objects (commands bar) – With objects selected in the composition view, this command will ungroup the objects. Ungrouped objects are able to be manipulated separate from other objects.

- Edit objects' color, gradients, stroke width... (commands bar) – This command opens the Fill and Stroke panel. The panel allows a selected object's properties to be modified. Commonly changed object properties are the fill color, stroke color, stroke style, and object opacity.

- View and select font family... **T** (commands bar) – This command opens the Text and Font dialog. This dialog allows you to set the font family, style, size, layout, and text of a selected text object.

- View Layers (commands bar) – This command opens the Layers panel. This panel displays all layers in the composition and allows you to set the layer name, visibility, opacity, and lock status. Additionally, you can add and remove layers, and set the draw order.

- Align and distribute objects (commands bar) – This command opens the Align and Distribute panel. This panel has numerous commands that will set the alignment and distribution of selected objects.

In general, an Inkscape document contains multiple layers of objects. Each object has multiple properties, such as color, stroke thickness, opacity, and position. Multiple objects can be grouped for control simultaneously, or ungrouped for finer, individual object control. Objects can be ungrouped to the component level. For instance, a square can be ungrouped so that the stroke (outline) is a single object, and the fill is a single, separate object. Grouping/ungrouping and layering objects allows for powerful, fine grained control over the Inkscape document and objects within.

Now that you have a brief overview of Inkscape's layout, we can get to work designing our map.

3.5   Task 3 Importing and Arranging Maps in Inkscape

We will design a colorful map of the USA in Inkscape that will be composed on an 11 inch x 8.5 inch piece of paper in landscape orientation. To prepare for the design, we will first set a few document properties, and then import the three maps we exported in Task 1. Each map will be imported to a separate layer.

1. In Inkscape, click File | Document Properties...

2. Click the Page tab and set the following properties:
    - Background color (click background color box): R: 255; G 255; B: 255; A: 0
        - This sets the background to fully transparent.
    - Page Size: US Letter 8.5 x 11.0 in
    - Orientation: Landscape
    - Show border shadow: unchecked
        - Removing the page border shadow reduces confusion as to where the actual page border is located.

3. Close the Document Properties—now we can import our PDF maps.

4. Click File | Import... or the Import button on the commands bar 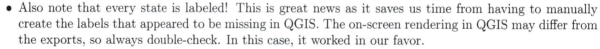. This will open the Import dialog.

5. Choose `Lower 48 States.pdf` from your exercise directory. Click Open. This will open the PDF Import Settings dialog.

6. Click OK to import the PDF as a new layer in the Inscape document.

7. You should now have your Lower 48 map displayed in Inkscape. Take a moment to use the Select tool to center the map on the page.
    - Also note that every state is labeled! This is great news as it saves us time from having to manually create the labels that appeared to be missing in QGIS. The on-screen rendering in QGIS may differ from the exports, so always double-check. In this case, it worked in our favor.

8. Click View layers button to open the Layer panel. Alternatively, you can click Layer | Layers from the menu bar to open the Layer panel. Note that there is a single layer listed, 'Layer 1' (shown in figure below).

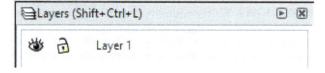

9. Click the visibility toggle 👁. The map will disappear.

10. Click the visibility toggle 👁. The map will re-appear. Turning layer visibility on and off helps de-clutter the document and makes it easier to focus on certain elements.

11. Double-click 'Layer 1' text to make it editable. Rename the layer 'Lower 48 States' then press Enter on your keyboard. The layer is now distinctly named which will make it easier to reference it later.

12. Click the lock toggle 🔒. This will lock the layer and prevent you from selecting or modifying the layer. Try selecting the layer with the select tool. You cannot. This is very handy when you wish to prevent a layer from being accidentally modified.

13. Click the lock toggle 🔒. This will unlock the layer and allow selection and modification.

With the Lower 48 imported, we will now import Hawaii and Alaska into Inkscape. Each map will be imported into a separate layer so we can manipulate them individually.

14. In the Layers panel, click Create a new layer ➕. This will open the Add Layer dialog.

15. Set the Layer name to 'Hawaii' and the Position to Above current.

16. Click Add to add the new layer.

17. Select the Hawaii layer in the Layers panel. A selected layer will have a blue background and will also be displayed in the status bar at the bottom of Inkscape. See the figure below for reference. The selected layer will be the target layer for imported files, as well as other reasons we are not concerned about right now.

18. Click File | Import... or the Import button on the commands bar . This will open the Import dialog.

19. Choose `Hawaii.pdf` from your exercise directory. Click Open. This will open the PDF Import Settings dialog.

20. Click OK to import the PDF as a new layer in the Inscape document. You will see Hawaii displayed on the Inkscape document.

    a. If the Lower 48 is obscured by a white background box in the Hawaii layer, remove the Hawaii layer, and re-visit steps in Task 1 to re-export the Hawaii layer with a transparent background.

21. Hold down the Control key on your keyboard. Use the Select tool ▶ and grab the scale arrows of a corner of the Hawaii layer (See figure below) and drag scale Hawaii down to a smaller size. Holding down the Control key maintains the aspect ratio as you are scaling. This means that Hawaii will maintain its correct shape when being scaled.

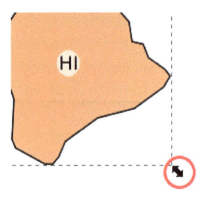

22. Use the Select tool ![cursor] to move Hawaii to the lower left-hand corner of the map. The placement of Hawaii should be below Texas and placed roughly in the same location shown in the figure below.

23. Repeat steps in this Task to import Alaska to its own layer and place it left of Hawaii. Your document should now look similar to the figure below.

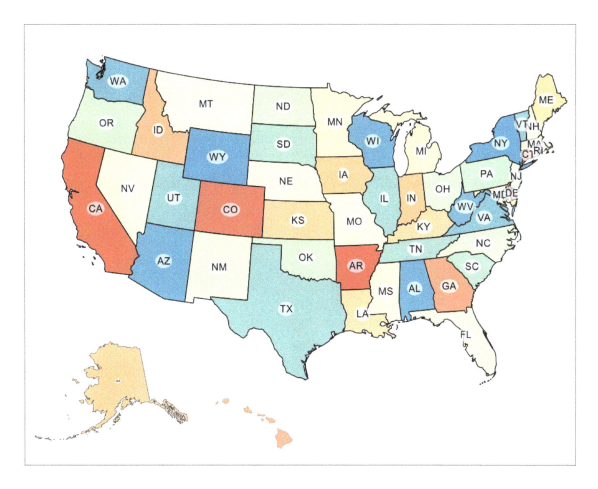

24. Take a moment to save your work in your exercise directory. Click File | **Save** and name your document `Colorful Map of the USA.svg` (Inkscape SVG format).

25. Click Save to save the document.

3.6 Task 4 Designing the Final Map Layout

In this task, you will complete the map design by adding a title, metadata, neatlines, adjusting line thicknesses for Alaska and Hawaii, and adjusting labels sizes and placement.

First, adjust the line thickness for Alaska and Hawaii.

1. In Inkscape, select the Alaska layer to make it the current layer.

2. Use the Select tool and select Alaska in the Composition View.

3. In the Command Bar, click the Edit object's colors... button 🖌 to open the Fill and Stroke Panel. Alternatively, click Object | Fill and Stroke from the menu bar.

4. Click the Stroke style tab in the Fill and Stroke Panel.

5. Set the Width to 1.417 which is the same width as the state boundary lines in the Lower 48.

   - I found the width of a state boundary by clicking the Edit paths by nodes button 🖉 on the Toolbox, then selecting a state. Inspecting the width in the Fill and Stroke Panel under the Stroke style tab shows the boundary width.

6. Repeat the steps to set the line width to 1.417 for Hawaii.

Next, we can change the placement of labels for Florida, Louisiana, Connecticut, Rhode Island, New Hampshire, and Vermont so they are more centrally placed and/or easier to read. To accomplish this, we will need to ungroup the Lower 48 so we can manipulate the individual label objects.

7. Use the Select tool and select the Lower 48 in the Composition View.

8. In the Commands Bar, click the Ungroup selected objects button 🔲 . This will separate the object in to multiple smaller objects. When this happens, you will see selection boxes appear around the labels and label ovals (shown in figure below). If you do not see the selection boxes around the labels, keep clicking the Ungroup selected objects button.

9. Press the Escape key on your keyboard to deselect everything. If you attempt to select a label with everything selected, it would not work. Instead, after you ungroup, you will need to deselect everything, then select the ungrouped object of interest.

10. Click the Zoom in or out tool 🔍 in the toolbox, then zoom in close to the northeastern states. Some of the labels are overlapping or too close to each other so we will separate them for readability.

11. Hold down the Shift key on your keyboard and use the Select tool to select the 'VT' label and the associated white ellipse. You may need to click a few times to get this to work. You can also drag a box around the label and ellipse, but make sure you do not select other labels or states. You will know you are successful when you see two selection boxes; one around VT and one around the ellipse (as shown in the figure below).

12. Press the Group selected objects button 🔲 on the commands bar to group the label and its background ellipse together. This will make the label easier to select in the future, if needed.

13. Move the VT label slightly up (north) so it does not crowd the NH label as much.

14. Select the NH label and ellipse, group it, and move it slightly down (south) so it does not crowd the VT label as much.

15. Move the MA, RI, CT, MD, and DE labels to more reasonable locations. The figure below shows a reasonable arrangement.

   • Here is an optional neat trick that may or may not be useful. If you select multiple labels that overlap, you can use the Move objects as little as possible so that their bounding boxes do not overlap button ▯▯▯ (whew! long button name!) in the Align and Distribute Panel. This will do exactly what the button says it will do and may produce a desirable result.

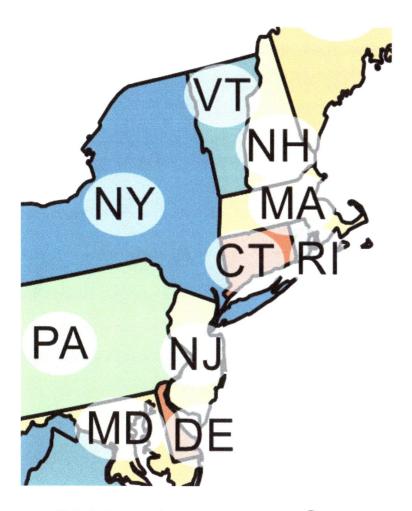

16. Click the Zoom to fit page in window button on the commands bar to zoom to the entire map. The 5 key on your keyboard is a shortcut for this command.

17. Move the LA and FL labels to locations that are more reasonable. You may need to zoom in to select more accurately. Feel free to move any other labels that you feel should be adjusted.

Now we can turn our attention to the labels for Alaska and Hawaii. They are quite small! They're small because they were scaled down when we scaled down the imported PDF in Task 3. We'll change these labels to the appropriate size again—there are two methods we can use.

18. Zoom in close to Alaska. Select then ungroup Alaska multiple times until you see the selection boxes around the label and ellipse.

19. Select the AK label and ellipse and press the Delete key on your keyboard. This will delete the label and ellipse. Alternatively, you could right-clicked on the selected objects and choose Delete from the context menu.

20. Click the Zoom to fit page in window button.

21. Zoom to Louisiana (LA).

22. Select the LA label and ellipse.

23. Click the Duplicate selected objects button on the commands bar. This will create a duplicate copy of the label and ellipse and place it on top of the existing label.

24. With the label still selected, zoom to the entire page, then move the duplicated label over Alaska. Oh no—the label disappeared behind Alaska! The reason this happened is because the duplicated object is still on the

Lower 48 layer, which is placed below the Alaska layer (reference the Layers Panel for draw order). We will need to move the duplicated label up to the Alaska layer so it will display correctly.

25. With the label selected, hold the Shift key and press the Page Up key two times. Notice that every time you press Page Up, the active layer in the Status bar changes to the layer that the object is now placed in. On the fifth press, you should reach Alaska as the active layer. If you go too far, hold Shift key and press Page Down key. You can also move the layers above and below using the Layer menu in the Menu bar.

    - If you unselected the label and it is hidden behind Alaska, turn off the Alaska layer visibility in the Layers panel, move the label to the Alaska layer (it should disappear when this happens), then turn the Alaska layer back on.

26. Zoom in close to the label on Alaska. Unfortunately the 'LA' label is not actually editable text. It is a path object (drawn lines having no textual meaning). Therefore, we will need to create a new text object, and make it the same size as the 'LA' symbol, then change it to 'AK'.

27. With Alaska still the active layer, click the **Create and edit text objects** tool **A** on the toolbar, then click above the LA label. This will create a new text object.

28. Type LA. LA will appear on the composition.

29. Use the **Select** tool to select the newly created text.

30. Click **Text | Text and Font** on the menu bar to open the Text and Font dialog.

31. Select Arial for the font family. Arial is the font we used to label the states in QGIS (I went back and checked, you can too!), so we are matching the font in Inkscape.

32. Click Apply then Close to set the font to Arial.

33. Ungroup the LA label from the ellipse.

34. Select both the LA label and the LA text you created using the text tool.

35. Open the Align and Distribute panel by clicking the **Align and distribute objects** button on the commands bar.

36. Set the following options and click the following buttons on the Align and Distribute Panel:

    - Relative to: Last Selected

    - Click the **Align bottom edges** button

    - Click the **Align left edges** button

37. With the origins of the labels together (shown in the figure below), you will now resize the text label (the larger one) to make it the same size as the path label (smaller one). Press the Escape key on your keyboard deselect everything.

38. Select the LA text (larger one), hold down the Control key on your keyboard, and use the top-right resize

arrows to make the larger text the same size as the smaller text. Holding down the Control key maintains the aspect ratio of the resizing object.

39. Re-open the Text and Font dialog (Text | Text and Font) and notice that the Font size is right around 18. Now we know which font size we are working with.

40. Set the Font size to 18.

41. Click the Text tab and then change the text to AK.

42. Click Apply then Close to close the Text and Font dialog.

43. Move the new text label off of the ellipse.

44. Select and delete the paths label on the ellipse. Now we will put the next text label exactly in the center of the ellipse.

45. Select both the text label and ellipse.

46. Open the Align and Distribute panel by clicking the Align and distribute objects button ⊟ on the commands bar.

47. Set the following options and click the following buttons on the Align and Distribute Panel (reference figure below):

   - Relative to: Last selected
   - Click the Center on vertical axis button ⊟
   - Click the Center on horizontal axis button ⊟

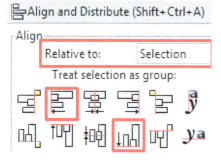

48. Notice that the ends of the A and K are touching the edges of the ellipse. We need to give the label more breathing room, so let's make the ellipse slightly larger. Select the ellipse. Hold down the shift key and drag a resize handle to make the ellipse slightly larger. Using the select key resizes the object about its centroid. See the figure below for reference.

49. Select both the text and ellipse and group them.

50. Move the newly created label to a reasonable location on Alaska.

Whew! Quite a few steps to change something so small! The reason I pulled you through all of those steps is so you can get some practice with selections, grouping, layers, aligning, and resizing. These simple commands are quite commonly used and powerful when designing a map.

Now we can try a second method to resize Hawaii's label that is much quicker, but may not produce completely accurate results.

51. Zoom in close to Hawaii. Select, then ungroup Hawaii multiple times until you see the selection boxes around the label and ellipse.

52. Select and group the HI label and ellipse.

53. Zoom to the IN (Indiana) label and select the label and ellipse.

54. Click Edit | Copy from the menu bar.

55. Zoom back to the HI label and select it.

56. Click Edit | Paste Size | Paste Size from the menu bar. Violà! The Hawaii label is now the same size as the Indiana label. Let's discuss the downsides to doing this for a moment. First, we chose the IN label because it was roughly the same shape and character width as HI, therefore, when it is scaled, the font size should be very close and the label should not appear unusually stretched. Had we chosen CA, for instance, you would notice the stretching of the HI label. The previous (long) method is a safer choice, however, this method will work in a pinch. Please check for consistency between like items (labels in this case) when you use this method.

57. Move the HI label to a reasonable location on Hawaii. Your map should look similar to the figure below at this point.

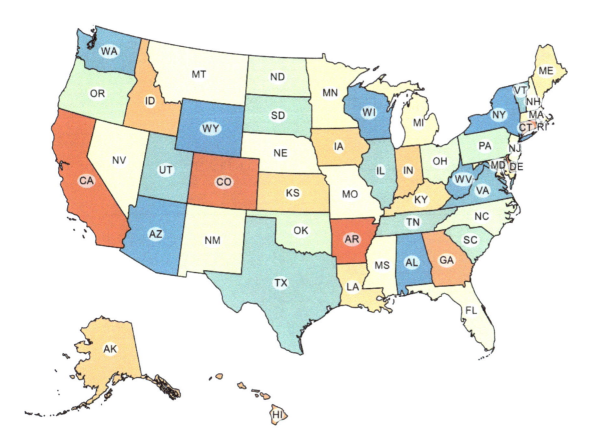

Now we will add a neatline around the entire map, and neatlines around Alaska and Hawaii.

58. Create a new layer, name it 'Neatlines', and place it at the top of the list of layers. If the layer needs to be moved up or down, select the target layer, then use the raise or lower buttons in the Layers Panel (see figure below).

59. With the Neatlines layer set as the active layer, select the Create rectangles and squares tool ▢ on the toolbox, and click and drag a box around the entire map, just inside the page border. A solid box will cover the entire map. Let's change the fill and line properties.

60. With the box still selected, click Edit objects' color, gradients... ✎ button on the commands bar. This will open the Fill and Stroke panel.

61. On the Fill tab, click the No paint button ✗. (Reference figure below).

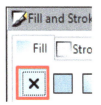

62. On the Stroke paint tab set the RGB values to 0, and Alpha to 255. This will make a black stroke that is fully opaque.

63. On the Stroke style tab, set the Width to 0.75 mm. This makes for a reasonably thick neatline.

64. Now we will align the neatline to the center of the page. Open the Align and Distribute panel and set the following:

   • Relative to: Page

   • Click the Center on vertical axis button ⊞.

   • Click the Center on horizontal axis button ⊞.

65. Resize your neatline to include all maps if the alignment made it overlap. Realign as necessary. Your map should look similar to the figure below.

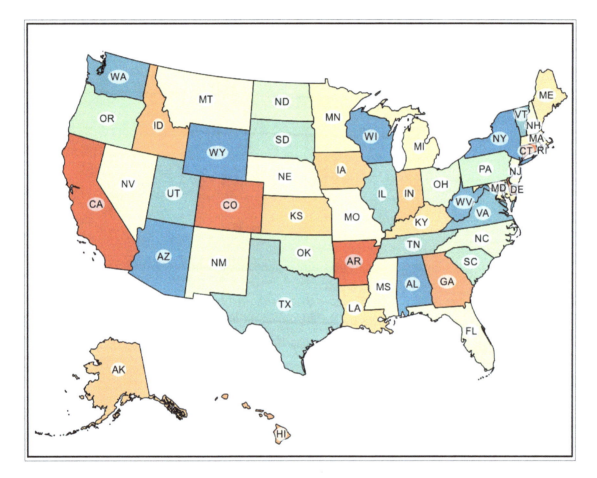

Now we'll add neatlines around Alaska and Hawaii. We can start with Alaska.

66. With the Neatlines layer set as the active layer, select the Create rectangles and squares tool ▢ on the toolbox, and click and drag a box around Alaska giving the state a little breathing room. Now we can change the fill and line properties.

67. With the box still selected, click Edit objects' color, gradients... 🖊 button on the commands bar. This will open the Fill and Stroke panel.

68. Set the following Fill and Stroke options:

   • Fill tab

   • No fill ✗

   • Stroke paint tab

– RGB: 0

– Alpha: 255

- Stroke style tab

  – Width: 0.5 mm

    * To give the appearance of a hierarchy in the map, we are making the interior neatlines 0.25 mm thinner than the map's neatline.

69. Select the Alaska neatline, then select the map neatline.

70. Open the Align and Distribute panel and do the following:

- Relative to: Last selected
- Click the Align bottom edges button
- Click the Align left edges button

71. Move the Alaska state and label if it no longer is inside the neatline, or, make the neatline larger. It may be useful to regroup the Alaska state and label so you can move it as one unit. Your Alaska neatline should look similar to the figure below.

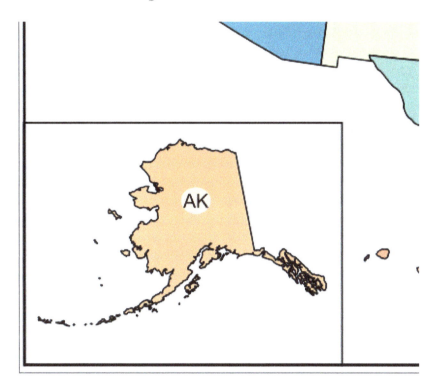

Now we will create a neatline around Hawaii. However, we won't create a boring square neatline, we will create a neatline that follows Hawaii's shape and, therefore, won't crowd Texas on the map.

72. Click the Draw Bezier curves and straight lines tool ✏️ in the toolbox.

73. Click once to the right of Hawaii and on the map neatline.

74. Hold down the Control key on your keyboard and move your mouse. Notice that the line rotates in 15° increments. This allows for nice, straight and diagonal line drawing.

75. Using the control key and mouse clicks, draw the neatline shown in the figure below. Double-click to complete the line drawing.

You can see which angle you are snapping to in the Status bar (see figure below). Make sure to connect the end of the neatline to the Alaska neatline. Don't worry about connecting exactly, we will address that in the next steps.

76. Using the Fill and Stroke panel, set the Hawaii neatline's properties to match Alaska's neatline properties. Reference step 68 above for a reminder.

77. Use the Align and Distribute panel to align Hawaii and the map's neatline to each other's bottom edges.

78. Zoom in close to where Alaska and Hawaii's neatlines touch.

79. Move the Hawaii neatline left or right to have it intersect with Alaska's neatline.

   - Alternatively, you can select the Hawaii neatline first then select the Alaska neatline, then, in the Align and Distribute panel, click **Align left edges of objects to the right edge of the anchor** button .

80. Open the Layers panel and lock the Neatlines layer. This will prevent us from accidentally selecting the neatlines as we place the title and metadata.

Now we'll add the title and metadata.

81. Create a new layer named 'Title and Metadata' and place it at the top of the Layers list.

82. Make sure 'Title and Metadata' is the active layer, then click the **Create and edit text objects** button **A** in the toolbox.

83. Click above the Lower 48 and enter the following title: 'United States of America'.

84. Select the title text then click **Text | Text and Font** from the menu bar. This will open the Text and Font dialog.

85. Set the following Text and Font properties:

   - Font family: Arial
   - Font size: 32

The title should be centered on the page, so, instead of trying to figure out where center is ourselves, we will use the Align and Distribute Panel to do it for us.

86. Select the title, then click the Align and distribute objects button in the commands bar. This will open the Align and Distribute Panel.

    - Set the following options (shown in figure below):
        - Relative to: Page
        - Click the Center on Vertical Axis button

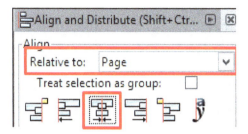

87. Use the Select tool to center the title halfway between the top of the Lower 48 and the neatline.

88. Make sure 'Title and Metadata' is the active layer, then click the Create and edit text objects button in the toolbox.

89. Click in the lower right-hand corner of the map and enter the following metadata, then press Enter on your keyboard.

    - Map Author: Made with Natural Earth. Free data at naturalearthdata.com.
        - It is not necessary to cite Natural Earth, however, I feel it is important to give credit for their amazing product. For more information, read their Terms of Use.

90. Select the metadata text, then click Text | Text and Font from the menu bar. This will open the Text and Font dialog.

91. Set the following Text and Font properties:

    - Font family: Arial
    - Font size: 10
    - Layout: Center lines

92. Click Apply then Close to apply the text and font properties.

93. Move the metadata so it is in the lower-right hand corner of the map.

94. Save the Inkscape document.

That is it! We are done designing the map! Your map should now look like the figure below.

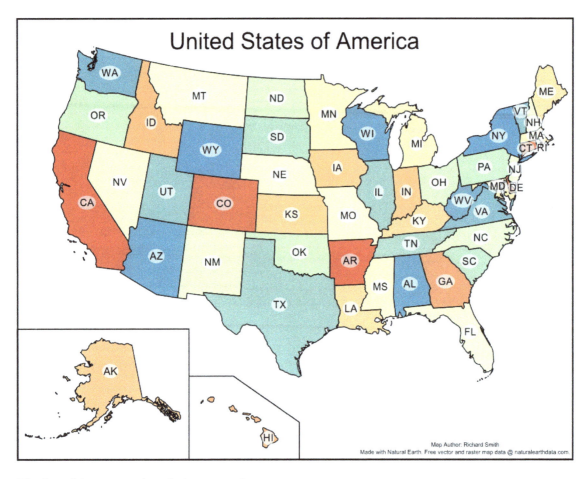

The last thing we need to do is export the map.

95. Click File | Save a Copy... from the menu bar.

96. Save the map as a Portable Document Format (.pdf) in your exercise directory. Name the map whatever you want, you made it, after all! Click Save. Another dialog will open.

97. Accept the defaults for the Portable Document Format dialog. Click OK to save the PDF.

3.7   Task 5 Challenge: Complete Challenge from Exercise 1 (optional)

Complete the challenge from Exercise 1. Compose a final map design in Inkscape.

Exercise 1 Challenge:

Now that you have designed a map at a national level, your next challenge is to choose a state that contains multiple smaller administrative units (e.g. county, parish) and make a colorful map of that state. In the map, choose a pleasing color scheme, and label all counties and the state. Additionally, make the state outline thicker than the county outlines; this may require some creative thinking on your part.

To accomplish this challenge, the 2013 TIGER County boundaries have been placed in the Exercise 1 directory. The county shapefile is named US Counties 2013 - TIGER.shp.

3.8   Conclusion

In this exercise, you learned how to use Inkscape to import PDFs, modify objects on those PDFs, create new layers, draw new objects, add text, and export the composition. While this exercise was long and, at times, tedious, the design skills and concepts are very common when designing maps and do transfer over to other software packages. Going forward in the exercise series in this course (and hopefully in your professional career), you will continue to utilize Inkscape to design two more maps beyond what QGIS could do alone.

3.9 Discussion Questions

1. Submit your exported colorful map of the USA for grading.

2. In Inkscape, click File | Document Properties | Snap tab. Set the Snap to objects | Snap distance to 50 then close the Document Properties. Zoom in close to a neatline. Click the Draw Bezier curves and straight lines tool. Click just outstide the neatline. Notice that the path snapped to the center of the path! Now, explore the Snap Controls bar and discuss what snapping is, and identify two places in this exercise where snapping would have come in useful.

3. We can add a little more pizazz to our map. Inkscape has a huge library of Filters that can do interesting things to our map. Your challenge is to apply a drop shadow to the map using the filter located at: Filters | Shadows and Glows | Drop Shadow... Add a drop shadow the the Lower 48, Alaska, and Hawaii. It may be useful to group everything on each of the three layers first, then apply the drop shadow to the selected group. To easily select everything in a layer, lock all other layers, then drag a large selection box around the objects to select. Export a PDF and submit the map with a drop shadow for grading. Your map may look similar to the one below.

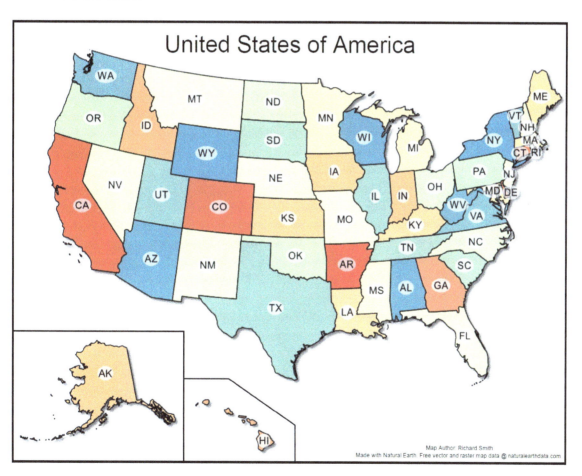

Exercise 4

IDP and Refugee Proportional Symbol Map

Objective - Design and construct a proportional symbol map in QGIS, then export the map for layout in Inkscape

4.1 Introduction

In this exercise, you'll learn how to design a proportional symbol map in QGIS. This map will show Syrian Internally Displaced Persons (IDPs) and Refugees. The figure below shows an example of the final product that will be completed by Exercise 5.

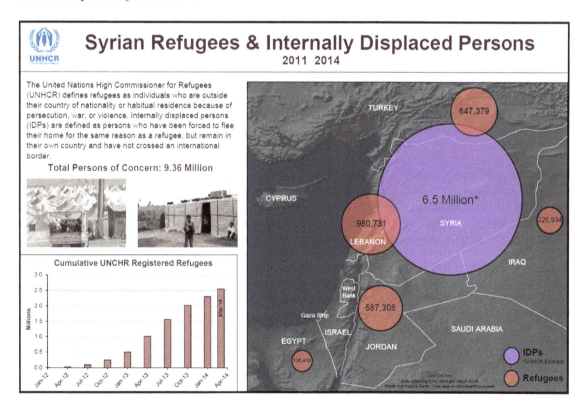

This exercise will focus primarily on setting colors, line thicknesses, layer drawing order, and proportional symbols. The secondary focus is exporting the map document and preparing a rough design in Inkscape.

The map designed in this exercise will be completed in Exercise 5. Additionally, the layout designed for this map may be partially reused for a related choropleth map designed later in Exercise 6.

It is assumed that you have completed Exercises 1, 2, and 3 in Part IV, Cartographic Design, on page 277, and have a working knowledge of Inkscape and QGIS. Because of this assumption, you'll be asked to complete tasks that were covered in the previous Exercises without being provided step-by-step instructions. Tasks that have not been covered in previous Exercises will be covered in detail as we go along.

Acknowledgement: The author would like to thank Mr. Olivert Garcia for allowing his Syria IDP and Refugee map design to be used as a teaching tool.

This exercise includes the following tasks:

- Task 1 – Rough Design of the Final Map

- Task 2 – Design a Proportional Symbol Map in QGIS

- Task 3 – Export Map by Layers

- Task 4 – Prepare Rough Map Design in Inkscape

- Challenge: Create Layout in QGIS

4.2   Objective: Utilize QGIS and Inkscape to Complete the Design of a Proportional Symbol Map Showing Syrian IDPs and Refugees

To achieve a properly designed map, the features on the map must be easily distinguishable, attractive to the map reader, and stand out from the grounds (supporting background information/data). In this exercise, you'll learn how to utilize QGIS and Inkscape to compose a well-designed proportional symbol map.

4.3   Task 1 Rough Design of the Final Map

At the outset, it's often useful to think of a rough design for your final map product. This is especially useful if your map will have multiple components, such as text, pictures, graphs, and so on. Map design is an iterative process. Though carefully planned designs at the beginning may not be what the final map ends up resembling, it is still worth going through the exercise of thinking through the parts of your map.

Normally this iterative map design process is organic and you'll often need to experiment with designs for a while until the map begins to take shape. However, you are at a disadvantage for these Exercises because as the exercise author, I've already designed the map I'm going to teach you how to make (shown in the previous). That doesn't mean you can't make changes to improve upon the design, but in order for you to follow the instructions, you'll need to at least first make the map as described, then tweak to make it your own.

With this caveat in mind, let's start by discussing the rough map design. First, let's consider the final map design, but focus on segmenting the page up for the components. The segmented final map is shown in the figure below. The blue lines are guidelines created in Inkscape by clicking and dragging from the ruler to the map. Making guidelines are a useful tool for making sure that items line up.

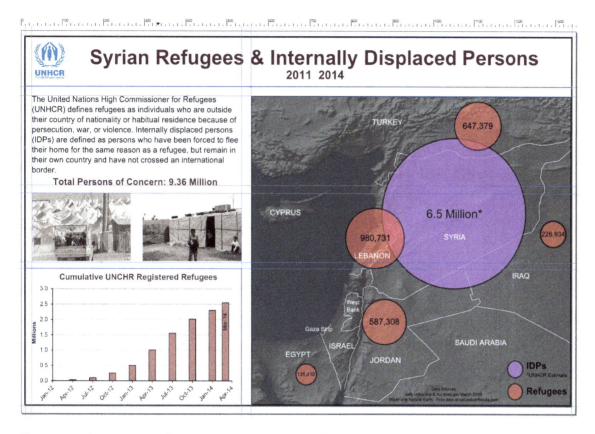

If we generalize our map design to get a rough idea of where things will go, we can create a sketch that looks like the figure below. Note that the measurements are nice round numbers, however, the final product does not need to follow those measurements precisely, as often times things may need to be transformed slightly so the map looks 'right'.

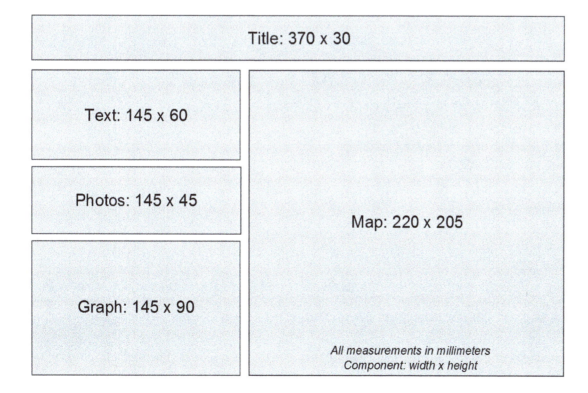

Out of the entire rough map design, what we need to set in stone now is the size of the map body. The reason we need to set this is that when we compose the map in QGIS Composer, it is best if we export the map in the exact dimensions that will be used in the final map design. By exporting in the exact dimensions, we can avoid having to scale the map, which may introduce artifacts. So, for this exercise, the map will be designed on a canvas of size 220 mm wide by 205 mm high.

With the map layout roughed in, we can now move towards creating the proportional symbol map in QGIS. We will revisit this map design in Task 4 when we put it into action in Inkscape.

4.4   Task 2 Design a Proportional Symbol Map in QGIS

In this task, you will design a proportional symbol map showing Syrian IDPs and refugees. In this Task, you'll design the base map and proportional symbols. Normally you would also create the labels, however, as there are so few, we will do this manually in the next exercise when we start finalizing the map design.

1. Open QGIS Desktop.

2. In QGIS Desktop, add the raster layer GRAY_HR_SR.tif to the project by clicking Layer | Add Layer | Add Raster Layer from the menu bar. This is a shaded relief of the world's land and will serve as a base layer for our map to provide a little terrain detail.

3. Rename the raster layer 'Shaded Relief'. (Layer Properties | General | Layer name).

4. Add the vector layer ne_10m_ocean.shp to the project.

5. Rename the newly added vector file 'Ocean' in the Layers panel.

6. Drag the Ocean layer above the Shaded Relief Layer in the Layers panel.

7. Set the following Style properties for the Ocean layer:
   - Symbol layer: Simple fill
     - Simple Fill Color:
       * Hue: 195
       * Sat: 16%
       * Val: 38%
   - Border style: No pen

8. Add the vector layer ne_10m_coastline.shp to the project. This layer will serve as the water boundary for the countries. It will essentially mask the color of the boundaries of the country layer we will add later.

9. Rename the newly added vector file 'Coastlines' in the Layers panel.

10. Drag the Coastlines layer below the Ocean layer.

11. Set the following Style properties for the Coastlines layer:
    - Symbol layers: Simple line
      - Color:
        * Hue: 195
        * Sat: 16%
        * Val: 38%
    - Pen width: 1.25

12. Add the vector layer Countries with IDP and Refugee Information.shp to the project. This layer will do triple-duty. It will serve as the basemap, the data for the refugee proportional symbols, and the data for the IDP proportional symbol. We will duplicate this layer twice so that we can have one layer for each use mentioned.

13. Right-click the newly added vector file, then click Duplicate. Do this a second time so that you now have three copies of the vector file in the Layers panel.

14. Drag the first duplicated layer with its visibility turned on beneath the Coastlines layer. Rename this layer 'Basemap'.

15. Rename another duplicated layer 'Refugees' and drag it to the top of the Layer list.

16. Rename the remaining duplicated layer 'IDPs' and drag it directly under the Refugees layer. Your layer list should look like the figure below. Keep the Refugees and IDPs layers' visibility off.

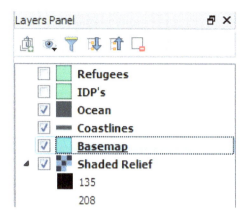

Now that we have all of our data loaded, let's work on setting the Basemap layer's properties so we can complete our basemap.

17. First, we want the hillshade to show on the map. Open the Layer Properties for the Basemap layer.

18. Click the Style tab.

19. Set the Layer transparency to 20.

20. Click Apply. You should see the hillshade become visible through the Basemap layer.

21. Set the following Style properties for the Basemap layer:

    - Symbol layers: Simple fill
        - Colors:
            * Fill:
                · Hue: 60
                · Sat: 10
                · Val: 40
            * Border:
                · Hue: 0
                · Sat: 0
                · Val: 25
        - Border width: 1.25

22. To make the country borders seem not so plain, we will add a thin light-grey fill stroke down the center of black border. This will help give the borders a little more definition.

23. Still in the Style properties for the Basemap layer, click the Add symbol layer button to add a new simple fill layer to the symbol.

    - If the new Simple fill layer is not at the top, select it and press the Move up button [▲] .

24. Select the newly added Simple fill. Set the following style properties:

- Colors:
    - Fill style: No Brush
    - Border:
        * Hue: 0
        * Sat: 0
        * Val: 75
- Border width: 0.75

25. It's time we zoom in to Syria so we can examine our work in detail. Zoom in to Syria and leave enough room to see part of the surrounding countries. Use the figure below as a rough guide.

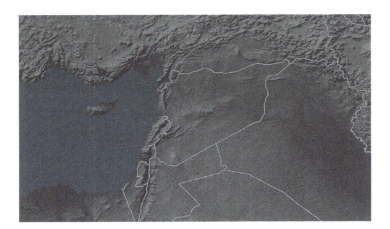

With the basemap now designed, let's turn our attention to creating the proportional symbols that represent the refugees and IDPs. Let's start with the refugee proportional symbols.

26. Turn on the 'Refugee' layer visibility. Your map will be temporarily ruined with an ugly default fill color. As we are only interested in having this layer display the proportional symbols, we will turn off the fill and border.

27. Set the following Style properties for the Refugee layer:

    - Symbol layer: Simple fill
        - Fill Style: No Brush
        - Border style: No pen

28. Click Apply to set the Style properties. The map is now back to its previous state. Now let's create the proportional symbols.

29. In the 'Refugee' Layer Properties, click the Diagrams tab.

30. Check the Show diagrams for this layer checkbox.

31. Choose Pie chart for the Diagram type. The plan is to create a pie chart with a single filling (Refugees) and have it scale proportional to the value of the Refugee field in the shapefile.

32. Click the Appearance tab.

33. Set Line width to 0.75.

34. Click on the Attribute tab.

35. In the Available attributes list, select 'Refugees' (bottom of list) then press the plus sign button . This will add the 'Refugees' attribute to the Assigned attributes list.

36. Double-click on the color bar next to the 'Refugees' attribute in the Assigned attributes box. This will open

the Select Color dialog.

37. Set the following color for the pie chart:

    - Hue: 4
    - Sat: 80
    - Val: 100

The Diagram properties should look like the figure below.

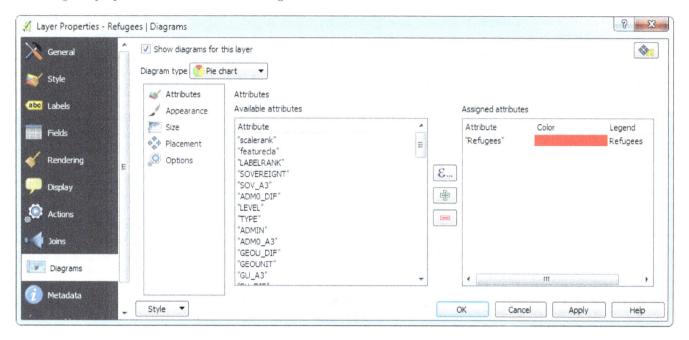

38. Click the Size tab.

39. Check Scaled size. As we want each proportional symbol to scale in relation to the refugee attribute. We will now set the properties for symbol scaling. In the Attribute dropdown box, choose 'Refugees'. Reference the figure below for the next three steps.

40. Click the Find maximum value button.

41. Set Size to 30.

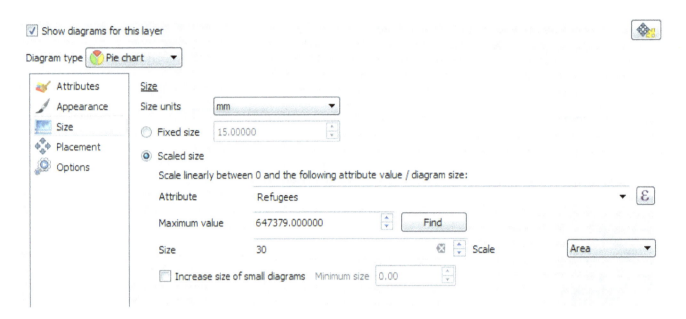

42. Click OK to complete the design of the refugee proportional symbols. Your map should look similar to the figure below. Note that there may be two symbols for Egypt and Turkey's symbol may be off the page (may vary slightly depending on your map extent and scale).

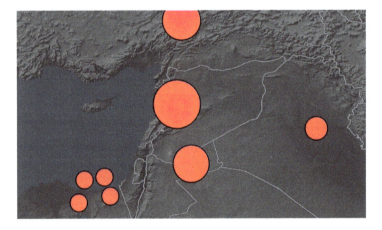

Now we can turn to creating the Syria proportional symbol. We really want to make an impact with the size of Syria's IDP proportional symbol, so we will have it dominate the map and be in a different color than the refugee symbols since we are talking about a different classification.

43. Turn on the IDPs layer visibility. Your map will be temporarily ruined with an ugly default fill color. As we are only interested in having this layer display the proportional symbol, we will turn off the fill and border.

44. Set the following Style properties for the IDPs layer:

- Symbol layer: Simple fill
    - Fill Style: No Brush
    - Border style: No pen

45. In the IDP Layer Properties, click the Diagrams tab.

46. Check the Show diagrams for this layer checkbox.

47. Choose Pie chart for the Diagram type.

48. Click the Appearance tab.

49. Set Line width to 0.75.

50. Click the Attributes tab.

51. In the Available attributes list, select 'IDPs' (bottom of list) then press the plus sign button .

52. Double-click on the color bar next to the 'IDPs' attribute in the Assigned attributes box. This will open the Select Color dialog.

53. Set the following color for the pie chart:

    - Hue: 270
    - Sat: 70
    - Val: 100

54. Click the Size tab.

55. Check Scaled size. If we kept Fixed size checked, even countries with NULL IDP attributes would have a circle displayed. Since we want to avoid that, we will still scale the size of the proportional symbols to the attribute value.

56. In the Attribute dropdown box, choose 'IDPs'.

57. Click the Find maximum value button. Notice that the maximum value is 6,500,000, roughly 6.5 times the amount of the country with the larger number of refugees (Lebanon – 980,731). If we set the size to be 6.5 times larger than the size of the largest refugee symbol (40 mm), it would be a staggering 260 mm! That would completely cover the map! (If you are curious, try 260 mm and see for yourself. I'll wait.) So, our options are to a) make the refugee circles smaller, or b) use some 'cartographic license' to scale down the IDP circle. If we choose option option a, the refugee circles may become too small to have an impact. If we choose option option b, we will not be scaling all circles proportionally. I recommend option option b because while we are not scaling proportionally, we will still make the IDP circle dominate the map and still leave an impact with the map reader.

58. Set size to 80.

59. Click OK. Your map should now look similar to the figure below.

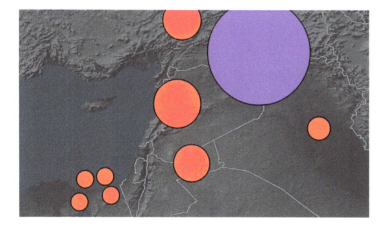

That's it for the map design. It looks sparse for now, but once we export the layers and import them into Inkscape, we can start arranging the circles and adding labels.

60. Save the QGIS Project as Syria Map.qgs in your exercise directory.

4.5   Task 3 Export Map by Layers

In this task, you will export the map in two parts: one for the base map, and the other for the proportional symbols. The reason two exports are required is the raster hillshade and the transparency effects of the vector layers cannot be exported to PDF as a vector file—to maintain these effects, the export must first be rasterized, which prevents us from getting access to the vector data. Therefore, we will export the proportional symbol layers separately as we will want to move and manipulate them.

1. In QGIS, with the Syria Map project loaded, turn off the visibility of the Refugees and IDPs layer so that only the basemap remains.

2. Click Project | New Print Composer.

3. Title the print composer 'Syria' then click OK. This will open the Print Composer.

4. Click the Composition tab in the information panel.

5. Set the following Paper and quality properties on the Composition tab:

    - Presets: Custom
    - Width: 220
    - Height: 205
    - Units: mm
    - Orientation: Landscape
    - Page background:
        - Symbol layers: Simple fill
            * Fill style: No Brush
                · Border style: No Pen
    - Print as raster: checked. This will be checked for our first export of the basemap. Since we won't need to modify the vector information on the basemap in Inkscape, we will rasterize it.

6. Click the Add new map button on the Composer Items toolbar. Drag a large box on the Composition View.

7. Click the Item properties tab and set the following properties:

    - Scale: 3500000 (3.5 million)
    - Position and Size:
        - X: 0
        - Y: 0
        - Width: 220
        - Height: 205
    - Background: unchecked

8. Use the Move item content tool  on the Composer Items toolbar to center the map around Syria. Your composition should look similar to the figure below.

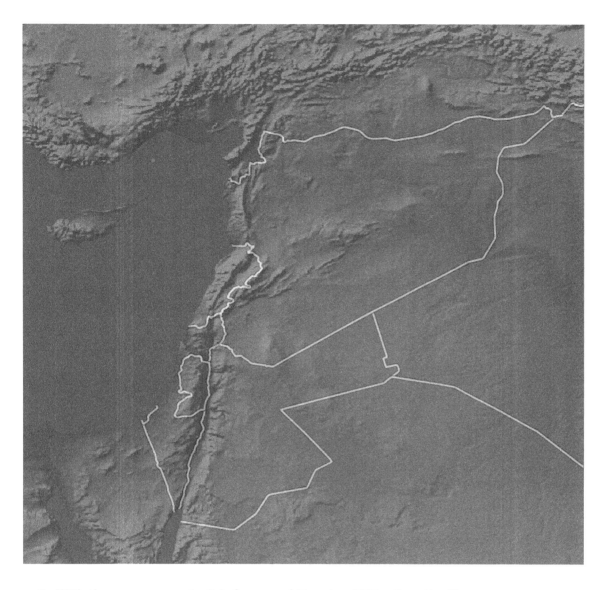

9. With the map composed, click Composer | Export as PDF... from the file menu.

10. Name the PDF `Syria Basemap.pdf` and save it in your exercise directory.

Now we will hide the basemap, only show the proportional symbols, and export the map as a vector PDF.

11. Close the Print Composer and return the QGIS.

12. Turn off the visibility for the basemap, shaded relief, ocean, and coastline layers, and turn on the visibility for Refugees and IDPs layers.

13. Click Project | Print Composers | Syria to reopen the print composer. Your map should look like the figure below.

  • If the composition does not update, select the map, then click the Item Properties | Update preview button.

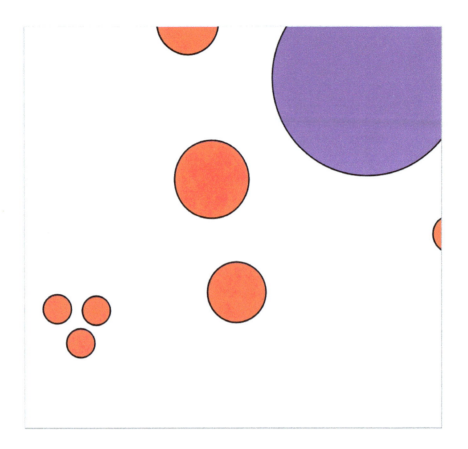

14. Click the Composition tab.

15. Uncheck Print as raster. We have this unchecked because we want to export these proportional symbols as vector objects in the PDF so we can manipulate them in Inkscape later.

16. With the proportional symbols composed, click Composer | Export as PDF... from the file menu.

   - If a Project contains composition effects window appears, uncheck Print as raster then click Close.

17. Name the PDF Syria Proportional Symbols.pdf and save it in your exercise directory.

That's all we need to do for composing the map in QGIS. Normally you would leave QGIS open so you can query the attributes for labeling the country names and proportional symbol values, however, this will be provided for you in the next exercise when you complete the map design, so you can close QGIS and Print Composer to save system resources.

4.6 Task 4 Prepare Rough Map Design in Inkscape

In this task, you will start the map design process in Inkscape by importing all of the resources needed to construct the map. You'll complete the map design in the next exercise.

1. Open Inkscape.

2. Click File | Document Properties. Click the Page tab.

3. The final map design is for a 15 in. wide by 10 in. tall piece of paper. We will set the page dimensions in this dialog. Set the following options:
   - Units: in
   - Width: 15.0
   - Height: 10.0

- Show border shadow: unchecked

4. Close the Document Properties dialog. The page size is now set.

5. From the menu bar choose Layer | Layers to open the Layers panel.

6. Rename 'Layer 1' to 'Basemap'.

7. Import the `Syria Basemap.pdf` that was exported in Task 3.

8. Click the Align and distribute objects button  on the command bar to open the Align and Distribute panel.

9. Align the basemap to the right and bottom of the page.

10. With the basemap in place, lock the Basemap layer by clicking the open lock next to the layer in the Layers panel. This will prevent us from accidentally selecting or moving the basemap.

11. Create a new layer, name it 'Proportional Symbols' and place it at the top of the Layer list.

12. Import `Syria Proportional Symbols.pdf` into the newly created layer.

13. Align the Proportional Symbols layer to the right and bottom of the page.

14. Lock the Proportional Symbols layer.

15. Create a new layer, name it 'Graph', and place it at the top of the Layer list.

16. Import `Bar Graph.jpg`. When prompted, choose embed and click OK to add the graph image to the composition.

17. The graph imports as a large image. We will scale it down to 145 mm x 90 mm as we had planned in Task 1 (refer to the layout sketch figure). In the tool controls bar (below the menu bar), we will set the W(idth) and H(eight) value. First, click the lock to maintain the aspect ratio, then set the units to 'mm', finally set the W(idth) to 145 and press Enter on your keyboard. The graph will resize. Refer to the figure below to see the final settings.

X 16.988   Y 3.722   W 145.000 🔒 H 89.352 mm ⌄

18. Align the graph to the left and bottom of the page. You can do this with the Align and Distribute panel, or, set the X and Y values next to the Width and Height values to 0,0 (X, Y value location shown in the figure above).

19. Lock the Graph layer.

20. Create a new layer, name it 'Pictures' and place it at the top of the Layer list.

21. Import and embed `Picture 1.jpg`, `Picture 2.jpg`, and `UNHCR Logo.jpg` into the Pictures layer.

22. Set the height of each picture to 45 mm with proportional scaling enabled (locked lock).

23. Place `Picture 1.jpg` and `Picture 2.jpg` above the Graph.

24. Set the proportionally scaled UNHCR logo to 30 mm high.

25. Place the UNHCR logo in the top left corner of the page.

26. Lock the Pictures layer.

27. Save the Inkscape document and name it `Syria Refugee and IDP Map.svg`.

28. Your map should resemble the figure below.

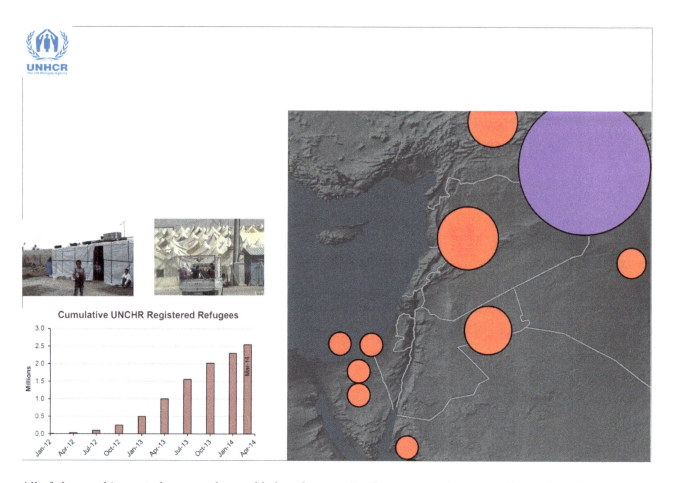

All of the graphic assets have now been added to the map. In the next exercise, you will complete the map design.

4.7   Task 5 Challenge: Create Layout in QGIS (optional)

While we are using Inkscape to complete final designs of our maps, QGIS does allow for some advanced map design. To do a comparison, create a new Print Composer and import all of the assets that were imported in Task 4, as well as the Syria map. See if you can re-create the map we created in Inkscape in QGIS's Print Composer. Export your design as a rasterized PDF and submit for grading.

4.8   Conclusion

In this exercise, you learned about the importance of thinking about the map design and layout for planning purposes. Next, you learned how to use QGIS to create a proportional symbol map and additional Print Composer options and export strategies. Lastly, in Inkscape, you learned how to import assets to different layers to create a rough map design. There is still quite a bit of work ahead of you in the next exercise where you will add text, neatlines, legend, labels, and modify the proportional symbols.

4.9   Discussion Questions

1. Save your Inkscape map as a PDF and submit it for grading.

2. The basemap was exported in QGIS as a raster file because transparency is not supported for vector data, and the hillshade is a raster. Suppose you wish to export the hillshade as a rasterized PDF and the ocean, coastline, and country boundaries as a separate vector PDF. Discover and list the steps required to achieve the transparency effect in Inkscape so the hillshade would show through the vector basemap layers.

3. In Inkscape, open the Align and Distribute panel. The Relative to: dropdown box lists seven options. Become comfortable with how each of these options change the way the alignment buttons work. List the seven Relative to: options and explain how each one works.

Exercise 5

IDP and Refugee Proportional Symbol Map – Designing the Final Map

Objective - Utilize Inkscape to Complete the Design of a Proportional Symbol Map Showing Syrian IDPs and Refugees

5.1 Introduction

In this exercise, you'll complete the map design discussed and started in Exercise 4. This map will show Syrian Internally Displaced Persons (IDPs) and Refugees. The figure below shows an example final product that will be completed in this exercise.

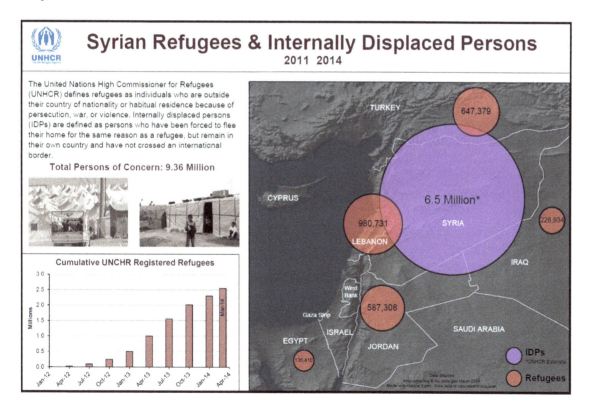

This exercise will focus primarily on arranging map elements, creating a legend, adding transparency effects, and properly aligning all map elements. The layout designed for this map may be partially reused for a related choropleth map designed later in Exercise 6.

For this exercise, it's assumed you've completed exercises 1-4 and have a working knowledge of Inkscape and QGIS. Because of this assumption, you'll be asked to complete tasks that were covered in the previous exercises without being provided step-by-step instructions. Tasks not covered in previous exercises will be covered in detail as we go along.

Acknowledgement: The author would like to thank Mr. Olivert Garcia for allowing his Syria IDP and Refugee map design to be used as a teaching tool.

This exercise includes the following tasks:

- Task 1 – Arrange Proportional Symbols and Apply Transparency

- Task 2 – Add Labels

- Task 3 – Create Legend, Metadata, Title, Ancillary Text, and Neatlines

- Task 4 – Final Checks for Alignment and Map Export

- Task 5 - Challenge: Add Refugee Camps to the Map

5.2   Objective: Utilize Inkscape to Complete the Design of a Proportional Symbol Map Showing Syrian IDPs and Refugees

To achieve a properly designed map, the features on the map must be easily distinguishable, attractive to the map reader, and stand out from the grounds (supporting background information/data). In this exercise, you'll learn how to utilize Inkscape to compose a well-designed proportional symbol map.

5.3   Task 1 Arrange Proportional Symbols and Apply Transparency

The first task we will tackle is completing the design and layout of the proportional symbols. There are four issues we need to resolve: addition of Iraq and Turkey symbols, removal of duplicated Egypt symbol, placement for symbols, and transparency of symbols. We will tackle these issues in the order listed.

One thing to note before you begin. Depending on the scale and extent of the map as set in QGIS, you may have more, or less circles than what is displayed and instructed in this exercise. If so, either add and scale, or remove symbols as appropriate.

1. There is no data for this exercise. You will use the `Syria Refugee and IDP Map.svg` Inkscape file that you completed in Exercise 4. Create a new exercise directory to store the output of this exercise.

2. Open Inkscape. Open `Syria Refugee and IDP Map.svg`. The figure below displays the map design at the end of Exercise 4.

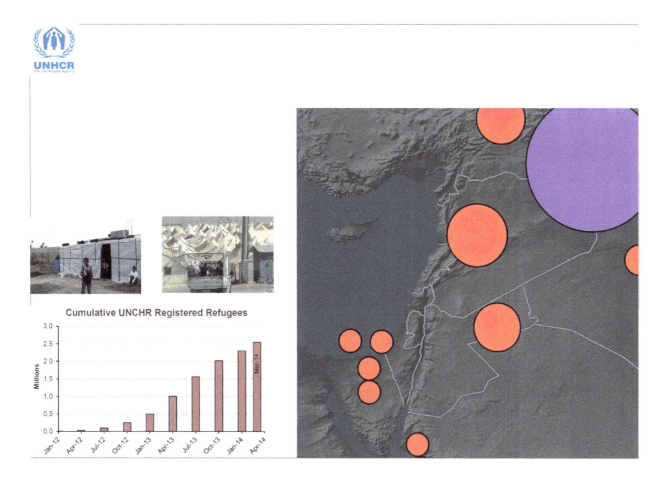

3. Open the Layers Panel and unlock the 'Proportional Symbols' layer. It is best to keep all other layers locked so you don't accidentally move or edit them.

4. You will move and arrange the Proportional symbols on the map for maximum impact and attractiveness.

5. Use the Select tool ⬆ to select the Proportional Symbol layer on the map.

6. Click the Ungroup selected groups button ⬚ multiple times until you see the selection boxes around the individual proportional symbols.

7. Select the proportional symbol representing Lebanon and move it so that it is better situated over Lebanon.

8. Repeat this step to better situate the symbols for Turkey, Iraq and Jordan.

Now we can remove the duplicate Egypt symbols.

9. Select one of the four Egypt symbols in the lower-left corner of the map.

10. Right-click on the selected symbol and choose Delete, or, press the 'Delete' key on your keyboard. This will delete the duplicate Egypt symbol.

Now you will address the position of the IDP symbol.

11. Move the purple IDP symbol over Syria.

12. If you need to make the purple symbol to sit underneath the red symbols, you can send it to the bottom of the draw order. Select the purple symbol, then click Object | Lower to Bottom from the File Menu.

13. Your map should now resemble the figure below.

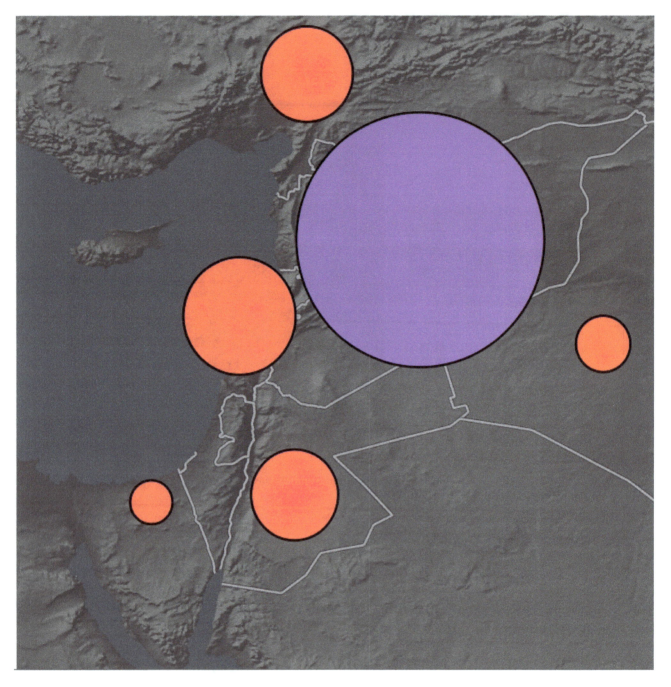

The last issue to tackle for the symbols is setting the transparency. While it is possible to set the transparency (opacity) for each individual symbol, we will set the layer's opacity, which will set it for every symbol at once. This provides a quick, simple way to apply a consistent opacity level to all objects on a layer.

14. Open the Layers Panel if it is not already open.
15. Select 'Proportional Symbols' layer.
16. Set Opacity, can see the borders and terrain underneath.
17. Lock the 'Proportional Symbols' layer so you don't accidentally modify it.

We now have our symbols in a good location, have the opacity set so you can see the terrain and boundaries behind them, and the red symbols cut into the purple symbol. We will now move on to labeling the countries and symbols.

5.4 Task 2 Add Labels

In this task, you will add labels for both the countries and proportional symbols. The countries will be labeled with their names in white and all capital letters, and the proportional symbols will be labeled with the number of IDPs or Refugees that they represent in black. You will create the country labels first.

1. In the Layers Panel, create a new layer named 'Map Labels'.

2. Place the layer at the top of the layer list.

3. Select the Text tool **A** in the Toolbox. The Tool Controls Bar will change to reflect that the Text tool has been selected.

4. Set the font to 'Arial' and font size to '13' in the Tool Controls Bar. Reference the figure below for the settings.

5. After typing text on the map, set the fill color to pure white by either:
   - Clicking the pure white on the palette at the bottom of Inkscape
   - Opening the Fill and Stroke Panel and setting the Fill RGB color to 255,255,255.

6. Label the following countries in all capital letters. All labels should be white and 13 point font, except where noted. Refer to the figure below for placement.
   - Turkey
   - Cyprus
   - Lebanon
   - West Bank -10 pt font size – Title Case
   - Gaza Strip - 10 pt font size – Title Case
   - Egypt
   - Israel
   - Jordan
   - Saudi Arabia
   - Iraq
   - Syria

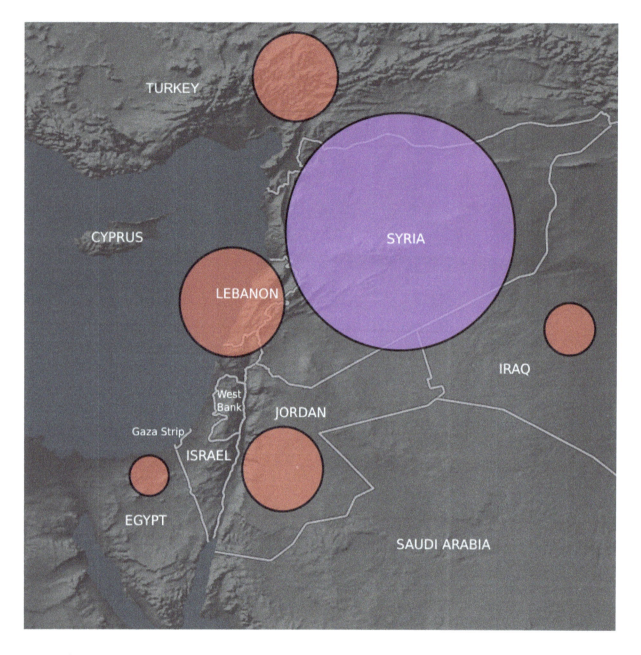

7. Label the proportional symbols with the following properties (reference the figure below for placement example):

   - Font: Arial
   - Color: Black
   - Font Size: 20
     - Syria: 6.5 Million
   - Font Size: 16
     - Lebanon: 980,731
     - Turkey: 647,379
     - Jordan: 587,308
   - Font Size: 12

- Iraq: 226,934
- Font Size: 9
- Egypt: 135,410

Great! The labels are now completed. Now we will align the proportional symbol labels to the center of each symbol, and readjust the locations of the country names, if required. I will demonstrate how to align Syria's purple proportional symbol label and symbol.

8. In the Layers Panel, unlock the 'Proportional Symbols' layer.

9. Open the Align and Distribute Panel by clicking the Align and distribute objects button on the Commands Bar.

10. Select the purple proportional symbol, then, holding down the Shift key on your keyboard, select the '6.5 Million' label.

11. In the Align and Distribute Panel, Set Relative to to First selected.

12. Click the Center on vertical axis button followed by the Center on horizontal axis button . This will align the label to the symbol.

    - If the symbol aligned to the label, undo the movement, and change from First selected to Last selected as order of selection counts and you selected the proportional symbol last. Then, set the alignment.

13. Align all other symbol labels to the horizontal and vertical centers of their associated symbols.

14. Lock the 'Proportional Symbols' layer again to prevent accidental modifications.

15. Move the country labels if they are crowding the symbol labels.

16. When done setting the label locations, lock the 'Map Labels' layer.

Your map body design is now completed. It should look similar to the figure below.

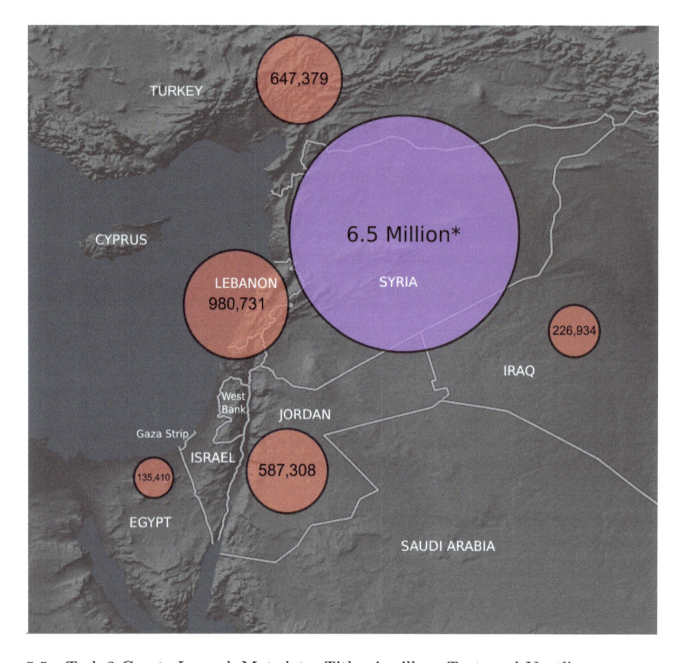

5.5 Task 3 Create Legend, Metadata, Title, Ancillary Text, and Neatlines

In this task, you will create the legend, metadata, title, ancillary text, and neatlines. We will continue to rough all of these items in and will fine tune the alignments in Task 4. Let's start by creating the Metadata.

1. Create a new layer and name it 'Metadata'. Make sure it is above at least Basemap in the layers list.

2. Use the Text tool **A** in the toolbox and the Text and Font Dialog **T** in the Commands Bar to add the following text with the associated properties: (as seen in the figure below)
   - Font: Arial
   - Font Size: 8
   - Color: Black
   - Layout: Center lines
   - Text:

– Data Sources: data.unhcr.org & hui.state.gov March 2014. Made with Natural Earth. Free data at naturalearthdata.com.

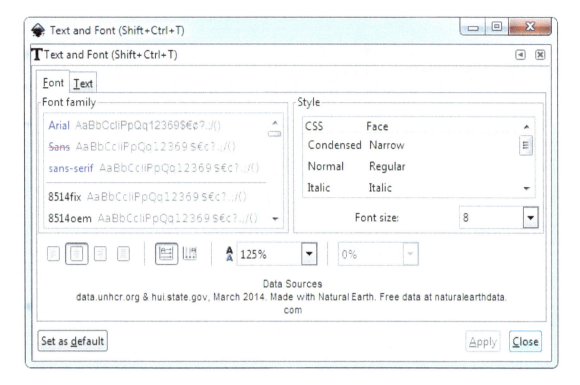

3. Place the metadata at the bottom of the map body, either centered or right of center.

4. Lock the Metadata layer.

Next, let's create the map legend, which will identify the meaning of the proportional symbol colors. The map legend will contain two circles, red and purple, which correspond to the two variables the proportional symbols represent. Next to the proportional symbols will be the text explanations. The figure below shows the legend design.

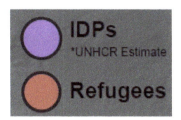

To accomplish this design, we can either: a) copy and paste one red and one purple symbol and reduce its size; or b) draw new circles and set their properties to match the proportional symbols. We'll look at both options—you choose whichever you want to use.

Option a: Copy and paste

1. Create a new layer named 'Legend' and place it at least above the Basemap layer.

2. Unlock the 'Proportional Symbols' layer.

3. Select a red symbol and click Edit | Copy from the file menu.

4. Select 'Legend' as the active layer by either selecting 'Layer' from the layer combo box in the Status Bar, or, selecting the layer in the Layer Panel.

5. Click Edit | Paste to paste the symbol on the 'Legend' layer. Turn the layer visibility off and on to verify that the symbol is on the 'Legend' layer. If it is not, select it, then hold Shift on your keyboard and press Page Up (or page down) until it is on the Legend layer.

6. Repeat steps 3-5 to copy the purple symbol.

7. Set the width and height of both legend symbols to 40px.

8. Set the Stroke Width of the legend symbol to 2.657 so it matches the stroke width of the larger symbols.

Option b: Draw new circles

1. Create a new layer named 'Legend' and place it at least above the Basemap layer.

2. Select the Ellipse tool ◯ from the Toolbox.

3. While holding Control key on your keyboard, click and drag to create a circle. The control key keeps the ratio to integers.

4. Select the ellipse and set the width and height to 50px.

5. Open the Fill and Stroke Panel and set the following options:
   - Fill tab:
     - R: 255
     - G: 58
     - B: 44
     - Opacity: 80
   - Stroke paint tab:
     - R: 0
     - G: 0
     - B: 0
   - Stroke style tab:
     - Width: 2.657 px

6. Repeat steps 2-4 to create a second ellipse and set the following options:
   - Fill tab:
     - R: 170
     - G: 85
     - B: 255
     - Opacity: 80
   - Stroke paint tab:
     - R: 0
     - G: 0
     - B: 0
   - Stroke style tab:
     - Width: 2.657 px

Note: In option b, we set the opacity for each symbol. In option a, we did not, because when we copy and pasted each symbol, it copied the opacity value from its parent layer's opacity value. Instead of setting each symbol's opacity in option b, you can simply set the 'Legend' layer's opacity to 80.

Complete the following steps after you complete option a or option b above.

1. Move the symbols to the bottom-right corner of the map body but leave room for the explanatory text.

2. Align the two legend symbols vertically to each other.

3. Add the following text next to the purple legend symbol:
   - Font: Arial
   - Font Size: 16
   - Font Style: Bold
     - Text: IDPs
   - Font Size: 10
   - Font Style: Normal
   - Location: Under 'IDPs' text.
     - Text: *UNHCR Estimate

4. Add the following text next to the red legend symbol:
   - Font: Arial
   - Font Size: 16
   - Font Style: Bold
     - Text: Refugees

5. Align the legend text to the horizontal center of their respective symbols.

6. Align the left character of each legend text to each other.

7. Move the entire legend to the lower-right corner of the map.

8. Lock the 'Legend' layer.

With the legend created, now let's turn our attention to the title.

9. Create a new layer named 'Title'.

10. At the top of the map layout, create the following title text with the following properties:
    - Font: Arial
    - Font Size: 36
    - Style: Bold
    - Color:
      - R: 99
      - G: 44
      - B: 40
    - Text: Syrian Refugees & Internally Displaced Persons

11. Below and vertically centered with the title, create the subtitle text with the following properties:
    - Font: Arial
    - Font Size: 20
    - Style: Bold
    - Color:
      - R: 99
      - G: 44
      - B: 40
    - Text: 2011 – 2014

12. Lock the 'Title' layer.

364EXERCISE 5. IDP AND REFUGEE PROPORTIONAL SYMBOL MAP – DESIGNING THE FINAL MAP

Next up is the ancillary text.

13. Create a new layer named 'Ancillary Text'.

14. Above the two photos, create the following text with the following properties:

    - Font: Arial
    - Font Size: 14
    - Color:
        - R: 0
        - G: 0
        - B: 0
    - Text: *The United Nations High Commissioner for Refugees (UNHCR) defines refugees as individuals who are outside their country of nationality or habitual residence because of persecution, war, or violence. Internally displaced persons (IDPs) are defined as persons who have been forced to flee their home for the same reason as a refugee, but remain in their own country and have not crossed an international border.*

15. Above the two photos, below and vertically centered with the ancillary text paragraph, create the following text with the following properties:

    - Font: Arial
    - Font Size: 16
    - Style: Bold
    - Color:
    - R: 99
    - G: 44
    - B: 40
    - Text: Total Persons of Concern: 9.36 Million

16. Lock the 'Ancillary Text' layer.

Your map should currently resemble the figure below.

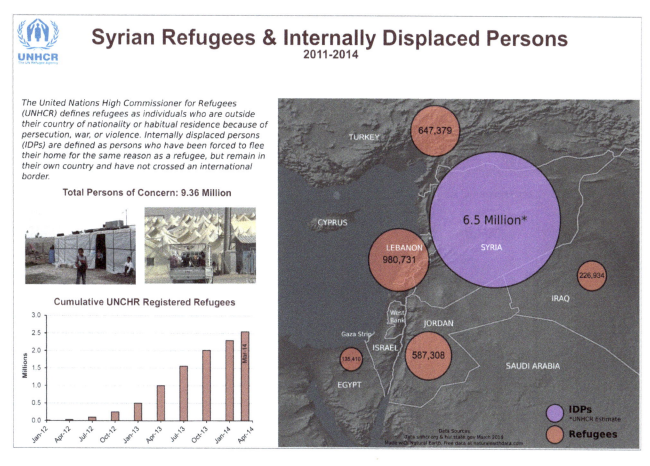

Last map element is the neatlines. There will be four neatlines on this map that surround the graph, title, map body, and entire map layout. Since we will use the neatline that surrounds the entire map layout as an anchor for the other neatlines, we will start there.

17. Create a new layer named 'Neatlines' and place it at the top of the layers list.

18. Select the Rectangles and squares tool ☐ from the Toolbox.

19. Draw a large rectangle on the map layout. Don't worry about having it completely surround the the elements, we will let Inkscape do that for us.

20. Set the size of the neatline to be 15 in wide and 10 in high. Set both the X and Y origins to 0. Remember you can set these properties on the Tool Controls Bar at the top of Inkscape when the neatline is selected. See the figure below.

21. Set the Fill color to No paint ✗ .

22. Set the Stroke Width to 3.5 px.

Now we will create a neatline around the title, graph, and map.

23. Use the Rectangles and squares tool ☐ to draw neatlines around the title, graph, and map body. Set the fill to No paint, and stroke width to 1.5px. Your neatlines should look similar to the ones in the figure below.

24. Lock the 'Neatlines' layer.

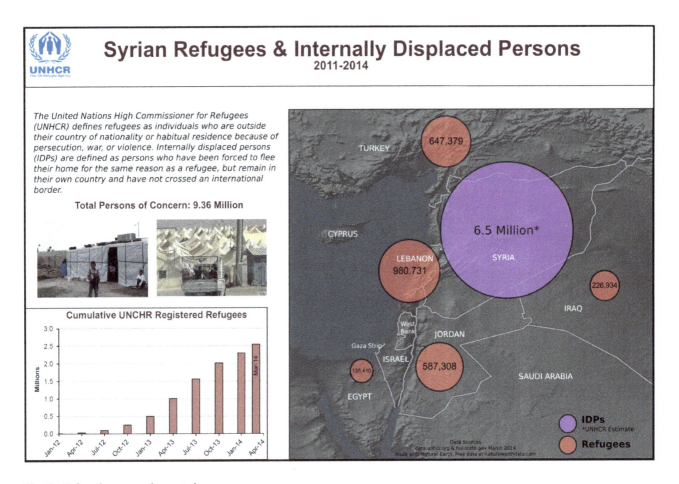

That's it for the map elements!

5.6   Task 4 Final Checks for Alignment and Map Export

Now that all of the map elements have been added to the map, we are ready for final tweaking of placement of elements and alignment between elements. In this Task, you will use the Align and Distribute Panel to align the map elements. Humans are really good at noticing slight mis-alignments, therefore, we want to avoid mis-alignments so map readers do not lose confidence in our map.

As you already have quite a bit of experience in aligning objects in Inkscape, this Task will provide general guidelines for aligning map elements. The figure below displays guidelines for the alignment of map elements and what is considered the final map design. Each guideline represents an alignment operation. The guidelines can be created by dragging from the left or top ruler down on to the composition. Guidelines can be deleted by selecting them then pressing Delete key on your keyboard.

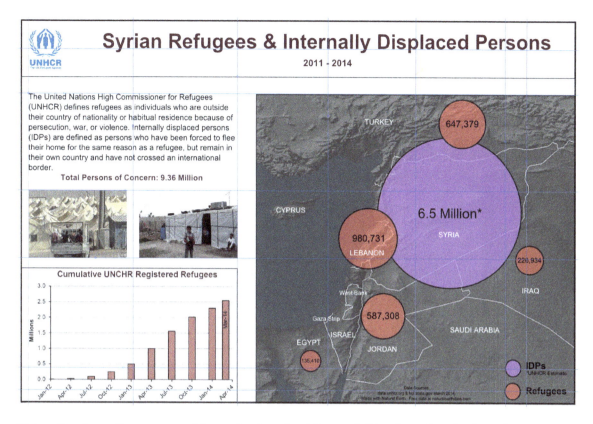

Using the above figure as a guide, and using the Align and Distribute Panel, align the map elements. You will need to unlock layers for alignment. If you want to manually move an element a small distance, select the element, then use the arrow keys on your keyboard to nudge the element in the related direction.

5.7 Task 5 Challenge: Add Refugee Camps to Map (optional)

The United States Department of State Humanitarian Information Unit provides GIS data of Syria Refugee Camps in Turkey, Iraq, and Jordan. The March 12th, 2014 data set is provided to you in Exercise 5 Data folder. Using QGIS and the Refugee Camp data, create a new layer for the map created in this exercise, and add it to the map, along with an associated legend and modified metadata statement. The new layer should show the locations of all camps, and the camps should have different symbology based on the designation in the 'DESIGNATION' field of the data.

The data was downloaded from https://hiu.state.gov/data/data.aspx

Here is the data's abstract:

> The "Syria Refugee Camps" dataset contains verified data about the geographic location (point geometry), name, and operational status of refugee camps hosting Syrian refugees in Turkey, Jordan, and Iraq. Only refugee camps operated by the United Nations High Commissioner for Refugees (UNHCR) or the Government of Turkey are included. Compiled by the U.S Department of State, Humanitarian Information Unit (INR/GGI/HIU), each attribute in the dataset (including name, location, and status) is verified against multiple sources. The name and status are obtained from the UNHCR data portal (accessible at http://data.unhcr.org/syrianrefugees/regional.php). The locations are obtained from the U.S. Department of State, Bureau of Population, Refugees, and Migration (PRM) and the National Geospatial-Intelligence Agency's GEOnet Names Server (GNS) (accessible at http://geonames.nga.mil/ggmagaz/). The name and status for each refugee camp is verified with PRM. Locations are verified using high-resolution commercial satellite imagery and/or known areas of population. Additionally, all data is checked against various news sources. Locations are only accurate

down to the city level. The designation field gives the type of site and the status of the site. Sites can be "Official Camps", camp settlements that are officially established and maintained by the United Nations or host country. Sites can also be "Transitional Camps", which is a typical camp structure but designed to be temporary or used on as needed basis. There can also be "Transitional Facilities"; these are facilities that are being used to temporarily house refugees. There can also be other sites such as host families or facilities, or other accommodations. Status of these sites can be Planned, Under Construction, Staged, Open, or Closed. The data contained herein is entirely unclassified and is current as of 12 March 2014. The data is updated as needed.

5.8   Conclusion

In this exercise, you used Inkscape to complete the map design of IDPs and Refugees of Syria. By separating the map elements by layer, you were able to logically place, lock, and modify properties of the layers' objects. In addition to map layout, you also added labels, copied and pasted objects, and aligned map elements for a clean, professional look. At this point, you know enough of Inkscape's commands to complete the majority of what would normally be done to complete a map.

5.9   Discussion Questions

1. Save your Inkscape map as a PDF and submit it for grading.

2. Discuss the lack of north arrow, scale bar, and locator map on the map you created in this exercise. Do you think leaving off these three map elements is a mistake? Why/why not? If you would include one of these map elements on the map, explain why and how you would expect your map reader to utilize the added map element.

3. If you were provided the data to create the Syrian Refugee & Internally Displaced Persons map, but were forbidden to create a proportional symbol map, what other map type would you choose to create this map? Why would your chosen map type be appropriate? Additionally, list one map type that would not be appropriate for portraying the data.

Exercise 6

Countries with Refugees and Internally Displaced Persons Over One Million Map Design

Objective - Utilize QGIS and Inkscape to Design a Choropleth Map Showing Refugees and IDPs Over One Million

6.1 Introduction

In this exercise, you'll construct a choropleth map showing worldwide refugee and internally displaced people (IDP). As this is the penultimate exercise for this series, this is where you'll be 'pushed from the nest' so-to-speak to complete the final map layout without any instruction from this exercise. This exercise will demonstrate how to design and export the final map (shown in figure below), and you'll be challenged to complete the map layout in Inkscape by modifying the layout designed in Exercise 5.

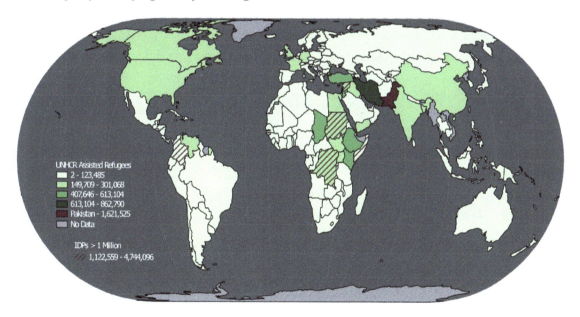

This exercise will focus primarily on data classification, symbolizing figures and grounds, creating a legend, and exporting the data to Inkscape.

It is assumed you've completed exercises 1-5 and have a working knowledge of Inkscape and QGIS. Because of this assumption, you'll be asked to complete tasks that were covered in the previous labs without being provided step-by-step instructions. Tasks that have not been covered in previous labs will be covered in detail in this exercise.

This exercise includes the following tasks:

- Task 1 – Load and Symbolize Basemap Data

- Task 2 – Classify and Symbolize Refugee Data

- Task 3 – Symbolize IDP Data

- Task 4 – Create Legend and Export Map

- Task 5 - Design Map Layout using Inkscape

6.2 Objective: Utilize QGIS and Inkscape to Complete the Design of a Choropleth Map Showing Worldwide IDPs and Refugees

To achieve a properly designed map, the features on the map must be easily distinguishable, attractive to the map reader, and stand out from the grounds (supporting background information/data). In this exercise, you'll learn how to utilize QGIS and Inkscape to compose a well-designed choropleth map.

6.3 Task 1 Load and Symbolize Basemap Data

The first task we will tackle is loading all of the basemap data and symbolizing it so we have a nice ground to contrast with our figures that we will add in Tasks 2 and 3.

1. Open QGIS Desktop.
2. In QGIS Desktop, add the following vector layers to the project. All of the layers have been projected in to EPSG:54012 - World_Eckert_IV, which is the projection we will use for this project.
   - Ocean.shp
   - Graticules 15 Degrees.shp
3. Order the Ocean layer below the Graticules 15 Degrees layer.
4. Set the following Style properties for the Ocean layer:
   - Symbol layer: Simple fill
     - Simple fill Color:
       * Hue: 195
       * Sat: 15
       * Val: 40
     - Border style: No pen
5. Set the following Style properties for the Graticules 15 Degrees layer:
   - Symbol layer: Simple fill
     - Simple line Color:
       * Hue: 60
       * Sat: 0
       * Val: 40
     - Pen width: 0.25

6.4 Task 2 Classify and Symbolize Refugee Data

In this task, you will add the dataset containing the refugee and IDP population information.

1. Add UNHCR Assisted IDPS and Refugees by Country.shp to the QGIS Project. Order this layer at the top of the Layers list. This dataset contains two attributes of interest:
   - Refugees: The number of refugees living within the country

- IDPs: The number of internally displaced persons (IDPs) living within the country.

2. Let's take a look at the descriptive statistics of the Refugee field to get a feeling for its form. Click Vector | Analysis Tools | Basic statistics to open the Basic statistics dialog. We will use this dialog to run basic descriptive statistics on the Refugee field.

3. Set the following options in the Basic statistics dialog, then Click OK to see the results shown in the figure below:

   - Input Vector Layer: 'UNHCR Assisted IDPS and Refugees by Country'
   - Target field: 'Refugees'

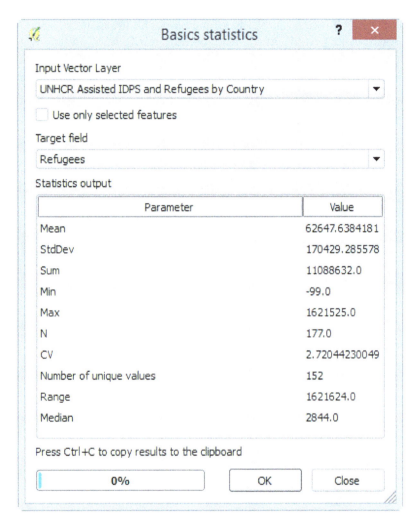

Reviewing the statistics, take note of the Mean, StdDev, Min, Max, and Median. Because the Median is significantly lower than the Mean, it tells us that the data is negatively skewed. The StdDev seems reasonable, if not a little large. Finally, notice that the Min value is -99. In this field, -99 represents a country with 'No Data' (aka NULL). Since -99 is a numeric value, it is being included in the basic statistics and is skewing our data. Additionally, the Max value is more than 9 times the standard deviation! This makes the maximum value seem like a prime candidate for being an outlier that we should handle separately.

4. Open the Attribute table and sort the Refugee field in descending order. Note that the largest value is almost twice the next largest value (shown in figure below).

Refugees
1621525
862790
613104
577212
550506

It turns out that Pakistan is the country with the largest refugee population. Because it is so much larger than the rest of the data, we will treat it separately for classification and statistics purposes. Additionally, we should exclude the -99 values when we run our basic statistics and classification. Let's do that now.

5. Right-click on the UNHCR... layer in the Layers list and choose Filter.... This opens a Query Builder dialog.

6. Enter the following expression to exclude Pakistan and -99 values.

   - "admin" != 'Pakistan' AND "Refugees" != -99

7. Click OK to apply the filter. Note that Pakistan and the countries with -99 refugees are now missing from the map and attribute table.

8. Rerun the Basic Statistics from steps 2 and 3. The results are shown in the figure below.

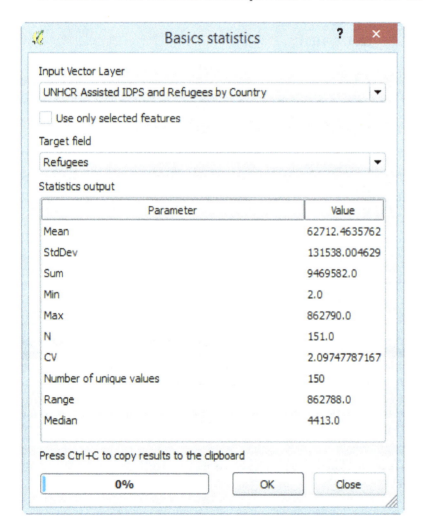

Review the basic statistics again. Note that they have changed quite significantly. The N value reduced from 177 to 151 which means that 26 countries were filtered out. While the Mean stayed roughly the same, the Median increased by 1,569, and the StdDev decreased by 38,891. This set of statistics gives us a better understanding of the nature of the data and will help guide us when classifying it. Let's classify the Refugee data now.

9. Close the Basic statistics dialog.

10. Open the Style properties for the UNHCR... layer.

11. Set the following Style properties (shown in figure below):

   - Classification type: Graduated
   - Column: Refugees
   - Symbol: Click the Change... button
     - Simple fill:
       * Border width: 0.3.
   - Classes: 5
   - Color ramp: Greens
   - Mode: Natural Breaks (Jenks)

12. Click the Classify button to classify the data.

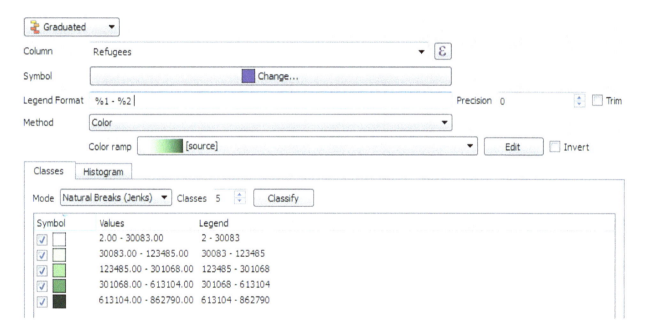

13. Click OK to apply the style to the map.

Notice there is quite a bit of white on the map that is a bit overpowering. Additionally, Pakistan and the -99 countries are still missing. Let's reintroduce and symbolize the missing countries while removing the white class.

14. Clear the Filter for the UNHCR layer.

15. Open the Style properties for the UNHCR... layer.

16. Uncheck Link class boundaries. This will allow us to introduce gaps between classes.

17. Since the first two classes only range from 2 to 123,485, which is within the first standard deviation, let's combine those two classes and reuse the lowest class for the -99 countries. Double-click on the values for the

lowest class (2.00 – 30083.00) to edit the class bounds.

18. Set the Lower value and Upper value both to -99 then click OK to set the new class bounds. See figure below for reference.

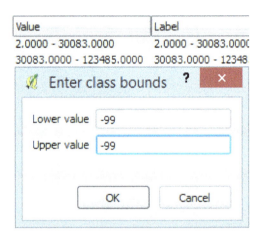

19. Double-click on the values for the second-lowest class (30083.0000 – 123485.0000) to edit the class bounds.

20. Set the Lower value to 2.0 then click OK to set the new Lower class bound.

21. Let's symbolize the -99 data as a grey color so it looks different from the refugee data; a different hue represents a different 'type' of thing, and, *no data* is different from data. Double-click on the symbol for the -99 - -99 class to open the Symbol selector.

   - Set the following Symbol properties:
     - Simple fill:
       * Fill Color:
         · Hue: 223
         · Sat: 10
         · Val: 65
       * Border width: 0.3

22. Click Add class to add a new class to the style. We will set this class to represent Pakistan.

23. Change the Lower value and Upper value of the class both to 1621525.

24. Let's symbolize Pakistan as a maroon color so it looks different from the refugee data and can have attention drawn to it. Double-click on the symbol for the 1621525.0000 – 1621525.0000 class to open the Symbol selector.

   - Set the following Symbol properties:
     - Simple fill:
       * Fill Color:
         · Hue: 4
         · Sat: 100
         · Val: 40
       * Border width: 0.3

25. Click OK to apply the style to the map. Your map should now resemble figure below.

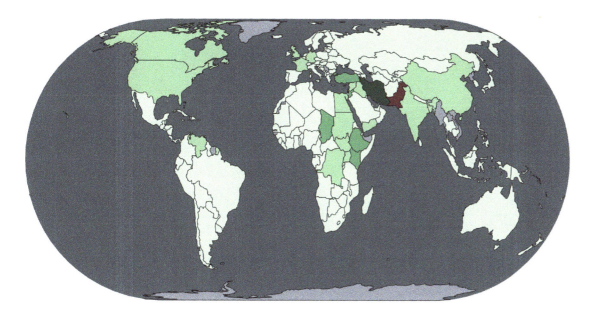

26. Re-open the style properties for the UNHCR... layer.

Let's review the classification as it stands now. Refer to the figure below for a screenshot of the classification. I'd like to make three observations: 1) the labels do not reflect the classification anymore; there are overlapping class boundaries (for example, which class does 301068.0000 below refer to?); 3) the class boundaries represent no gaps between the classes (i.e. the class boundaries do not always represent actual data values).

Symbol	Value	Label
	1621525.0000 - 1621525.00...	0.0 - 0.0
	-99.0000 - -99.0000	2.0000 - 30083.0000
	2.0000 - 123485.0000	30083.0000 - 123485.0000
	123485.0000 - 301068.0000	123485.0000 - 301068.0000
	301068.0000 - 613104.0000	301068.0000 - 613104.0000
	613104.0000 - 862790.0000	613104.0000 - 862790.0000

Let's address all three observations by a) changing the class boundaries to represent actual minimum and maximum values, b) updating the labels to represent the new class boundaries. By sorting the Refugee column values in the attribute table, we can see that the lower boundaries for the top three classes are all wrong (123485 and 301068 do not exist, and 613104 is the upper boundary for the previous class). Let's change them.

27. Set the lower boundary values for the top three classes so the classes are the same as shown in the figure below.

Symbol	Value
	1621525.0000 - 1621525.00...
	-99.0000 - -99.0000
	2.0000 - 123485.0000
	149709.0000 - 301068.0000
	407646.0000 - 613104.0000
	862790.0000 - 862790.0000

28. Now that all of the classes are set, we should update the Label field to reflect the changes we made. Set the following label values as shown in the figure below. Essentially you are:

- removing the decimal numbers

- adding thousands separators

- changing -99 to No Data

- identifying Pakistan and Iran by name since they are in classes by themselves and, as they are the highest values, might be countries of interest and easy identification.

Symbol	Value	Label
	1621525.0000 - 1621525.00...	1,621,525 (Pakistan)
	-99.0000 - -99.0000	No Data
	2.0000 - 123485.0000	2 - 123,485
	149709.0000 - 301068.0000	149,709 - 301,068
	407646.0000 - 613104.0000	407,646 - 613,104
	862790.0000 - 862790.0000	862,790 (Iran)

6.5   Task 3 Symbolize IDP Data

With the refugees mapped, now we will map the countries with IDPs numbering over 250,000 so we can bring special attention to them. As we have already assigned a fill color to each country, we need to get creative in how we can show which countries have over 250,000 IDPs. Let's overlay a hachure on the countries with high IDP values.

1. Duplicate the UNHCR... layer by right-clicking the UNHCR... layer in the Layers list then choosing Duplicate.

2. Turn on layer visibility for the original UNHCR... layer.

3. Rename the top UNHCR... layer to 'High IDP Countries'.

4. Open the style properties for the 'High IDP Countries'.

5. For Column, change from 'Refugees' to 'IDPs'.

6. Click the Delete all button to remove all classes.

7. Click the Add class button to add a single class.

8. Set the Lower value to 250000 and the Upper value to 4744096 (highest IDP value).

9. Change the class label to 'More than 250,000 IDPs'

10. Double-click on the symbol for the class to open the Symbol selector.

11. Set the following Symbol properties (shown in two figures below):

    - Simple fill:

        – Symbol layer type: Line pattern fill

        – Distance: 2.0

        – Line:

    - Simple line:

        – Color:

            * Hue: 0

            * Sat: 0

            * Val: 0

        – Pen width: 0.25

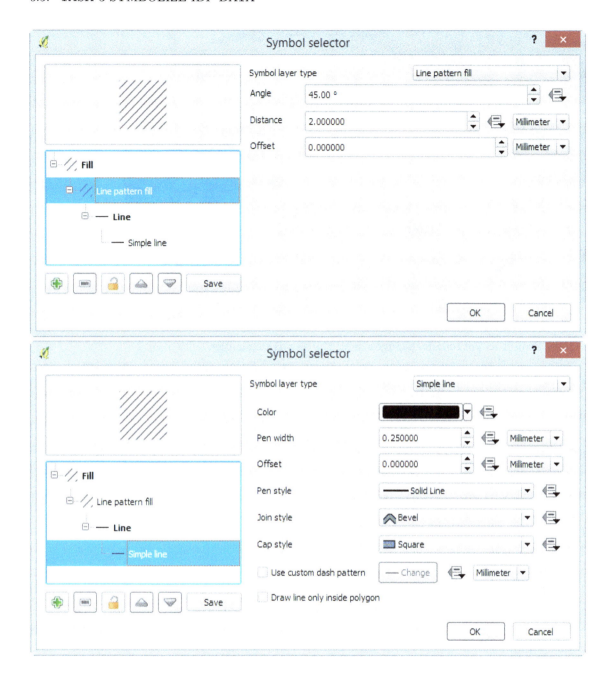

With all of the symbology now set, your map should look like the figure below.

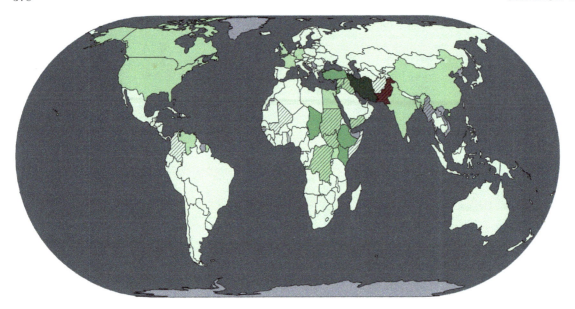

12. Save your QGIS Project as `Worldwide Refugee and IDP Population.qgs`.

6.6 Task 4 Create Legend and Export Map

With the map design complete, let's create a legend then export the map to Inkscape.

1. Click Project | New Print Composer and name it 'Worldwide IDPs and Refugees'.

2. In the Composition Panel, under the Composition tab, set the following properties:
    - Paper and quality
        - Presets: ANSI A (Letter; 8.5x11 in)
        - Orientation: Landscape
        - Page background:
            * Transparency: 100%
        - Print as raster: unchecked

3. Add the map to the composition and make it the same size as the page. Center the world on the page.

4. With the map selected, in the Composition panel, under the Item properties tab, uncheck Background so that the background is transparent.

Now we will add the legend.

5. Click the Add new legend button and click on the map. This will add the legend to the map. Let's change some basic legend properties before we dive in deeper.

6. With the legend selected, in the Composition panel, under the Item properties tab, set the following properties:
    - Main properties
        - Title: (none)
        - Background: unchecked
        - Fonts:
            * Subgroup font...
                · Font: Arial

        · Size: 11

       * Item font...

         · Font: Arial

         · Size: 10

       * Font color...

         · Hue: 0

         · Sat: 0

         · Val: 100

     – Symbol:

       * Symbol width: 6.00 mm

       * Symbol height: 4.00 mm

7. Now let's remove the Ocean and Graticules from the legend. In the Item properties tab, under Legend items group:

- Uncheck Auto update. This will allow us to change the contents of the legend.

- Select the `Graticules 15 Degrees` entry then press the remove button . This will remove it from the legend.

- Remove the Ocean entry from the legend.

8. Let's shorten the name for the Refugees layer and reorder the classes (the figure below shows the final configuration).

- Select UNHCR... entry and press the edit button .

- Change the Item text to 'UNHCR Assisted Refugees'.

- Click OK.

- Select the No Data class, then press the Move down button ![down arrow] repeatedly until it is at the bottom.

- Move the Pakistan class just above the No Data class.

High IDP Countries
   More than 250,000 IDP's

UNHCR Assisted Refugees
   2 - 123,485
   147,909 - 301,068
   407,646 - 613,104
   862790 (Iran)
   1,621,525 (Pakistan)
   No Data

9. Place the legend on top of the world map, West of South America. Your map should resemble the figure below.

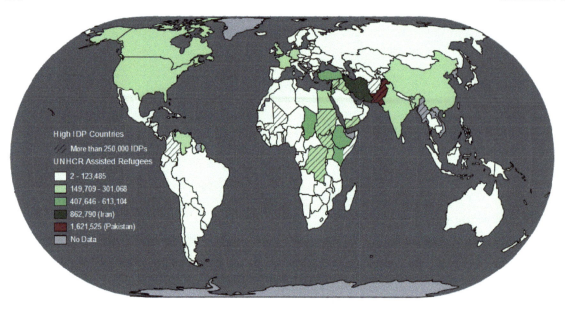

10. Export the map as a PDF named `Worldwide Refugee and IDP Population.pdf`.

6.7   Task 5: Design Map Layout using Inkscape

Using what you have learned in all of the exercises up to this point, design a final map layout in Inkscape. In your layout, use any page size and orientation you feel would be appropriate for the map. Be sure to add ancillary text and metadata to explain your map. Feel free to do some research online to add interesting text/pictures/graphs (cite your sources!). You may want to start by modifying the layout you designed in Exercise 5 so that both maps look like they are part of the same map series, but this is not a requirement.

Additionally, modify the legend so that it looks like the legend in the figure below (*hint*: ungroup a few times to get access to the legend, then move it to its own layer).

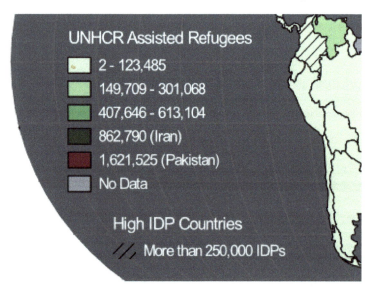

Example ancillary text:

> The United Nations High Commissioner for Refugees (UNHCR) defines refugees as individuals who are outside their country of nationality or habitual residence because of persecution, war, or violence.

Internally displaced persons (IDPs) are defined as persons who have been forced to flee their home for the same reason as a refugee, but remain in their own country and have not crossed an international border. This map shows the number of refugees each country contains and IDPs in their respective countries of origin. All data are current as of mid-2013 or the latest available estimates.

Example metadata:

Data Sources:
data.unhcr.org
naturalearthdata.com

6.8 Conclusion

In this exercise, you viewed the descriptive statistics for an attribute, classified data, modified the classification, designed a hachure symbol for multivariate mapping, designed a legend, and exported a map. Additionally, you were challenged to create a map design in Inkscape.

6.9 Discussion Questions

1. Save your Inkscape map from Task 5 as a PDF and submit it for grading.

2. In this exercise, we used hachures to show the IDP variable. What other visual variable could you have used to show the IDP variable on the map? What would be the positives and negatives of the visual variable you chose?

3. The World Eckert IV map projection was used in this exercise. Was this a good choice for mapping at a global scale? Identify at least two more map projections that would be appropriate for this type of thematic mapping. For each map projection, list the projection properties and explain why it would be appropriate.

4. How would you change the classification for the refugee variable? Would you lump countries with less than 100 refugees in with countries with 123,000 refugees? Would you separate out Iran and Pakistan? Design a different classification scheme and explain how yours is an improvement on the one designed in this exercise.

Exercise 7

Design and Label a Downtown Street Map

Objective – Utilize QGIS and Inkscape to Design and Label a Street Map of a Downtown Area

7.1 Introduction

In this exercise, you'll design and label a 1:2,500 scale downtown street map. This exercise will focus on teaching you basic and advanced labeling techniques in QGIS. Next, on your own, you'll design a downtown street map of any city in Massachusetts. The final map design should be designed using all techniques and concepts covered in this course.

It is assumed you've completed exercises 1-6 and have a working knowledge of Inkscape and QGIS. Because of this assumption, the you'll be asked to complete tasks that were covered in the previous labs without being provided step-by-step instructions. Tasks that have not been covered in previous labs will be covered in detail in this exercise.

This exercise includes the following tasks:

- Task 1 – Label Features using Basic QGIS Labeling Functions

- Task 2 – Improve Labels using Advanced QGIS Labeling Functions

- Task 3 – Complete Final Map Design

- Task 4 - Challenge: Design and Label a 1:2,500 Scale Downtown Street Map

7.2 Objective: Utilize QGIS and Inkscape to Design and Label a Street Map of a Downtown Area

Labeling a map is one of the most time consuming, frustrating, poorly automated, and *important* tasks a cartographer undertakes. Labels should provide the map reader with important attribute information to assist them in properly using the map. Poorly designed or missing labels can destroy a map's usefulness and undermine its authority. In this exercise, you'll learn how to utilize QGIS to label features using both basic and advanced QGIS labeling functions. The final product will be a well-designed street map of a downtown area.

7.3 Task 1 Label Features using Basic QGIS Labeling Functions

In this task, you'll label roads, water, and parks using basic labeling techniques. In Task 2, you will improve the labeling using advanced labeling techniques.

1. Open QGIS Desktop.

2. Open the `Salem Downtown.qgs` project. This project contains multiple OpenStreetMap layers that have been clipped to downtown Salem, Massachusetts (shown in the figure below). The map is set to 1:2,500 which is the planned print scale (if the scale is not 1:2,500, change it now). Therefore, every design decision made must be with respect to producing at this scale, and this scale only.

3. Open the Label Properties for the 'Waterways' layer by right-clicking on the layer in the Layers list, then choosing Properties from the contextual menu, then choosing the Labels tab.

4. Check Label this layer with and choose 'name' as the labeling attribute.

5. Set the following label properties (shown in the figure below):

   - Text:
     - Font: Arial
     - Style: Italic
     - Size: 9.0 points
     - Color:
       * Hue: 200
       * Sat: 100
       * Val: 100
   - Placement:
     - Position:
       * Above line: unchecked
       * On line: checked

6. Click OK. Look at the South River label in the bottom-right corner of the map. Notice that it overlaps with the road (shown in the figure below). This is not a desirable label placement. Unfortunately, with the basic labeling options, we cannot do anything about this, however, we'll address this problem in Task 2.

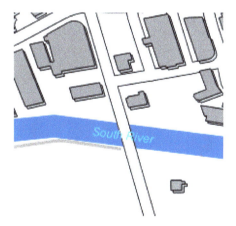

Now that the Waterways are labeled, we will label the Natural areas, which all happen to be parks in our map.

7. Open the Label Properties for the 'Natural' layer.

8. Check Label this layer with and choose 'name' as the labeling attribute.

9. Set the following label properties:

- Text:
    - Font: Arial
    - Style: Italic
    - Size: 9.0 points

- Color:
  - * Hue: 123
  - * Sat: 75
  - * Val: 30
- Placement: Around centroid
- Centroid: visible polygon

10. Click OK.

Find Armory Park just east of the center of the map (shown in the figure below). Notice that the label runs over on to the adjacent building. Again, not much we can do about this with basic labeling, so we will address the problem in Task 2.

Lastly, for this Task, let's label the Roads layer.

11. Open the Label Properties for the Roads layer.

12. Check Label this layer with and choose 'name' as the labeling attribute.

13. Set the following label properties:
- Text:
  - Font: Arial
  - Style: Normal
  - Size: 9.0 points
  - Color:
    - * Hue: 0
    - * Sat: 0
    - * Val: 0
- Placement:
  - Position:
    - * Above line: unchecked
    - * On line: checked

14. Click OK to set the Road labels. The basic labeling does a pretty good job in labeling the roads. There are a few issues, however, that need attention. Four examples are shown in the figure below.

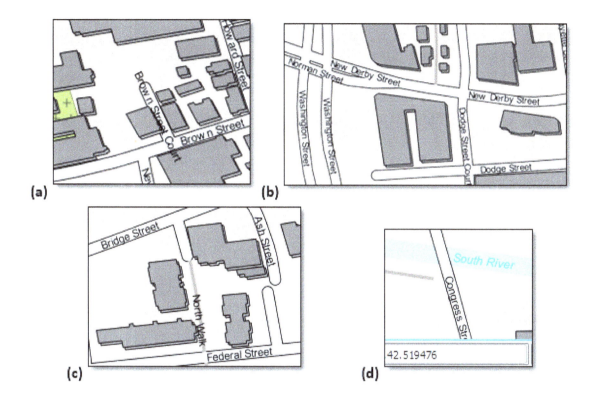

- (a) displays an example of a street label overrunning the street it is labeling.

- (b) displays a street being labeled multiple times and both labels being in close proximity to each other.

- (c) displays North Walk, a path, being labeled the same way as a road. This path could/should have a different label style since it is a different type of road.

- (d) displays Congress Street label running off the map. It should be moved or removed. Note that the South River label has moved off of the road and is in a better spot, however, it is crowding Congress Street and could still be placed in a better location.

We can address (b) from the figure above by changing a labeling property. Let's do this now.

15. Open the Label Properties for the Roads layer.
16. Set the following Label properties:
    - Rendering:
        - Feature options:
            * Merge connected lines to avoid duplicate labels: checked
17. Click OK to see the results. Notice that the amount of labels has been reduced and the multiple labels of the same roads have, for the most part, been removed.
18. Save the QGIS Project in your exercise directory.

7.4 Task 2 Improve Labels using Advanced QGIS Labeling Functions

Labeling a map increases its usefulness to the map reader if the labels are done well. The Salem Downtown map labels are decent for as little work that we put in to labeling the features, however, the map labels are far from publishable quality. This task will teach you how to use Data Defined Overrides to improve placement, define different labeling properties for records of different types, and, among other things, hide labels.

First, let's determine what a Data Defined Override is, and how to identify where they can be set. A Data Defined Override sets a layer property to a value stored in an attribute field in the layer. For example, a layer's label font, style, size, size unit, and color can all be set by referencing attribute values for the layer that is being labeled. Each text property that can be set with a Data Defined Override will have this button next to the property: ⬅ The figure below shows a small example of where the Data Defined Override buttons are located and which properties can be set with the Overrides.

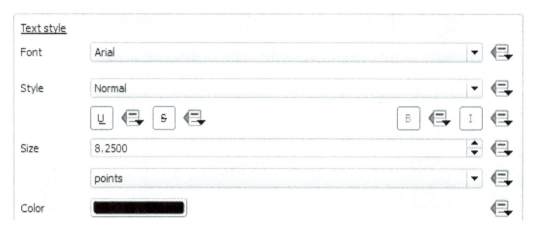

To set an Override, click the Override button, choose Field type, then the name of the field containing the override value. The figure below shows an override being set for the layer's Font property. This Font field contains the name of the font to be used to label its record.

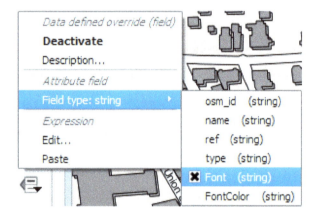

To get a description of what each Data Defined Override does, the expected input, valid input types, and current definition, click the Override button, then choose Description... For example, the figure below shows the Override description for the Font property.

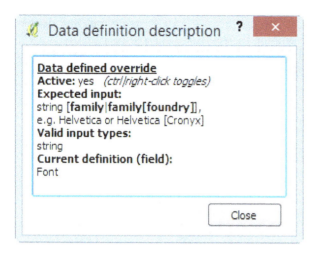

Note that for the font property being overridden, it expects a string input that contains the font family name. Additionally, it will only accept a string field (other properties may accept multiple field formats). Therefore, if we wish to have our record labeled using the Arial font family, we would create a field named 'Font' of format 'string', and store the string 'Arial' in the field for the record we want to label (example in figure below).

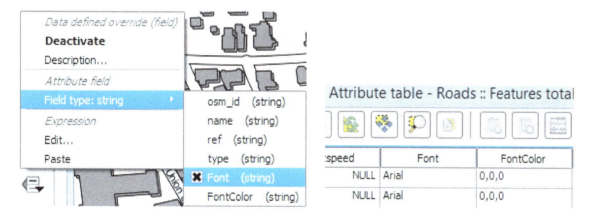

Let's start with moving the South River label to a more reasonable location. This will be achieved in three steps:

- Step 1. Create attribute columns to store the label's
    - X coordinate
    - Y coordinate
    - Rotation value

- Step 2. Assign the attributes created in Step 1 to Data Defined Overrides.

- Step 3. Start editing and use the Move Label and Rotate Label buttons on the Label toolbar to modify the South River label.

With the attribute columns created, let's make an observation.

1. Open the Label Properties for the Waterways layer.

2. Select the Placement tab. Note that in the Data define section, Coordinate X, Y, and Rotation can all be set with Data Defined Overrides (because all three have the Override button).

3. Look at the Data Defined Override Description for Coordinate X, Y, and Rotation. Pay special attention to the Valid input types.

You should have noticed that for the coordinates and rotation, it accepts fields of format string, int, and double. We will create three fields: two for the coordinates (X, Y) and one for the rotation. For the coordinates, we will store them as a double with a precision of six, so we can precisely position the label. For the rotation, we will store this as an integer, as that should give us enough precision. Let's create these fields now.

4. Close the Label properties.

5. Open the Attribute Table for the Waterways layer.

6. Start editing by clicking the edit mode toggle .

7. Create a new column by clicking the New column button .

8. Set the following properties for the new column:
   - Name: Label_X
   - Comment: X coordinate of label's position
   - Type: Decimal number (real)
   - Width: 9
   - Precision: 6

9. Click OK to create the field.

10. Create a second field for the label's Y coordinate. Create it with similar settings as the Label_X field.

11. Create a third field to store the rotation value. It's type should be a Whole number with a width of 3.

12. Save your edits and stop editing.

Now with the proper fields created, let's link them to the Data Defined Overrides.

13. Open the Label properties for the Waterways layer.

14. Choose the Placement tab.

15. Click the Data Defined Override button next to Coordinate X | Field type... | Label_X. You will know the Override has been set when the Override button changes to a yellow fill color Coordinate X.

16. Set the Override for Coordinate Y and Rotation to the appropriate attribute fields.

17. Click OK to set the overrides.

Now we can do the final step, which is editing the label's placement.

18. Turn on the Labels toolbar if it is turned off.

19. Start editing the Waterways layer by selecting the layer in the Layers list and choosing Layer | Toggle Editing. When you toggle editing on, commands on the Labels toolbar (reference the figure below) will be activated.

Let's take a moment and explore the activated labels toolbar. From left-to-right, the buttons represent:

- Labeling options – opens a dialog box allowing you to change the labeling properties.
- Highlight pinned labels – any labels that have been modified (moved, rotated, etc. . .) and have values stored in the data defined override attribute fields is considered to be 'pinned'. Pinned labels will be highlighted when this button is toggled on.

- Pin/Unpin labels – with this button toggled on, if you click a label, it will become, or stay, pinned (location stored in data defined override attribute values). If you hold the shift-key on your keyboard and click a pinned label, the data defined override attribute values will be erased, the label will no longer be pinned, and it will return to its original location.

- Show/hide labels (shown disabled) – with this button toggled on, if you click a label, it will become invisible. Shift-clicking the label will make it visible again.

- Move label – allows you to click and drag a label to define a new location.

- Rotate label – allows you to click and drag to rotate a label. Holding the Control key on your keyboard while rotating, rotates the label in 15° increments.

- Change label – allows you to change the text of the label and any data defined override values you have enabled.

We will use the Move and Rotate commands to move the South River label to a more desirable location.

20. Click on the Move Label button to enable the command.
21. Click on the South River label and drag it further east or west (your choice).
22. When you release the South River label, you'll notice that the rotation of the label is now horizontal (i.e., the rotation value has been lost and reset to 0.) Click the Rotate Label button to enable the command.
23. Click and drag the South River label to rotate it so that it is parallel with the centerline of the river segment that the label is on top of.
    - After you rotate the label, you may need to move the label again to have it properly placed on the river.

Your label, properly placed, should resemble the figure below.

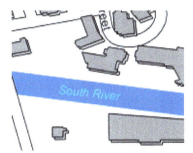

24. Save your edits and stop the editing session.
25. Open the Waterways Attribute Table and note that values have now been stored in the Label_X, Label_Y, and Rotation fields.

At this point, you could add the Waterways layer to another QGIS project, enable labeling on the name field, and enable Data Defined Overrides using the three fields created in this Task, to have the label show up in the exact location you just set. If you use the Waterways layer in another QGIS project and do not enabled Data Defined Overrides, then the Waterways layer will be labeled using the basic labeling engine.

Now let's turn our attention to the Natural layer, which represents the parks in downtown Salem. Note that multiple park labels are wider than the park. To help mitigate this, let's do three things:

- Define a Data Defined Override for the position of the label.

- Define a font size for the labels.

- Wrap the text to a new line based on specific character(s) in the text.

26. Using what you learned above, create attributes, and define Data Defined Overrides for the X and Y position of the Natural labels.

27. Create a new attribute field to hold the font size and set the value for every row to: 9.0

   - Set the following properties for the new attribute field:
      - Name: LFontSize
      - Comment: Label's font size in points.
      - Type: Decimal number (real)
      - Width: 3
      - Precision: 1 (this allows for 1/10th of a point sizing)

28. Save your edits and stop editing.

29. Open the Label properties for the Natural Layer.

30. Choose the Placement tab.

31. Set the Data Defined Override for the Coordinate X and Coordinate Y to the fields you created.

32. Select the Text tab.

33. For the Font Size property, set the Data Defined Override to the LFontSize field you just created.

34. Click OK. The map should look the same, since the Natural layer was already labeled with size of 9.0 point labels.

Before we change label size of individual parks, let's set up the text wrapping so we can change both the font size and label wrap at once later.

35. Reopen the Label properties for the Natural layer.

36. Select the Formatting tab.

37. Set Wrap on character to '\n' (without the quotes). The property should look like the figure below. The '\n' character sequence is a common way to denote that a carriage return and line feed should be inserted at that location in a string of text. We will use that sequence to identify locations in label text where the label should continue on the next line.

With the font size and wrap on text properties set, let's change a park's label to see how they work.

38. Click OK to save and close the Natural layer's properties if you haven't already.

39. Start editing on the Natural layer.

40. On the Labels Toolbar, click the Change Label button abc to toggle it on.

41. Click the Lappin Park label (you may need to zoom out to find the park). This will open the Label properties dialog box.

42. Change the following label properties (shown changed in figure below):

   - Text: Lappin\nPark (no spaces anywhere in the text)
   - Font:

    − Size: 7.0

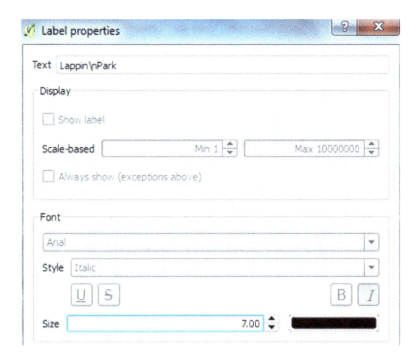

43. With the properties set, click OK to save the label properties. Note that the Lappin Park label is now on two separate lines and is small enough to fit inside the park polygon at this scale.

44. Move the Lappin Park label so that it is completely inside the park.

45. Using your judgment, modify the other park labels so they are properly placed.

With the waterways and parks labeled, all that is left to label are the roads. To properly label the roads, we will use a Data Defined Override value for the position, rotation, visibility, font, font color, and font size. Additionally, we will wrap the text on the '\n' characters. Let's get started.

46. Using what you learned above, for the Roads layer, create attributes, and define Data Defined Overrides for the following:

   • X and Y position

   • Rotation value

   • Font Size

47. Set the Wrap on text property to '\n' (without the quotes).

48. Create a new attribute with the following properties:

   • Name: LVisibility

   • Comment: Label's visibility

   • Type: Whole Number (integer)

   • Width: 1

49. Set every row value for the LVisibility layer to '1'. This field holds a boolean value. A value of 1 represents 'True' and indicates to QGIS that you wish the label to be visible. A value of 0, or, 'False', hides the label.

50. To set the visibility Data Defined Override, open the Road layer's label properties and select the Rendering tab.

51. In the Label options section, set Show label property's Data Defined Override to the LVisibility attribute

(refer to figure below).

52. Click OK to set the Data Defined Override.

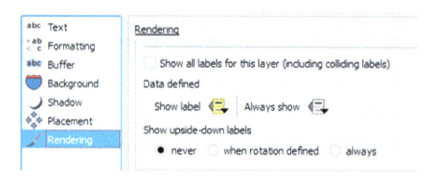

To show or hide a label, you will start editing the layer, then, on the Label toolbar, click the Show/hide label button , then click on a label to show it, or shift-click a label to hide it. We won't do that now, however, you may wish to do this in Task 3.

53. Create a new attribute with the following properties:

    • Name: LabelFont

    • Comment: Label's Font

    • Type: Text (string)

    • Width: 10

54. Set every row value for the LabelFont layer to 'Arial'. With this field, we could set different fonts for the records, however, in our case, we will set all fonts to Arial.

55. To set the font Data Defined Override, open the Road layer's label properties and select the Text tab.

56. In the Text style section, set Font property's Data Defined Override to the LabelFont attribute.

57. Click OK to set the Data Defined Override. All labels will now use the Arial font.

The last labeling option we will set with a Data Defined Override is the font color. This override needs a short explanation on how the values should be stored in the attribute. First, let's look at the data definition description for the font color property, shown in the figure below.

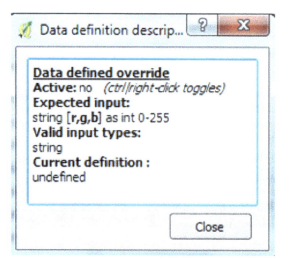

For the expected input, it was a list of three values (red, green, and blue), and each value ranging between the numbers 0 and 255. The attribute field should be of type Text (string). So, as an example, to specify the color white, we would store in the attribute this string: 255,255,255. For black, the value would be: 0,0,0. So, what we need to figure out is what is the maximum number of characters that we would need to hold in our new attribute field? Well, since white uses the maximum value of 255 for red, green, and blue, we can count 11 characters (nine numbers, plus two commas). So, with that sorted, let's create the attribute field to hold the label color.

58. Create a new attribute with the following properties:

 - Name: LabelColor
 - Comment: Label's RGB Color Value
 - Type: Text (string)
 - Width: 11

With this field, we could set different font colors for the records, however, in our case, we will leave the values as NULL for now as the black color set in the label properties will display if it sees a NULL value in the Data Defined Override field.

59. To set the font Data Defined Override, open the Road layer's label properties and select the Text tab.

60. In the Text style section, set Color property's Data Defined Override to the LabelColor attribute.

61. Click OK to set the Data Defined Override.

Let's set the roads with the type attribute of footway, path, pedestrian, or track to a different color from the roads. To do this, we will first select these types of roads, then use the field calculator to set the selected records' LabelColor to 75, 67, 64.

62. Open the Roads layer Attribute Table.

63. Press the Select Features button to open the Select by Expression dialog box.

64. Set the following expression (shown in figure below):"type" = 'footway' OR "type" = 'path' OR "type" = 'pedestrian' OR "type" = 'track'

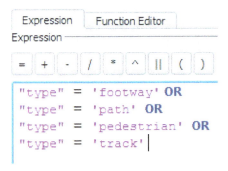

65. Click the Select button to select 26 records.

66. Click the Close button to dismiss the Select by Expression dialog box.

67. With the attribute table still open, start editing, and open the field calculator and set the following values (also shown in figure below):

 - Only update 26 selected features: checked
 - Update existing field: checked
 - Existing field dropdown box: LabelColor
 - Expression: '75,67,64' (include the single quotes)

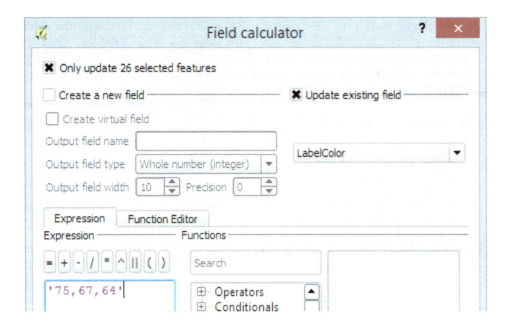

68. Click OK to set the value of the selected records' LabelColor attributes to 75,67,64. The labels for the selected records will now be dark grey, and the other road features will still be black (0,0,0).

69. Save the QGIS Project.

7.5   Task 3 Complete Final Map Design

With those Data Defined Overrides set for the Road layer, you should have the capability to modify the road labels so that they are properly positioned. Once that is completed, the map is ready for the other map elements to be added (e.g. title, north arrow, scale bar, legend, etc. . .).

For this task, complete the labeling of the roads, design a map layout, and export the map as a PDF, and submit for grading. You may do the layout design in QGIS, or use Inkscape for the final layout.

7.6   Task 4 Challenge: Design and Label a 1:2,500 Scale Downtown Street Map (optional)

In the exercise folder, there is a subfolder named Massachusetts OSM Data that contains Open Street Map data for the entire state of Massachusetts. Using what you have learned in this exercise, complete the following:

- Identify a new downtown area of a city in Massachusetts that you would like to map at 1:2,500 scale. Clip this downtown area to new shapefiles.

- Fully symbolize the data.

- Fully label the data and do at least the following:

  - Use Data Defined Overrides for some of the label properties.
  - Label the roads differently based on their type.

- Complete the map layout and export as a PDF and submit for grading.

7.7 Conclusion

In this exercise, you learned how to label features in QGIS using both basic and advanced labeling options. To enable the advanced labeling, you created new attribute fields to hold values that are read by the Data Defined Overrides.

7.8 Discussion Questions

1. Save maps from Tasks 3 and 4 (if Task 4 was attempted) as PDFs and submit them for grading.

2. Identify two other label properties you feel would be useful to set a Data Defined Override. Describe how you would create a Data Defined Override for the two properties, specifically listing the properties of the new fields. Give an example of a value you would set for each of the properties.

3. For the Roads layer, open the Style properties. Notice that the Feature blending mode is set to 'Lighten'. Research then explain what the feature blending mode does. How might you use the feature blending mode with labels?

Part V

Remote Sensing

Exercise 1

Image Composite, Mosaic, and Subset

Objective – Overview of Basic GRASS GIS Raster Functionality inside QGIS

1.1 Introduction

This exercise will provide an introduction and overview of some of the basic functionality of GRASS GIS inside QGIS for working with raw image data to add and view image data sets. You're encouraged to become familiar with working with, and finding information on, GRASS GIS help topics.

This exercise includes the following tasks:

- Task 1 – Learn Basics of GRASS GIS inside QGIS

- Task 2 – Image Composite

- Task 3 – Image Mosaic

- Task 4 – Image Subset

- Task 5 – Calculate NDVI

- Task 6 – Challenge: Image Subset with r.patch

1.2 Objective: Overview of Basic GRASS Raster Functionality inside QGIS

While QGIS has a large amount of functionality, it only goes so far before its limits are reached. To extend the functionality of QGIS, the capabilities of GRASS GIS (or simply GRASS), have been made available through the *GRASS 7* plugin. GRASS is a free and open source GIS software package containing over 350 modules to display, analyze, and manipulate vector and raster data. While GRASS is a separate, standalone GIS software package, in this exercise series we will use QGIS as a front-end to GRASS.

At this point you're familiar with the vector-based GIS functions found within QGIS. This exercise introduces you to the raster analysis functions in GRASS to: create some simple multiband image composites from existing remotely sensed imagery, create subsets (clipping) of rasters, and create a mosaic.

1.3 Task 1 – Learn Basics of GRASS GIS inside QGIS

GRASS GIS is installed by default when you install QGIS Desktop. While GRASS is a completely standalone GIS software package, its capabilities are made available via a core QGIS plugin. This task will teach you the basic terminology and concepts of how GRASS manages data, as well as how to work with GRASS data within QGIS.

First, let's start with some terminology and concepts. Working with GRASS data is different than how you may be used to working with data using QGIS or other GIS software packages. Since the storage paradigm is significantly different than what you have seen in prior GIS software, we will discuss how GRASS stores data first. Refer to the figure below during the following explanation for a graphic representation of the storage concepts.

In order for GRASS to start a project, it must first connect to a **Database** (also called a GISDBase). The Database is simply a folder on your computer that has special subdirectories. Once GRASS connects to a Database, it then needs to access a Location.

A **Location** is a child directory of the Database and stores the coordinate system or map projection that all enclosed Mapsets will use. Think of a Location as a common container for a project.

A **Mapset** is a child directory of a Location that represents a geographical subset of its parent Location. Mapsets contain geographic data in their directories. There are two types of mapsets: *Permanent* and *owner*.

- A **Permanent mapset** usually contains read-only geographic data that can be used by anyone. The Permanent mapset may also contain other information about the Location that is not stored anywhere else, therefore, the Permanent mapset must exist in every Location.

- **Owner mapsets** are user-created and represent specific areas or study sites within the Location. Think of a mapset as a collection of geographic data that is project or user specific. Owner mapsets can be named whatever logical name is desired. Examples of mapset names are 'user1' and 'Nueces County', where 'user1' represents a mapset created by, or created for a user on the system, and 'Nueces County' represents a project dealing with Nueces County, Texas.

Last, there is the concept of a **Region**. A Region is a subset of a Location defined by a rectangular bounding box. The Region is important for raster operations as it bounds the area (region) that will participate in any raster operations executed in GRASS. A Region is an operating parameter set when working in GRASS.

If all of the above explanation was a little confusing, don't worry, with practice in these exercises, it will start to make more sense.

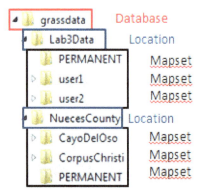

As you saw in Part 2 - Exercise 6, on page 171, there is a GRASS 7 plugin, and GRASS databases can be browsed via the QGIS Browser Panel. This QGIS-GRASS integration was completed in the fall of 2015 with QGIS v2.12. GRASS vector data can now be edited directly via the standard QGIS interface.

To open a GRASS Mapset, use the QGIS Browser Panel to right-click on a mapset and use the mapset context menu action **Open mapset**. When a Mapset is open, the GRASS Tools panel items will become enabled.

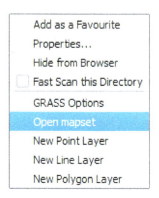

The GRASS Tools panel has two tabs: Modules and Region. Modules allows you to access GRASS tools organized by theme. Region shows the GRASS Region settings.

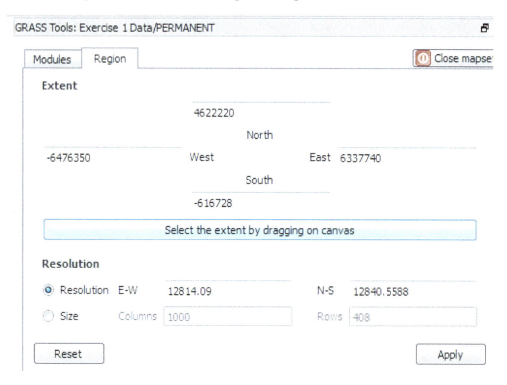

You can click the Close Mapset button ⬛️Close mapset in the GRASS Tools panel to close the open Mapset.

New locations can be created via the Create new GRASS location and transfer data into it option at the top of the GRASS tools modules tab.

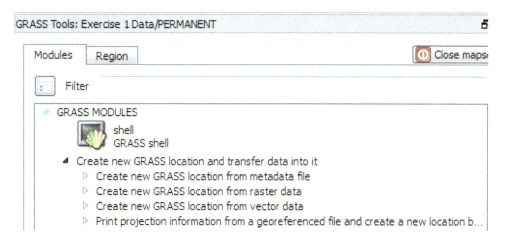

New mapsets can be created by right clicking on a GRASS database in the QGIS Browser panel and choosing New mapset from the context menu.

This task provided a brief overview of how GRASS can be used within QGIS. This, and the subsequent exercises in this workbook, will only use a small subset of GRASS's capabilities. To learn more about GRASS GIS, visit the official webpage at http://grass.osgeo.org/

1.4   Task 2 - Image Composite

An image composite consists of taking individual bands and putting them together into a single multiband image data set. In many cases, downloaded image data is provided this way where the end-user will need the ability to put it together.

1. Start QGIS and enable the 'GRASS 7' plugin and panel.

2. Open the Browser Panel and navigate to the Exercise 1 Data folder.

3. Right-click on the user 1 mapset and choose Open mapset from the context menu.

4. Load the following image bands from the user 1 mapset into QGIS by dragging them onto the map canvas.

   - tm_sacsub1.tif
   - tm_sacsub2.tif
   - tm_sacsub3.tif
   - tm_sacsub4.tif
   - tm_sacsub5.tif
   - tm_sacsub7.tif

The six images represent different bands are from a Landsat TM satellite subset. These will show up in the QGIS Layers Panel.

5. In the GRASS Tools panel select the Modules tab.

6. Expand the tree to find r.composite tool.

   - GRASS Modules
     - Raster
       * Manage map colors
         · r.composite

7. Click on r.composite tool to open it.

8. Set the following options. Refer to the figure below.

   - Name of raster map to be used for <red>: tm_sacsuub3
     - Click 'Use region of this map' button ⬜
   - Name of raster map to be used for <green>: tm_sacsuub2
   - Name of raster map to be used for <blue>: tm_sacsuub1
   - (1-256): 32 (represents number of values for red)
   - (1-256): 32 (represents number of values for green)
   - (1-256): 32 (represents number of values for blue)
   - Name for output raster map: Composite_32_TM_123

9. Click the Run button to run the tool. The dialog will switch to the Output tab to show the results of the tool. If it does not say 'Successfully finished', recheck that you entered the options correctly, and run again.

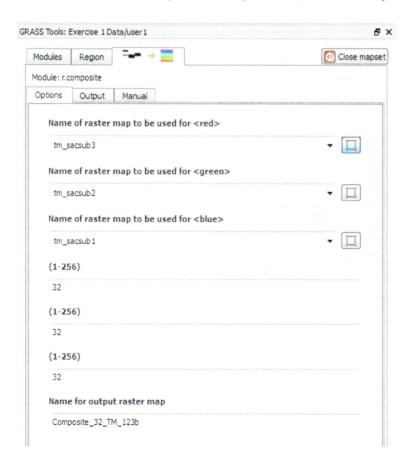

10. On the Output tab, with the r.composite tool successfully run, click the View output button to add the composite raster to the QGIS Layers list. You should now see a true color 3-band raster.

Let's investigate this new raster a little more by viewing details about it in the Browser Panel.

11. Open the Browser Panel.

12. Right click on the newly created compsite raster (Composite_32_TM_123) and choose Properties.

If you do not see the newly created compsite raster (Composite_32_TM_123), click the Refresh button .

13. The Layer Properties window opens.

What are the Properties for the following?

- Min value

- Max value

- Data type

14. Using the same procedure as above, create a new composite raster using bands 4, 5, and 7. You can simply click the Options tab for the r.composite tool in the GRASS Tools panel, change the settings, and re-run the tool. Use the following band assignments:
    - Red: tm_sacsub4
    - Green: tm_sacsub5
    - Blue: tm_sacsub7

Your output composite should look like the figure below.

Create new composites to answer the following three questions.

15. Change the display to show a true color band combination (Red Display = Band 3, Green Display =Band 2, and Blue Display = Band 1). Describe what you see and the colors of the features. This is a "natural color" band combination.

16. Change the band combination to (Red Display = Band 4, Green Display to Band 3, and the Blue Display to Band 2). Describe what you see and the colors of the features. This combination is generally referred to as a false color composite.

17. Change the band combination to (Red Display = Band 4, Green Display to Band 5, and the Blue Display to Band 3). Describe what you see and the colors of the features. This combination shows moisture differences, and is useful for analysis of soil and vegetation.

1.5   Task 3 - Image Mosaic

This task will walk through the steps to generate a simple image mosaic to merge adjacent images from the same sensor with the same number of bands.

1. Start QGIS and enable the GRASS 7 plugin and GRASS Tools panel. If QGIS is already open, create a new, empty project.

2. Switch to the Browser Panel. Navigate to the `Exercise 1 Data` folder and open the `user 2` mapset.

3. Load the following image bands from the `user 2` mapset into QGIS:

   - subset1
   - subset2
   - subset3
   - subset4

4. Zoom to full extent on the map canvas.

Note that the four rasters are adjacent and represent one larger square area. Before we mosaic the rasters together, we first need to define the region that our newly mosaicked raster will fill. A region can be thought of as a working window for raster processing.

5. On the GRASS Tools panel switch to the Modules tab.

6. In the Filter search box, enter 'region'.

7. Click on the g.region.multiple.raster tool to open it.

8. Select subset1, subset2, subset3, and subset4 from the drop down layers list.

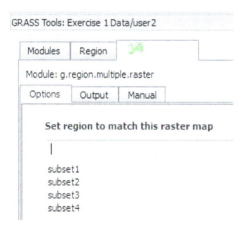

9. Click the Run button to execute the tool. Close the g.region.multiple.rasters tool.

10. Zoom to full extent on the map canvas.

Notice that there is now a red outline surrounding the extents of the four subset rasters. This red outline represents the current raster processing region. The figure below illustrates what the region extent should look like (note that subset4 has been turned off to better illustrate the red outline).

Now that the region has been set, we will mosaic the rasters together into a single, new raster. To do this, we will utilize the r.patch tool. The r.patch tool sets the current region's cell values with the values of the specified rasters. Therefore, since the current region is filled by our four rasters, the values from each of the four rasters will transfer to the new, moasiced raster is the same size as the current region.

11. Select the Modules tab in the GRASS Tools panel.

12. In the Filter search box, enter 'patch' to quickly find the r.patch tool.

13. Click on the r.patch tool to open it.

14. Select the four rasters to mosaic. (refer to figure below):

- Name of raster maps to be patched together: subset1, subset2, subset3, subset4

- Name for resultant raster map: mosaic

15. Click 'Run' button to execute the patch tool.

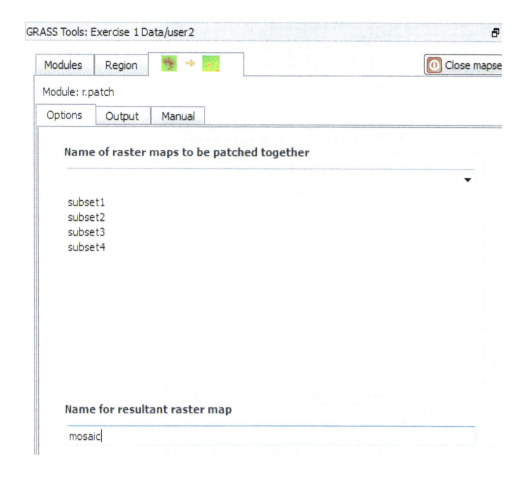

16. Add the newly created mosaic to the QGIS canvas to view it. Turn off the visibility of the subset rasters to verify that the mosaic is complete.

1.6 Task 4 - Image Subset

This task will walk through the steps to generate an Image Subset.

1. Start QGIS and enable the GRASS 7 plugin and GRASS Tools panel. If QGIS is already open, create a new, empty project.
2. Switch to the Browser Panel. Navigate to the `Exercise 1 Data` folder and open the `user 2` mapset as you did in Task 3.
3. Load the mosaic raster from Task 3.
4. On the GRASS Tools panel, select the Region tab.

The current region can be set manually using this tab. It allows you to drag a box on the map canvas to set the four extent values. We will use this technique here.

5. Click the Select the extent by dragging on canvas button.
6. Drag a box inside the mosaic that is smaller than the mosaic.
7. Click Apply on the Region tab.
8. See the figure below for an example.

The extent values are updated to match the extent of the drawn box.

The Resolution setting determines what cell size will be used in the region. As we wish to stay at the same cell size, we will set the Cell width and Cell height to 30.

9. On the GRASS Region tab, set the following:

    • Cell width: 30

    • Cell height: 30

        – *Note that the sizes may change slightly when you move between input boxes; this is normal.*

10. Click Apply to set the new region.

11. Switch to the Modules tab on the GRASS Tools panel.

12. Using the search box find and open the r.resample tool.

13. Click on the Manual tab of the tool and read the manual. Every GRASS tool has a manual worth referencing to learn about their functionality.

14. Click the Options tab of the tool and set the following options:

    • Name of an input layer: mosaic

    • Name of an output layer: smaller_mosaic

15. Click Run to execute the tool and click View output.

16. Verify that the `smaller_mosaic` was successfully created.

1.7 Task 5 - Calculate Normalized Difference Vegetation Index (NDVI)

This task will teach you how to calculate NDVI.

1. Start QGIS and enable the GRASS 7 plugin and GRASS Tools panel. If QGIS is already open, create a new, empty project.

2. Switch to the Browser Panel. Navigate to the `Exercise 1 Data` folder and open the `user 1` mapset as you did in Task 2.

3. Load the following image bands from the user 1 mapset into QGIS:

   - tm_sacsub3 – represents the red band
   - tm_sacsub4 – represents the near infrared band

4. Find and open the r.mapcalculator tool. Set the following options:

   - A: tm_sacsub3
   - Use region of this map : selected
   - B: tm_sacsub4
   - Formula: float(B-A)/float(B+A)
   - Name for output raster map: NDVI

5. Run the tool and add the output to the map canvas.

At this point, you should have a black and white image that looks like the figure below. While this is the calculated NDVI, it can be more visually appealing to assist the map reader in understanding where the healthy vegetation is located. To do this, we will apply a color table to the NDVI raster.

6. In the Modules tab, find and open r.colors.table. Set the following options:

   - Name of input raster map: NDVI
   - Type of color table: Normalized Difference Vegetation Index colors

7. Run the tool. The raster will now look like the figure below. If it does not, remove and re-add the NDVI raster to the map canvas.

1.8 Task 6 - Challenge: Image Subset with r.patch (optional)

Now that you know how to create an image subset with r.resample, determine how you would create an image subset with r.patch.

1.9   Conclusion

In this exercise, you have learned the basics of using GRASS Tools inside of QGIS to complete a composite, mosaic, subset, and NDVI. This exercise just scratches the surface in terms of GRASS's capabilities. Future exercises will delve deeper into GRASS.

1.10   Discussion Questions

1. Answer the questions from Task 2 (copied below).

   • Create new composites to answer the following three questions.

     a) Change the display to show a true color band combination (Red Display = Band 3, Green Display =Band 2, and Blue Display = Band 1). Describe what you see and the colors of the features. This is a "natural color" band combination.

     b) Change the band combination to (Red Display = Band 4, Green Display to Band 3, and the Blue Display to Band 2). Describe what you see and the colors of the features. This combination is generally referred to as a false color composite.

     c) Change the band combination to (Red Display = Band 4, Green Display to Band 5, and the Blue Display to Band 3). Describe what you see and the colors of the features. This combination shows moisture differences, and is useful for analysis of soil and vegetation.

Exercise 2

Image Rectification

Objective – Perform an Image Rectification

2.1 Introduction

Although many photogrammetric processes require specialized photogrammetric software, this exercise reviews how to perform an image rectification, which is one of the fundamental methods used in photogrammetry. In a real-world setting, additional training and education would be required in addition to an investment in photogrammetric software. Many ortho imaging and analysis firms make the necessary investments to perform photogrammetric processes.

This exercise includes the following tasks:

- Task 1 – Set Up Referencing Environment
- Task 2 – Select Common Control Points
- Task 3 – Rectify the Image
- Task 4 – Post-Rectification Steps

2.2 Objective: Perform an Image Rectification

In this exercise you'll walk through the processes of conducting an image rectification using 2009 6 inch ortho rectified aerial photography to rectify a 2005 1m Color IR USGS image.

2.3 Task 1 – Set Up Referencing Environment

In this task, we will set up our referencing environment to prepare for image rectification.

To perform the image rectification, you will be using the QGIS Georeferencer Plugin and a reference image. In Part 1 - Exercise 3, on page 57 you used benchmarks to georeference an image. Here you will choose the control points interactively. The reference image will be used to pick control points and match them with the image we will be georeferencing.

Note for Mac users:

You will need to download and install the MrSID plugin from http://j-vh.me/XfKiEd (located about halfway down the page) to open .sid files (and, therefore, complete this exercise). Make sure you read the post-install read-me text file as you will need to create a free account at LizardTech, download an SDK, unzip and copy the files to the System Library GDAL folder.

1. Open QGIS Desktop.

2. Click the Add Raster Layer button and add SAC_13.sid to the map canvas.

SAC_13.sid is a MrSID compressed image. It is an ortho image from the City of Sacramento from 2009. The pixel size is six inches and the coordinate system is NAD 1983 California State Plane II FIPS 0402 Feet, EPSG: 102642. This image will serve as the reference layer for our rectification.

Now we will enable the Georeferencer Plugin and toolbar.

3. From the menu bar, choose Plugins | Manage and Install Plugins.

4. The Plugins manager will open.

5. Click on Installed and check the box next to Georeferencer GDAL (see figure below). Click Close.

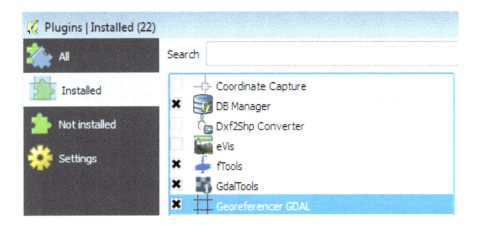

6. To open the Georeferencer plugin go to the menu bar choose Raster | Georeferencer | Georeferencer.

7. The Georeferencer window opens. Click the Open Raster button at the upper left hand side (see figure below).

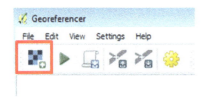

8. Navigate to the Exercise 2 folder, select the SAC1_CIR.img, and click Open. *Note: If the Coordinate Reference System Selector window opens click Cancel to close. This dataset does not yet have an Earth-based coordinate system.*

SAC1_CIR.img is an image of Sacramento covering a smaller area than our reference image we loaded above. It is in the ERDAS Imagine format with an undefined coordinate system as it needs to be georeferenced.

You should now have the image to be rectified loaded as shown in the figure below.

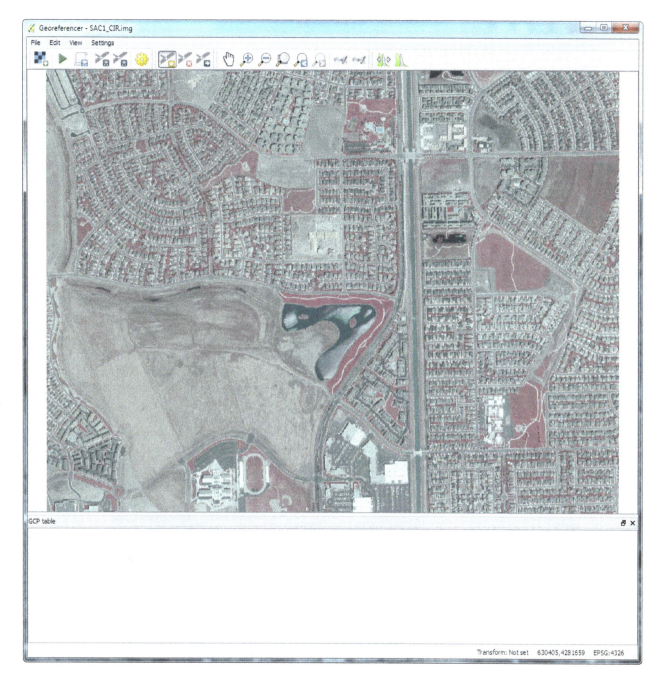

9. Arrange the Georeferencer window to the left of your screen (or preferably a second monitor if you have one) so that you can see both the source image and the image to be rectified. This will allow for easier identification of common points between images. See the figure below for reference.

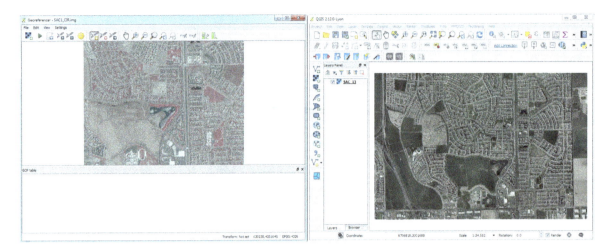

The referencing environment setup is now complete and we can move on to referencing the image.

2.4   Task 2 - Select Common Control Points

In this task, we will rectify the SAC1_CIR.img image to the source SAC_13.sid image. To do this, you will locate common features in each image and add control points in each image. Typically, you should find mutually identifiable points in at least the four corners and center of the image for best results. Only identifying points in one portion of the image will not yield optimal results, so it is best to spread the control points around the image as evenly as possible.

The figure below illustrates where we will focus on finding common features in both images.

1. Use the Zoom and Pan tools in both the Georeferencer window and the QGIS window to zoom to the upper-left corner of both images denoted as Area 1 in the figure above.

2. Find a common reference point in both images. The figure below shows an acceptable common reference point where a sidewalk forks in the backyard of a house with a pool.

   - Note: You will likely need to zoom very close to the feature found in each image. Examples of acceptable common features can include permanent features such as street corners, bases of flag poles, bases of buildings (not the roof tops), etc. The goal is to try and find the exact location in each image.

3. With a common reference point located, in the Georeferencer window, click the Add Point button .

4. Click on the image to be referenced on the common reference point. Try and be accurate and precise with your click. When you click on the image, the Enter map coordinates dialog will appear (shown below).

5. Click the From map canvas button. This will allow us to select a coordinate from the reference image rather than manually entering the coordinates.

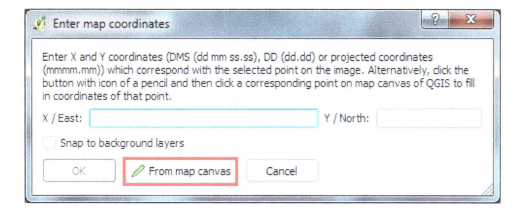

6. Click on the exact same reference point location on the reference image on the QGIS map canvas. Take care to click in the exact same location (or as close as you can get, resolution allowing). When you do this, the Enter map coordinates dialog will reappear, but with the selected coordinates entered (see the figure below for an example).

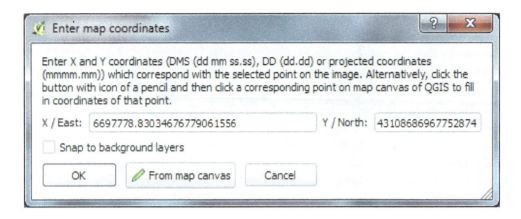

7. Click OK to accept the coordinates. When you do this, the Ground Control Point (GCP) table will contain the new created control point (shown in the figure below).

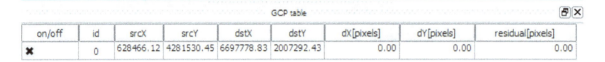

on/off	id	srcX	srcY	dstX	dstY	dX[pixels]	dY[pixels]	residual[pixels]
✘	0	628466.12	4281530.45	6697778.83	2007292.43	0.00	0.00	0.00

The GCP table contains a list of all control points you created. If you wish to remove a control point, you can right-click on its entry in the table, then choose Remove from the contextual menu. If you wish to keep the control point, but not apply it to the rectification, you can click the on/off box in the first column. Additionally, if you wish to manually change any of the values, double-click on the cell you wish to change to make it editable.

8. Repeat the above steps four more times to collect five control points. Reference the figure above to determine the areas where the control points should be located. When you have completed this, you should have five points on both images, and five entries in your GCP table. See the figure below for an example.

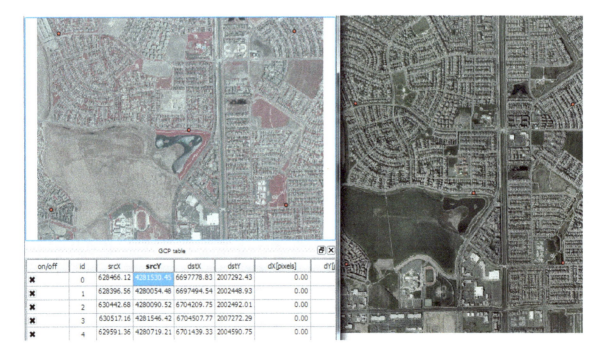

2.5 Task 3 – Rectify the Image

Now that you have your control points set, we will move on to rectifying the image.

1. To perform the rectification click the **Start georeferencing** button ▶ in the Georeferencer window.

2. The **Transformation settings** window will open (see figure below). If beforehand you get a message saying 'Please set transformation type' click OK.

   - In the Transformation window choose Polynomial 1 as the **Transformation type**.

   - Choose **Nearest neighbour** as the **Resampling method**. This is the standard raster resampling method for discrete data such as a scanned map.

   - Click the browse button to the right of **Output raster**. Navigate to your exercise Folder and name the file SAC1_CIR_modified_spcs.tif.

   - Click the browse button to the right of **Target SRS**. Type 102642 into the **Filter** and then double click the NAD_1983_StatePlane...0402_Feet CRS to make it the Selected CRS.

   - Click OK to set the CRS.

   - Check Load in QGIS when done.

   - Click OK to perform the rectification.

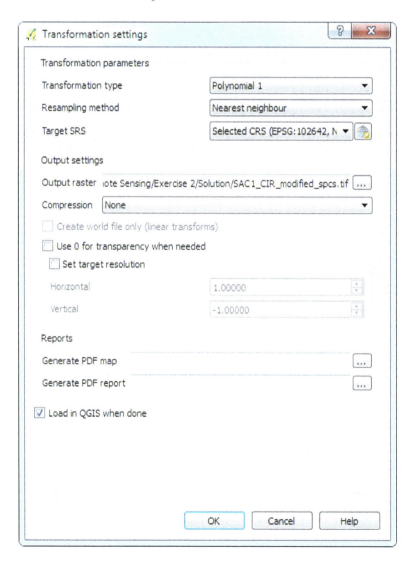

When the rectification is performed, two things will happen. First, the rectified image will be added to the QGIS map canvas relative to the selected ground control points. This is shown in the figure below.

The second thing that happens when the image is rectified, is the residual values will appear in the GCP table in the Georeferencer window. This is shown in the figure below. The dX and dY columns report the difference in location between the reference image and the rectified image in pixels. The residual column reports the residual value for the control point. Below the GCP table is the transformation (rectification) mean error.

| | | | | | | | GCP table | ⊟✕ |
on/off	id	srcX	srcY	dstX	dstY	dX[pixels]	dY[pixels]	residual[pixels]
✖	0	628465.78	4281529.99	6697778.35	2007292.46	-0.00	-0.03	0.03
✖	1	628383.64	4280116.08	6697455.76	2002654.44	0.08	0.02	0.08
✖	2	629724.35	4280694.18	6701875.85	2004502.52	-0.18	0.03	0.18
✖	3	630714.14	4281475.76	6705153.86	2007031.43	0.08	0.02	0.08
✖	4	630443.25	4280079.00	6704212.15	2002457.02	0.03	-0.04	0.05

Ideally, you will try to obtain a residual value less than 0.5 pixel width or less than some small acceptable tolerance. Ideally the mean error would be less than 2.0.

If the residual is less than 0.5 pixels and/or the mean error is less than 2.0, the rectified image is probably pretty good. If the residual is greater than 0.5 pixels or the mean error is greater than 2.0, then delete or readjust the existing ground control to make the residual better. Try adding more ground control points and see what effect this has on the residuals.

Notice that small changes and not choosing the exact pixel between the two images can have dramatic effect on the resulting residuals and hence the quality of the final rectified image output.

2.6 Task 4 – Post-Rectification Steps

With the image successfully rectified to an acceptable residual, there are a few cleanup steps left to complete the rectification process: save the ground control points and remove the rectified image's white border.

1. In the Georeferencer window, click the Save GCP points as' button . This will open a Save GCP points dialog.
2. Save the GCP points as SAC1_CIR.img.points in your exercise directory.
3. Click File | Quit to close the Georeferencer window.

The saved GCP points can be loaded into the Georeferencer window at a later time to re-rectify our image.

Next, we will remove the white border around the image for display purposes.

4. Open the Properties for the rectified image.
5. Select the Transparency tab.
6. Uncheck No data value.
7. Enter 255 as an Additional no data value (shown in the figure below). 255 represents the RGB code for white, which is the color we wish to exclude.
8. Click OK to set the no data value. The white border will now be transparent.
   - Note: Typically, these borders are either white (RGB:255) or black (RGB:0), so choose the appropriate no data value when needed.

▼ No data value

☐ No data value: 0

Additional no data value 255

2.7 Conclusion

You have completed the fundamental image rectification process that is common throughout many photogrammetric processes. Although image rectification is much more involved than this exercise, the same principles of identifying and collecting high quality ground control that are then used to rectify image data is important. In addition, being able to review and determine the accuracy of the image rectification process and how to take subsequent steps to improve the output is equally important.

2.8 Discussion Questions

1. Describe how the rectified image compares to the 2009 reference imagery. How effective was the rectification? How might you improve the rectification?
2. What challenges did you face when choosing common control points between the two images? What strategies did you employee to mitigate those challenges?
3. Why did the white border show up on the rectified image when added to the QGIS map canvas?

Exercise 3

Unsupervised Classification

Objective – Perform an Unsupervised Classification

3.1 Introduction

As you learned in Part 1 - Exercise 4, on page 75, the unsupervised classification method is one of the two commonly used traditional image classification routines. This method (and the supervised classification) is often used with medium (> 20m) and coarse (> 1km) resolution multispectral remotely sensed imagery. More commonly, the unsupervised and supervised classification methods are used together to form a hybrid image classification process to categorize pixels into land cover or land use types.

This exercise includes the following tasks:

- Task 1 – Define New GRASS Location and Mapset

- Task 2 – Learn GRASS Graphical User Interface and Concepts

- Task 3 – Import and Group Imagery, and Set Region

- Task 4 – Perform Unsupervised Classification

- Task 5 – Interpret Results

- Task 6 – Challenge: Perform 15 Class Unsupervised Classification

3.2 Objective: Perform an Unsupervised Classification

In this exercise you'll be introduced to the unsupervised classification method.

QGIS and GRASS Tools do not provide access to GRASS's classification functions, therefore, in this exercise, we'll learn how to classify an image using the GRASS GIS Graphical User Interface (GUI).

A simple classification scheme will be used for the exercise:

- Water

- Agriculture

- Fallow

- Grassland

- Forest

- Urban

- Barren

3.3 Task 1 Define New GRASS Location

In this task, we will define a new GRASS Location and Mapset to serve as our working environment for the unsupervised classification. First, let's briefly review a few storage concepts. For a more detailed overview, revisit Task 1 in Exercise 1, on page 401 of this Remote Sensing section, or, read the GRASS GIS documentation at http://grass.osgeo.org/".

In order for GRASS to start a project, it must first connect to a Database (also called a GISDBase or a GIS Data Directory). Again, the Database is simply a folder on your computer that has special subdirectories. Once GRASS connects to a Database, it needs to access a Location. A Location is a child directory of the Database and stores the coordinate system or map projection that all enclosed Mapsets will use. A Mapset is a child directory of a Location that represents a geographical subset of its parent Location. Mapsets contain geographic data in their directories. There are two types of mapsets: Permanent and owner.

Let's create the Location and Mapset.

1. Open GRASS 7.0.3 GUI. In Windows, this can be found at Start | All Programs | GRASS GIS 7.0.3 | GRASS 7.0.3 GUI. If you installed QGIS using OSGEO4W, then it can be found at Start | All Programs | OSGEO4W | GRASS GIS 7.0.3 GUI.

This will open the 'Welcome to GRASS GIS' window (shown in the figure below) and possibly a command prompt. You can ignore the command prompt for this exercise. We will use this Welcome window to create our new location.

2. Click the Browse button and navigate to the `Exercise 3 Data` folder.

3. Create a new folder named `grassdata` in your exercise directory and select the new folder as the database.

4. Click the New button on the 'Welcome to GRASS GIS' window. This will open the Define new GRASS Location wizard.

5. Verify that the GIS Data Directory points to the exercise directory.

6. Set the Project Location and Location Title both to 'Sacramento'.

7. Press Next.

8. Select Select EPSG code of spatial reference system.

9. Click Next.

10. Search for EPSG code 3309. Select 3309 NAD27 / California Albers. (shown in figure below).

Choose EPSG Code

Path to the EPSG-codes file:	ROGRA~2\QGISVA~1\share\proj\epsg
EPSG code:	

Q 3309|

Code	Description
3309	NAD27 / California Albers

11. Click Next to set the CRS. The Select datum transformation window will appear.

12. Choose 1: Used in whole nad27 region as the datum transformation.

13. Click OK to set the datum transformation.

14. Click Finish on the summary to return to the GRASS Welcome window.

   - Note: If you receive a dialog telling you to change the default GIS data directory, press OK to dismiss.

15. A dialog box named Location <Sacramento> created will appear asking if we wish to set the default region extents and resolution now. Click No.

16. A dialog box named Create new mapset will appear asking if we wish to create a new mapset. Enter 'Classification', then press OK to create the mapset.

You should now have the Sacramento and two Mapsets created in the GIS Database (shown in the figure below). We can now start our GRASS GIS Project.

Choose project location and mapset

Project location (projection/coordinate system)	Accessible mapsets (directories of GIS files)
Sacramento	Classification PERMANENT

17. Select Classification from the Accessible mapsets list then click the Start GRASS session button. This will open the GRASS GUI.

3.4   Task 2 Learn GRASS Graphical User Interface and Concepts

When the GRASS GUI program starts, you are presented with two separate windows: The Layer Manger and the Map Display (shown in the figure below).

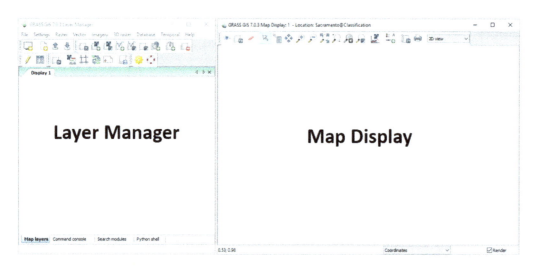

The Layer Manager is composed of:

- Menu Bar

- Toolbars

- Four Tabs

  - Map layers
  - Command console
  - Search module
  - Python shell

Let's discuss these items in detail appropriate for what you will use in this exercise.

- Menu Bar – Provides access to all of GRASS's functions. In this exercise, we will use the File, Settings, Raster, and Imagery menus.

- Toolbars – Provides convenient access to commonly used GRASS functions. We will not use any of these buttons for this exercise, but will instead opt to use the Menu Bar.

- Map layers tab – Manages the draw order and visibility of map layers. We will use this to access information about loaded map layers.

- Command console tab – Displays the output of commands that are run. Also allows the user to type in commands to execute. We will review output of command runs in this tab throughout the exercise.

- Search module tab – Similar to the GRASS Tools Modules Tree, it provides a hierarchical listing of all GRASS functions for logical browsing. You can find modules by description, keyword, or command by using the filter box. We will not use this tab in the exercise.

- Python shell tab - Provides access to the Python interpreter for sending commands. We will not use this tab in the exercise.

Now let's take a closer look at the Map Display. It is composed of:

- Toolbar – Provides access to the Map Display functions. This is roughly analogous to the QGIS Map Canvas controls. We will use this toolbar to explore map layers loaded in the Map layers tab of the Layer Manager window.

- Information bar – Located along the bottom of the Map Display window, it displays a multitude of information depending on which option is selected in the dropdown box. Map rendering can be enabled or disabled on this bar.

The Layer Manager is the core part of the GRASS GUI as it provides access to all of GRASS's functionality. During this exercise, we will access quite a few menu items from the Layer Manager to set up our analysis environment, and then view the results in the Map Display for interpretation and interaction.

One last note about GRASS's modules. A GRASS module (which I will refer to as a module, tool, or function) can be thought of as a small supporting program that can be executed to perform useful actions. Examples of such actions are importing raster maps, rectifying images, creating composites, and performing cluster analysis.

As we select modules to run, you will notice that the module names are preceded by a single letter and a dot (e.g. r.composite). The single letter and dot, represents which category of actions the module belongs to. Below is a listing of categories of actions and their associated single letters that we will use in this exercise. Other categories exist, but we will not access them in this exercise.

- g – General functions, such as file management, mapset management, and projection management. These functions are primarily found in the Menu Bar under File, Settings, and Help.

- r – Raster related functions, such as importing rasters, terrain analysis, color management, and interpolation to name a few. These functions are primarily found in the Menu Bar under Raster.

- v – Vector related functions, such as importing vectors, topology maintenance, feature queries, and attribute management. These functions are primarily found in the Menu Bar under Vector.

- i – Imagery related functions, such as classification, image grouping, transformations, and filtering. These functions are found in the Menu Bar under Imagery.

3.5   Task 3 Import and Group Imagery, and Set Region

In this task, we will import the raster file that we will perform an unsupervised classification on, and create an image group. This will prepare the imagery for input for classification.

1. Click File | Import Raster Data | Common formats import [r.in.gdal]. This will open the Import raster data module window.

2. Set the following options (see the figure below for reference):
   - Source Type: File
   - Source settings
     - Format: Erdas Imagine Images (.img)
     - File: tm_sacsub.img
   - List of GDAL layers
     - tm_sacsub.img: checked
     - Add imported layers into layer tree: unchecked

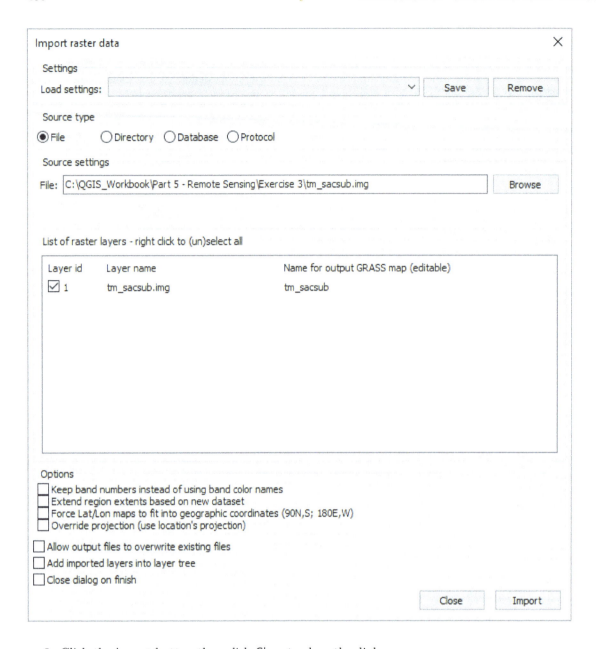

3. Click the Import button then click Close to close the dialog.

4. Select the Layer Manager window and select the Command console tab if it is not already selected (shown in the figure below). The console displays the results of the import function.

```
(Sat Apr 09 09:52:00 2016)
r.in.gdal input=C:\QGIS_Workbook\Part 5 - Remote Sensing\Exerc
Proceeding with import of 6 raster bands...
Importing raster map <tm_sacsub.1>...
Importing raster map <tm_sacsub.2>...
Importing raster map <tm_sacsub.3>...
Importing raster map <tm_sacsub.4>...
Importing raster map <tm_sacsub.5>...
Importing raster map <tm_sacsub.6>...
(Sat Apr 09 09:52:01 2016) Command finished (0 sec)
```

Note that the tool imported six rasters; one raster for each raster band. GRASS treats each band as a separate raster map. Each band can be visualized separately, or, if desired, a composite can be created, such as the composite created in Part 5 Remote Sensing - Exercise 1, on page 401.

To perform an image classification, the raster maps (bands) must be combined into a group and subgroup. A group is a collection of raster maps. A subgroup is a subset of the group's raster maps that will be utilized in the image classification. So, for instance, if you had a group of bands 1, 2, 3, 4, 5, 6, but only wanted to use bands 3 and 4 for analysis, you would create a subgroup containing only bands 3 and 4.

When we imported tm_sacsub, GRASS created a group for us named tm_sacsub. We will edit the group containing all six raster maps to add a subgroup containing all of the maps, since we will use all bands for our unsupervised classification.

5. Click Imagery | Develop images and groups | Create/edit group [i.group]. This will open the Create or edit imagery groups tool.

6. Enter tm_sacsub_group as the group name in the top dropdown box. The Layers in selected group should automatically populate with the six tm_sacsub raster maps (see the figure below).

   - If the layers do not populate, click Add and check the boxes next to the six tm_sacsub maps.

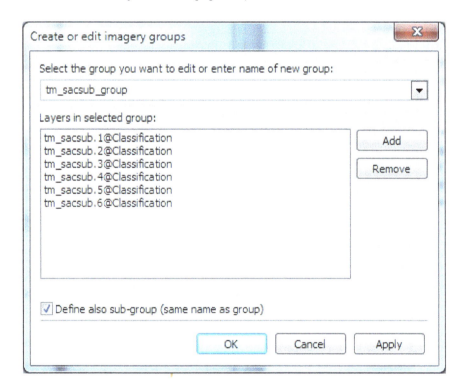

7. Check Edit create sub-group....

8. Click Select all to add the subgroup and OK dismiss the tool.

Now that the imagery has been loaded, and a group and subgroup have been specified, the last step is to set the region. If you recall from Exercise 1, a Region is a subset of a Location defined by a rectangular bounding box. The Region is important for raster and imagery operations as it bounds the area (region) that will participate in any raster and imagery operations executed in GRASS. A Region is an operating parameter set when working in GRASS.

Let's set the region equal to one of the tm_sacsub raster maps.

9. Click Settings | Region | Set region [region] on the Layer Manager window. This will open the region tool.

10. Set the following options:

    • [multiple] Set region to match this raster map: tm_ sacsub.1@Classification

      – Note: The '@Classification' denotes that tm_sacsub.1 is stored in the 'Classification' mapset.

11. Click Run. The tool will switch to the Command output tab. If you do not see any line that begins with the word 'ERROR', then the region has been successfully set.

12. Click Close to close the region tool.

With the imagery loaded, group and subgroup defined, and region set, we can now perform the unsupervised classification.

3.6   Task 4 Perform Unsupervised Classification

In this task, we will perform an unsupervised classification using two tools: i.cluster, and i.maxlik. Let's get started.

1. Click Imagery | Classify image | Clustering input for unsupervised classification [i.cluster] from the Layer Manager menu bar. This will open the cluster tool.

To understand what a tool will do, it is important to refer to the tool's manual. Luckily for us, the majority of tools in GRASS GUI have a Manual tab that displays the manual. Let's explore the i.cluster manual now to understand how this tool works.

2. Click Manual tab in the cluster tool. This will display the cluster tool's manual. You may want to maximize the window to view all of the manual's content without having to scroll.

3. Read the following manual sections:

    • Name

    • Description

    • Parameters (second Parameters list under Description, which has more verbose descriptions).

Now that you have an understanding of what the tool will do, and the fact that it is the first of two steps of the unsupervised classification process (i.maxlik being the second), let's set tool options to run the classification.

4. Click the Required tab.

5. Set the following options:

    • Name of input imagery group: `tm_sacsub@Classification`

    • Name of input imagery subgroup: `tm_sacsub_group`

    • Name for output file containing result signatures: `cluster10`

6. Click the Settings tab.

    • Initial number of classes: 10

7. Click the Optional tab.

    • Name for output file containing final report: `cluster10_report`

8. Click Run to execute the tool. It will switch to the Command output tab and display the results of the cluster tool (shown in the figure below).

```
(Sat Apr 09 09:59:12 2016)
i.cluster group=tm_sacsub@Classification subgroup=tm_sacsub_g
Reading raster maps...
i.cluster complete. File <cluster10> created.
(Sat Apr 09 09:59:13 2016) Command finished (0 sec)
```

9. Review the Command output for any errors. If there are errors, double-check the steps above and run the cluster tool again.

The cluster tool creates two files of interest to us: the result signatures file (`cluster10`), and the final report (`cluster10_report`). Let's view the `cluster10_report` to see what it contains.

10. Open a text editor, such as Notepad and open `cluster10_report`.

This report contains detailed information about the results of the cluster tool as it iterated over the input subgroup multiple times to reach its convergence goal. It reports the class means, standard deviations, class distribution, class separation, and how many classes were created.

11. Take a few moments to review the `cluster10_report`. Take note of the number of created classes (located at the bottom of the report).

12. Close the `cluster10_report`.

Now let's view the result (spectral) signatures file.

13. Open a text editor, such as Notepad and open
    `\Sacramento\Classification\group\tm_sacsub_group\subgroup\tm_sacsub\sig\cluster10`. (Wow! What a long path!) A portion of the `cluster10` file is shown in the figure below.

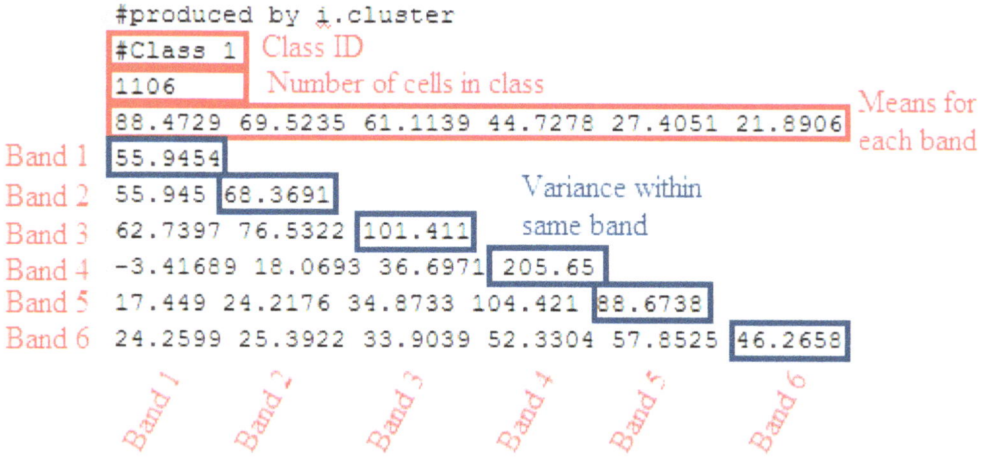

The spectral signature file can be reviewed to see the signature statistics for each of the spectral classes that were created from the unsupervised classification process. The spectral signature file shows a Class ID (the spectral class number, which are unknown cover types at this point), the number of cells in the class, the means for each set of pixels that make up the spectral class, and an associated covariance matrix. The covariance matrix is a set of values that compare how similar or different the pixel values that make up the spectral class are between the image bands. The diagonal values represent the variance for a set of pixels for the specific band number. Large values indicate that the pixel values are different; small variance values indicate that the pixels values that make up the spectral class are similar (or are homogeneous).

The spectral signature file can be used in conjunction with reviewing different spectral classes within the image to help determine what other steps might need to be taken to make further refinements on the image classification. The spectral signature file may help determine that a different unsupervised classification is needed that contains a larger number of spectral classes to be created. The spectral signature file may also provide some insight on how similar or different some spectral classes are from one another and provide some insight where the individual spectral classes need to be merged. The spectral differences between some cover types may not be large enough to separate out or identify one of the unique land cover types in the classification scheme.

The spectral signature file is another piece of information that may provide some insight and the you can decide if creating and reviewing this file is worth the effort during the unsupervised classification process. The spectral signature file will be discussed again in the supervised classification exercise.

With the clustering complete, we can now move on to the second step of the unsupervised classification: running the i.maxlik tool.

14. Click Imagery | Classify Image | Maximum likelihood classification (MLC) [i.maxlik]. This will open the MLC tool.

15. Click the Manual tab and read the manual for the MLC tool. When you are done reading the manual, proceed to the next step.

16. Click the Required tab and set the following options:

    • Name of input imagery group: tm_sacsub@Classification

    • Name of input imagery subgroup: tm_sacsub_group

    • Name of file containing signatures: cluster10

    • Name for raster map holding classification results: tm_sacsub_un_sup_class

    • Add created map(s) into layer tree: checked

17. Click Run to execute the MLC tool.

18. Check the Command output for errors. If none exist, click Close to close the MLC tool.

19. On the Layer Manager window and click Map layers. You should see our classified image listed. On the Map Display, you should see the classified image (shown in the figure below).

    • Note: if you do not see the image in the map display, right-click on the layer in the Map Layers list, and choose Zoom to selected map(s) from the context menu.

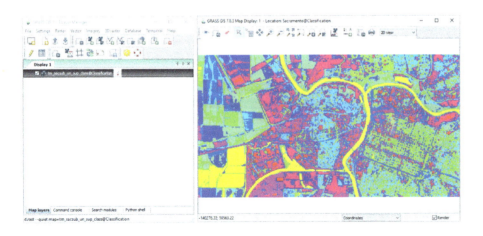

With the classification completed, we will now move to interpreting the result.

3.7 Task 5 Interpret Results

The resulting image (which represent spectral classes) was created without much involvement. Our next steps involve making sense of the result. Generally, some of the spectral classes might make sense, but others are likely a mix of cover types. Normally, some field work would be conducted or other data is available to help make some determinations in land cover types. In addition, some manual processes to change groups of pixels can be expected. The interpretation and revision of the results are often involved and can easily take weeks or months of time, not just days.

- Look at the obvious.

Water oftentimes is represented as a single class or maybe two classes. To make it easier for us to understand what the classes are representing, let's add a color composite of `tm_sacsub` to the map display for comparison purposes.

1. Click Raster | Manage colors | Create RGB [r.composite]. This will open the composite tool.
2. Set the following options (shown in Figure below):
   - Name of raster map to be used for <red>: `tm_sacsub.3@Classification`
   - Name of raster map to be used for <green>: `tm_sacsub.2@Classification`
   - Name of raster map to be used for <blue>: `tm_sacsub.1@Classification`
   - Name for output raster map: `tm_sacsub_RGB`
   - Add created map(s) into layer tree: checked
3. Click Run to execute the composite tool.

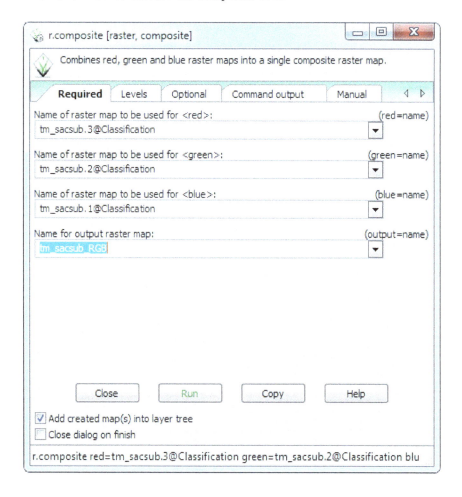

4. If no errors are shown in the Command output, click Close to close the tool.

5. View the Map Display. Note that you can now see the true color composite. Let's have it draw underneath the classification image.

6. In the Layer Manager, select the Map layers tab.

7. Drag `tm_sacsub_un_sup_class` above `tm_sacsub_RGB` to rearrange the draw order. You should now see the classified image in the Map Display.

8. Toggle the visibility of the classified image by checking and unchecking the checkbox next to the layer name in the Layer Manager. While toggling the visibility, determine which color represents the water features.

Now that you have identified which color represents water (yellow in our case (see the figure above of cluster10 Result File Showing First Class), let's determine which class in the raster represents water.

9. In the Layer Manager, select `tm_sacsub_un_sup_class`, then in the Map Display, click the Query raster/vector maps button ▨.

10. Click on a cell in the Map Display that represents water features.

11. Open the Command console tab on the Layer Manager. This will display the results of our query. In our case, Class 1 represents water features (shown in the figure below).

```
(Tue Jul 15 17:54:56 2014)
r.what --v -f -n input=tm_sacsub_un_sup_class@Classificat
easting|northing|site_name|tm_sacsub_un_sup_class@Classif
-135528.391304|66794.521739||1|Class 1
(Tue Jul 15 17:54:57 2014) Command finished (0 sec)
```

Now that we know that Class 1 represents water features, let's only apply a color to that class to easily see where water was identified.

12. Click Raster | Manage colors | Color tables [r.colors]. This will open the color tables tool.

13. Click on the Manual tab and read the following sections:

    • Name

    • Description

    • Examples

14. Click the Required tab.

15. Set Name of input raster map to `tm_sacsub_un_sup_class`.

16. Click the Colors tab.

17. In or enter values interactively, enter:

    • 1 yellow

    • default grey

18. Press Run to set the color table. You should see the figure below displayed in the Map Display.

Most of the Spectral Class 1 falls along the river and is likely correct; however, some pixels in class 1 fall on agricultural fields in the South West corner.

When an image analyst is evaluating and trying to determine the land cover types in an unsupervised classification, it can be useful to label the spectral classes to prospective land cover types.

NOTE: Most of the spectral classes will not represent a single land cover class. This is because a human creates the land cover classification scheme whereas the unsupervised classification is categorizing pixels into similar spectral groups (which may or may not relate to specific land cover types).

Since the land cover types are not known when the unsupervised classification is run, additional work and investigation is required to refine the spectral classes into specific land cover types. To make a "first attempt" at determining the land cover types, the analyst can label possible land cover types for each spectral class.

For Spectral Class 1, since this category seems to represent Water cover types, this spectral class can be labeled "Water".

Now that we know that Class 1 represents water, let's re-colorize all classes, then change the class label from '1' to 'Water'.

19. Using the r.colors tool opened in Step 1 above, clear the or enter values interactively values on the Colors tab.

20. For Type of color table, choose 'rainbow'.

21. Click Run. This will revert the classified image back to its original colors.

22. Click Close to close the r.color tool.

23. Click Raster | Change category values and labels | Reclassify [r.reclass].

24. Click on the Manual tab and read the manual to understand what this tool does.

25. Set the following options:

   - Required tab

      - Raster map to be reclassified: `tm_sacsub_un_sup_class`

      - Name for output raster map: `tm_sacsub_un_sup_class_reclass`

      - Add created map(s) into layer tree: checked

- Optional tab (shown in Figure 14)
  - Or enter values interactively:
    * 1 = 1 Water
    * * = *

or enter values interactively
_____

1 = 1 Water
* = *

26. Click Run to reclassify the raster.

27. Click Close to close the tool.

You probably noticed that the newly added reclassified layer looks exactly the same as the original raster. That is normal. What has changed is the class label. Let's take a look.

28. In the Map layers tab, select `tm_sacsub_un_sup_class_reclass`, then in the Map Display, click the Query raster/vector maps button.

29. Click on a Water feature cell then inspect the Command console to see what was returned (shown in the figure below).

```
(Tue Jul 15 21:00:31 2014)
r.what --v -f -n input=tm_sacsub_un_sup_class_recla
easting|northing|site_name|tm_sacsub_un_sup_class_r
-132314.478261|62064.956522||1|Water
(Tue Jul 15 21:00:31 2014) Command finished (0 sec)
```

Reclassifying the raster map makes it more intuitive when trying to understand or query the layer in future operations.

The other classes can be assigned in a similar fashion.

30. Use the methods above to turn on/off other layers and review the geographic extent to determine if one or more land cover types make up the spectral class.

31. Assign the a useful name for each spectral class.

32. Provide a list of land cover types assigned to the ten classes in the classified image. **Submit this list for Discussion Question 1 in this exercise.**

This can be time consuming and often takes some serious review and visual analysis and consultation of "ancillary" or reference data and often field work.

To get more practice, work on some of the other classes using the same methods to label the spectral classes at this point. No additional ancillary information exists to continue this exercise.

If you're not familiar with the Sacramento area, you can use Google Maps or Google Earth to review high resolution image data that can help assign the spectral classes to prospective land cover types.

3.8   Task 6 Challenge: Perform a 15 Class Unsupervised Classification (optional)

Perform another unsupervised classification on the same data, however, this time, use 15 classes instead of 10. Assign land cover classes in the same manner as above, perhaps combining a few classes together (if appropriate) using the r.reclass tool.

Discuss the following:

1. Briefly describe your observations of assigning land cover types to the spectral classes.

2. Compare the two image classification results (after the land cover types have been assigned). Assign useful colors to each classified image and provide screen shots of each of your colorized image classifications. Use the first land cover type to assign a color if you have multiple land cover labels for a single spectral class. Describe some of the similarities and differences. Do you think either resulting image classification is better than the other? Describe.

3.9 Conclusion

This completes the unsupervised classification process. You've learned how to implement the unsupervised classification as well as observe some of the issues and additional work that is required to refine and improve the unsupervised classification.

3.10 Discussion Questions

1. Submit the 10 class land types you assigned in Task 5 **highlighted above**.

2. When working on assigning the 10 land types to the 10 classes in Task 5, **highlighted above**, briefly summarize the observations discovered when assigning the land types.

3. Find, learn, and use the i.histogram tool on the reclassified raster. Describe what the histogram is displaying and how it might be a useful visualization for interpreting the classification results.

Exercise 4

Supervised Classification

Objective – Perform Supervised Classification

4.1 Introduction

The Supervised classification method is another of the two commonly used "traditional" image classification routines. This method (as well as the unsupervised method) is often used with medium (> 20m) and coarse (> 1km) resolution multispectral remotely sensed imagery. More commonly the unsupervised and supervised classification methods are used together to form a hybrid image classification process to categorize pixels into land cover or land use types.

The primary difference between the unsupervised and the supervised methods is the supervised classification process requires a spectral signature file (sometimes referred to as the "training samples" or "training signatures"). .. Creating and evaluating spectral signatures were discussed in the lecture material. This exercise will provide an opportunity for you to learn how to create and evaluate spectral signatures that can be used in a supervised image classification.

This exercise includes the following tasks:

- Task 1 – Define New GRASS Location

- Task 2 – Import and Group Imagery, and Set Region

- Task 3 – Create Training Dataset

- Task 4 – Perform Supervised Classification

- Task 5 – Reclassify Spectral Classes to Information Classes

- Task 6 – Perform a Second Class Supervised Classification

4.2 Objective: Perform a Supervised Classification

QGIS and GRASS Tools do not provide access to GRASS's classification functions, therefore, in this exercise, the you'll learn how to classify an image using the GRASS GIS Graphical User Interface (GUI).

The primary objectives of this exercise are:

1. Create and Evaluate Spectral Signatures
2. Perform a Supervised Classification
3. Recode Spectral Classes to Information Classes

A simple classification scheme will be used for the exercise:

- Water

- Agriculture

- Grassland

- Forest

- Urban

4.3   Task 1 Define New GRASS Location

In this task, we will define a new GRASS Location and Mapset to serve as our working environment for the unsupervised classification.

Let's create the Location and Mapset.

1. Open GRASS 7.0.3 GUI. In Windows, this can be found at Start | All Programs | GRASS GIS 7.0.3 | GRASS 7.0.3 GUI. If you installed QGIS using OSGEO4W, then it can be found at Start | All Programs | OSGEO4W | GRASS GIS 7.0.3 GUI.

This will open the 'Welcome to GRASS GIS' window (shown in the figure below) and possibly a command prompt. You can ignore the command prompt for this exercise. We will use this Welcome window to create our new location.

2. Click the Browse button and navigate to the `Exercise 4 Data` folder.

3. Create a new folder named `grassdata` in your exercise directory and select the new folder as the database.

4. Click the New button on the 'Welcome to GRASS GIS' window. This will open the Define new GRASS Location wizard.

5. Verify that the GIS Data Directory points to the `grassdata` directory.

6. Set the Project Location and Location Title both to 'Sacramento'.

7. Press Next.

8. Select Select EPSG code of spatial reference system.

9. Click Next.

10. Search for EPSG code 3309. Select 3309 NAD27 / California Albers. (Shown in figure below).

Choose EPSG Code

Path to the EPSG-codes file:　　ROGRA~2\QGISVA~1\share\proj\epsg

EPSG code:

Q 3309|

Code	Description
3309	NAD27 / California Albers

11. Click Next to set the CRS. The Select datum transformation window will appear.

12. Choose 1: Used in whole nad27 region as the datum transformation.

13. Click OK to set the datum transformation.

14. Click Finish on the summary to return to the GRASS Welcome window.

   - Note: If you receive a dialog telling you to change the default GIS data directory, press OK to dismiss.

15. A dialog box named Location created will appear asking if we wish to set the default region extents and resolution now. Click No.

16. A dialog box named Create new mapset will appear asking if we wish to create a new mapset. Enter 'Classification', then press OK to create the mapset.

You should now have the Sacramento Location and two Mapsets created in the GIS Database (shown in the figure below). We can now start our GRASS GIS Project.

Choose project location and mapset

Project location (projection/coordinate system)	Accessible mapsets (directories of GIS files)
Sacramento	Classification PERMANENT

17. Select Classification from the Accessible mapsets list then click the Start GRASS session button. This will open the GRASS GUI.

4.4   Task 2 Import and Group Imagery, and Set Region

In this task, we'll import the raster file that we will perform a supervised classification on, and create an image group. This will prepare the imagery for input for classification.

1. Click File | Import Raster Data | Common formats import [r.in.gdal]. This will open the Import raster data module window.

2. Set the following options (see figure below for reference):
   - Source Type: File
   - Source settings
     - Format: Erdas Imagine Images (.img)
     - File: tm_sacsub.img
   - List of GDAL layers
     - tm_sacsub.img: checked
   - Add imported layers into layer tree: unchecked

3. Click the Import button then click the Close button to close the dialog.

4. Select the Layer Manager window and select the Command console tab if it is not already selected (shown in figure below). The console displays the results of the import function

```
(Sat Apr 09 09:52:00 2016)
r.in.gdal input=C:\QGIS_Workbook\Part 5 - Remote Sensing\Exerc
Proceeding with import of 6 raster bands...
Importing raster map <tm_sacsub.1>...
Importing raster map <tm_sacsub.2>...
Importing raster map <tm_sacsub.3>...
Importing raster map <tm_sacsub.4>...
Importing raster map <tm_sacsub.5>...
Importing raster map <tm_sacsub.6>...
(Sat Apr 09 09:52:01 2016) Command finished (0 sec)
```

Just as in the previous exercise, the tool imported six rasters; one raster for each raster band. GRASS treats each band as a separate raster map. Each band can be visualized separately, or, if desired, a composite can be created, such as the composite created in Part 5 Remote Sensing - Exercise 1, on page 401.

Again, to perform an image classification, the raster maps (bands) must be combined into a group and subgroup. When we imported **tm_sacsub**, GRASS created a group for us named **tm_sacsub**. We will edit the group containing all six raster maps to add a subgroup containing all of the raster maps, since we will use all bands for our unsupervised classification.

5. Click Imagery | Develop images and groups | Create/edit group [i.group]. This will open the Create or edit imagery groups tool.

6. Enter **tm_sacsub** as the group name in the top dropdown box. The Layers in selected group should automatically populate with the six **tm_sacsub** raster maps (see figure below). *Note*: If the layers do not populate, click Add and check the boxes next to the six tm_sacsub.n maps.

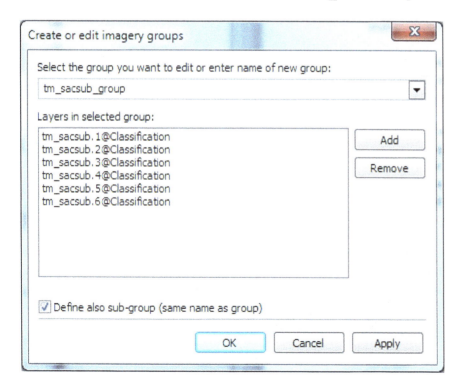

7. Check Edit-Create sub-group

8. Enter 'SacsubGroup' as the group name.

9. Click OK to add the sub-group and dismiss the tool.

Now that the imagery has been loaded, and a group and subgroup have been specified—the last step is to set the region. Let's set the region equal to one of the tm_sacsub raster maps.

10. Click Settings | Region | Set region [region] on the Layer Manager window. This will open the region tool.

11. Set the following options:

    - [multiple] Set region to match this raster map: tm_sacsub.1@Classification

12. Click Run. The tool will switch to the Command output tab. If you do not see any line that begins with the word 'ERROR', then the region has been successfully set.

13. Click Close to close the region tool.

With the imagery loaded, group and subgroup defined, and region set, we can now perform the unsupervised classification.

4.5   Task 3 Create Training Dataset

In this task, we will perform a supervised classification. There are two steps when performing a supervised classification: training, and classification. In the training step, a training dataset is created that classifies sample portions of the input imagery. This training dataset will then be passed to step two where it will be used when determining how to classify the image. You can think of it as the user (you) showing the computer a few examples of how you would like have the image classified, and then letting the computer rely on your examples to classify the rest of the image based on what it learned from you.

For the first step, training, we will create a new vector map and digitize a few sample areas of the image and set the classes we wish to have similar areas classified as when the computer performs the supervised classification. Next, we will convert the vector map to a raster map which will then be passed to step two for use in classification. Let's perform the training step now.

1. Click Vector | Develop vector map | Create new vector map from the Layer Manager menu bar. This will open the Create new vector map dialog.

2. Set the following options:

    - Name: Training
    - Create attribute table: checked
      - Key column: category
    - Add created map into layer tree: checked

3. Click OK to create the Training vector map and add it to the layer tree.

4. In the layer tree, right-click on the Training vector map and choose Show attribute data from the context menu. This will open the GRASS GIS Attribute Table Manager window which allows for display, query, and modification of the vector map's attribute table.

5. Click the Manage tables tab. This tab allows us to create, remove, and rename attribute table columns. We will create a new column to store the description of the categories that we will assign to our training dataset.

6. In the Add column section, create a new column with the following properties (as shown in the figure below):

    - Column: Descr
    - Type: varchar
    - Length: 10

7. Click the Add button to create the column. The new column will appear in the Table list. If you make a mistake, you can right-click on a column and choose Drop selected column to delete it from the table.

8. Click the Close button to close the table manager. Now that we have the vector map created, we need to display the raster map that we wish to digitize our training areas from. Instead of creating a new raster composite, we will create a new, temporary RGB display raster.

9. In the Layer Manager, click the Add various raster map layers button, then select Add RGB map layer from the context menu. This will open the d.rgb tool.

10. Set the following parameters:

   - Required tab:

     – Name of raster map to be used for <red>: tm_sacsub.4@Classification

     – Name of raster map to be used for <green>: tm_sacsub.5@Classification

     – Name of raster map to be used for <blue>: tm_sacsub.3@Classification

11. Click the OK button to create the RGB temporary raster overlay and add it to the map layers list (shown in figure below). You may need to right-click on the layer and choose Zoom to selected map.

Note: The Training@Classification vector map may be hidden behind the RGB raster overlay in the map layers list (shown in figure below). If this happens, simply click on a different tab in the Layer Manager window, then click back to the Map layers tab.

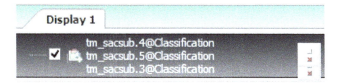

12. Drag the Training@Classification map above the raster overlay in the map layers list to have the vector map display on top of the raster map (you won't notice a difference now, but you will when we start editing the vector map).

Now we are set to create our training dataset. We will create five training records for five classes (agriculture, water, grass, forest, urban). We will then evaluate the spectral signatures, and then add additional spectral signatures.

13. In the map layers list, right-click on Training@Classification and choose Start editing from the context menu.

This will enable and display the digitizer toolbar in the Map Display window (shown below).

We will use this toolbar to create new training areas and set the `Category` and `Descr` attributes to the appropriate values.

14. Zoom to the field shown below. This is an agriculture field we will specify as our first training area.

15. Click the Digitize new area button on the Digitizer toolbar to select the tool.

In general, the tools on the Digitizer toolbar perform actions with a left-click, undo actions with a control-click, and confirm/complete actions with a right-click. Therefore, to create an area with four vertices, we would left-click five times to place the four vertices and the fifth vertex at the same location as the first vertex (to close the area), then right-click to complete the area.

16. Using the figure below as a guide, left-click four times to create the four vertices for the area, then left-click a fifth time on top of the first vertex to close the area, then right-click to complete the area. When the area is created, the Define attributes dialog will appear.

17. In the Define attributes dialog, set the Descr attribute value to 'AG1'.

18. Click the Submit button to save the attribute and close the window. If the window does not close, click the Cancel button.

19. Create four more training areas using the next four figures as guides. Set the descriptions of these training areas to 'Water1', 'Grass1', 'Forest1', and 'Urban1' respectively.

If you make a mistake when digitizing, you can use the Delete feature(s) tool to remove unwanted features. To use the tool, first, left-click on the outline (or line, or vertex) of the feature you wish to remove, then right-click to confirm and complete the delete action.

Water1 Training Area

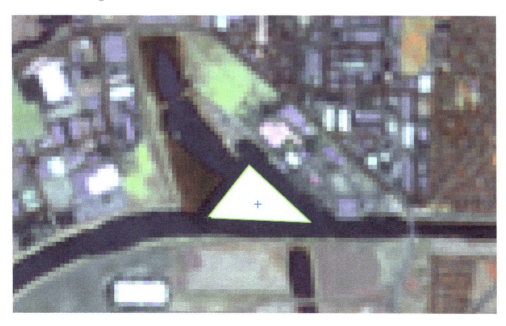

Grass1 Training Area

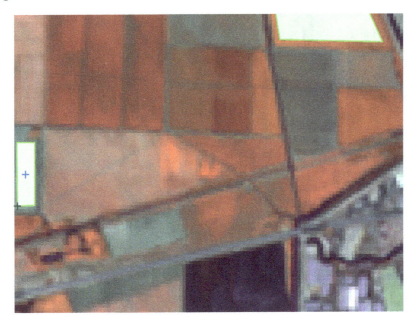

Forest1 Training Area

Urban1 Training Area

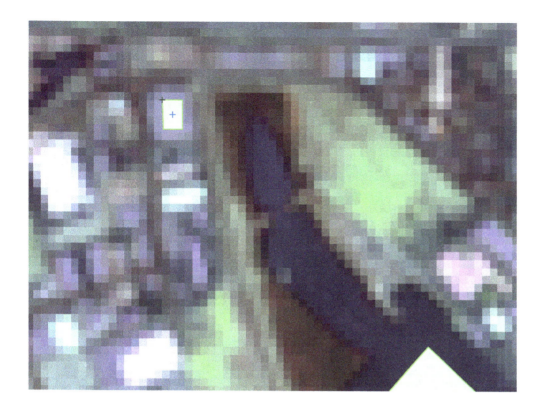

20. When you have completed digitizing all five training areas, click the Quit digitizer button ⏻.

21. Click Yes to the Save changes? dialog to save your digitized training areas. The digitized areas will now display in a bland grey color letting you know that they have been saved to the vector map.

With the vector training map completed, the next step is to convert it to a raster map so it can be used for input into the first pass (i.gensig) of the supervised classification process.

22. Click Vector | Map type conversions | Vector to raster (v.to.rast) on the Layer Manager window. This will open the v.to.rast tool.

23. Set the following parameters:

   - Required tab:
       – Name of input vector map: Training@Classification
       – Name for output raster map: TrainingAreas
       – Source of raster values: attr
   - Attributes tab:
       – Name of column for 'attr' parameter: category
       – Name of column...category labels: Descr
   - Add created map(s) into layer tree: checked

24. Click the Run button to execute the tool, then close the tool. The TrainingAreas raster will be added to the map layers list and displayed in the Map Display (see figure below).

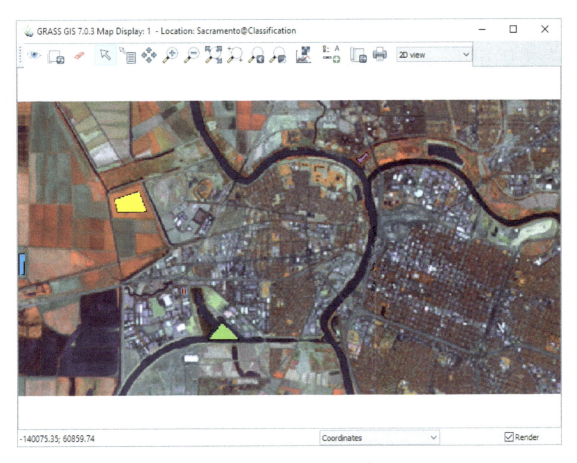

The TrainingAreas raster map may display the NULL cells as white and obscure the view of the underlying imagery. If so, you can make the NULL cells transparent so you can see where the training areas lay on top of the imagery.

25. Right-click on TrainingAreas in the map layers list then choose Properties from the contextual menu.

26. Click the Null cells tab.

27. Check Overlay (non-null values only).

28. Click the OK button to apply and close the dialog.

29. In the Map Display, click the Query raster/vector maps button' button to select the tool. This tool will display the attributes of the raster or vector that you click on the map display.

30. Click on one of the training areas to display its attributes. When you do this, the result of the Query tool will display (example figure below). What you should verify is that the category and Descr are stored in the training area properly (example circled in the figure below). If you are not getting the expected results, you may need to revisit previous steps above.

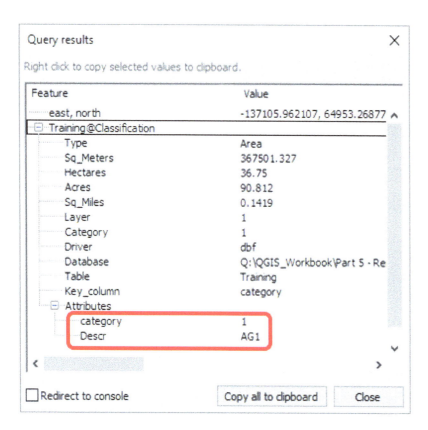

4.6   Task 4 Perform Supervised Classification

In this task, we will perform the second step of a supervised classification. In this step, we will first generate and review the spectral signatures of the training areas that we created Task 3. Next, we will perform the supervised classification and review the results. Let's start with generating the spectral signatures.

1. Click Imagery | Classify image | Input for supervised MLC (i.gensig) on the Layer Manager window. This will open the i.gensig tool.

2. Read the manual for the i.gensig tool to learn what it does and what parameters it expects.

3. Set the following parameters for the i.gensig tool:
   - Required tab:
     – Ground truth training map: `TrainingAreas`
     – Name of input imagery group: `tm_sacsub`
     – Name of input imagery subgroup: `sacsub_group`
     – Name for output file...: `TrainingSignatures`

4. Click the Run button to execute the tool. If no errors were reported, close the i.gensig dialog.

5. Open a text editor, such as Notepad and open:
   `\grassdata\Sacramento\Classification\group\tm_sacsub\subgroup\SacsubGroup\sig\TrainingSignatures`

The tree structure is shown in the figure below.

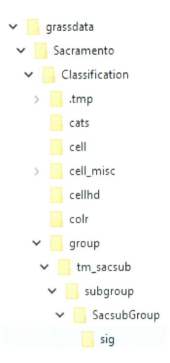

Let's take a few moments to review and discuss the spectral signatures file partially shown in the figure below. Once the spectral signature is created, it can be evaluated to see if it looks like a high quality signature (that is, one that has a single bell-shaped histogram, and small standard deviations, and variances for each band).

```
#AG1
409
77.1002 61.7775 43.8582 207.325 89.4914
1.24728
0.502751 1.34498
0.63925 0.919351 2.39651
-0.179737 0.820078 -4.09348 85.5337
0.744732 1.33265 1.413 6.65843 3.75544
```

The first line display the text label of the class, in this case, 'AG1' representing agriculture. The second line reports the number of cells in the class. The third line is the mean values per band of the class. The remaining lines are the semi-matrix of band-band covariance.

Remember, the covariance matrix shows both the variance for a specific image band as well as how the spectral signature varies between different image bands.

Ideally, each spectral signature will have a single 'hump', or peak value, on the diagonal, which tends to indicate a high quality spectral signature. If multiple 'humps' were returned, or the standard deviations and variances are very large, that would support the theory that the signature may be comprised of more than one land cover type.

6. Review the remaining classes in the spectral signature file. If any signatures seem to be a low quality signature, take note of them for discussion later.

Normally, you would re-create the training areas to gain a higher quality spectral signature, but for the purposes of learning, we will continue as you will be provided with a full set of training areas for the next few steps.

A full set of training areas has been provided for you in the exercise folder. We will import the vector training areas and convert them to a raster.

7. Click File | Import Vector Data | Common formats import [v.in.ogr]. This will open the Import vector data module window.

8. Set the following options:
   - Source Type: File
   - Source settings
     - File:
       Spectral_Sigs_Training.shp
   - List of vector layers
     - Spectral_Sigs_Training: checked
   - Add imported layers into layer tree: unchecked

9. Click the Import button then click Close to close the dialog.

10. Click Vector | Map type conversions | Vector to raster (v.to.rast) on the Layer Manager window. This will open the v.to.rast tool.

11. Set the following parameters:
    - Required tab:
      - Name of input vector map: Spectral_Sigs_ Training@Classification
      - Name for output raster map: TrainingAreas
      - Source of raster values: attr
    - Attributes tab:
      - Name of column for 'attr' parameter: Classvalue
      - Name of column...category labels: Classname
    - Optional tab:
      - Allow output files to overwrite existing files: checked
    - Add created map(s) into layer tree: checked

12. Click the Run button to execute the tool then close the tool. The TrainingAreas raster will be added to the map layers list.

13. You may need to open the Properties for this layer, select the Null cells tab and check Overlay to make null cells transparent.

14. The new training areas will be displayed in the Map Display (see figure below). You will use this raster map going forward in this exercise.

We will first regenerate the spectral signatures file using the full set of training areas, then move forward to the supervised classification.

15. Click Imagery | Classify image | Input for supervised MLC (i.gensig) on the Layer Manager window. This will open the i.gensig tool.

16. Set the following parameters for the i.gensig tool:

    - Required tab:

        – Ground truth training map: `TrainingAreas@Classification`
        – Name of input imagery group: `tm_sacsub_group`
        – Name of input imagery subgroup: `SacsubGroup`
        – Name for output file...: `TrainingSignatures`

17. Click the Run button to execute the tool. If no errors were reported, Close i.gensig dialog.

18. Review the newly created spectral signature file. Note that we now have 4 or 5 classes for each type of land cover.

With the spectral signature file review complete, we can now move on to the next step of the unsupervised classification: running the i.maxlik tool.

19. Click Imagery | Classify Image | Maximum likelihood classification (MLC) [i.maxlik]. This will open the MLC tool.

20. Click the Required tab and set the following options:

    - Name of input imagery group: `tm_sacsub@Classification`
    - Name of input imagery subgroup: `SacsubGroup`
    - Name of file containing signatures: `TrainingSignatures`
    - Name for raster map holding classification results: `tm_sacsub_sup_class`
    - Add created map(s) into layer tree: checked

21. Click Run to execute the MLC tool.

22. Check the Command output for errors. If none exist, click Close to close the MLC tool.

23. On the Layer Manager window, click Map layers. You should see our classified image listed. On the Map Display, you should see the classified image (shown in the figure below).

    - Note: if you do not see the image in the map display, right-click on the layer in the Map layers list, and choose Zoom to selected map(s) from the context menu.

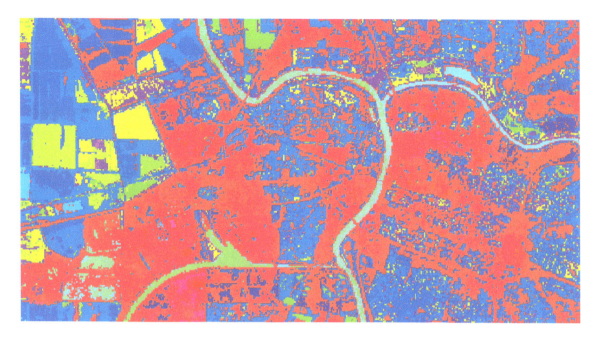

With the classification completed, we will now move to interpreting the result.

4.7 Task 5 Reclassify Spectral Classes to Information Classes

The final step in an image classification (and before an accuracy assessment is conducted) is to reclassify the spectral classes—that is the individual classes that represent the same land cover type to information classes (a single class for each unique land cover type).

Recoding the spectral classes to information classes can be accomplished using the r.reclass tool.

The following list can be used to reclassify existing spectral classes to information classes. Review the table, then let's perform the reclassification.

Spectral Class Number Information Class Number:

```
1-5   2 - Agriculture
6-9   1 - Water
10-14 3 - Grass
15-16 4 - Forest
19-23 5 - Urban
```

1. Click Raster | Change category values and labels | Reclassify (r.reclass) to open the Reclassify tool.
2. Set the following parameters:
    - Required tab:
        – Raster map to be reclassified: tm_sacsub_sup_class
        – Name for output raster map: tm_sacsub_sup_reclass
        – or enter values directly:

or enter values interactively

1 thru 5 = 2 Agricultre
6 thru 9 = 1 Water
10 thru 14 = 3 Grass
15 thru 16 = 4 Forest
19 thru 23 = 5 Urban

3. Continue to set the parameters

- Add created map(s) into layer tree: checked

- Click the Run button to execute the reclassification.

4. View the reclassified raster map in the Map Display. You may need to rearrange or toggle visibility of other maps in the map layers list to view the reclassified raster map (shown in the figure below).

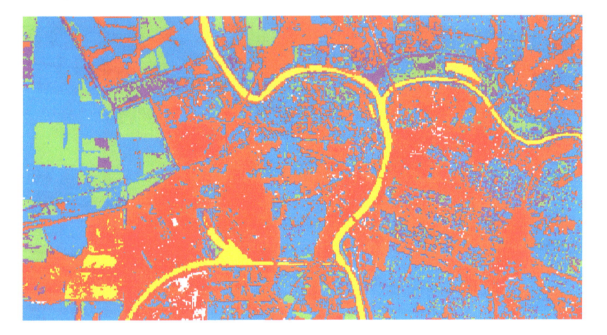

5. Query a few cells to view the values. Notice that there are only five classes (and colors) represented in the raster map. This makes it easier to understand what is being classified in the raster.

The colors do not make much sense, since they are randomly assigned. Since each value represents one of the unique land cover types in the classification scheme, the colors should be changed to be more intuitive. We will make those changes now by creating a new color table.

6. Click Raster | Manage colors | Color tables (r.colors) to open the color tables tool.

7. Read the r.colors manual to understand what a color table is and what this tool does.

8. Set the following parameters:

- Required tab:

  - Name of input raster map: tm_sacsub_sup_reclass

- Color tab:

  - or enter values interactively:

or enter values interactively

1 blue
2 252:252:158
3 138:239:21
4 71:123:11
5 grey

9. You can optionally save the color rules by clicking the Save As... button. These can later be loaded by clicking the Load button.

10. Click the Run button to set the color table for the raster map. If no errors are displayed, close the Color tables dialog. You should now see the reclassified and recolored raster shown in the figure below.

4.8   Task 6 Perform a Second Class Supervised Classification

Perform another supervised classification on the same data, however, this time, choose training areas you think would best represent the five land cover classes. Use as many training areas you see fit to get optimal results. Assign land cover classes in the same manner as above, perhaps combining a few classes together (if appropriate) using the r.reclass tool.

Discuss the following:

1. Briefly describe your strategy in defining suitable training areas.

2. Compare your classified image to the classified image completed in Task 5. Were you able to achieve a more accurate classification (based on your observations)? How and why did you deviate from what you did previously? Did your deviations improve or degrade the classification? Why/why not?

4.9   Conclusion

This exercise has introduced the primary steps to perform a supervised classification:

- Creating and evaluating spectral signatures.

- The supervised classification method was implemented which uses the spectral signature file.

- The Reclass and Color Table tools were used to convert spectral classes and better represent the classes visually.

You should have a good understanding of the steps and processes required to create a categorized image based on the supervised classification method.

At the end of this exercise, the final image classification is ready for an accuracy assessment. The accuracy assessment will be performed in Exercise 5.

4.10 Discussion Questions

1. Submit your answers to the Task 6 questions. Include a map image of your classified image.

2. Describe the characteristics that define a 'high quality' spectral signature.

3. What is the purpose of performing a recode or reclassification?

4. In this exercise, we digitized the training areas using GRASS GIS. This can also be done in QGIS. List the steps required to digitize the training areas in QGIS and how you would import them into your GRASS Mapset.

Exercise 5

Accuracy Assessment

Objective – Perform an Accuracy Assessment

5.1 Introduction

A primary aspect of image classification is to quantitatively validate the resulting land cover data set. A common method to do this is to perform an accuracy assessment that uses an Error Matrix to compute a number of quantitative measures on the land cover data set. For this exercise, you'll use a built-in accuracy assessment routine that functions within GRASS GIS.

This exercise includes the following tasks:

- Task 1 – Review Input Data in GRASS GIS

- Task 2 – Run the Accuracy Assessment Tool

- Task 3 – Review and Interpret the Kappa Report

- Task 4 – Challenge: Improve the Supervised Classification (optional)

5.2 Objective: Perform an Accuracy Assessment

Using an accuracy assessment routine, you'll perform an accuracy assessment on a classified image. The results will be reviewed and interpreted to determine how well the image classification performed. The image classification has already been performed and the accuracy assessments sites required to compute the accuracy assessment is provided.

5.3 Task 1 Review Input Data in GRASS GIS

In this Task, we will quickly get familiar with the data that we will use to conduct an accuracy assessment.

1. Open GRASS 7.0.3 GUI. In Windows, this can be found at Start | All Programs | GRASS GIS 7.0.3 | GRASS 7.0.3 GUI. If you installed QGIS using OSGEO4W, then it can be found at Start | All Programs | OSGEO4W | GRASS GIS 7.0.3 GUI.

2. Set the GIS Data Directory to `Exercise 5\grass7data`. (NOTE: a GRASS6 Db is also provided for use with GRASS 6.x.x.)

3. Open the `user1` mapset in the `AccuracyAssessment` Location.

4. Click File | Workspace | Open to open the Choose workspace file dialog.

5. Select `\grass7data\Exercise5 Workspace.gxw` and click the Open button. This will load the workspace into the GRASS GUI.

A GRASS workspace is a file that stores the loaded map layers and display options. A GRASS GIS workspace has been created for you that contains a small subset of a Landsat TM image (displayed as a RGB using bands 4, 5, 3 respectively) as well as a classified image (MLClass), and a reclassified image (Reclass_ML).

The Reclass_ML contains five land cover types:

- Agriculture

- Water

- Grassland

- Forest

- Urban

6. Right-click on Reclass_ML then choose Histogram from the context menu. This will open the Histogramming Tool (d.histogram), displaying how many instances of each cell value are contained in the raster map (shown in the figure below).

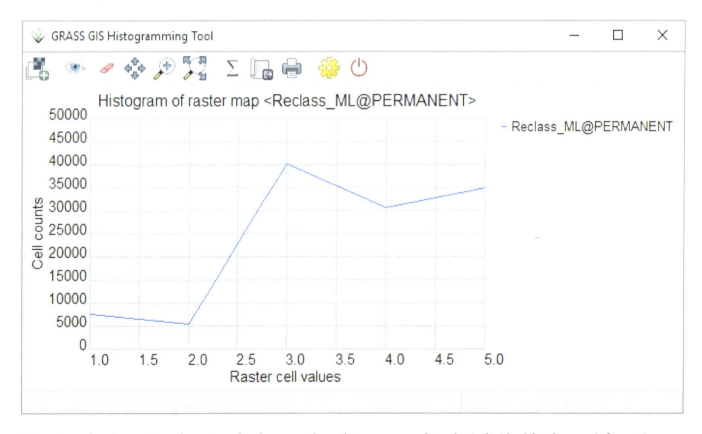

The value of each contains the unique land cover values that correspond to the individual land cover information classes.

The MLClass file represents a typical output from the maximum likelihood image classification (i.maxlik) where every spectral class is categorized in the output. The Reclass_ML file is the recoded version of the ML_class where the spectral classes have been recoded to the five information classes shown above.

Reclass_ML is the image that will be used in the accuracy assessment.

In addition to the images, two raster maps are provided. The Spectral_Sigs_Raster raster map represents the sites that were used to generate the training sites that were used to produce the MLClass. The AA_Sites_Raster are the accuracy assessment areas and will be used in the accuracy assessment.

7. Take a few moments to view the histograms for each raster map. Make sure you understand the relationship between the raster maps and how the reclassified raster maps (AA_Sites_Raster, Reclass_ML) relate to the original classification output (MLClass) using the input training set (Spectral_Sigs_Raster). Consider the number of training cells per class versus the number of classified cells per class.

5.4 Task 2 Run the Accuracy Assessment Tool

In this task, we will run the accuracy assessment tool to generate an accuracy report.

1. Click Imagery | Report and statistics | Kappa analysis [r.kappa]. This will open the kappa analysis tool.
2. Set the following parameters:
   - Required tab:
     - Name ... containing classification result: `Reclass_ML`
     - Name ... containing reference classes: `AA_Sites_Raster`
   - Optional tab:
     - Name for output file. . . kappa: `\KappaReport.txt`
3. Click the Run button to execute the tool.
4. If no errors are reported, click the Close button to close the r.kappa tool.

5.5 Task 3 Review and Interpret the Kappa Report

In this task, we will open, review, and interpret the Kappa Report generated in Task 2 above.

1. Use a text editor (like Notepad) to open `KappaReport.txt` to view the created report.

The first section (five lines in our case) shown in the figure below displays the header information identifying the title, location, date, mask, and input maps for the kappa analysis.

```
1              ACCURACY ASSESSMENT
2  LOCATION: AccuracyAssessment              Mon Aug 11 21:19:00 2014
3  MASK: none
4  MAPS: MAP1 = Rasterized vector map from labels (AA_Sites_Raster@user1 in user1)
5        MAP2 = (untitled) (Reclass_ML@PERMANENT in PERMANENT)
```

The second section (lines 7-24) shown in the figure below displays the error matrix between Map1 (identified as "AA_Sites_Raster" in the header section) and Map2 (identified as `Reclass_ML`).

```
 7  Error Matrix
 8  Panel #1 of 1
 9                  MAP1
10        cat#    1    2    3    4    5
11   M     1    168   5    0    1    0
12   A     2      1  44    0    5    0
13   P     3      0  16  271    1   12
14   2     4     42 247    0   42    0
15         5      0   0   15    0   30
16  Col Sum      211 312 286   49   42
17
18  cat#     Row Sum
19  R    1       168        5        0        1        0    174
20  e    2         1       44        0        5        0    398
21  c    3         0       16      271        1       12    922
22  l    4        42      247        0       42        0   1777
23  a    5         0        0       15        0       30   2677
24        5948
```

Let's consider the error matrix for a moment (lines 9-16). The columns are the reference data (the supervised classification we did by hand), while the rows are predicted classifications (classification done by the computer). So, for example, if we look at the category 1 column, it reports that 168 cells were classified as category 1 when they were category 1 (so, classified correctly). However, 1 cell was classified as category 2, when it was, in fact, category 1 (classified incorrectly). Additionally, 42 cells were classified as category 4, when they were actually category 1 cells.

If we sum the diagonal (168+44+271+42+30), we get 555, which represents the number of cells that were classified correctly. If we sum the Col Sum (211+312+286+49+42), we get 900, which represents the total number of reference cells (all considered to be correctly classified). So, if we divide the number of cells classified correctly, by the number of reference cells, we get 555/900 = .6166, which represents a 61.66% accuracy rating of the unsupervised classification. This is reported in lines 36-37 in the report (shown in the figure below). Essentially, this is the overall accuracy measure from the kappa report.

```
36  Obs Correct  Total Obs   % Observed Correct
37  555          900         61.666667
```

If we just stopped reading the report at the Observation Percentage section, we would be missing an important section that will explain where the classification is getting poor results. If we understand where the classification is getting confused, we can, perhaps, improve our training data to improve the overall accuracy.

Observe the Error Statistics section of our report (lines 26-34) shown in the figure below.

```
26  Cats      % Commission      % Ommission Estimated Kappa
27  1    3.448276      20.379147    0.954957
28  2    12.000000     85.897436    0.816327
29  3    9.666667      5.244755     0.858306
30  4    87.311178     14.285714    0.076615
31  5    33.333333     28.571429    0.650350
32
33  Kappa           Kappa Variance
34  0.525067        0.000350
```

Consider the Percent Commission column (second column). The percent commission reports what percentage of each class was confused with another class (i.e. misclassification percentage). So, for example, class 4 (Forest) was confused with other classes 87.31% of the time! Refer back to the Error Matrix section of the report and look at the column for category 2 from Map1. Here, 247 cells were mistakenly classified as class 4 (forest), when they were actually class 2 (Water). Compared to the other classes, this percentage is very, very high, which explains a large percentage of our classification error.

The Percent Omission column (third column) reports what percentage of each class was mistakenly classified as the wrong class. Think of this column as the opposite case from the Percent Commission column. For each category row, Percent Commission reports how many cells were placed into its class incorrectly, where Percent Omission reports how many cells were not placed into its class correctly (placed incorrectly into other classes).

The third column represents the estimated kappa coefficient. The kappa coefficient is a statistical measure of agreement between two different classifiers of the same data (in our case, how well the training dataset and supervised classification agreed in their classifications). The kappa coefficient takes into account the agreement of classification versus the possibility that the agreement is just from sheer chance (both classifiers are just randomly guessing the classes). If the classifiers completely agree on all classifications, then kappa would equal 1. If the classifiers do not agree other than what would be expected by sheer chance, then kappa would equal 0. So, in our case, the kappa coefficient is reported as 0.525067 in line 34 of the report. This could be considered a moderate amount of agreement between the two classifiers, however, there is no universally agreed-upon range of values that would consider a kappa coefficient to be excellent, good, moderate, poor, or otherwise. Therefore, when reviewing the kappa coefficient, you should also wholly consider the report when determining whether the classification is acceptable enough for your purposes.

The remaining section of the report (lines 39-51) displays the category descriptions as provided in the raster maps.

5.6 Task 4 Challenge: Improve the Supervised Classification (optional)

Now that you have assessed the kappa report and understand which classes are contributing the most error, create a new classification training set, and reclassify the `tm_sacsub_group` imagery. Use as many training areas you see fit to get optimal results. Reclassify the resulting classification and training data into the same five classes used for this exercise (outlined in Task 1).

Discuss the following:

1. Briefly describe your strategy in defining suitable training areas. Which classes did you pay particular attention to when choosing training areas? Why?

2. Run a kappa report on your reclassified training and classified image. Report your Percent Observed Correct value and your Kappa Coefficient. Additionally, discuss how your report differed from the first report and explain why the reports differed based on how you chose your training areas.

3. (If you completed the Challenge Task in Exercise 4): Compare your training strategy for this exercise, versus the training strategy you undertook in the Challenge Task in Exercise 4. Did the kappa report change your strategy? Run a kappa report on the classification you completed for the Exercise 4 Challenge. Compare the results with the kappa report from this exercise's Challenge.

5.7   Conclusion

This completes the quantitative analysis of an image classification data set. You performed a simple image classification and were able to observe and interpret the overall accuracy measures of the supervised classification.

5.8   Discussion Questions

1. Which class has the most confusion for a given column? How do you know?

2. Which row (1-5) has the most confusion? How do you know?

3. Is there anything suspect about this error matrix? Describe and explain.

4. Given the accuracy assessment outlined in Task 3, would you think the accuracy assessment is valid and useable? Why or why not? Justify your answer.

5. Submit your answers to the Task 4 questions (if attempted).

Conclusion

Congratulations, you have completed the GeoAcademy labs! Now that you have developed a well-rounded skill set, I encourage you to continue learning how QGIS, GRASS GIS, and other FOSS4G tools can be used to analyze and visualize spatial data. QGIS in particular, is undergoing rapid development with new features being introduced regularly. Below are some resources for staying abreast of the latest developments, and continuing your geospatial education.

Learn more skills via the QGIS Training Manual: https://www.qgis.org/en/site/forusers/trainingmaterial/index.html

Refer to the QGIS User Manual when technical questions arise: https://www.qgis.org/en/docs/index.html

Subscribe to a QGIS Mailing List: https://www.qgis.org/en/site/getinvolved/mailinglists.html#qgis-mailinglists

Read about, "How to ask a QGIS question" before posing your first question to a mailing list (listserv): https://www.qgis.org/en/site/getinvolved/faq/index.html#how-to-ask-a-qgis-question

Read about how others have used QGIS in QGIS Case Studies: https://www.qgis.org/en/site/about/case_studies/index.html

Explore maps others have made using QGIS: https://www.qgis.org/en/site/about/screenshots.html

Read blog entries about new features and how-tos: http://plugins.qgis.org/planet/

Explore other QGIS Applications: https://www.qgis.org/en/site/about/features.html

For GRASS GIS you can visit the website to find documentation and additional tutorials, mailing lists, and other resources: https://grass.osgeo.org/

Visit the Open Source GeoSpatial Foundation (OSGeo) website, to stay abreast of other FOSS4G project news and conference announcements: http://www.osgeo.org/

Index

Books from Locate Press

QGIS Map Design

USE QGIS TO TAKE YOUR CARTOGRAPHIC PRODUCTS TO THE HIGHEST LEVEL.

With step-by-step instructions for creating the most modern print map designs seen in any instructional materials to-date, this book covers everything from basic styling and labeling to advanced techniques like illuminated contours and dynamic masking.

See how QGIS is rapidly surpassing the cartographic capabilities of any other geoware available today with its data-driven overrides, flexible expression functions, multitudinous color tools, blend modes, and atlasing capabilities. A prior familiarity with basic QGIS capabilities is assumed. All example data and project files are included.

Written by two of the leading experts in the realm of open source mapping, Anita and Gretchen are experienced authors who pour their wealth of knowledge into the book. Get ready to bump up your mapping experience!

The PyQGIS Programmer's Guide

EXTENDING QGIS JUST GOT EASIER!

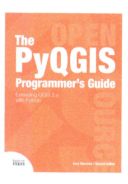

This book is your fast track to getting started with PyQGIS. After a brief introduction to Python, you'll learn how to understand the QGIS Application Programmer Interface (API), write scripts, and build a plugin. The book is designed to allow you to work through the examples as you go along. At the end of each chapter you'll find a set of exercises you can do to enhance your learning experience.

The PyQGIS Programmer's Guide is compatible with the version 2.0 API released with QGIS 2.x. All code samples and data are freely available from the book's website. Get started learning PyQGIS today!

Geospatial Power Tools

EVERYONE LOVES POWER TOOLS!

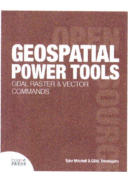

The GDAL and OGR utilities are the power tools of the GIS world, and best of all, they're free.

The utilities include tools for examining, converting, transforming, building and analysing data. This book is a collection of the GDAL and OGR documentation, but also includes substantial new content designed to help guide you in using the utilities to solve your current data problems.

Inside you'll find a quick reference for looking up the right syntax and example usage quickly. The book is divided into three parts: *Workflows and examples, GDAL raster utilities,* and *OGR vector utilities.*

Once you get a taste of the power the GDAL/OGR suite provides, you'll wonder how you ever got along without them. This book will get you on the fast track to becoming more efficient in your GIS data processing efforts.

Be sure to visit http://locatepress.com for information on new and upcoming titles.

For a 50% discount on the PDF, see locatepress.com/dqw_pdf.   651508003a2

www.ingramcontent.com/pod-product-compliance
Lightning Source LLC
Chambersburg PA
CBHW080135060326
40689CB00018B/3798